Digital Revolutions in Public Finance

Editors
Sanjeev Gupta, Michael Keen, Alpa Shah, and
Geneviève Verdier

INTERNATIONAL MONETARY FUND

Cover design: Jessie Sanchez Art & Design

Cataloging-in-Publication Data
Joint Bank-Fund Library

Names: Gupta, Sanjeev. | Keen, Michael. | Shah, Alpa. | Verdier, Geneviève. |
International Monetary Fund.
Title: Digital revolutions in public finance / editors: Sanjeev Gupta, Michael
Keen, Alpa Shah, and Geneviève Verdier.
Description: [Washington, DC] : International Monetary Fund, 2017. |
Includes bibliographical references.
Identifiers: ISBN 9781484315224 (paperback)
Subjects: LCSH: Fiscal policy. | Finance, Public. | Tax administration and
procedure.
Classification: LCC HJ192.5.D534 2017

Disclaimer: The views expressed in this book are those of the authors and do
not necessarily represent the views of the International Monetary Fund, its
Executive Board, or management.

Please send orders to:
International Monetary Fund, Publication Services
P.O. Box 92780, Washington, DC 20090, U.S.A.
Tel.: (202) 623-7430   Fax: (202) 623-7201
E-mail: publications@imf.org
Internet: www.elibrary.imf.org
www.bookstore.imf.org

Contents

Acknowledgments

This book has been a collective endeavor and has benefited from contributions from both inside and outside the IMF. We would like to thank the contributing authors for their close collaboration and enthusiasm for the topic. The research presented in this book was the subject of the IMF's Fiscal Affairs Department Fiscal Forum *Digital Revolutions in Public Finance* held in April 2017 in Washington, DC, during the IMF–World Bank Spring Meetings. The chapters greatly benefited from valuable feedback received during the Fiscal Forum, and several chapters have also benefited from the comments by staff of the IMF's Fiscal Affairs Department and the Bill & Melinda Gates Foundation.

Linda Kean and Linda Long of the IMF's Communications Department efficiently managed all aspects related to the production of the book, and we are grateful for their excellent work. Liza Prado and Ana Popovich also provided excellent administrative assistance during the many steps needed to bring a book to completion. Katy Whipple performed layout services for the book.

This publication and the conference on which it is based have been made possible thanks to the generous financial support of the Bill & Melinda Gates Foundation. We would like to thank Vishal Gujadhur of the Gates Foundation for his skillful coordination of our collaboration with the foundation.

Sanjeev Gupta
Michael Keen
Alpa Shah
Geneviève Verdier
Editors

Foreword

Fiscal policy has a significant impact on us all. How governments mobilize resources and spend them on public goods and services, and how fiscal policy is used to steer the economy, are critical for the well-being of societies. The better equipped countries are to formulate and execute fiscal policies, the better people's lives will be.

The digital revolution holds vast potential to improve fiscal policy. By transforming the way countries collect, process, and act on information, digital technology can reshape the way governments design and implement their tax, spending, and macro-fiscal policies. If technology is used in a smart way, fiscal policy will be more efficient, transparent, equitable, and impactful—improving lives all over the world. The potential benefits are huge.

Governments now have access to *better data*. Digitalization allows for greater storage and tracking of information through electronic records, linking of data registries between different parts of government, and enhanced capabilities to handle and analyze large data sets. With these new data and new capabilities come *better systems*. Many countries are already finding that it costs less to collect taxes, deliver public services, administer social programs, and manage public finances. This has opened *new policy options*, including a more innovative and progressive design of tax systems. Who knows what cognitive systems and artificial intelligence have in store for tax systems and public service delivery in the future?

Most importantly, new policies and better systems can have a *greater impact* on people's lives. The digital revolution in public finance now underway can be transformative for governments *and* for the people they represent and serve.

Each country will need to chart its own path—either by taking incremental steps to digitalize or by leapfrogging to newer and more sophisticated policies and implementation methods. We must not underestimate the institutional challenges and capacity constraints along the way, and the design of new policies must be equitable and inclusive. There are also privacy and cybersecurity concerns and new avenues for fraud, which call for international cooperation and regulation as information increasingly travels across borders. Yet the potential benefits far outweigh the risks.

The IMF and the Bill & Melinda Gates Foundation are proud to be partners in taking forward this important agenda. We share a vision of the future in which technological innovation helps the poorest and most vulnerable lead healthy, productive lives. In terms of fiscal policy, this means a future in which governments use technology to collect and deploy resources to the benefit of all their citizens.

We hope that this book will take us closer to that future. Together we can harness new technology to achieve better fiscal policy outcomes for all.

Melinda Gates
Co-Chair
Bill & Melinda Gates Foundation

Christine Lagarde
Managing Director
International Monetary Fund

Contributors

Jenny Aker is an associate professor of development economics at the Fletcher School and Economics Department at Tufts University, working on development economics in sub-Saharan Africa. She previously worked for the International Food Policy Research Institute, the Center for Global Development, and Catholic Relief Services. Ms. Aker has conducted research on a range of issues, including the impact of information technology on development outcomes, agricultural market efficiency, barriers to adult education, and social protection programs. She earned a Ph.D. in agricultural economics from the University of California-Berkeley in 2008. She has an M.A. from the Fletcher School and a B.A. from Duke University.

Aqib Aslam is an economist in the IMF's Fiscal Affairs Department, having previously worked in the European and Research Departments. Before that, he worked at Goldman Sachs International, the Bank of England, and the U.K. Government Economic Service. He has a Ph.D. from the University of Cambridge, an M.Sc. from University College London, and a B.A. (Hons) from the University of Oxford. His research interests include applied macroeconomics and econometrics.

Solomon Assefa is director of IBM Research Africa. He is responsible for IBM's research labs in Kenya and South Africa and heads the company's research strategy and partnership across the African continent. Previously, he was the director of research strategy and growth initiatives for Africa. He was also program manager in the Office of Science and Technology. As a research scientist, Dr. Assefa has worked on IBM's nanophotonics technology with responsibilities spanning research, development, and technology transfer to commercial foundry. He has coauthored more than 150 publications in peer-reviewed journals and conference proceedings and has more than 50 patents. He is also a fellow of the Ethiopian Academy of Sciences, and an honorary professor at University of Witwatersrand in South Africa. Dr. Assefa received a bachelor's degree in Physics and a bachelor's degree, M.S., and Ph.D. in electrical engineering and computer science from the Massachusetts Institute of Technology.

Marco Cangiano is a former assistant director of the IMF and is currently an independent consultant affiliated with the London-based Overseas Development Institute and the United Nations Capital Development Fund. He has consulted for the IMF and the Italian Ministry for the Economy and Finance, among others. Between 1991 and 2016, he held various positions at the IMF. Among these, between 2008 and 2015 he was head of the divisions responsible for public financial management in the Fiscal Affairs Department; prior to that he headed the Budget Strategy Division of the IMF Office of Budget and Planning. He has presented and lectured on a range of fiscal topics in Washington and abroad, including at the OECD Senior Budget Officers' meetings, the Joint Vienna Institute, the Ljubljana Centre for Excellence in Finance, the Harvard Kennedy School of Government, and New York University's Wagner Graduate School for Public Service. He is a graduate of La Sapienza University in Rome and holds an M.Sc. in economics from the University of York. He has been on the steering committee of the multi-donor Public Expenditure and Financial Accountability program; published on energy economics, pension reforms, fiscal transparency, and tax policy; and coedited *Public Financial Management and Its Emerging Architecture* published by the IMF in 2013.

Jingnan (Cecilia) Chen is a lecturer (assistant professor) of economics at the University of Exeter in the United Kingdom. She received a B.A. in finance at Shanghai Jiao Tong University and a Ph.D. in economics at George Mason University. Her research combines experimental methodology, game theory, and insights from psychology and sociology. Her primary research interest is behavioral and experimental economics, including topics such as tax compliance, deception, and gender.

Michael Devereux is director at the Oxford University Centre for Business Taxation; professor of Business Taxation, Saïd Business School, University of Oxford; and professorial fellow at Oriel College, Oxford. He is research director of the European Tax Policy Forum and research fellow of the Centre for Economic Policy Research and CESifo. He is assistant editor of the *British Tax Review* and is a member of the editorial board of the *World Tax Journal*. He is a member of the Business Forum on Tax and Competitiveness, chaired by the exchequer secretary, and in 2014 was a member of the European Commission High Level Expert Group on Taxation of the Digital Economy.

Martin Fleming is IBM's chief analytics officer and chief economist. As chief analytics officer, Dr. Fleming leads IBM's data science center of competency, focused on improving the company's business performance and achieving its financial goals. As IBM's chief economist, he provides regular macroeconomic insight and analysis to the company's senior leaders and engages with select IBM clients. Dr. Fleming also leads IBM's data science profession with the mission to drive the growth and expertise of its skilled data science professionals. His work has been published in professional journals and general interest publications including *The Economist, The New York Times*, and the *Wall Street Journal*. He has testified before various U.S. congressional committees, including the Joint Economic Committee. Dr. Fleming holds an M.A. and Ph.D. in economics from Tufts University and a B.Sc. cum laude in mathematics from the University of Massachusetts Lowell.

Alan Gelb is senior fellow and director of studies at the Center for Global Development. He previously held positions at the World Bank, including director of development policy, chief economist for the Africa Region, and staff director for the 1996 World Development Report *From Plan to Market*. His recent areas of research include the development applications of digital identification systems and biometric technology, the special development challenges of resource-rich countries, the growth and diversification of African economies, and results-based aid. He serves on the board of advisors for ID4Africa, a multi-stakeholder movement that promotes the transparent and responsible adoption of digital identity in the service of development in Africa. Prior to joining the World Bank, he held academic positions at the University of Essex and Queen's University. He holds a D.Phil. and B.Phil. from Oxford University and a B.Sc. from the University of KwaZulu Natal (South Africa).

Ruth Goodwin-Groen is managing director of the Better Than Cash Alliance, which is a global partnership of governments, companies, and international organizations accelerating the shift from cash to digital payments, housed at the United Nations. Prior to leading the Alliance, Ms. Goodwin-Groen was the Australian co-chair for the G20's Global Partnership for Financial Inclusion and financial inclusion advisor to the Australian government. She holds a Ph.D. from the University of Bath, United Kingdom; an M.B.A. from Harvard Business School; and a B.Sc. Hons. from the University of Western Australia. She led her own consulting business for 15 years with a focus on financial inclusion, financial sector, and institutional development issues.

Shaun Grimshaw is an economics Ph.D. student at the University of Exeter, where he is part of the Tax Administration Research Centre. His current research interests include experimental investigations of behavioral aspects of tax evasion and cheating. Prior to joining the research center, he worked as a manager in credit derivatives technology at Deutsche Bank and holds a D.Phil. in chemistry from the University of Oxford.

Sanjeev Gupta is deputy director of the Fiscal Affairs Department of the IMF and previously was in its African Department and European Department. Mr. Gupta has led IMF missions to some 25 countries in Africa, Asia, Europe, and the Middle East and represented the institution in numerous international meetings and conferences. Prior to joining the IMF, he was a fellow of the Kiel Institute of World Economics, Germany; professor in the Administrative Staff College of India, Hyderabad; and secretary of the Federation of Indian Chambers of Commerce and Industry. Mr. Gupta has authored/coauthored more than 150 papers on macroeconomic and fiscal issues and authored/coauthored/coedited 12 books; the most recent, published by the IMF, are "The Economics of Public Health Care Reform in Advanced and Emerging Economies," 2012; "Energy Subsidy Reform: Lessons and Implications," 2013; "Equitable and

Sustainable Pensions: Challenges and Experiences," 2014; "Fiscal Policy and Inequality," September 2015; and "Fiscal Politics," 2017.

Bas Jacobs has been professor of economics and public finance since 2007 at the Erasmus School of Economics of the Erasmus University Rotterdam, Netherlands. He is a research fellow of the Tinbergen Institute and CESifo, academic partner of the CPB Netherlands Bureau for Economic Policy Analysis, and president of the Royal Netherlands Economics Association. His research crosses the borders of public finance, optimal taxation, macroeconomics, human capital theory, and labor economics. Professor Jacobs has written about optimal labor income taxation, optimal capital income taxation, inverse optimal taxation, human capital theory, optimal education policy, optimal taxation in labor markets with trade unions and minimum wages, the marginal cost of public funds, environmental and corrective taxation, wage inequality, fiscal policy, productivity growth, and technical change. He holds an M.A. and a Ph.D. in economics from the University of Amsterdam.

Ravi Kanbur is T.H. Lee Professor of World Affairs, international professor of applied economics and management, and professor of economics at Cornell University. He has served on the senior staff of the World Bank, including as chief economist for Africa. He is president of the Human Development and Capabilities Association, chair of the board of UNU-WIDER, co-chair of the Scientific Council of the International Panel on Social Progress, and member of the OECD High Level Expert Group on the Measurement of Economic Performance. He is also past-president of the Society for the Study of Economic Inequality, past-member of the High Level Advisory Council of the Climate Justice Dialogue, and past-member of the Core Group of the Commission on Global Poverty.

Michael Keen is deputy director of the Fiscal Affairs Department of the IMF, where he was previously head of the Tax Policy and Tax Coordination divisions. Before joining the IMF, he was professor of economics at the University of Essex and visiting professor at Kyoto University. He was awarded the CESifo-IIPF Musgrave prize in 2010, delivered the 2012 Chelliah lecture at the National Institute of Public Finance and Policy in New Delhi, and is honorary president of the International Institute of Public Finance (of which he was elected president from 2003 to 2006). He has led technical assistance missions to over 30 countries on a wide range of issues in tax policy, and has consulted for the World Bank, European Commission, and the private sector. He has served on the board of the National Tax Association in the United States, and on the editorial boards of *American Economic Journal: Economic Policy*, *International Tax and Public Finance* (of which he was joint founder), *Journal of Public Economics*, *Review of Economic Studies*, and many other journals. He is coauthor of books on the modern VAT, the taxation of petroleum and minerals, and changing customs. Recent publications also appear in the *American Economic Review*,

Economic Policy, Journal of Public Economics, Journal of Development Economics, and *National Tax Journal.*

Lamya Kejji is an information management assistant in the Statistics Department of the IMF, working on data collection and database management. She was previously a project officer in the IMF's Information Technology Department. She holds an engineering degree in computer science from Telecom Nancy, a French Grande École.

Arvind Krishna is senior vice president, Hybrid Cloud, and director of IBM Research. He was previously general manager of IBM Systems and Technology Group development and manufacturing, general manager of IBM Information Management, and vice president of strategy for IBM Software. Dr. Krishna leads IBM's Hybrid Cloud Unit, which has $10 billion in annual revenues and oversees research for a broad portfolio of next-generation projects in cognitive computing, cloud and platform services, semiconductors, data-driven solutions, and blockchain, among others. An electrical engineer and business leader, Dr. Krishna has major technical achievements in wireless networking, security, databases, systems, and research. He was instrumental in developing the world's first operational wireless systems. He pioneered IBM's security software business and created new database technologies. He is the architect of IBM Research's blockchain strategy and the use of open source and open standards for this emerging technology. Dr. Krishna has coauthored 26 articles in peer-reviewed journals and conference proceedings and holds 15 patents. He received an undergraduate degree from the Indian Institute of Technology, Kanpur, and a Ph.D. in electrical engineering from the University of Illinois at Urbana-Champaign.

Jason Lamb is deputy director with the Digital Enabling Environment on the Financial Services for the Poor initiative at the Bill & Melinda Gates Foundation. He leads the team's engagement with global organizations seeking to bring financial services to everyone, including those living on $2/day or less. During his tenure at the foundation he has served as board chair and board member of the Better Than Cash Alliance. He is currently serving on the board of the Alliance for Financial Inclusion. He also coauthored the seminal report *Fighting Poverty Profitably* in 2013 that quantified the cost savings of reaching consumers with digital financial services. Prior to joining the foundation, Mr. Lamb spent six years at Washington Mutual Bank where he managed the consumer checking portfolio. He gained his initial experience in the financial sector and emerging economies during his seven years at McKinsey & Company, where he spent time advising banks in Central and Eastern Europe, Africa, and North America. He was a founding member of the McKinsey Budapest office. Mr. Lamb holds a B.A. in economics and history from the University of California, Davis and an M.B.A. from the Ross School of Business at the University of Michigan.

Susan Lund is a partner of McKinsey & Company and a leader of the McKinsey Global Institute, conducting research on international financial markets and globalization. Her latest research provides new evidence on the retrenchment of global banks and state of financial globalization. Recent reports assessed the potential economic impact of digital finance and mobile money in developing countries; examined how globalization is evolving in the digital era; and assessed the risks associated with the accumulation of debt in countries around the world, with a focus on China. Dr. Lund is a board member of the National Association of Business Economists and a member of the Council on Foreign Relations, the Bretton Woods Committee, and the Conference of Business Economists. She holds a Ph.D. from Stanford University in applied economics and a B.A. from Northwestern University.

Florian Misch is an economist in the Fiscal Affairs Department of the IMF, where he has been working on a range of analytical projects as well as on fiscal issues in European countries and in Mexico. Prior to joining the IMF, he was deputy head of department at a major think tank in Germany, and worked as a consultant for various organizations, including the World Bank, the German International Cooperation, and the New Zealand Treasury. His research interests cover macroeconomics, public finance, and development economics. He holds a Ph.D. in economics from the University of Nottingham.

Gareth Myles is professor of economics and head of the school at the University of Adelaide and a research fellow of the Institute for Fiscal Studies. He was previously a lecturer at the University of Warwick, and professor of economics and director of the Tax Administration Research Centre at the University of Exeter. He is a managing editor of the *Journal of Public Economic Theory* and was managing editor of fiscal studies from 1998 to 2013. His major research interest is in public economics and his publications include *Public Economics* (1995), *Intermediate Public Economics* (2006), and numerous papers in *International Tax and Public Finance*, *Journal of Public Economic Theory*, and *Journal of Public Economics*. He was one of the authors of the *Mirrlees Review of the UK Tax System*.

Njuguna Ndung'u is an associate professor of economics at the University of Nairobi, Kenya (on leave of absence). He is the immediate former governor of the Central Bank of Kenya, where he served for two four-year terms as required by law, from 2007 to 2015. He has been a member of Global Advisory Council of the World Economic Forum and a visiting fellow of practice at the Blavatnik School of Government, Oxford University. Prior to his appointment as governor, he was the director of training at the African Economic Research Consortium, a pan-African premier capacity-building network. He also worked at the International Development Research Centre of Canada, as a regional programme specialist for the Eastern and Southern Africa Regional Office, and at the Kenya Institute for Public Policy Research and Analysis as a principal analyst/researcher. In the latter, he led a team to develop the Kenyan macromodel that has been in use for forecasting growth and fiscal stance since 2001. He obtained his Ph.D. at the University of Gothenburg, Sweden. He has lectured in advanced economic theory and econometrics at the University of Nairobi. In addition, he has published widely in international journals as well as chapters in various books on economic policy issues. Currently, he is a member of the Brookings Africa Growth Initiative Distinguished Advisory Group; a member of the Advisory Committee of the Alliance for Financial Inclusion, which coordinates financial inclusion policies in Africa, Asia, and Latin America; and a senior advisor for the UN-based Better Than Cash Alliance.

Brian Olden is deputy division chief in the IMF Fiscal Affairs Department's Public Financial Management 1 Division. He has been with the IMF since 2003. From 2009 to 2012, he served as the IMF's regional public financial management advisor in southeastern Europe. Prior to joining the IMF, he worked as a director of a consultancy firm specializing in public financial management, a senior treasury manager in the Irish National Treasury Management Agency, and an official in the Irish Department of Finance. Mr. Olden has produced numerous articles and book contributions on issues related to public financial management and debt management and significant inputs to IMF policy papers. Mr. Olden has an M.Sc. in investment and treasury from Dublin City University and a B. Comm. from University College Dublin.

Marcos Poplawski-Ribeiro is a senior economist in the Research Department of the IMF. He has previously held positions in the IMF's Fiscal Affairs and African Departments. Before the IMF, he worked and lectured in various institutions and universities in Brazil, Europe, and the United States, including the United Nations, the University of Amsterdam, the Centre d'Etudes Prospectives et d'Informations Internationales, and Sciences Po in Paris. Mr. Poplawski-Ribeiro holds a Ph.D. in economics from the University of Amsterdam. He has published in leading academic and policy-oriented journals on several topics in the fields of public finance, macroeconomics, international economics, and development.

Suyash Rai is a senior consultant at the National Institute of Public Finance and Policy, New Delhi, where he works on issues of financial regulation, infrastructure regulation, and public finance. He has served on government committees and given research and advisory support to various government agencies. He previously worked at ICICI Bank, a private sector bank, and IFMR Trust, a microfinance organization. He has also been a consultant to Consultative Group to Assist the Poor, a World Bank initiative. He has written for various popular media outlets. He has a graduate degree in management and an undergraduate degree in computer science.

Rathin Roy is director and CEO of the National Institute of Public Finance and Policy, New Delhi, an autonomous research institute under the Ministry of Finance of the Government of India. Dr. Roy has served as economic advisor with the Thirteenth Finance Commission, Government of India; as member on the FRBM Review Committee; and as member of the Seventh Central Pay Commission. He was previously regional manager and director Asia Pacific Regional Centre, United Nations Development Programme Bangkok; director of the International Policy Centre for Inclusive Growth, Brazil; and public finance economist at UNDP headquarters. Prior to joining the UNDP, he was tenured at the Department of Economics, School of Oriental and African Studies, University of London, and taught at the University of Manchester. Dr. Roy's policy interests and publications have mainly focused on fiscal and macroeconomic issues pertinent to human development in developing and emerging economies. He has written extensively on fiscal space for human development, inter-government fiscal issues, fiscal marksmanship, macroeconomic conditionality, and IMF Article IV policy analyses. Dr. Roy holds a Ph.D. in economics from the University of Cambridge, an M.A. in economics from the Jawaharlal Nehru University, and a B.A. (Hons.) in economics from St. Stephen's College, University of Delhi.

Alpa Shah is an economist in the Tax Policy Division of the Fiscal Affairs Department at the IMF. Her work encompasses a range of technical assistance, research, and analysis on income, consumption, and natural resource tax policy issues. Prior to joining the IMF, she worked in the investment banking sector in London in infrastructure finance, and subsequently for the Government of Liberia under the Overseas Development Institute Fellowship, advising on the negotiation and monitoring of investment agreements with its international investors. She holds an M.A. in economics from the University of Cambridge and an M.Sc. from the School of Oriental and African Studies, University of London.

John Vella is an associate professor of taxation law in the Faculty of Law at the University of Oxford, a fellow of Harris Manchester College, and a program director at the Oxford University Centre for Business Taxation. Mr. Vella studied law at the University of Malta (B.A. and L.L.D.) and the University of Cambridge (L.L.M. and Ph.D.). After completing his doctorate, he moved to Oxford first as Norton Rose Career Development Fellow in company law at the Faculty of Law and then as a senior research fellow at the Oxford University Centre for Business Taxation. His recent research has focused on the taxation of multinationals, financial sector taxation, and tax compliance and administration.

Geneviève Verdier is the deputy division chief of the Expenditure Policy Division of the IMF's Fiscal Affairs Department. Prior to joining the IMF, she was an assistant professor at Texas A&M University. She previously worked as an economist in the Research Department of the Bank of Canada, as well as the IMF's Strategy, Policy, and Review Department; African Department; and Institute for Capacity Development. She earned a Ph.D. from the University of British Columbia. Her work to date and publications in IMF research and policy publications, books, and peer-reviewed journals cover a wide range of macroeconomic issues related to public spending efficiency, public investment, sovereign debt restructuring, economic growth, international macroeconomics, and financial development.

Olivia White is a partner in the San Francisco office of McKinsey & Company, working on financial inclusion topics in emerging markets. She also works with U.S. and European financial institutions, particularly in risk management, and leads McKinsey's service line on Enterprise Risk Management. Ms. White has published across a wide range of topics and is an author of the McKinsey Global Institute publication *Digital Finance for All: Powering Inclusive Growth in Emerging Economies* (2016). Before joining McKinsey, she was a Pappalardo Fellow in Physics at Massachusetts Institute of Technology. She holds a Ph.D. in physics from Harvard University; an M.Sc. in mathematics from Oxford University, where she was a Rhodes Scholar; and a B.A. in physics and mathematics from Stanford University.

CHAPTER 1

Introduction

Reshaping Public Finance

Sanjeev Gupta, Michael Keen, Alpa Shah, and Geneviève Verdier

The effectiveness of fiscal policy—the collection and use of resources to stabilize the economic cycle, pursue distributional objectives, and enable public spending—depends crucially on the information and technologies available to government, and how it exploits them. Governments stimulate the economy during recessions and retrench during booms. They tax in order to finance social safety nets, health and education services, infrastructure, and so on. The design and implementation of fiscal policy is therefore fundamentally shaped by the reliability, timeliness, and detail of the information available to the government about the economy and its actors. This includes taxpayers' incomes and assets, the identity and circumstances of social program beneficiaries, the employment status of workers, the size of the output gap, and the magnitude and timing of government transactions. By transforming the way in which governments can collect, process, and act on information, digitalization[1] is reshaping the formulation and implementation of these policies—a process that has only just begun. This reshaping is the topic of this book.

Computerization—the use of computers to perform human tasks—has become as familiar and routine in government as anywhere else. But now it is yielding to the inherently more profound process of digitalization. And deep-learning technologies are pushing the boundaries of digitalization one step further, with artificial intelligence machines now able to learn by themselves based on information fed to them. Using such technology, computers are now capable of designing industrial objects, generating scientific hypotheses, and even composing music (McAfee and Brynjolfsson 2017).

Digitalization has also vastly increased the possibilities for data collection and storage. In 2000 only 25 percent of data were stored digitally; by 2007 this metric

---

[1]Though the two terms are often used interchangeably, we use *digitization* to refer to the transformation of information storage into digital formats (a series of binary numbers) for use by computers and *digitalization* to refer to the integration of digital technologies into everyday life, including government systems. So the core concern of this book is with digitalization.

had risen to 94 percent (Ross 2016). With multiple means to access and share information—computers, tablets, phones—this revolution has left virtually no corner of the world untouched: in 2014, 90 percent of the world's population had access to a mobile phone (ITU 2014; GSMA 2013). This digital revolution is having a wide-reaching impact, presenting markets, society, and governments with the challenges of responding to and absorbing this continual change.

This chapter first argues that while the digital revolution offers exciting new opportunities for public finance (better information, systems, and policy)—which are the focus of the next section—it is not without significant challenges and limitations. These are taken up in the second section. The third section discusses how countries will need to take steps based on their own circumstances, and highlights the need for them to cooperate in tackling emerging challenges. The remainder of the chapter details the contributions of the book.

NEW OPPORTUNITIES

Through digitalization, government can potentially conduct current fiscal policy more effectively—doing what we do now, but better—and perhaps before too long, design policy in new ways—doing things, that is, that we do not, and cannot, do now. They can have better information, build better systems, and design and implement better policies.

Better Information

Of the digital revolution's many potential benefits, the most visible and crucial may well be the ability to collect, process, and disseminate more timely, easily accessible, and transparent information on economic activity. Greater storage capacity and computing power means that governments can now collect *more* information, by tracking and recording a vast range and volume of transactions and interactions.

Tax authorities are increasingly gaining access to the vast amount of information held by the private sector—such as data on bank transactions and interest income—through the use of digital systems, standardized reporting formats, and electronic interfaces. Systems for sharing information have also improved. The increasing trend toward single-view online portals or digital platforms allows fiscal authorities access to data across government departments. New norms in global tax transparency have led to the development of a global reporting standard on automatic exchange of information on the financial records of nonresidents with the tax authorities in their country of residence.

Governments can now collect more *timely* information. Tax authorities in Australia and the United Kingdom are now receiving real-time reporting of payroll information, and, in Brazil and Russia, electronic invoicing systems allow immediate access to data on firm sales. With the automation of public finance management, a number of governments can now access high-frequency fiscal data through their information technology systems. Some countries—such as Brazil and the United States—even make these daily cash operations avail-able to the public.

Digitalization also allows for more *precise* identification of individuals and their associated activities. New technology to monitor and record biometric char-acteristics provides a unique, secure, and less-costly alternative to more traditional paper-based official documentation systems. In many developing countries, this technology has given governments and citizens the means to authenticate official identity, strengthening civil registries and national ID card systems using various physical traits, including fingerprints, iris scans, vein patterns, and DNA. Gelb and Clark (2013) find projects to biometrically identify people—small and large, by governments and by nongovernment organizations—in more than 80 coun-tries. Latin America leads the way in biometric-enabled national identity systems, but other regions are not far behind. Africa, Angola, Ghana, Nigeria, and South Africa have established or are planning such systems. Countries in South Asia such as Afghanistan, Bangladesh, Nepal, and Pakistan are following suit. India's *Aadhaar* is the world's largest biometric identification system, with more than 1.1 billion citizens registered.

In the private sector, the constant recording of digital information in real time has given rise to a data economy, with individuals leaving a digital trail with every internet search, retail transaction, and activity that is carried out using digital means. Businesses are already buying and selling these data, and using them in conjunction with artificial intelligence algorithms to better target their advertising efforts. Governments are already starting to catch on, and such big data and cognitive computing may also expand policy and enforcement options.

Better Systems

With new information and new capabilities, a wide range of new possibilities emerge for enhanced implementation of tax and spending policies. These include lower costs of tax collection and compliance, as well as of delivering public ser-vices, administering social programs, and managing public finances.

Tax Administration

Electronic filing of tax returns has reduced the cost of compliance for taxpayers and of administration for the government. Many countries began experimenting with electronic filing of tax returns, for example, as early as 10 to 15 years ago (OECD 2006; Deloitte 2013). Furthermore, access to third-party information has allowed governments increasingly to "prepopulate" tax returns, easing the compliance burden even further, with taxpayers simply having to verify the infor-mation they are presented with. And access to additional information sources and capabilities to link existing information in various government systems is helping tax authorities to better detect evasion or avoidance.

Digitalization has allowed governments to implement electronic tracking of business activity. For example, tracking of sales through the use of e-invoices has facilitated more efficient administration of indirect taxes, a common area of fraud and revenue leakage. Russia has seen the rollout of online cash registers that record information on each transaction, which is then transferred immediately to a server where tax authorities can access it. For decades, massive cross-checking of value-added tax (VAT) invoices (to verify that sellers have been charged the tax for which they seek a credit) was presumed to be technically impossible; now China is showing that it can be done.[2] In Brazil, the Public System of Digital Bookkeeping or SPED system allows tax authorities to determine a company's income tax obligation based on information the business enters into an annual digital bookkeeping report.

With data being collected in more standardized formats, increased processing capabilities have allowed tax authorities to assess taxpayer risks by analyzing large data sets and by combining different sources of data (for example, firm-level input and output data for VAT purposes). In the United Kingdom, HM Revenue and Customs' Connect computer draws on information from a wide range of government and corporate sources, as well as individual digital footprints, to create a profile of each taxpayer's total income. Such analytical capability could even be used to assess the behavioral impact of new tax and spending policies.

Digital systems present new roles for consumers and third parties in facilitating enhanced compliance. The emerging peer-to-peer (P2P) economy, in which a digital platform intermediates transactions between individual buyers and sellers, has introduced organization and formalization to previously informal and perhaps undocumented activities. Such platforms record large volumes of consumption and income data that, if accessible by tax authorities, could play an important role in tax administration (as discussed in Chapter 3 by Aslam and Shah). Estonia, for instance, uses the platform technology to connect Uber drivers directly with the tax office, adding income from rides directly to their tax return. Offering a role for consumers as auditors, the *Nota Fiscal Paulista* program in São Paulo, Brazil, using a digital payments system, is designed to encourage better enforcement of the VAT at the final consumer stage by providing a 30 percent tax rebate and monthly lottery prizes to consumers who ask for receipts.[3]

Public Spending, Service Delivery, and Administration

Digitalization can help improve public service delivery. First, governments can take advantage of greater capabilities to disseminate important information. Studies have found that sharing information through text messaging about best agricultural practices and commodity prices can improve farmer knowledge. Similarly, information about breastfeeding and sexual and reproductive health shared through mobile phones has increased recipients' knowledge (see Chapter 8 by Aker). Estonia stands out in its use of digital platforms for delivering government services. Using an electronic identity card, citizens can vote online and consult medical records—just a few of the 600 e-services that the government

---

[2]See for instance Fan and others (2017).

[3]See Naritomi (2015) for an assessment.

offers (see Chapter 12 by Cangiano, Gelb, and Goodwin-Groen). Digital technology can also help improve the quality of services. Results from impact evaluations in Haiti, India, Pakistan, and Uganda suggest that digital monitoring can reduce the pervasive absenteeism of some key public service workers, including nurses, doctors, and teachers (World Bank 2016).

The use of electronic payment systems has helped cut bureaucratic inefficiencies, produce fiscal savings, and facilitated the delivery of benefits (see Chapters 8, 11, and 12 by Aker; Roy and Rai; and Cangiano, Gelb, and Goodwin-Groen, respectively). In Haiti and the Philippines, for instance, the cost per transaction of some social assistance programs fell by close to or more than 50 percent per transaction once payments had been digitalized (Zimmerman, Bohling, and Rotman Parker 2014). Governments are now extensively using biometric technology to expand coverage of social benefits and improve targeting. Launched in 2013, the Indian government's Direct Benefit Transfer program significantly changed the delivery system of subsidy and welfare benefits by transferring payments directly into bank accounts linked to beneficiaries' Aadhaar biometric ID (see Chapter 11 by Roy and Rai and Chapter 12 by Cangiano, Gelb, and Goodwin-Groen).

At the same time, digitalization of government payments has often reduced fraud and corruption (see Chapter 13 by Lund, White, and Lamb). In Sierra Leone, the introduction of e-payments through mobile wallets during the Ebola crisis restored payments to health care workers whose salaries had often been stolen (Bangura 2016). In Côte d'Ivoire, most secondary school students pay their school fees digitally, virtually eliminating the high levels of theft and bribery that were commonplace after the country's civil war (Frydrych, Scharwatt, and Vonthron 2015).

A world in which databases are linked across government agencies and relevant third parties offers opportunities to expand benefit coverage. Attempts to fight poverty through redistribution are often thwarted by the failure of many eligible citizens to register for benefits. Non-take-up rates can be high: a 2016 study for the French National Assembly estimated that one-third of eligible citizens failed to take up guaranteed minimum income benefits (prior to its 2016 reform).[4] The non-take-up rate for in-work benefits was higher, at two-thirds of eligible citizens. If information about individuals is synchronized across public agencies and employers—with digital authentication (biometric if necessary) linked to banking information—changes in individual circumstances automatically captured in these data could immediately trigger coverage and benefit payment without requiring lengthy and possibly stigmatizing procedures for proving eligibility that involve filling in forms and standing in queues. Coverage inclusion as the default—rather than exclusion—would more closely align with the original policy objective and reduce poverty, though possibly at a higher fiscal cost.

---

[4]See http://www.assemblee-nationale.fr/14/rap-info/i4158.asp for more information.

Better Policies

Greater access to information and enhanced digital systems and processing capabilities could also open up new policy options.

The ability to monitor and unify information on taxpayers' income, consumption, and wealth on a timely basis offers scope to rethink the design of tax policy. For example, current systems have arbitrarily imposed a one-year period as the normal basis for income taxation, but with better access to and ease of manipulating data, something closer to a lifetime basis—arguably more equitable, and potentially more efficient too—may become possible. While for practical reasons, capital gains under current tax systems are often taxed only on realization, technology can now allow regular tracking and recording of asset values to allow gains to be taxed upon accrual.

The increased scope for individual taxpayer information exchange and matching across countries might even, ultimately, be used to impose capital income taxation directly on shareholders, eliminating the role of the corporate tax as a device for withholding tax on final shareholders. Technology that allows electronic tracking and tagging of individual consumer purchases could pave the way to more innovative and progressive systems of consumption tax, for example, by tracking (and taxing) lifetime consumption.

The availability of high-frequency fiscal data presents significant opportunities for fiscal policymakers, such as better forecasting of revenues and budget preparation. Daily fiscal data can be particularly useful to policymakers attempting to stabilize the business cycle, allowing governments to monitor economic activity in real time. With increased capacity to store and analyze data, governments can exploit the correlation of tax receipts with the business cycle to anticipate a crisis or monitor cash balances to better assess liquidity and borrowing needs (see Chapter 6 by Misch, Olden, Poplawski-Ribeiro, and Kejji).

In many countries, digitalization is also enabling improvements in governance and fiscal transparency, allowing citizens easy access to information on government revenues and spending, such as through data.gov.uk in the United Kingdom, or encouraging public participation in the budget process, as through D-Brain in Korea.[5] In this regard, the so-called Digital 5 countries—Estonia, Israel, New Zealand, Korea, and the United Kingdom[6]—have committed to build better digital public services based on the principles of open standards, open source systems, open markets, and transparency in government.

---

[5]See Chambers, Dimitrova, and Pollock (2016) for a report on outcomes.

[6]See the Digital 5 Charter at https://www.ict.govt.nz/assets/Uploads/D5Charter-signed-accessible.pdf.

NEW CHALLENGES—AND OLD ONES THAT WON'T GO AWAY

While the book illustrates the many potential benefits of the digital revolution, it also stresses that digitalization reforms require careful design and safeguards, and a clear understanding of the challenges and limitations.

Old and Familiar Challenges

Government Adoption of Technology

The implementation of new technology by governments must be appropriate to their capacity. Countries have absorbed new innovations at differing paces, reflecting the challenges of adopting technology in the public sector. Political, institutional, and human capacity constraints will continue to hinder government innovation and uptake of advanced technological solutions.

Past failures in introducing integrated financial management information systems, particularly in developing countries, illustrate some of these constraints.[7] In many countries, obstacles to successful implementation of such systems included institutional bureaucratic resistance, limited capacity of governments to adopt innovative systems, as well as exploitation of new technologies for personal gain (Diamond and Khemani 2005; USAID 2008). There is no shortage of warnings to be drawn from examples of governments failing to reap the potential advantages of technological transformation.

Digital Inclusion

In order to digitally administer tax payment and spending systems, governments must ensure that as many individuals and businesses as possible are able to access the digital world and are taking up digital technology. This may involve financial inclusion initiatives to ensure that citizens have access to a formal banking system or—perhaps more risky given the possibility of foregoing revenue unnecessarily—tax incentives such as reduced VAT or turnover tax rates to encourage the use of digital payment systems over cash payments, as seen in Argentina, Korea, and Uruguay. Other countries (China, United Arab Emirates) have launched digital wallet or mobile money initiatives to provide an alternative to cash for those without access to bank accounts.

The rollout of new technology and initiatives must be carefully designed, recognizing the transition time and costs for adoption by individuals and businesses. For example, new electronic-reporting requirements may impose a high burden on small businesses, and some individuals may have no access to digital technology, requiring alternative arrangements. The November 2016 surprise

---

[7]Integrated financial management information systems computerize and automate budget and accounting operations, enabling access to reliable operations data and increasing fiscal transparency and control.

demonetization in India is a case in point. The seemingly overnight decision to remove large-denomination notes—while intended to reduce the scale of illegal transactions conducted with "black" money and accelerate the digitalization of the Indian economy—caused widespread disruption in retail markets for small businesses and consumers alike.

Complementary Institutional Reforms

Taking full advantage of the opportunities of digitalization can require government to organize itself differently and move away from traditional skill mixes. For instance, digitalization eases the more complete integration of tax and social benefit systems (recognizing that social support payments are simply negative taxes). Indeed, many tax administrations increasingly find themselves not only collecting money, but paying it out as well. And that can require quite different skills and processes. Sorting out a complex tax case can take months or years, to no very great harm. But complex and rapidly changing personal circumstances—the mother who finds herself suddenly homeless—need quick response, and personal skills required to deal with such emergencies can be quite different from those needed to explain VAT refund entitlement. At a wider level too, linking information across government agencies—between the tax administration and health services, for instance—and between government and private institutions—the tax administration and P2P enterprises, for example—can require developing new channels and protocols for such exchange.

New Challenges

Revolutions are not easy times to live through and can have their nastier aspects. The digital revolutions discussed in this book are no exception.

New Taxation Problems

Governments might approach the digital revolution with some caution and vigilance, with some awareness that innovations can often incentivize individual and corporate behavior in directions that make effective taxation harder, not easier.

There is no shortage of examples of tax fraudsters undermining or even exploiting governments' deployment of new technologies. The use of electronic cash registers, for instance, led to the development of "zappers": software that simply deletes the records of some sales in ways intended to be undetectable. In 2009, the Emissions Trading System of the European Union (buying and selling of rights to emit carbon) was brought to a halt by VAT fraud—at a revenue loss put by Europol at €5 billion—that exploited online trading and was in part hidden behind the cover of the sheer speed and volume of derivatives trading. And some European countries have been attacked by VAT schemes that involved automated submission of multiple fraudulent VAT refund claims, each too small by itself for the tax administration to focus its attention on, but, through their sheer number, significant in aggregate. Criminal attacks, it is important to bear in mind, can be extraordinarily sophisticated. It will not be easy for governments to keep one step ahead.

In the corporate sphere, much recent attention has been given to the tax planning strategies used by multinationals to reduce their tax base (IMF 2014; OECD 2013). Over recent years, digitalization has intensified these challenges by enabling an increasing number of companies, including many household names, to operate and sell electronically in multiple jurisdictions without having much of a physical presence there. As discussed in Chapter 4 by Devereux and Vella, one approach to this problem is to widen the current notion of what it means to be active in a country for tax purposes—a "doing what we do now but better" approach. A more radical alternative, also explored in that chapter, is to change the nature of the corporate tax more profoundly, so as to impose the tax liability where consumers or shareholders are located, rather than where the business has a production-related presence—very much a "doing things differently" approach.

As information becomes valuable and readily traded, questions arise as to whether it should be an object of taxation in itself. It could be argued, for instance, that information about the behaviors and preferences of a country's citizens is a collective asset of that country in much the same way as would be any oil, gold, or other natural resource asset lying within its borders. From that, it is a short step to see a potential taxing right akin to that widely recognized and exercised in relation to natural resources. This, again, would be a radical departure from current norms.

Getting the Information

The impact of digitalization depends heavily on the accuracy and timeliness of information collected. Prepopulation of tax returns, for instance, might be an attractive option for reducing compliance and administration costs, but the system must be carefully designed and implemented to ensure that it does not provide opportunities and motivation for cheating. If the prepopulated information is unduly favorable to the taxpayer, for instance, one might not expect the taxpayer to voluntarily correct it: psychologically, prepopulation transfers "ownership" of errors from the taxpayer to the revenue agency (see Chapter 5 by Chen, Grimshaw, and Myles).

Ensuring adequate data quality requires appropriate incentives for revealing such information. Those wishing to avoid prosecution or large tax bills, for instance, have an incentive to find ways not to leave a digital trail of their transactions. One route to this is the use of cash, and eliminating this opportunity for concealment is a key merit of the movement to a cashless economy notably urged by Rogoff (2016). Several countries have taken steps to "demonetize" or withdraw large-denomination notes from circulation to stamp out undocumented activity and encourage use of digital money transfers, with India, discussed in Chapter 11 by Roy and Rai, being the prime example. The dark web, however, has shown private initiative to be adept in developing ways to transact online without leaving traceable footprints. While this will become less attractive as the ease of traceable digital transactions continues to increase, reducing incentives to use untraceable alternatives, such as decentralized cryptocurrencies, will remain a key concern.

Privacy

While increased information provides opportunities for more targeted design and implementation of tax and spending policy, there are significant sensitivities surrounding the collection of detailed individual and corporate information. The real-time recording of digital information on individuals and the use of such data by businesses in their marketing efforts have raised concerns about how the management and use of information should be regulated and protected. And while people often readily provide their data to retail companies or leave digital footprints in the form of social media activity, government recording and management of individual data is often met with Orwellian unease.

As noted earlier, some countries are now moving to a single-platform approach, connecting information on citizens held by different government ministries and centralizing storage and processing in a handful of data centers. While such data systems can be used for more efficient and targeted tax and spending policies, in the wrong hands they could easily be used to cause social and economic disruption. Indeed, recent years have seen intrusions of privacy with hacking, leaks, and ransom attacks at major government institutions worldwide, highlighting the vulnerability of government systems to outside intrusion.

In the end, the nature and extent of possible data collection is a function of institutional and sociopolitical factors and may be more limited in countries where trust in government or rule of law is weak. However, what is clear is that to envisage the enhanced fiscal policies conceptualized in this book, government oversight of citizens may require a new level of scrutiny if citizens are to trust in how oversight is exercised.

Fundamental Limits

While the digital revolution undoubtedly expands the fiscal policy frontier, solving some institutional or development problems may remain beyond the scope of technology. Electronic payment systems tighten controls and can reduce fraud and corruption. But one must not be naive. Criminals have already proved remarkably adept in attacking tax systems. Bribery and theft can occur after transfers made electronically to a government worker have been cashed at the local bank. Farmers may receive better information about agricultural practices but will still need access to roads and markets to sell their commodities. Blockchain technology may allow for more secure management of land registries, but this will be of little use in a country whose original paper-based registry has been destroyed. Capital gains will remain difficult to tax on accrual for assets that are not regularly traded, and so are hard to value. In other words, digitalization will not remove the institutional constraints under which fiscal policy must often operate, for example, where public and private incentives are not aligned, access to markets is limited for large segments of the population, or property rights are ill-defined.

Moreover, digitalization does not solve one fundamental problem of public finance: the inability to observe private information to distinguish between individual ability, effort, and luck. An ideal tax and transfer system would be based not on an individual's income, but rather on her initial circumstances and characteristics. The debate has only just begun as to whether these characteristics might at some point become observable, and then subject to manipulation.[8]

LOOKING FORWARD

The digital revolution is already well under way. Governments must respond or be left behind.

Each country's path to digitalization must depend on its circumstances. While most advanced economies are choosing more incremental approaches, for developing countries, technological advances offer the potential to "leapfrog" to newer and more sophisticated policy formulation, design, and implementation.

Countries with more basic infrastructure may be able to leapfrog directly to the latest digital technologies. For example, some countries without universal fixed landline infrastructure have jumped to more sophisticated and accessible mobile phone and internet technology. Kenya—which has pioneered the use of mobile-phone-based money transfer through M-Pesa—now even allows the direct payment of taxes and for government services by mobile phone (see Chapter 10 by Ndung'u). Such technology has been extended to fragile states such as Afghanistan, where the ability to raise revenues is hampered by conflict and corruption. Estonia, starting from a low infrastructure base after independence from the Soviet Union, jumped over several stages of development, now operating in a fully digitalized environment, using blockchain-distributed ledger technology to keep systems secure, and a "data embassy" housed in Luxembourg, capable of rebooting the country in case of cyberattack.

The digital revolution is raising hard questions around inequality and redistribution. Digitalization comes with an increased automation of manual labor jobs, with software and robots performing some jobs partially, or even, at times, entirely (Acemoglu and Restrepo 2016). This can have important implications across countries too: automation may have adverse effects for developing countries, for example, where a large amount of low-cost labor is employed by multinational companies to carry out manufacturing work. And as digitalization allows scope for substantial profit generation, there will be implications for employment and income distribution as the greatest benefits are likely to be enjoyed by the providers of intellectual and financial capital.

These changing employment and distributional trends are already starting to raise questions about the appropriate fiscal policy response. One example is the suggestion that the increased use of labor-replacing "robot capital" should be

---

[8]This is touched on in Chapter 2 by Jacobs and Chapter 5 by Chen, Grimshaw, and Myles, which take contrasting positions.

taxed.[9] Another approach, more in line with economists' reluctance to forgo improvements in the efficiency of production, would be to ensure a fairer distribution of ownership and to tax the economic value created by robots. More immediately, the possibility of increasing job destruction and structural unemployment is raising anew the question of whether it is time to move toward adoption of a universal basic income (IMF 2017).[10] Others are more optimistic. Brynjolfsson and McAfee (2014) present a vision of a future in which we can shape technology rather than the opposite and in which policy can increase overall economic growth to improve job prospects for all, even as digitalization takes hold, by investing in education, research and development, and infrastructure.

The digital revolution also underscores the importance of international cooperation. Information is now flowing across borders with unprecedented pace and volume, with significant impacts on innovation, global supply chains, international trade, and capital flows.[11] Serious cybersecurity threats and concerns have highlighted the vulnerability of systems to widespread and costly disruption of economic activity and the importance of international cooperation in an interdependent digital economy, including to address these threats. In an ever more-interconnected global system, greater coordination may well also be necessary to resolve the international tax challenges exacerbated by the digital revolution.

The challenges that lie ahead for governments, if they are to realize the full potential of digitalization, will try the established ways in which they have gone about their business—and even how they think about what that business is.

WHAT DOES THIS BOOK COVER?

This book is divided into five parts. Part I explores the new frontiers in tax policy and revenue administration, starting with a broader look at the implications of digitalization for tax policy design before focusing on the emerging P2P economy, challenges of corporate taxation in an increasingly digitalized economy, and the use of prepopulation and online guidance for tax administration. Part II discusses the transformative potential of digitalization for broader fiscal management, from the availability of daily fiscal data to blockchain and artificial intelligence. Part III turns to spending policy and discusses how even simple and now-ubiquitous technology and information—mobile phones, biometric data—can help improve public service delivery and perhaps even the targeting of social

---

[9]The Korean government is proposing something along these lines, not introducing a tax, but scaling back tax incentives for investment in automation (see The Telegraph 2017).

[10]In its most commonly used definition, a universal basic income is a uniform transfer given to all citizens on a regular basis. Most prominently, some form of a universal basic income has been advocated by Atkinson (2015). IMF (2017) also discusses universal basic income as a policy option for tackling inequality.

[11]See He and others (2017) for a discussion of the impact of new technological innovations in the financial sector, in particular in the area of cross-border payments, including possible regulatory challenges and areas for international cooperation.

benefits, while also stressing that they do not in themselves necessarily solve or sidestep deeper institutional problems. Part IV describes and reviews experiences with digitalization in a number of countries, including, notably, Kenya and India. Part V concludes by quantifying the size of the potential benefit from the digital revolution.

Part I: Pushing the Frontiers in Tax Policy and Revenue Administration

Bas Jacobs opens in Chapter 2 by exploring the implications of expanded information and analytical capacity presented by the digital revolution for tax policy and enforcement. These can be profound, since information constraints lie at the heart of the traditional economic analysis of taxation. For the optimal tax theorist, in an ideal world, governments would be able to completely verify all relevant fixed economic characteristics of taxpayers at zero cost. In such a world, nondistortionary individualized lump-sum taxes would be available to redistribute income and raise revenue: information being perfect, tax avoidance and evasion would be impossible. In reality, of course, the government does not have such perfect information, and taxpayers may misrepresent their income, consumption, wealth, or bequests to avoid or even evade taxes. To alleviate these problems, the government uses tax audits to verify economic outcomes, along with penalties for noncompliance.

So, what does the digital revolution mean for tax policy design and enforcement? First, *Jacobs* argues that digitalization can help improve the enforcement capacity of tax authorities by providing more possibilities to verify the true economic outcomes of taxpayers. For instance, greater use of digital payment methods may provide the government with more information on total individual consumption expenditures, allowing tax authorities to verify more effectively than at present whether reported (labor and capital) income and wealth holdings are in line with observed consumption levels. Digitalization could also help improve compliance by creating and linking data registers on wealth and capital incomes, with financial institutions acting as third-party reporters—indeed this is to some degree already happening.

Second, digitalization can allow governments to implement more sophisticated tax systems than are currently in place. For example, tax liabilities could be conditioned not only on the taxpayer's current yearly income, but also on income earned in different periods, income earned by spouses, asset holdings, and so on. By conditioning tax schedules on more information, the government can target income redistribution better and potentially in more efficient ways. Of course, whether governments will actually implement such tax reforms is determined not only by the economic benefits of having better tax enforcement or more efficient tax systems, but also by horizontal-equity considerations and citizens' concerns over privacy and the potential abuse of state powers. Indeed, these concerns might be the reason why many of the suggested tax reforms have not been implemented so far. Nonetheless, as the author concludes, understanding the new position of the tax policy frontier is important for policymakers in an increasingly digitalized world.

In addition to recognizing the potential opportunities for tax policy, governments must also position themselves to adequately respond to new types of economic activity generated in this increasingly digital world, particularly where such activity presents challenges for domestic revenue mobilization.

In Chapter 3, *Aqib Aslam* and *Alpa Shah* take up a leading instance of this, exploring the tax policy and administration issues associated with digitally intermediated P2P activities—facilitated through online platforms—that have emerged as an increasingly popular way to organize activity and provide goods and services. They review the key features of the P2P economy that could be deciding factors in its future tax treatment. Importantly, they argue that the emergence of P2P activities does not necessarily require a radical rethink of the existing tax system or the principles on which it is based.

Instead, the P2P economy—should it continue to grow—is forcing tax policy and administration to reconsider old trade-offs in a new light. Specifically, as the P2P sector continues to grow, the number of new small businesses is increasing, particularly at the lower end of the income distribution. Should this continue, existing well-known challenges for taxing large numbers of small businesses will only increase. Furthermore, these new entrants could displace larger firms, while at the same time formalizing previously undocumented activity.

Happily, the P2P economy also presents an important and distinct opportunity. Digital platforms can already act as custodians for tax administrations by withholding various taxes (potentially including both sales taxes and income tax on those providing the intermediated services), a role that could help ease both compliance and administration while raising revenue, particularly in low-capacity countries. In addition, as online intermediaries, P2P platforms are recording data on the myriad of transactions taking place in their virtual markets. If governments were to cooperate with them to access these data, this could alleviate information constraints and strengthen tax enforcement and allow for better quantification of activity that has until now been undocumented.

In Chapter 4, *Michael Devereux* and *John Vella* explore the challenges created by digitalization for the taxation of the profits of multinational enterprises. Under the current international tax architecture, source countries are allocated primary taxing rights on businesses' active income and residence countries on the primary taxing rights on passive income, such as dividends, royalties, and interest. However, the actual allocation of taxable profit depends on the nature and extent of avoidance—"profit shifting"—activities undertaken by multinationals.

The authors explore the ways in which digitalization has increased the internationalization of business, generating increasingly complex supply chains that expand the possibilities for profit shifting and challenge traditional notions of a strong physical presence in a country being required for a company to be liable to corporate tax there, posing serious challenges for the national taxation of such multinational corporations. Digital businesses are at the forefront of these concerns, seeming to be particularly adept at shifting profit to low-tax jurisdictions.

The chapter calls for fundamental reform to address the stresses now placed on the international corporate tax system, arguing that they point instead to some system in which taxation is based on relatively immobile factors—so limiting opportunities for the tax base to be shifted elsewhere. It raises and explores two possibilities: to tax where shareholders are located or where consumers are located. (For the first of these, digitalization may eventually come to help implementation, enabling profits to be directly attached to shareholders, as noted earlier, and taxed at their level.) It also discusses the distinct and highly contentious corporate tax challenges posed by certain types of digital business that offer their services for "free" to one side of the market they serve.

In Chapter 5, *Jingnan Chen, Shaun Grimshaw*, and *Gareth Myles* report direct evidence from laboratory experiments in the United Kingdom on the behavioral implications of digital interventions to improve taxpayer compliance. One experiment relates to the prepopulation of tax returns, which is already practiced in several advanced economies (such as Australia, Denmark, and the Netherlands). Here the issue they examine is how taxpayers are likely to react when the information they are presented with is incorrect. When the mistake is in the taxpayers' favor, it emerges that taxpayers tend not to correct it. This does not in itself mean that, overall, prepopulation is bad for compliance—that seems unlikely to be the case, and there are clear advantages in terms of reducing the taxpayers' costs of complying with their obligations—but it does caution that inaccurate or incomplete prepopulation carries dangers in signaling weaknesses in the information available to the revenue service. Perhaps surprisingly, the results also suggest that when the error is in the direction of imposing too much tax, taxpayers tend to accept this too. The second issue they examine is the relative effectiveness of providing information to taxpayers online rather than on paper. This proved less significant than the nature of the guidance itself—online guidance, in that sense, is not necessarily in itself better.

The chapter thus provides a very tangible reminder that digitalization is not perfection, that established practices and concerns can remain important in checking the full accuracy of the final return, and that convenience of obtaining information is not a substitute for its clarity. The chapter also stresses the importance of rigorously evaluating digital innovations, with lab experiments among the most important tools to this end.

Part II: Innovations in Fiscal Management

The second section of the book explores the practical application of new technology in macroeconomic policy and public finance.

In Chapter 6, *Florian Misch, Brian Olden, Marcos Poplawski-Ribeiro,* and *Lamya Kejji* explore how digitalization of public finances and public financial management (PFM) tools have facilitated the construction of disaggregated and high-frequency fiscal data (in this case, daily). Many countries have implemented information technology systems to automate the management of their public finances. These systems record daily government transactions—tax receipts, wage payments, debt issuance, and so on. The authors argue that such data are accessible and can be exploited for policy purposes by complementing lower-frequency conventional macroeconomic aggregates for real-time macroeconomic analysis. The chapter makes two main contributions. First, it demonstrates that digitalization has made daily fiscal data accessible in many countries. Second, the authors argue that removing noise from the data is relatively easy, facilitating its practical use in fiscal policy analysis.

The chapter presents several case studies and examples to illustrate the usefulness of daily fiscal data to monitor tax revenue, assess fiscal vulnerabilities, and monitor economic activity using cash balances and payroll receipts in real time. The authors acknowledge possible drawbacks. Safeguards must be in place to ensure that false alarms are not triggered through misinterpretation of short-term volatility in the data. In addition, information systems reflect only cash transactions and may not capture some important fiscal operations. Nevertheless, the chapter makes a strong case for exploiting this underused source of fiscal information, given proper safeguards and capacity building.

Arvind Krishna, Martin Fleming, and *Solomon Assefa* explore in Chapter 7 two emerging digital technologies, blockchain and cognitive computing, and potential applications to government and public finance. Blockchain technology can reduce frictions and increase trust in transaction systems by putting data into shared, distributed ledgers—synchronized databases—that allow every participant access to the system of record for a transaction. Cognitive systems can process and analyze these data to gain insight and detect patterns. They argue that the advent of digitalization and cloud computing gives government and industry access to advanced technical solutions through the internet. This reduces the need for large, capital-intensive investments in infrastructure and lowers cost.

The authors examine how blockchain and cognitive computing could, individually and in combination, help governments improve certain core functions, for example, digital citizen identity, tax collection, and benefit payments. With billions of people lacking proper identification, blockchain offers the possibility of establishing permanent, immutable records of identity for citizens that cannot be lost or stolen. In fact, Estonia already offers its citizens a digital identity card based on blockchain technology. Blockchain could also be used in revenue collection, which is currently a separate process from the commercial transactions on which it depends. With blockchain, companies would not be required to submit a return, as their tax account could be continuously maintained and settlement automated. The existing separation between the commercial transactions and their tax component encourages both deliberate and accidental underreporting. Cognitive systems can spot this underreporting by looking at the patterns of commercial transactions and their relative tax generation. Furthermore, blockchain technology can also help improve the payment of welfare benefits—in the United Kingdom, for example, the Department of Work and Pensions is engaged in a pilot program to record benefit payment transactions on a distributed ledger to improve their management and reduce overpayment of claims.

The authors offer a series of recommendations on how best to prepare to harness these emerging technologies. In particular, they emphasize the need for governments to increase their capacity to manage and standardize data and processes. This includes the ability to maintain large-scale, high-quality standardized data sets that will facilitate data sharing and collection—a core requirement for blockchain and cognitive computing—and the willingness to standardize processes for work flow, document management, authentication, and certification. More importantly, governments must invest in human capital—a key to success in adopting disruptive technologies.

Part III: Modernizing Public Service Delivery and Spending

The third section considers the impact of technology on spending policies and public service delivery. Indeed, the growth of digital technology worldwide has generated considerable optimism about its scope for alleviating key market failures associated with public service provision. Over the past decade, the number of digitally based public service initiatives has increased substantially, with an estimated 400 deployments as of 2017. Yet research on the impact of these initiatives is still limited, often focusing on particular countries and sectors, so with little sense of its general applicability.

Jenny Aker reviews some of these initiatives in Chapter 8, focusing on mobile phone technology in developing countries across a range of sectors including health, education, and agriculture. Mobile phones are used in a variety of ways, including as pedagogical devices in the classroom, as platforms to distribute social transfers, as medical recordkeeping devices, and as communication devices for key agricultural information on the weather or commodity prices.

She finds that such initiatives can, at times, be successful along certain dimensions. For example, in social protection, they have increased the efficiency of provision—that is, to lower the cost of providing a public service of a given quality. In education, research finds that digitalization can improve effectiveness—ensuring that programs meet their stated goals. Results are mixed, however, in agriculture and health. While mobile devices offer new opportunities, they also add new challenges—text requires literacy, and voice platforms are costly. In addition, they do not always overcome structural barriers to development, such as lack of access to other essential infrastructure, such as roads or property rights.

The chapter concludes that digital public service provision should build on a thorough understanding of the market failures—information asymmetries, transactions costs—that are a binding constraint to technology adoption and public service provision.

In Chapter 9, *Ravi Kanbur* cautions against overoptimism in viewing technology as a solution for difficulties in targeting public expenditure for poverty reduction. His chapter revisits the fundamentals of the theory of targeting to pinpoint the possible impacts of the digital revolution on three key dimensions of fine targeting—information costs, high implicit marginal tax rates, and political economy. For example, he argues that while biometric information may provide a unique identifier, fine targeting requires detailed information on income and consumption, which will remain scarce in developing countries with large informal sectors, even with efforts to digitalize. Similarly, digitalization will not solve the problem of high implicit marginal tax rates required by fine targeting.

Finally, digitalization may not necessarily eliminate constraints brought about by political economy considerations, norms, and existing institutions. Middle-income citizens may object to spending that benefits the poor with little benefit to them; corrupt officials may bypass the digital system meant to reduce leakage. However, digitally based social protection programs have often successfully lowered the program's costs. This seems to suggest a need for empirical studies based on household data to examine the trade-offs involved in the kind of finer targeting that digitalization may enable.

Part IV: Country Case Studies

This section presents country case studies and offers lessons for those seeking to embark on a path of digital reform.

Njuguna Ndung'u describes in Chapter 10 how the digital revolution in Kenya has paved the way for significant changes in tax policy design and administration. This revolution was set in motion by the creation of *M-Pesa*, a money-transfer system that gradually advanced into a real-time retail payments system and further into a virtual savings and credit supply platform. These developments fostered a dramatic increase in financial inclusion and have provided a springboard for the tax authorities to devise more efficient systems for tax payments, including web-enabled application systems for the administration of domestic taxes (the iTax system) and a mobile phone application that facilitates tax payment and taxpayers' access to tax information (the M-Service platform).

The chapter describes these innovations, detailing the critical role of the monetary authorities and the telecommunications regulator in providing an appropriate legal and regulatory framework, and the importance of the modernization efforts of the Kenya Revenue Authority prior to the implementation of the iTax and M-Service systems. While sufficient data are not available to quantify the impact of these digitalization efforts on tax collections, the chapter argues that digitalization of the tax system has reduced direct interaction between taxpayers and tax officers, thus reducing the opportunities for bribery and fraud, and has allowed the revenue authority to reduce the costs of tax collection, with many small and previously undocumented businesses now using mobile phones for tax payments. The Kenyan case illustrates that widespread use of digital financial services and greater financial inclusion can be an important impetus to the digitalization of public finances.

In Chapter 11, *Rathin Roy* and *Suyash Rai* focus on the fiscal policy consequences of digitalization of the Indian economy. They review the steps taken to facilitate digitalization, including the demonetization decision in 2016. With the introduction of *Aadhaar*, the government has sought to improve the effectiveness of public expenditure, especially transfers. Successful financial inclusion programs were essential to these efforts—under the *Pradhan Mantri Jan Dhan Yojana,* more than 280 million bank accounts were opened between 2014 and 2017, allowing the delivery of social benefits payments directly to beneficiaries' bank accounts. In addition, the government has developed an online system of public procurement and sought to use digital technology to improve tax collection and enforcement.

The best-known and most internationally publicized demonetization initiative of recent years is probably that of India. In a November 2016 surprise announcement, the government declared its decision to withdraw large-denomination notes—about 87 percent of currency in circulation—to expand the tax base and reduce the use of cash and illegal cash holdings (so-called black money). The government hoped for a permanent shift of a predominantly cash-based economy to digital payments resulting from demonetization.

The authors note that it is too early to fully measure the impact of most of these initiatives, although available evidence suggests that the use of biometric information has delivered less-corrupt payment systems and a reduction in leakage. Preliminary evidence also suggests that the direct delivery of social benefits to beneficiaries can generate nontrivial fiscal savings. And while demonetization and its surprise rollout may have weakened economic activity in the short term, it is too early to assess its full impact on the informal economy and on digitalization in India.

Marco Cangiano, Alan Gelb, and *Ruth Goodwin-Groen* document in Chapter 12 the promise of digitalization in PFM. They argue that it is time to mainstream digitalization of payments as part of a functional PFM system to better achieve both PFM and broader reform goals. In so doing, care should be exercised to avoid common mistakes incurred in implementing government financial management information systems. Case studies illustrate the benefits of integrating digitalization of payments with a government's PFM.

In India, the government has combined the use of unique biometric identifiers (the *Aadhaar* program) and financial inclusion for both efficiency and effectiveness in social benefits and to reduce the number of illegitimate beneficiaries under welfare programs. In Mexico, aligning the policy objectives of digitalization and centralization of payments through a "single treasury account" has improved the efficiency and effectiveness of both and contributed to financial inclusion. By creating X-Road—a data exchange layer that enables secure internet-based data exchange between information systems—and an advanced digital identity system, Estonia has significantly enhanced the effectiveness of government. Ghana's efforts to standardize digital identification and shift away from a cash-based economy are still facing challenges, but have contributed to a reduction of ghost workers included in public payrolls.

These cases point to key success factors for digitalization and PFM integration: first, high-level leadership, needed to neutralize opposition that will inevitably arise with lengthy reforms; second, an integrated comprehensive approach to building a digital and regulatory infrastructure for PFM; and finally, an appreciation of the risks of the digital economy, which requires attention to data privacy and security.

Part V: How Much Is It All Worth?

To conclude the book, in Chapter 13, *Susan Lund, Olivia White,* and *Jason Lamb* quantify the potential value at stake when government payment transactions shift from cash to digital. They focus on savings stemming from reducing leakage in government payments and tax receipts, reducing fraudulent payments and tax evasion, and cost savings from digitalizing payment processes. They find that digitalizing government payments in developing countries could save roughly 1 percent of GDP, equivalent to $220–$320 billion in value annually. This is equal to 1.5 percent of the value of all government payment transactions. Of this total, roughly 0.5 percent of GDP—about $105–$155 billion each year—would accrue directly to the government and improve fiscal balances, while the remainder would benefit individuals and businesses as government spending reaches its intended targets. These estimates may well underestimate the value of digitalizing public finances, as they leave aside potentially significant second-order effects arising from the improvement in government service delivery, including encouraging more widespread use of digital finance in the private sector, and shifting of economic activity from the informal to the formal sector.

Clearly, much remains to be done in understanding the likely implications of the digital revolutions now under way in the design and conduct of fiscal policies—and quantifying them will be even harder. The implications are also likely to vary widely across countries: in some cases, for instance, they may enable the size of government to increase so as to address unmet spending needs and achievement of the Sustainable Development Goals; in others, it may be a matter of raising and spending much the same in aggregate but doing both more effectively.

Although the outcomes of revolutions are inherently hard to predict, the chapters in this book make it clear that the effects of current and future digital revolutions are likely to be profound.

REFERENCES

Acemoglu, Daron, and Pascual Restrepo. 2016. "Robots and Jobs: Evidence from U.S. Labor Markets." MIT Working Paper, Massachusetts Institute of Technology, Cambridge, MA.

Atkinson, Anthony. 2015. *Inequality: What Can Be Done?* Cambridge, MA: Harvard University Press.

Bangura, Joe Abass. 2016. "Saving Money, Saving Lives: A Case Study on the Benefits of Digitizing Payments to Ebola Response Workers in Sierra Leone." Better Than Cash Alliance, New York.

Brynjolfsson, Erik, and Andrew McAfee. 2014. *The Second Machine Age: Work, Progress, and Prosperity in a Time of Brilliant Technologies.* New York: W. W. Norton & Company.

Chambers, Lucy, Velichka Dimitrova, and Rufus Pollock. 2016. "Technology for Transparent and Accountable Public Finance." Report, Open Knowledge Foundation, Cambridge, United Kingdom.

Deloitte. 2013. "Comparative Study of the Personal Income Tax Return Process in Belgium and 33 Other Countries." London.

Diamond, Jack, and Pokar Khemani. 2005. "Introducing Financial Management Information Systems in Developing Countries." IMF Working Paper 05/196, International Monetary Fund, Washington, DC.

Fan, Haichao, Yu Liu, Nancy Qian, and Jaya Wen. 2017. "The Short- and Medium-Run Effects of Computerized VAT Invoices on Tax Revenues in China." Unpublished, Fudan University, Shanghai, China.

Frydrych, Jennifer, Claire Scharwatt, and Nicolas Vonthron. 2015. "Paying School Fees with Mobile Money in Côte d'Ivoire: A Public-Private Partnership to Achieve Greater Efficiency." Case Study, GSMA, London.

Gelb, Alan, and Julia Clark. 2013. "Identification for Development: The Biometrics Revolution." Working Paper 315, Center for Global Development, Washington, DC.

GSMA. 2013. "The Mobile Economy 2013." London.

He, Dong, Ross Leckow, Vikram Haksar, Tommaso Mancini-Griffoli, Nigel Jenkinson, Mikari Kashima, Tanai Khiaonarong, Celine Rochon, and Herve Tourpe. 2017. *Fintech and Financial Services: Initial Considerations.* IMF Staff Discussion Note 17/05, International Monetary Fund, Washington, DC.

International Monetary Fund (IMF). 2014. "Spillovers in International Corporate Taxation." IMF Policy Paper, Washington, DC.

———. 2017. *Fiscal Monitor: Tackling Inequality.* Washington, DC, October.

International Telecommunications Union (ITU). 2014. *Measuring the Information Society Report.* Geneva.

McAfee, Andrew, and Erik Brynjolfsson. 2017. *Machine, Platform, Crowd: Harnessing Our Digital Future.* New York: W.W. Norton & Company.

Naritomi, Joana. 2015. "Consumers as Tax Auditors." Working Paper, London School of Economics, London.

Organisation for Economic Co-operation and Development (OECD). 2006. "Using Third Party Information Reports to Assist Taxpayers Meet Their Return Filing Obligations—Country Experiences with the Use of Pre-Populated Personal Tax Returns." Information Note, Forum on Tax Administration Taxpayer Sub-Group, Paris.

———. 2013. "Base Erosion and Profit Shifting Action Plan." Note by the Secretariat, Paris.

Rogoff, K. S. 2016. *The Curse of Cash.* Princeton, NJ: Princeton University Press.

Ross, Alec. 2016. *The Industries of the Future.* New York: Simon & Schuster.

The Telegraph. 2017. "South Korea Introduces World's First 'Robot Tax.'" August 9.

US Agency for International Development (USAID). 2008. "Integrated Financial Management Information Systems: A Practical Guide." USAID Paper, Washington, DC.

World Bank. 2016. *World Development Report: Digital Dividends.* Washington, DC.

Zimmerman, Jamie M., Kristy Bohling, and Sarah Rotman Parker. 2014. "Electronic G2P Payments: Evidence from Four Lower-Income Countries." Focus Note 93, Consultative Group to Assist the Poor, Washington, DC.

PART I

Pushing the Frontiers in Tax Policy and Revenue Administration

CHAPTER 2

Digitalization and Taxation

BAS JACOBS

INTRODUCTION

In an ideal world, governments would be able to completely verify all relevant economic outcomes and characteristics of taxpayers at zero cost. In such a world, non-distortionary, individualized lump-sum taxes would be available to redistribute income and to raise revenue. Indeed, the government could then condition its tax policy on all the characteristics of taxpayers on which it likes to base income redistribution: earning ability, needs, initial endowments, inheritances, luck, and so on. Moreover, if information were perfect, tax avoidance and evasion would not exist. Governments would just know how much individuals earn, save, and consume. If markets were perfect as well (no externalities, no monopoly, complete contracts, symmetric information, complete markets, and zero transaction costs), the second fundamental theorem of welfare economics would apply: governments could completely separate issues of allocation and distribution, since any efficient market outcome could be achieved with suitable redistributions using individualized lump-sum taxes and transfers.

The world is not ideal, however, since information on economic outcomes and characteristics of taxpayers is not perfect. Information constraints lie at the heart of the traditional economic analysis of taxation. Government is not able to verify all economic outcomes of individuals or households. Indeed, taxpayers may misrepresent their incomes, consumption, wealth, or bequests to avoid or even evade paying taxes. Information constraints determine a government's tax enforcement capacity. Governments use costly verification of economic outcomes (tax audits) and penalties for noncompliance, to alleviate information problems in verifying economic outcomes. The taxpayer's willingness to tolerate risk, the size of penalties if caught evading, and the tax enforcement technology determine the extent of tax avoidance (Allingham and Sandmo 1972).

The chapter benefited from numerous comments and useful suggestions from Aqib Aslam, Mike Devereux, Vitor Gaspar, Michael Keen, Ruud de Mooij, Victoria Perry, Alpa Shah, Geneviève Verdier, and Philippe Wingender.

Furthermore, governments cannot verify important characteristics (such as earning abilities) and economic behaviors of individuals and firms (such as work effort). As a result, non-distortionary, individualized lump-sum taxes are not feasible and government must rely on taxing verifiable economic outcomes such as income (output), consumption, savings, and bequests. Information constraints imply that government inevitably distorts incentives to earn income, to consume, to save, and to leave a bequest. Such constraints are, therefore, the fundamental reason for the ultimate trade-off between equity and efficiency (Mirrlees 1971).[1]

Information constraints thus determine the opportunities for tax avoidance and evasion and shape the inescapable trade-off between equity and efficiency. This chapter argues that digitalization can help alleviate these constraints in two ways.

First, digitalization can help relax information constraints through better ways to verify the true economic outcomes of taxpayers. Digitalization makes it easier for governments to link existing information in various parts of the tax system to better detect evasion or avoidance. Digitalization can thus be seen *as improving the tax enforcement technology* of the government. Better tax enforcement allows governments to raise the same revenue with lower taxes (more efficiency) or to raise more tax revenue with the same taxes.

Second, digitalization can allow governments to implement more sophisticated tax systems. For example, tax liabilities can be conditioned not only on current yearly (labor) income, but also on income earned in different periods, income earned by spouses, asset holdings, and so on. By conditioning tax schedules on more information, government can better target income redistribution. Consequently, the same income redistribution can be achieved with lower tax rates, or the same tax rates can achieve more income redistribution. By using more information in the design of tax systems, digitalization can thus *alleviate the equity-efficiency trade-off*.

Importantly, however, digitalization can never negate the equity-efficiency trade-off. Important economic behaviors remain the private information of taxpayers and therefore unobservable to tax authorities (such as work effort). This remains so even in a fully digitized world, and even if there were no tax avoidance or evasion. However, by conditioning tax schedules on variables that go beyond current incomes, governments can improve the equity-efficiency trade-off while respecting the fundamental information constraints on the non-verifiability of certain economic behaviors.

This chapter follows a classical public finance approach, which is firmly rooted in welfare economics. The main goal is to identify desirable tax policies as if they are set by an enlightened dictator. Naturally, enlightened dictators do not exist and discussions on taxation cannot be seen in isolation from political economy,

---

[1]At low levels of taxation, the trade-off between equity and efficiency might not be present if income redistribution enhances economic efficiency, such as by providing income insurance or alleviating capital market failures (for example, promoting investment in education). Moreover, if tax systems are not optimized there may not be a trade-off between equity and efficiency. Removing the inefficiency can then enhance both equity and efficiency.

legal (horizontal equity), and privacy concerns. Nevertheless, this chapter aims to provide information to policymakers on whether it would be possible to improve tax policies. This is important policy information, irrespective of whether political and other concerns would ultimately prevent societies from implementing welfare-improving tax reforms.

Digitalization affects both the public and private sectors. Digitalization may foster stronger tax avoidance and evasion and raise behavioral responses to taxation, such as through more aggressive tax planning. Digitalization can therefore also raise the efficiency costs of taxation, which tend to lower optimal taxes. Moreover, by fostering tax avoidance and evasion, digitalization can contribute to rising inequality in income and wealth, both of which tend to increase optimal taxes. As such, digitalization in the private sector is likely to raise both the efficiency costs and the equity gains of redistributive taxes, and it is not clear whether digitalization in the private sector should result in lower or higher optimal tax rates. The analysis here remains applicable, however, since better use of information in the *public* sector allows for more efficient tax systems for all possible efficiency costs and distributional gains of taxation.

What does digitalization imply for optimal tax design? The chapter analyzes the promise of digitalization for (1) reducing tax avoidance and evasion and (2) the optimal design of taxes on labor, capital, and consumption. It provides 13 policy ideas to improve existing tax systems. Five ideas relate to improving the tax enforcement technology of the government by exploiting more information on taxpayers' economic outcomes. Eight ideas relate to alleviating the equity-efficiency trade-off in current tax systems by exploiting more available information in designing tax schedules.

This chapter discusses digitalization and tax enforcement, followed by a look at digitalization and tax design, and concluding with a summary of policy proposals on digitalization and taxation and reflections on tax policy and digitalization.

DIGITALIZATION AND TAX ENFORCEMENT

Allingham and Sandmo (1972) is the classic contribution on the economics of tax evasion. In their analysis, taxpayers need to report their income to the tax authorities. They can conceal part of their income, but at the cost of a penalty when they are caught evading taxes. The informational constraint is that the government does not know the true income of taxpayers and it can only figure out whether taxpayers are cheating by auditing them, at some cost. In Allingham and Sandmo (1972) taxpayers are audited with a given probability. The optimal strategy of the taxpayers is to underreport income if expected penalties are low enough compared to the tax savings on undeclared income.

Audits are a costly state-verification or monitoring device, the state being the true income of the taxpayers. The *tax enforcement technology* describes how efficient the government is in verifying the true incomes of taxpayers. The tax enforcement technology thus tells us how much tax evasion is detected for a given amount of resources spent on auditing and enforcing tax compliance. Trivially, the tax enforcement technology becomes perfect, that is, nearly costless, if the government can impose infinitely large penalties on cheating taxpayers, no matter how low auditing probabilities are (Mirrlees 1999). In that case, no taxpayer finds it in its interest to underreport income. However, the law constrains the penalties that governments can impose, for example, because the government can also make mistakes in correctly applying the tax laws. Given that infinite penalties on tax evaders are impossible, the enforcement technology is primarily determined by the effectiveness with which tax authorities can process information on taxpayers to detect evasion.[2]

Digitalization holds the promise of improving the tax enforcement technology of the government. In particular, digitalization allows the government to process more information on the different economic outcomes of taxpayers, such as their earnings, capital incomes, consumption expenditures, gifts, and bequests. Information from various sources can thus be used to more easily identify taxpayers who evade taxes. Consequently, if digitalization improves the enforcement technology, digitalization can lower tax evasion. Hence, government revenue increases for the same statutory tax structure.

How can digitalization help improve the enforcement technology? To fix ideas, consider the budget constraint of a particular individual in a particular year. The individual budget constraint implies that increases in net wealth Δa, plus net bequests/gifts received b^* equals net capital income r^*a plus net labor income w^*l minus net consumption expenditures p^*c minus net bequests/gifts made g: $\Delta a + b^* = r^*a + w^*l - p^*c - g$, where an asterisk denotes an after-tax value. Tax authorities collect information on many parts of the household budget constraint. Whether such information is available depends on whether income from labor and capital and bequests are taxed.

What information is currently available to tax authorities? Nearly all countries levy taxes on labor income, hence tax authorities need to verify before-tax labor earnings wl. Typically, most developed countries have third-party reporting by firms on labor income earned by employees. However, perfect verification of labor earnings is not feasible, which holds especially for the self-employed, where third-party reporting is difficult or even impossible. Similarly, most countries also levy taxes on capital income, which requires verifiability of before-tax capital incomes ra. Verifying capital income can be more complicated than verifying labor income in view of the larger international mobility of capital. Nevertheless, there is also third-party reporting by financial firms on various sorts of capital incomes of individuals. This information mainly concerns deposits (including interest) in bank accounts, assets and their returns in investment funds, assets and returns on these assets from insurance policies and in pension funds. By using the

---

[2]Keen and Slemrod (2016) analyze the optimal enforcement of taxes. Governments need to make a trade-off between the benefits of larger tax revenue and the public costs of better tax enforcement.

information from financial institutions, governments can also exchange information internationally. However, some important parts of capital income—housing and pensions—are generally taxed very lightly or not taxed at all. Many countries collect information on property values in property registers, often at the local level of government. Governments may also resort to land and satellite imagery to enforce property taxes.

Moreover, in most countries, not all elements of the individual budget constraint can be observed, because no taxes are levied at the individual level, especially on consumption pc. Most consumption taxes (value-added tax [VAT], sales tax) are levied as a withholding tax at the firm level. Third-party reporting on consumption from consumer transactions data and customs is sometimes observed. Moreover, most countries do not levy wealth taxes, and as a result, information on wealth accrual Δa at the individual level may not be available. Finally, bequests or gifts g might only be lightly taxed, if at all. The more items in the individual budget constraint are non-verifiable to the government, the easier it is for individual taxpayers to avoid or evade paying taxes.

The individual budget constraint can also be written in lifetime, rather than yearly, terms. The net present value of lifetime consumption C plus the net present value of bequests made net of bequests received B equals the net present value of earnings Y: $C + B = Y$. If tax authorities had the information on lifetime income Y and lifetime consumption C, it would be much easier to detect evasion or avoidance in taxes on bequests and gifts B. Indeed, at any period during the lifecycle, if the net present value of consumption C substantially deviates from the net present value of income Y, tax authorities may expect avoidance or evasion of taxes on bequests or gifts.

Although it is perhaps not a surprising or novel idea, digitalization still has the potential to reduce tax evasion and avoidance by gathering more information on the economic outcomes of taxpayers. Digitalization may be useful to gather information on individual or household consumption levels, individual or household capital incomes or assets, and individual or household bequests and gifts. Moreover, digitalization may facilitate third-party reporting, not only on labor income, but also on consumption, capital income, and assets. The remainder of this section gives five ways improve tax enforcement.

Linking Data on Consumption

Digitalization may provide the government with more information on total individual consumption expenditures, for example, due to greater use of digital payment methods. Indeed, in the future all consumption transactions may eventually become electronic and cash may be abolished (Rogoff 2016).[3] By definition, total consumption plus accrued wealth (including bequests) equals labor

---

[3]Abolishing cash and relying only on electronic consumer transactions make barter exchange more profitable. This form of tax evasion needs to be taken into account when designing tax systems in cashless economies.

income plus capital income. Consumption is typically not observed at the individual level. However, by recording consumption transactions, digitalization provides possibilities to link total individual consumption expenditure to data on labor income, capital income, and wealth.

Suppose that the government could indeed verify total consumption at the individual level. Then, from the yearly budget constraint of an individual, it follows that tax authorities could verify whether reported (labor and capital) income and wealth holdings were in line with observed consumption levels. If not, tax authorities might check whether this taxpayer avoids income taxes. Tax authorities may already rely on consumption measurements to detect evasion in income taxation. However, systematic recording of all consumption transactions would greatly enhance the measurement of total consumption expenditures of individuals. This is relevant not only for wealthy taxpayers, but also for the big group of poor taxpayers that never files for income taxation, because their taxable incomes are too low to pay tax, for example, due to the general tax exemption or various (income-dependent) tax credits.

Moreover, if information on individual consumption were available, tax authorities could also verify whether reported wealth (increases in wealth) were in line with income and consumption data. If reported wealth levels are too low to be consistent with observed income and consumption levels, tax authorities can check whether the taxpayer evaded taxes by moving wealth toward the unofficial sector or abroad. International coordination and information exchange is then needed to verify whether taxpayers are indeed shifting wealth abroad.

If all consumption and income were recorded every year, then tax authorities could also calculate the differential between the present value of consumption and the present value of labor earnings of a taxpayer until a particular moment in time. If asset holdings in that year and the bequest and gift behavior of the taxpayer until that year are incompatible with these measures, tax authorities might check whether the taxpayer used avoidance vehicles to transfer wealth to his or her spouse or children or moved wealth toward the unofficial sector or abroad. Hence, if digitalization made individual consumption verifiable, the government would be able to reduce tax avoidance and evasion in taxes on income, wealth, bequests, and gifts.[4]

Linking Data on Wealth and Capital Income

Digitalization could help to create and link data registers on wealth and capital incomes—savings, publicly traded assets, closely held assets, homeownership, pensions, and bequests/estates. By combining various sources of information on taxable wealth, capital incomes, and bequests, the government can reduce tax

---

[4]Moreover, making all consumption transactions electronic by abolishing cash transactions, governments can reduce the informal economy and conduct macroeconomic management in liquidity-trap conditions more effectively by helping to overcome the zero lower bound on nominal interest rates (Buiter and Rahbari 2015; Rogoff 2016).

avoidance and evasion. Verification of all assets and returns on assets requires information on home ownership, which can be made available from (local) property registers.[5] Tax authorities may also gain relatively easy access to information on pension entitlements and pension benefits of individuals in public pension plans. Digitalization can thus help verify total capital incomes and wealth levels of taxpayers, and thereby tax capital income and wealth more effectively (see also sections on Corporate Taxation and Optimal Taxation of Capital Income).

Cross-Border Linking of Data on Wealth and Capital

Taxpayers can avoid paying taxes on wealth and capital income by moving their assets abroad. Tax evasion can be reduced by Taxation Information Exchange Agreements, where countries share information on individuals' and firms' financial accounts in certain financial institutions. Many countries participating in the Organisation for Economic Co-operation and Development (OECD) Convention on Mutual Administrative Assistance in Tax Matters have reached bilateral agreements to share information on request for all types of investment income (including interest, dividends, income from certain insurance contracts, and other similar types of income), but also account balances and proceeds from sales of financial assets. Financial institutions include banks, custodians, brokers, certain collective investment vehicles, and certain insurance companies. Digitalization can help further to build and link international registers for asset ownership (shares, property, pensions) and capital incomes (interest, dividends, capital gains, property values, pension accrual) (Zucman 2015).

Naturally, such information exchanges are complicated by beneficial ownerships, bearer shares, and bearer bonds, and it is not clear whether digitalization can be helpful in these cases. Nevertheless, more complete registers and further information sharing between tax authorities would render tax avoidance much more difficult. Moreover, exchange of information makes it much easier for governments to tax capital income on a residence basis rather than on a source basis. Indeed, if it were possible to verify all assets and their returns at the individual level, then there would be no need for corporate income taxes. Corporate income tax could remain to serve as a withholding tax for individual capital income (see also section on Corporate Taxation).[6]

Financial Institutions as Third-Party Reporters

Information on capital income and asset holdings helps governments detect tax avoidance and evasion in taxing capital income. Although digitalization is not required for information exchange, it has the potential to substantially lower the costs of doing so, especially if countries would exchange financial information

---

[5]Returns on property are not directly measurable, and imputation of returns to property is necessary if the returns are to be taxed.

[6]Devereux and Vella (2017) discuss the implications of digitalization for the corporate tax in more detail.

automatically. Currently, 100 countries have agreed to automatically share financial information from the bilateral Tax Information Exchange Agreements by 2017 or 2018 (OECD 2016a). Digitalization allows financial institutions—banks, insurance companies, investment funds, pension funds, and so on—to act as third-party reporters on capital incomes and wealth for the government. Moreover, financial transaction taxes can help generate additional information on taxpayer assets.

Consumers as Third-Party Reporters

If most consumer transactions are digitized, consumers can act as third-party reporters for the VAT or sales tax. In a cashless economy, as advocated by Rogoff (2016), all consumer transactions would be digital. Governments could then employ electronic payment information (such as through debit and credit card payments) or use information on consumption from digital platforms (Chapter 3) to estimate the aggregate sales of particular firms. Information on sales of individual companies can help governments reduce tax avoidance and evasion of firms in the VAT or sales tax. However, firms that are evading taxes have strong incentives to transact in cash rather than electronically. Hence, digitalization brings only limited reduction of tax evasion if a large volume of consumer transactions remains in cash.

DIGITALIZATION AND TAX DESIGN

Optimal Taxation of Labor Income

The Nobel-prize winning article of Mirrlees (1971) shows how information constraints determine the inescapable trade-off between equity and efficiency. Mirrlees' static model analyzes optimal nonlinear taxation of labor income. One may view the Mirrlees model in broad terms as a theory of optimal income redistribution or, even broader, as a theory of the optimal welfare state. The Mirrlees framework determines how *effective* marginal tax rates should optimally vary with income. The effective marginal tax rates on labor income include statutory tax rates, as well as the impact of all income-dependent transfers, tax credits, tax deductions, and benefits aimed at redistributing income. The government aims to optimally set the effective marginal tax rate at each level of labor income. Individuals are different in their earning ability, which equals their productivity per hour worked. Individuals trade off the benefits of consumption and the costs of supplying work effort.[7] The government redistributes income from high-ability

---

[7] These costs may be narrowly interpreted as forgone leisure, but also more broadly as encompassing the costs of forgone household production or forgone income from the informal or black labor market. Consequently, elasticities of taxable income are bigger if the possibility of working in the informal sector strengthens behavioral responses to taxation.

to low-ability individuals. Social preferences for income redistribution are exogenously given.

The fundamental information constraint in the Mirrlees (1971) framework is that both earning ability and work effort are private information and are thus non-verifiable by the government. Indeed, all the government can verify is total labor income, which is the product of earning ability and work effort. Due to information constraints, the second theorem of welfare economics breaks down, since non-distortionary individualized lump-sum taxes based on earning ability cannot be implemented. The government can only redistribute income through a distortionary nonlinear tax schedule on labor income. By taxing labor income, the government not only redistributes the rents from earning ability, but also the fruits of labor effort. Hence, income redistribution distorts incentives to work.

Mirrlees (1971) theoretically derives the optimal nonlinear income tax schedule. The optimal marginal tax rate at each point in the income distribution is set such that the marginal distributional benefits of a higher marginal tax rate are equal to the associated marginal deadweight losses of distorting work effort. Recent literature has shown that the optimal tax schedule typically features a U-shape with income. The economic logic behind the U-shape is as follows. The redistributional benefits of setting a higher marginal tax rate at a particular income level always decline with income. Intuitively, an increase in marginal tax rates yields less additional tax progression if the rate is raised at a higher income level. Raising the tax at a higher income level gives lower revenues than raising the tax rate at lower income levels. Given that revenues are lower, tax credits, transfers, or deductions cannot be raised as much if marginal tax rates are increased at higher income levels. At the same time, the tax distortions of a higher marginal tax rate follow the shape of the income distribution: the tax base first increases with income and then decreases with income for most empirical distributions of income. For a given elasticity of taxable income, the same marginal tax rate thus yields low distortions at low incomes, highest distortions for middle-income groups, and then lower distortions for the high-income groups. This is standard Ramsey logic. Therefore, marginal tax rates start out high at low-income levels (high distributional benefits–low distortions), then decline toward the mode of the earnings distribution (lower distributional benefits–higher distortions), increase again after the mode (lower distributional benefits, but also lower distortions), and gradually converge to a constant top rate for high income earners.[8]

A crucial insight into the potential of digitalization follows directly from Mirrlees (1971): digitalization does *not* have any potential to improve the tax system under the assumptions of the Mirrlees framework. If earning ability (labor effort) is fundamentally non-verifiable, as Mirrlees assumes, then digitalization cannot change this fundamental information constraint: earning ability and labor effort remain non-verifiable even in a fully digitized world. Hence, digitalization

---

[8]For more elaborate explanation of the shape of the nonlinear tax schedule, see also Mirrlees (1971), Diamond (1998), and Saez (2001).

has no power to alleviate the equity-efficiency trade-off. This is in line with remarks in Kanbur (2017).[9] Another way to interpret this is that, if income redistribution is optimized through the nonlinear tax on labor earnings, the government fully exploits all available information on taxpayers' labor earnings. Moreover, digitalization cannot help to improve tax enforcement, since tax enforcement is already assumed to be perfect. That is, labor earnings are assumed to be completely verifiable in Mirrlees (1971).

Digitalization and Progressive Consumption Taxes

The Mirrlees (1971) model of optimal income taxation is not readily applicable to developing countries, where tax enforcement is generally too weak to verify labor incomes. Therefore, most developing countries have a strong reliance on consumption taxes to raise revenue or to redistribute income. Digitalization may help to alleviate the equity-efficiency trade-off if earned income is not verifiable to the government and the government is forced to tax consumption.

Electronic transaction systems and biometric identification technology could help to implement a non-individualized, lump-sum transfer besides the consumption tax.[10] Therefore, digitalization allows the government to implement a *progressive* consumption tax instead of a proportional consumption tax, even if income is not verifiable and untaxed. A progressive consumption tax can thus redistribute more income for the same consumption tax rates or lower consumption tax rates can be set for the same amount of income redistribution. Therefore, digitalization can improve the redistributive powers of the commodity tax system.

---

[9]In contrast, Chen, Grimshaw, and Myles (2017) argue that digitalization may, in the future allow the government to verify individual earning ability. If earning ability would indeed become verifiable, the incentive problem that is central to optimal tax theory vanishes, and first-best outcomes can be achieved. One should, however, be skeptical about this idea for a number of reasons. First, it is not immediately clear what should be the proper measure for exogenous earning ability. For example, earnings per hour worked are endogenous and the result of investments in education, occupational choices, on-the-job training, intensity of work effort, luck in the labor market, and so on. Second, it is hard to find truly exogenous measures for earning ability, since even supposedly exogenous measures, such as IQ or genes, may be malleable. This would introduce new behavioral responses, as Chen, Grimshaw, and Myles (2017) also point out. Third, finding measures for earning ability raise a host of philosophical, political, and legal issues as to what the proper measures of earning ability ought to be. Fourth, even if a tax on ability would be possible, a time-consistency problem in taxation emerges. Individuals anticipating fully individualized lump-sum taxation after they revealed their earning ability to the government, have strong incentives to misrepresent their earning ability or to game the tax system to prevent such first-best individualized lump-sum taxation (Roberts 1984).

[10]Consider a budget constraint of an individual that earns wl, where w is the wage and l is labor effort. This individual spends earned income on consumption c which is taxed at rate τ: $wl = (1 + \tau)c$. Clearly, if a non-individualized lump-sum transfer g could be provided to individuals, based on electronic transactions or biometric identification, the budget constraint would become: $wl + g = (1 + \tau)c$. This would change the consumption tax from a proportional to a progressive one, provided the transfer g is positive.

Many countries also rely on differentiated commodity taxes to redistribute income, such as through low VAT-rates on necessities. In the absence of an income tax, such a policy can be desirable for redistributive reasons. However, if the tax system would allow for a non-individualized, lump-sum transfer, besides linear consumption taxes, the government might be able to optimally reduce the reliance on low VAT rates to redistribute incomes.[11] Thus, the government could organize more income redistribution through a linear consumption tax supplemented with a lump-sum component, which would avoid the distortions associated with differentiated consumption taxes, such as low VAT rates.

Optimal Income and Commodity Taxation

The stylized Mirrlees model of optimal nonlinear income taxation considers only two commodities (consumption and leisure) and the government receives only one signal of earning ability: labor income. However, individuals in the real world may make many more choices: they choose between different consumption goods at one time, between consumption at different points in time (their savings), they choose how to save (portfolio choices), investments in education, and so on. Moreover, individuals may differ in more than their earning ability: their preferences, such as the preference for different commodities (rental housing, health care), time preference (for saving or borrowing), or risk aversion. Consequently, how should tax systems be optimized when individuals face choices among multiple commodities and may differ in their preferences? And, can digitalization help improve the equity-efficiency trade-off in tax systems that tax different consumption goods and consumption in different periods?

The starting point in the theory of optimal commodity taxation is the Atkinson-Stiglitz (AS) theorem, which derives the conditions under which government can organize all desired income redistribution with only a nonlinear tax on labor income, without resorting to commodity tax differentiation (Atkinson and Stiglitz 1976). The AS theorem is an important benchmark. If there is no need to differentiate commodity taxes, all redistribution can be carried out through nonlinear income taxes. With perfect enforcement of income taxes, as the AS theorem assumes, there is no need to have commodity taxation at all. Exactly the same economic outcomes can be achieved by setting all (uniform) commodity taxes to zero and proportionally adjusting the tax on labor income. How should taxes then be optimally divided between taxes on labor income and consumption? Under the conditions of the AS theorem, the distinction between taxes on income and consumption is immaterial. In practice, however, the

---

[11]Indeed, if individual preferences are of the Gorman polar form, which includes the Cobb-Douglas, constant elasticity of substitution (CES), Stone-Geary, linear expenditure system (LES), and iso-elastic utility functions, then the government optimally sets uniform consumption taxes even if the poor spend a disproportionate fraction of their income on necessities (Deaton 1977).

reliance on both income and consumption taxes presumably relies on issues of tax enforcement.[12]

The AS theorem shows that commodity taxes should be uniform if (1) individuals only differ in their earning ability, (2) earning ability only affects labor income, (3) individuals have identical preferences over various commodities, and (4) utility from commodities is weakly separable from utility of leisure (Atkinson and Stiglitz 1976; Laroque 2005; Jacobs and Boadway 2014). Weak separability implies that the willingness to supply labor is independent of how individuals like to spend their income. In particular, commodity demands are identical for all individuals earning the same income. Commodity demands thus do not reveal any more information on earning ability than is already present in labor earnings. Consequently, differentiated commodity taxes cannot redistribute any more income than the nonlinear income tax can, but in addition also distort commodity demands. Another (but equivalent) way to think about the AS theorem is that weak separability implies that all commodities are equally complementary to work (or leisure), because commodity demands are the same for everyone with the same labor earnings. Hence, differentiated commodity taxes cannot alleviate distortions on labor supply by taxing goods that are complementary to leisure (complementary to work) at higher (lower) rates, but only distort commodity demands.

Under the conditions of the AS theorem, digitalization has no promise to improve upon pre-existing tax schedules, since all redistribution should be carried out through the nonlinear tax on labor income. As argued above, digitalization has no promise under the conditions of the Mirrlees (1971) framework with only two commodities (consumption and leisure). A corollary to this result is that digitalization has no promise either to improve existing tax systems in the Atkinson and Stiglitz (1976) framework with multiple commodities if the conditions for the AS theorem indeed apply. Under these conditions, it is socially optimal to organize all redistribution through the nonlinear income tax and commodity taxes are superfluous. Consequently, any promise for digitalization to improve on the equity-efficiency trade-off relies on the breakdown of the AS theorem.

All the conditions underlying the AS theorem are expected to fail in the real world: even if individuals differ in only one "deep" characteristic—their earning ability—heterogeneity in earning ability may also determine their preferences for different commodities or parts of their income other than their labor income (such as capital income). Furthermore, individuals' preferences do not need to be

---

[12]Tax administration and enforcement of nonlinear income taxes can be more costly than that of linear consumption taxes. Most consumption taxes need to be linear, since individual consumption transactions are anonymous. However, linear consumption taxes are inferior instruments for income redistribution compared to nonlinear income taxes. Consequently, governments may want to use both linear consumption taxes and nonlinear income taxes to balance the costs of tax evasion and avoidance in income taxes with the distributional losses of consumption taxes (Boadway, Marchand, and Pestieau 1994).

weakly separable between labor and all other commodities, so that commodity demands interact with labor choices. Moreover, the AS theorem also breaks down if individuals differ in more than one "deep" characteristic. Think of health, time preference, and so on. In all these cases, commodity taxes are not redundant. If commodity taxes are not superfluous, there is potential for digitalization to improve the equity-efficiency trade-off.

A later section turns to the (complex) question of how taxes should optimally be set if individuals differ in multiple deep characteristics. The following sections focus on the case where heterogeneity is still one-dimensional, but affects more than only labor earnings. In particular, it focuses on commodity taxation and taxation of capital income.

Digitalization and Commodity Taxation

If the conditions for the AS theorem fail, commodities should be taxed besides labor income, possibly under a nonlinear schedule. This is the case if heterogeneity in ability—besides labor income—also determines preferences for commodities or capital (or other) income. Commodity demands then reflect not only differences in labor earnings, but also preferences for commodities or the other source of income. For example, earning ability can be correlated with endowments, capital income, or inheritances.

It is optimal to tax commodities at higher rates if commodity demand—conditional in labor income—correlates positively with earning ability, which is due to the correlation of earning ability with initial endowments of commodities (Cremer, Pestieau, and Rochet 2001; Gerritsen and others 2017).

Moreover, individual preference may depend on ability. Commodities should be taxed at higher rates if the high-ability individuals like to consume these commodities more than low-ability individuals—conditional on labor income (Mirrlees 1976; Saez 2002). Intuitively, if commodity demands differ by individual, then commodity demands reveal additional information on earning ability, besides the information obtained by observing labor earnings.

Furthermore, even if preferences for certain commodities are the same for all individuals, but not weakly separable from labor, then some commodities are stronger (weaker) complements to work than others. Hence, the willingness to consume certain goods varies by individuals' labor effort. The government then optimally lowers (increases) the tax on commodities that are complementary to work (leisure) to alleviate the distortions of the income tax on labor supply (Corlett and Hague 1953; Atkinson and Stiglitz 1976; Jacobs and Boadway 2014).[13]

Optimal commodity taxes should be nonlinear and depend on individual commodity demands (Atkinson and Stiglitz 1976; Mirrlees 1976). Of course,

[13]The Ramsey inverse elasticity rule is a special case of the Corlett-Hague motive for commodity tax differentiation; the most elastic goods are the goods that are the strongest complements to work (Ramsey 1927).

commodity tax differentiation—whether for redistributional or efficiency reasons—always comes at a cost in terms of distorted commodity demands.

How, then, does digitalization affect the setting of optimal commodity taxes, provided that commodity tax differentiation is indeed desirable? Nonlinear commodity taxation requires that the government can verify individual commodity demands. Digitalization may be especially helpful if it helps to collect information on individual consumption, as argued above. If all consumption transactions were verifiable, through electronic payment systems, for example, then governments could be in the position to levy individualized, nonlinear consumption taxes. Important examples of such commodities are water, electricity, and gas. Nonlinear taxes (subsidies) are also often levied on many services, such as health care, education, and (house) rentals.

However, in practice, most taxes on commodities are linear. Nonlinear taxation of commodities is impossible if commodities can be traded in secondary markets, and if these trades cannot be verified by the government. Secondary markets exist for commodities that are transportable, durable, and storable. Hence, individuals paying different nonlinear commodity taxes trade on secondary markets until all net price differentials are arbitraged away. Non-verifiable trades in secondary markets effectively make individual commodity demands non-verifiable so that only linear commodity taxes can be implemented.[14] Commodities that are non-transportable, perishable, and non-storable are difficult to trade in secondary markets, and, hence, these commodity demands can be verifiable to the government. Consequently, these commodities can be taxed nonlinearly.[15]

Digitalization may, therefore, complement existing commodity tax systems by allowing for nonlinear taxes on individual commodity demands of verifiable commodities. Nonlinear commodity taxes redistribute income at lower efficiency cost than linear commodity taxes—provided individual commodity demands can be verified. Although a theoretical case for nonlinear commodity taxation can be made easily, it is not clear which commodities should be taxed and how commodity taxes should then be differentiated. Empirical literature clearly rejects the conditions for the AS theorem.[16] At the same time, the literature provides very little guidance for the setting of commodity taxes. More empirical research on

[14]Diamond and Mirrlees (1971a, b), Atkinson and Stiglitz (1976), Saez (2002), Mirrlees (1976), and Jacobs and Boadway (2014) show that optimal linear commodity taxes need to be used for redistributive reasons—if taxes on income are constrained to be linear or if preferences are heterogeneous and, for efficiency reasons, to reduce labor-tax induced distortions on labor supply.

[15]Secondhand markets also become increasingly more digitized, such as through online platforms for secondhand commodities. However, it is unlikely that this would allow for nonlinear consumption taxes on the goods traded on these platforms, since the characteristics of the commodities do not change as a result of trading them on secondhand platforms. In particular, nonlinear commodity taxation would induce tax arbitrage because the commodities are still durable, transportable, and storable.

[16]For example, see Browning and Meghir (1991); Crawford, Keen, and Smith (2010); Gordon and Kopczuk (2014); and Pirttilä and Suoniemi (2014).

commodity demands is, therefore, needed to inform the policy discussion on the optimal setting of consumption taxes in a digitized world.

Taxation of Corporate Income

The corporate income tax is presumably the most distortionary tax in most modern tax systems. Indeed, optimal tax theory provides no solid welfare-economic basis for taxing capital income at source. Taxing capital income at source interferes with production efficiency, as it distorts a firm's investment, leverage, and location decisions. Production inefficiencies should preferably be avoided, even in second-best settings with distortionary taxation (Diamond and Mirrlees 1971a, b).[17]

Arguably, the most important task of the corporate income tax is to act as a "backstop" for the personal income tax. It is more difficult for governments to tax each shareholder individually under the personal income tax than to tax firms paying out dividends to many different shareholders. Moreover, taxing shareholders individually is more difficult in a financially globalized world, where individuals have their assets located in many countries. Hence, if taxing capital income on a residence basis is too difficult or costly to implement, then taxing at source may be the only way to tax capital income.[18]

Digitalization would hold a big promise to tax shareholders directly if international registers would be set up in which information on all assets and asset incomes were collected. If individual capital incomes can be verified by governments, then capital income can be taxed on residence basis rather than on source basis. Moreover, if assets and capital incomes are registered digitally, substantial improvements in tax collection can be achieved. The corporate income tax might then no longer be needed to backstop personal income tax.

In its most radical form the corporate income tax can be abolished entirely. Alternatively, the corporate income tax can still be used as a withholding tax on dividend incomes, as it was originally intended when introduced (Zucman 2015). In doing so, the government could rely on third-party reports on dividend payouts of firms, and thereby reduce tax evasion in reported capital incomes. Moreover, by levying a withholding tax at the corporate level, rather than at many

---

[17]The production efficiency theorem relies, however, on a number of important assumptions, which need not be met in reality (Diamond and Mirrlees 1971a). First, the government needs to verify all factor payments in all production sectors of the economy. Hence, the production efficiency theorem breaks down if there are untaxed informal or black sectors. Second, all labor types (or occupations) need to be perfect substitutes in production, such that all wage rates per hour worked are symmetrically affected by production distortions. If labor types are not perfectly substitutable, the government needs to set a labor type (occupation)-specific labor tax schedule (Scheuer and Werning 2016). Third, there need to be constant returns to scale in production (zero profits) or the government needs to have access to a 100 percent tax on pure profits.

[18]Alternatively, the corporate income tax could be viewed as a benefit tax to compensate governments for investments in infrastructure, human capital, institutions, and so on. Furthermore, the corporate income tax could be seen as a way to shift part of the tax burden to foreign shareholders. The latter argument becomes less important in practice due to high and increasing capital mobility.

shareholders in the personal income tax, there can still be economies of scale in the collection of taxes on dividends.

Removal of source-based taxes on corporate income would eliminate the substantial economic distortions generated by the corporate income tax. In particular, most countries have adopted a "classical" corporate tax system, where the costs of equity finance (dividends) are not deductible from the corporate income tax, whereas costs of debt finance (interest) are. Consequently, by taxing the normal and above-normal returns to equity, the corporate income tax raises the user cost of capital as long as not all investments are financed with debt, so that the corporate income tax reduces corporate investment. Moreover, due to the asymmetric tax treatment of debt and equity, corporations have tax-induced incentives to finance their activities relatively more with debt. This "debt bias" not only distorts the optimal capital and risk allocation in economies, but high leverage also promotes financial instability and fragility (IMF 2016). Further, differentials in corporate income tax rates across countries provide incentives to relocate real economic activities to lower-taxed countries or to shift profits to lower-taxed countries through transfer price manipulation, debt shifting, or licensing. If capital income were taxed on a residence basis, rather than at source, all these distortions would disappear. Tax arbitrage through the corporate income tax would stop as well.

Moreover, taxing capital income on a residence basis would end tax competition in the corporate income tax. Countries may respond strategically to the setting of corporate income tax rates of other, neighboring countries to attract economic activity (Keen and Konrad 2013). Empirically, tax rates are found to be strategic complements, especially in the European Union, which implies that countries lower their corporate income tax rates if other countries do so (Devereux and Loretz 2013). Therefore, tax competition may result in a "race to the bottom," where corporate income tax rates are driven down to very low or even zero levels. Such fears are stoked by observed declines in corporate income tax rates in most of the Western world in recent decades. If taxation of capital income were no longer at source, but on a residence basis, part of the tax competition for mobile capital would presumably move from the corporate income tax to the personal income tax, as countries might lower taxes on interest, dividends, and capital gains in the personal income tax to attract high-net-worth individuals instead of firms.

Optimal Taxation of Capital Income

The AS theorem also provides the foundation for the well-known theoretical result that the (normal return to) capital income should not be taxed in the personal income tax if preferences are identical and weakly separable between labor and consumption in different periods, and heterogeneity in earning ability only affects labor income.[19] However, as with commodity taxes, these conditions for zero capital taxation are not met in practice. Taxes on capital income should be positive for a number of equity reasons, because of the following:

- discount rates decrease with earning ability (Mirrlees 1976; Saez 2002; Banks and Diamond 2010; Diamond and Spinnewijn 2011)
- initial assets or bequests typically increase with earning ability (Cremer, Pestieau, and Rochet 2001; Piketty and Saez 2013)
- asset returns increase with earning ability (Gerritsen and others 2017)
- assets or bequests increase with positive shocks in earning ability (Jacobs and Schindler 2012).

Consequently, capital incomes are higher for high-ability individuals—even if labor earnings would be the same. Positive taxes on capital income are therefore optimal for income redistribution.

Optimal taxes on capital income should also be positive for a number of efficiency reasons. In particular, taxes on capital income are desirable because they accomplish the following:

- prevent tax arbitrage with labor taxation (Christiansen and Tuomala 2008; Reis 2011);
- tax rents (Correia 1996)
- reduce labor supply distortions (Corlett and Hague 1953; Atkinson and Stiglitz 1976; Erosa and Gervais 2002; Conesa, Kitao, and Krueger 2009; Jacobs and Boadway 2014)
- reduce human capital distortions (Jacobs and Bovenberg 2010)
- alleviate capital market failures (Aiyagari 1995)
- alleviate insurance market failures (Golosov, Kocherlakota, and Tsyvinski 2003; Golosov, Troshkin, and Tsyvinski 2016; Jacobs and Schindler 2012; Fahri and Werning 2012).

There are thus good economic reasons to tax capital income at a positive rate, disposing of the theoretical argument for a consumption (or expenditure) tax that implies no taxation of (the normal return to) capital income. However, there is no reason to presume that taxes on capital income should be the same as taxes on labor income (a synthetic income tax), given that taxes on labor and capital income have both different excess burdens and different distributional benefits. Hence, a dual-income-tax system, where labor and capital income are taxed under separate schedules, is likely to be optimal (Jacobs 2013).

---

[19]Chamley (1986) and Judd (1985) also find that the optimal tax on capital income is zero in the long run. Jacobs and Rusu (2017) show that this result ultimately derives from optimal commodity tax principles. In particular, the long-term tax on capital income is zero because consumption over time has become equally complementary to leisure. Hence, taxing capital income has no benefit in terms of lower labor market distortions, but only costs in terms of saving distortions. Consequently, Chamley (1986) and Judd (1985) can be interpreted as a special case of the AS theorem.

By the same argument, one would expect that differential taxation of various sources of capital income—interest on saving deposits and loans, dividends and capital gains on traded shares and non-traded closely held shares, rent and capital gains from housing, and asset accrual in pension funds—would be desirable. However, a differential tax treatment of various assets is likely to provoke large-scale tax arbitrage among asset classes, since it is easy to transform one asset into another, for example, through investment funds, housing, pensions, and firm ownerships. Therefore, all capital income probably needs to be taxed under a uniform tax regime.

Most tax systems apply differing tax rates on the various sources of capital incomes and wealth (Harding 2013; OECD 2011, 2016b). Housing is often subsidized (mortgage rent deductibility, very low or no taxation of imputed rent). Pensions are generally subsidized (often tax-exempt pension accrual, various tax advantages in the personal income tax). Interest income, dividends and capital gains are generally taxed in the personal income tax, although some countries do not tax capital gains. Asset income from personal businesses often receives a separate tax treatment, and generally entails various tax advantages. For example, countries that tax capital gains on a realization basis—on traded shares or closely held shares—generally do not account for interest accrued on unrealized capital gains (Auerbach 1991).

The differential tax treatment of various sources of capital income opens the door to tax arbitrage, between asset classes, between persons or legal entities, and over time (such as through pension constructions). Moreover, a patchwork of capital taxes creates all sorts of economic distortions. A non-exhaustive list includes too-high leverage in household financing decisions as a result of debt bias (in housing and sole proprietorships), and distorted risk allocations due to poorly diversified household portfolios (such as over-exposure to housing market risk, too high investment in illiquid pension wealth). Low taxes on capital incomes (or even subsidies) result in greater distortions in labor markets as the tax burden is shifted to labor income or consumption. Higher taxes on both labor income and consumption weaken incentives to supply work effort, to participate in the labor market, to invest in human capital, and to retire later.

Digitalization allows governments to create and link data registers on wealth and capital incomes—savings, publicly traded assets, closely held assets, homeownership, pensions, and bequests/estates. Digitalization therefore makes it possible to implement a dual-income-tax system in which "comprehensive" capital income and wealth can be linked and taxed symmetrically under a single overall regime for capital income: a "synthetic capital income tax." Under this regime, all capital income would be added and taxed under a single schedule. This schedule would preferably entail a flat tax rate that is applied to all capital income above a certain tax-free exemption.[20] This tax change is desirable to reduce tax arbitrage

---

[20]The government may provide tax incentives to save for retirement by introducing a larger tax-free exemption for the tax on capital income. The government then provides incentives for retirement saving irrespective of how individuals save for retirement: whether through personal

and raise the efficiency and equity of current personal income tax systems. A single rate on all sources of capital income eliminates arbitrage across all sources of capital income, over time, and between persons or legal entities. Moreover, capital and risk allocations would no longer be distorted. Finally, the government could more easily achieve an optimal mix of taxes on labor and capital income.

Jointness in Tax Systems

Real-world tax systems are generally quite simple. In its most simple form, all sources of income are taxed under one progressive tax schedule (synthetic income tax). However, various countries levy separate tax schedules on different sources of income. These tax schedules are generally independent or "disjoint" from each other. For example, the marginal tax rate on labor earnings depends on only labor income and is independent of the level of capital income or wealth. Similarly, the marginal tax rate on capital income—in a dual-tax system—depends on only capital income and not on labor income.

Of course, exceptions do exist. Although tax rates on labor earnings are generally independent of capital income (in dual-tax systems) or assets (in synthetic-tax systems), many countries apply asset tests in benefits or sickness, disability, unemployment, or welfare. Hence, the tax-benefit schedule features "jointness": the effective marginal tax rate (that is, including the impact of benefits, tax deductions, and tax credits) on labor income depends on wealth. The question is then whether cross-dependencies—or jointness—in tax schedules are socially desirable. If they are, then digitalization can be very useful to administer and implement these much more complex tax systems.

The starting point to think about cross-dependencies in tax schedules is Mirrlees' (1976) analysis of optimal income and commodity taxation. Mirrlees assumed that earning ability is the only "deep" primitive parameter that determines all heterogeneity among individuals in not only labor earnings, but potentially also their preferences, endowments, and so on. Mirrlees already showed that it is optimal to levy *separate* nonlinear taxes on income and commodities. Hence, if individuals differ in only one deep characteristic, cross-dependencies in tax schedules are superfluous (see also Renes and Zoutman 2016b). Consequently, digitalization would once more not be helpful in improving existing tax systems by being able to create jointness in tax schedules.

Jointness in tax schedules is desirable if individuals differ in *more* dimensions than just their earning ability. Kleven, Kreiner, and Saez (2009); Golosov, Tsyvinski, and Werquin (2014); Renes and Zoutman (2016a, b); and Spiritus (2017) build on Mirrlees (1976) to analyze optimal nonlinear taxes in models in which individuals may differ in more than one characteristic, such as their earning ability, participation costs, health status, time preference, risk aversion, and so on. Consequently, not all heterogeneity between individuals can be reduced to

---

savings and stock market investments, through their house, through personal businesses, or through pension funds.

one underlying factor, as in nearly the entire optimal tax literature. These authors all derive that optimal tax systems feature cross-dependencies in tax schedules. For example, the optimal tax rate on labor earnings depends on capital income or assets (and vice versa). Similarly, the tax rate on certain commodities depends on labor income and capital income or assets. Cross-dependencies thus become desirable if individuals differ in more than one dimension than their earning ability.

As a rule of thumb, an optimal tax system has a number of interdependencies among tax schedules that is equal to the number of characteristics in which people differ (that is, the dimensionality of the type space).[21] Intuitively, the role of introducing cross-dependencies in tax schedules is to reduce the economic distortions of tax systems. If individuals differ in multiple dimensions, they can adjust their behavior in multiple dimensions, making it harder for governments to target income redistribution toward the individuals it likes to support. However, by introducing jointness in tax schedules, governments can more effectively "control" the behavioral responses to income redistribution. In terms of optimal tax jargon: multidimensional heterogeneity allows individuals to "game" the tax system by making profitable ("double" or "joint" deviations).[22] Introducing jointness in tax schedules makes these joint deviations less attractive. Hence, incentive constraints associated with income redistribution are relaxed. Consequently, introducing joint tax schedules allows governments to achieve the same (more) redistribution at lower (the same) efficiency costs.

To see how jointness in tax systems can be desirable, consider the following simple example, inspired by Diamond and Spinnewijn (2011). Suppose that labor income is taxed and capital income is not. Then, the individuals with both a high earning ability and a strong time preference can work less tomorrow and save more today to reduce labor income taxes and increase leisure tomorrow, while sacrificing some consumption today. This strategy is desirable if the individual ultimately pays less labor tax by simultaneously changing labor supply and saving behavior. Therefore, for any marginal tax rate on earnings, the labor tax achieves less income redistribution. Now, if the government conditions the tax

---

[21]Intuitively, the optimal tax function must implement the second-best allocation of a direct mechanism in which the government designs a resource-feasible and incentive-compatible allocation, in which each individual truthfully reveals all hidden characteristics by a particular choice of commodities. To have full revelation of J hidden characteristics, the optimal wedge on each good should also be a function of the demand of at least J commodities.

[22]It is not guaranteed that joint schedules can in fact be implemented. Implementation problems arise because individuals can make combinations of commodities using market transactions that would be unavailable to them in an optimal direct mechanism. This is again the problem of "joint deviations." Renes and Zoutman (2016b) derive that implementation of joint schedules is possible in two classes of tax problems. In the first class of tax problems, the allocations should be (second-best) Pareto efficient and there should be no externalities. In the second class of tax problems, the second-best allocation should be surjective onto the choice space, so that implementability conditions coincide with incentive compatibility constraints. Golosov, Tsyvinski, and Werquin (2014) and Spiritus (2017) *assume* that all given joint tax schedules are implementable for any set of model primitives. These authors only analyze the optimality properties of optimal tax systems.

rate on labor income on capital income, such that individuals with higher incomes pay a positive marginal tax on saving, then the individual is discouraged from making the double deviation of saving more and working less to reduce its tax bill. Hence, there will be smaller behavioral responses to income redistribution, so that the government can alleviate the equity-efficiency trade-off by introducing a joint schedule on labor income and assets.

An important policy question is: How should optimal taxes be designed when individuals are heterogeneous in more than one dimension? The remainder of this section considers several suggestions where jointness can improve existing tax systems. However, not much is known theoretically and empirically about how such joint schedules should be designed. More research is needed to identify the potential welfare gains of implementing joint tax systems and how they should be designed in practice.

Taxation of Lifetime Income

The main insight of the previous section—tax systems should optimally have as many cross-dependencies as characteristics of individuals—generalizes to settings in which individuals have different earning abilities at different moments in time. Hence, a joint tax schedule based on the entire history of earnings is optimal. Jointness implies that the marginal tax rate on earnings in year t depends not only on the earnings in year t, but also on all earnings in all other years $s \neq t$. The optimal tax rate on labor income in each year thus depends on the entire history of labor earnings, including all future earnings. Roughly speaking, earnings in a given year are a reflection but not a perfect indicator of "average earning ability" over the life-cycle or "lifetime earning ability." Hence, by basing taxation on each year's labor earnings, the government can redistribute better toward the individuals who have, on average, lower earnings ability and thus lower lifetime earnings. Earnings in each period provide useful information on the lifetime earning ability of individuals. Consequently, by using the entire history of earnings, the government employs more signals of lifetime earning ability in setting taxes. Thus, governments can tax labor income with lower efficiency costs—for given distributional objectives—by conditioning tax schedules on the entire history of labor income.

If individuals do indeed have different earnings ability in each year of their lifecycle, under which conditions is a time-invariant (or age-independent) non-linear income tax optimal? Werning (2007) shows that optimal marginal tax rates over time are generally not constant, since neither tax distortions nor distributional gains of income taxes are constant over time. Tax schedules are only constant over time ("tax smoothing") with power utility functions—resulting in constant elasticities—and age-earnings profiles that are parallel across individuals. The latter implies that there is really only *one* underlying source of heterogeneity (Werning 2007). Hence, only in this special case is it sufficient to have a tax schedule based on yearly earnings only.

The discussion of taxing the history of labor earnings is also related to an old idea of Vickrey (1939, 1947) to base income taxation on cumulative averaging of income. Horizontal equity principles suggest that lifetime taxation is preferable over yearly taxation. Intuitively, individuals with the same average lifetime income, but with more fluctuations in their incomes, will pay more tax under a progressive income tax system based on yearly income. Moving toward lifetime taxation would remove this inequity. Yearly income may also be poor measure for lifetime income in the presence of strongly changing earnings profiles over the lifecycle, insurance market failures (no insurance of risk in labor and capital income), and incomplete capital markets (borrowing/liquidity constraints). Consequently, lifetime taxation may redistribute income more effectively and alleviate some of the capital and insurance market imperfections by lowering tax burdens in low-income phases/states and raising the tax burden in high-income phases/states. Moreover, progressive yearly tax systems create incentives for shifting incomes over time from periods with high tax rates toward periods with low tax rates, particularly capital income. These disincentives can be avoided by moving to a lifetime tax system.

Vickrey (1939, 1947) proposed to tax the yearly average of taxable income, as if all taxable incomes had been constant over time.[23] Very little attention has been paid to taxation of the cumulative average of earnings in the tax literature. An exception is Liebman (2003) who analyzes income averaging in taxing labor income if there is no taxation of capital income. He shows that cumulative averaging of labor taxes can produce small equity gains and substantial efficiency gains in terms of lower labor supply distortions and better smoothing of consumption in the presence of present bias or borrowing constraints. In many countries, electronic tax files are available for many years for individual taxpayers. Digitalization therefore makes it possible to implement Vickrey's (1947) proposal for an average tax on cumulative income, which converges to the taxation of lifetime income. No country has until now implemented Vickrey's tax cumulative earnings.[24] Alternatively, digitalization may allow for marginal tax rates dependent on entire earnings histories. Doing so can raise social welfare by achieving distributional objectives at lower efficiency costs by targeting income redistribution better toward the lifetime poor.

Joint Taxation of Labor and Capital Income

As argued above, if individuals differ in more than one characteristic, then cross dependencies in tax schedules are generally optimal. The so-called New Dynamic Public Finance literature (Golosov, Kocherlakota, and Tsyvinski 2003; Kocherlakota 2005, 2010; Golosov, Tsyvinski, and Werning 2007)

---

[23]Since Vickrey (1939, 1947) discussed a traditional synthetic income tax, he proposed provisions to account for taxing interest on unrealized capital gains so that all incentives for deferral of capital gains would be removed. See also Auerbach and Bradford (2004) for more on this.

[24]Vickrey (1939) shows that one requires only two consecutive tax returns to practically implement a tax on the cumulative average of income. Hence, the "digitalization" requirements to implement such a system are minimal (or even absent).

analyzes nonlinear taxes on income, consumption, and capital in models where individuals are heterogeneous in their earning ability in every period of their lifecycle.[25] This entire literature demonstrates that optimal taxes on labor income generally depend on the level of assets or capital income and vice versa. Consequently, some form of asset testing is optimal. Intuitively, by conditioning income redistribution on the level of assets (or capital incomes), individuals get weaker incentives to jointly distort labor supply and saving behavior to benefit from the redistributive schemes aimed at the (lifetime) poor. For example, Golosov and Tsyvinski (2006) show that individuals may save more income in early periods of the lifecycle to falsely claim disability benefits in later stages of their lifecycle. Asset testing of disability benefits makes this "joint deviation" (saving more and falsely claiming disability) less attractive. Their simulations demonstrate that the potential welfare gains from asset testing are substantial.[26]

Digitalization makes it potentially easier to levy sophisticated joint tax schedules over labor and capital income or wealth, where marginal tax rates on labor income can depend on capital income or wealth and vice versa. Indeed, in many countries income support programs are often means tested not only on labor and capital income, but also on wealth. By introducing jointness in tax schedules, the equity-efficiency trade-off can be improved. Digitalization thus holds the promise to more precisely target income support to the lifetime poor, which raises equity (more redistribution for given tax rates), efficiency (lower tax rates for given redistribution), or both.

Joint Taxation of Individual and Household Income

Most tax systems tax either individual incomes or household incomes. The distinction between individual and household taxation is generally not precise. Many countries with individual-based tax systems also allow for dependencies on household income, such as in income support for housing, health care, tax credits, or welfare benefits. Similarly, tax systems are generally not purely based on household income, due to individual-specific elements in tax-benefit systems. In

---

[25]Earning ability is typically modeled as a stochastic variable, which evolves over time as a Markov-process, possibly exhibiting persistence. In addition, these models may allow for aggregate productivity shocks.

[26]The implementation of optimal second-best allocations requires very complex tax schedules (see also footnote 24). Since insurance markets are missing, externalities are present and implementations of optimal allocations with separate tax schedules generally do not exist (Renes and Zoutman 2016b). Albanesi and Sleet (2006) analyze a version of the New Dynamic Public Finance model with preference shocks (to the disutility of work) rather than skill shocks. If preference shocks are independent and identically distributed, then the optimal nonlinear joint tax schedule depends on current labor income and wealth. Simulations show that marginal labor taxes are declining in wealth. Expected wealth taxes are at most 2 percent, which is quite substantial. Kocherlakota (2005, 2010) allows for general processes of skill shocks and aggregate risks as in the canonical New Dynamic Public Finance model. Optimal nonlinear labor taxes and linear taxes on wealth are shown to be functions of the entire history of earnings. Moreover, the optimal wealth tax is zero in expectation. But these results depend on the particular implementation chosen.

the economics literature, there is a long-standing economic debate on whether it is better to levy taxes based on individual or on household income (such as Boskin and Sheshinski 1983; Kleven, Kreiner, and Saez 2009). This debate has not been settled, since it is fraught with conceptual difficulties as to what the proper objective of policy should be: should it be based on individual or on household welfare? However, even without delving into these discussions, and adhering to a strictly individualistic approach to social welfare, the problem of optimal taxation of individuals in different households is a complex one.

The standard Mirrlees (1971) framework assumes that earning ability is private information and is the only source of heterogeneity. However, if we would allow for households consisting of different individuals, not only is earning ability private information, so are the transfers among household members. If primary earners transfer resources to secondary earners, individual incomes are a poor proxy for individual consumption, and thus for individual welfare. Moreover, income tax schedules cannot be conditioned on individual income after intra-household transfers. A tax system based on household income implicitly takes intra-household transfers into account by basing the total tax liability on joint earnings.

How does the tax system affect efficiency and redistribution if it is based on either individual or household income? To understand the differences between individual and household taxation, assume that a household consists of two income earners. The primary ("male") earner has—by definition—a higher income than the secondary ("female") earner. Furthermore, assume that the secondary earner is more elastic in its labor supply decisions than the primary earner. Suppose furthermore that tax systems are progressive and feature increasing tax rates with income. All these assumptions are empirically valid. Taxation of household income under a progressive tax schedule raises tax rates of the secondary earner and lowers tax rates of primary earners compared to a system of individual taxation—assuming the ordering of incomes of primary and secondary earners remains the same. Given that secondary earners are more elastic in their labor supply decisions, incentives to work will be weaker under a system of household taxation compared to a system of individual taxation. At the same time, a progressive individual tax system puts a larger tax burden on households with a more unequal distribution of labor income ("traditional couples") than on households with a more equal distribution of labor income ("modern couples") if household income is the same in both traditional and modern couples.[27] Hence, a move from a tax system based on individual income to a tax system based on household income redistributes income from "modern" to "traditional" couples. This is the mirror image of the larger labor-supply distortions—on average—implied by household tax system compared to the individual tax system.

---

[27]This is similar to the notion that progressive tax systems imply a higher average tax burden on more volatile incomes for the same average incomes.

Kleven, Kreiner, and Saez (2009) analyze the joint taxation of households where the primary earner supplies labor on the intensive margin and the secondary earner on the extensive margin. They show that, if two-earner households are better (worse) off than single-earner households, the optimal income tax schedule features a positive tax (subsidy) on labor participation of the secondary earner. The tax schedule displays jointness, since the optimal participation tax on the secondary earner depends on the labor income of the primary earner. In particular, there is negative (positive) jointness if the participation tax (subsidy) decreases in the income of the primary earner. The participation tax converges to zero for very high incomes of primary earners.

Renes and Zoutman (2016a) also provide an example of the optimal joint taxation of couples. They demonstrate that the optimal tax schedule on labor income of the primary (secondary) earner strongly depends on the income of the secondary (primary) earner. Simulations indicate that the marginal tax rate of a top-income primary earner with a spouse having nearly zero earnings faces a marginal tax rate of about 25 percent. However, if both spouses are top income earners their marginal tax rate is about 65 percent. Hence, optimal tax schedules feature (positive) jointness in the income of primary and secondary earners.

Digitalization may allow tax authorities to more easily implement and administer more complex tax schedules that are based on both individual and household income. This is equivalent to conditioning tax schedules on incomes from primary and secondary earners. By levying a joint tax schedule on individual and household (or, equivalently, partner) income, the government can achieve its distributional goals at lower efficiency costs. Such tax systems generate fewer distortions, more equity or a combination of both compared to purely individual-based or household-based tax systems.

Tagging in Nonlinear Tax Schedules

In general, nonlinear tax schedules should be conditioned on immutable household characteristics that can be verified and that are correlated with earning ability—age, gender, unemployment, illness—or related to distributional objectives ("needs")—children, non-working dependents, disability, health. This is the old idea of "tagging" of Akerlof (1978). Indeed, practically all tax countries in the world apply tagging in their tax-transfer systems through tax credits and deductions, and benefits for particular groups that are considered to be more deserving or have larger needs.

However, there is ample room for improving existing tax schedules. The most obvious areas where policy could improve is to implement age- and gender-based nonlinear taxes on earnings. Furthermore, tax schedules could be made (more) dependent on the number of household members. Digitalization could help administer and implement such "tag-dependent tax schedules" based on individual or household characteristics, other than labor or capital income or wealth, that are correlated with ability or need. Intuitively, it is better to levy tag-specific nonlinear tax schedules than to levy one nonlinear income tax schedule supplemented with various income- or needs-based programs. By introducing separate tax schedules based on individual or household characteristics, governments could once more achieve distributional objectives at lower efficiency costs. Indeed, age-based taxation is shown to substantially improve the equity-efficiency trade-off in Weinzierl (2011); Bastani, Blomquist, and Micheletto (2013); and Fahri and Werning (2013). Similarly, Boskin and Sheshinski (1983) and Cremer Gahvari, and Lozachmeur (2010) demonstrate that gender-based tax schedules can substantially improve equity, efficiency, or both.

Interactions between Tax Complexity and Costs of Tax Enforcement

Digitalization may allow governments to implement more sophisticated tax systems that improve the equity-efficiency trade off. If tax systems are made more complex and sophisticated, as indicated in various policy suggestions, the costs of tax enforcement and tax compliance increase. A related concern is that tax systems would become less transparent and more difficult to understand for taxpayers.

Digitalization may also be useful to make tax systems more transparent and easier to understand. For example, digitalization could help taxpayers gain direct access to their tax returns. Furthermore, governments could provide sophisticated online tax-benefit calculators to assist individual taxpayers with their financial planning. Moreover, as argued above, digitalization potentially also reduces the cost of tax enforcement and compliance. Hence, digitalization may potentially allow for more complex tax systems.

Nevertheless, it is not guaranteed that more complex tax systems are socially desirable. The costs of greater complexity always need to be traded off against the welfare gains of better tax systems in terms of an improved equity-efficiency trade-off. Only if the costs of higher complexity and resulting lack of transparency are sufficiently low will it be socially desirable to implement more complex and sophisticated tax schedules.

CONCLUSION

Digitalization may improve the tax enforcement technology by collecting more and more reliable information on the economic outcomes of taxpayers, and improve the equity-efficiency trade-off by implementing more complex tax systems to better target income redistribution. In doing so, digitalization potentially allows governments to lower tax rates to collect the same amount of revenue or to redistribute the same amount of income as in current tax systems.

The chapter identified five proposals to improve the tax enforcement technology of the government:

1. Digitalization may provide the government with greater information on individual consumption, such as due to increased use of digital payment methods and the phasing out of cash payments.

2. Digitalization can help to generate information on and improve existing links between wealth (traded and non-traded assets, homeownership, pensions) and capital incomes (interest, dividends, capital gains, property income, pension accrual).

3. International information exchange can be made automatic and can be improved by creating international registers for asset ownership and capital incomes.

4. Digitalization allows financial institutions to act better as third-party reporters on capital incomes and wealth for the government.

5. Digitalization makes it possible for consumers to act as third-party reporters for the VAT or sales tax, for example, by using electronic payment information (such as debit and credit card payments).

Moreover, the chapter identified eight proposals to improve the equity-efficiency trade-off by designing more efficient tax systems—more efficient in the sense that distributional objectives can be achieved with lower tax rates and thus lower efficiency costs.

1. International registers of asset ownership and shareholders allow for taxation of capital income on residence rather than on source basis. The corporate income tax could be used as a withholding tax on dividend income or abolished altogether.

2. By combining information on all assets and capital incomes, a dual-income-tax system could be introduced, under which all capital incomes and wealth are linked and taxed under a single tax schedule: a synthetic capital income tax.

3. In developing economies, biometric identification and electronic transaction systems could allow progressive consumption taxes, reducing the need for low VAT rates on necessities for income redistribution.

4. Nonlinear consumption taxes could be levied on goods that are perishable, non-storable, and non-transportable.

5. Vickrey's (1947) proposal for an average tax on cumulative income could be implemented. Alternatively, marginal tax rates could be made dependent on entire earnings histories.

6. Tax schedules could jointly tax labor and capital income or wealth.

7. Tax schedules could jointly tax individual and household income.

8. Separate tax schedules could be introduced based on individual or household characteristics, such as gender, age, disability, health, or children ("tagging"; Akerlof 1978).

Whether governments would like to implement such tax reforms is determined not only by the economic benefits of having better tax enforcement or more efficient tax systems, but also by horizontal equity, privacy concerns and avoiding abuse of state powers. Indeed, these concerns might be the reason many of the suggested tax reforms have not been implemented so far, such as age-dependent or gender-based tax schedules. Moreover, political-economy constraints can prevent moving to the second-best frontier as identified by optimal tax analysis. However, information on the second-best frontier is important for policymakers, irrespective of whether political constraints prevent reaching this frontier.

Clearly, political distortions are important in real-world policymaking, but the literature does not provide crystallized ideas how political constraints interact with tax distortions. Government can use the information provided by digitalization for both good and bad. Digitalization raises issues about the quality of government institutions and the protection of the privacy of citizens. Digitalization can improve tax systems, increase economic efficiency, and promote equity in countries with good institutions, well-functioning democracies, enforcement of the rule of law, and strict protection of the privacy of citizens. However, more digitalization may well prove counterproductive in countries with bad institutions, greater corruption, more authoritarian regimes, little or no rule of law, and no protection of the privacy of its citizens. Indeed, greater use of information can also enable bad governments to better realize bad policy objectives.

REFERENCES

Aiyagari, Rao S. 1995. "Optimal Capital Income Taxation with Incomplete Markets, Borrowing Constraints, and Constant Discounting." *Journal of Political Economy* 103 (6): 1158–75.

Akerlof, George A. 1978. "The Economics of 'Tagging' as Applied to the Optimal Income Tax, Welfare Programs, and Manpower Planning." *American Economic Review* 68 (1): 8–19.

Albanesi, Stefania, and Christopher Sleet. 2006. "Dynamic Optimal Taxation with Private Information." *Review of Economic Studies* 73 (1): 1–30.

Allingham, Michael G., and Agnar Sandmo. 1972. "Income Tax Evasion: A Theoretical Analysis." *Journal of Public Economics* 1 (1): 323–338.

Aslam, Aqib, and Alpa Shah. 2017. "Taxation and the Peer-to-Peer Economy." IMF Fiscal Forum 2017: Digital Revolutions in Public Finance, International Monetary Fund, Washington, DC.

Atkinson, Anthony B., and Joseph E. Stiglitz. 1976. "The Design of Tax Structure: Direct versus Indirect Taxation." *Journal of Public Economics* 6 (1–2): 55–75.

Auerbach, Alan J. 1991. "Retrospective Capital Gains Taxation." *American Economic Review* 81 (1): 167–78.

———, and David F. Bradford. 2004. "Generalized Cash-Flow Taxation." *Journal of Public Economics* 88 (5): 957–80.

Banks, James, and Peter. A. Diamond. 2010. "The Base for Direct Taxation." In *The Mirrlees Review. Dimensions of Tax Design*, edited by S. Adam, T. Besley, R. Blundell, S. Bond, R. Chote, M. Gammie, P. Johnson, G. Myles, and J. M. Poterba. Oxford: Oxford University Press, 548–648.

Bastani, Spencer, Sören Blomquist, and Luca Micheletto. 2013. "The Welfare Gains of Age-Related Optimal Taxation." *International Economic Review* 54 (4): 1219–49.

Boadway, Robin, Maurice Marchand, and Pierre Pestieau. 1994. "Toward a Theory of the Direct-Indirect Tax Mix." *Journal of Public Economics* 55 (1): 71–78.

Boskin, Michael J., and Eytan Sheshinski. 1983. "Optimal Tax Treatment of the Family: Married Couples." *Journal of Public Economics* 20 (3): 281–97.

Browning, Martin, and Costas Meghir. 1991. "The Effects of Male and Female Labour Supply on Commodity Demands." *Econometrica* 59 (4): 925–51.

Buiter, Willem H., and Ebrahim Rahbari. 2015. "High Time to Get Low: Getting Rid of the Lower Bound on Nominal Interest Rates." Global Economics View, Citi Bank Research. April 9.

Chamley, Christophe. 1986. "Optimal Taxation of Capital Income in General Equilibrium with Infinite Lives." *Econometrica* 54 (3): 607–22.

Chen, Jingnan C., Shaun Grimshaw, and Gareth D. Myles. 2017. "Testing and Implementing Digital Tax Administration." IMF Fiscal Forum 2017: Digital Revolutions in Public Finance, International Monetary Fund, Washington, DC.

Christiansen, Vidar, and Matti Tuomala. 2008. "On Taxing Capital Income with Income Shifting." *International Tax and Public Finance* 15 (4): 527–45.

Conesa, Juan Carlos, Sagiri Kitao, and Dirk Krueger. 2009. "Taxing Capital? Not a Bad Idea After All." *American Economic Review* 99 (1): 25–48.

Corlett, Wilfred J., and Douglas C. Hague. 1953. "Complementarity and the Excess Burden of Taxation." *Review of Economic Studies* 21 (1): 21–30.

Correia, Isabel H. 1996. "Should Capital Income Be Taxed in the Steady State?" *Journal of Public Economics* 60 (1): 147–51.

Crawford, Ian, Michael Keen, and Stephen Smith. 2010. "Value Added Tax and Excises." In *The Mirrlees Review. Dimensions of Tax Design*, edited by S. Adam, T. Besley, R. Blundell, S. Bond, R. Chote, M. Gammie, P. Johnson, G. Myles, and J. M. Poterba. Oxford: Oxford University Press: 275–362.

Cremer, Helmuth, Firouz Gahvari, and Jean-Marie Lozachmeur. 2010. "Tagging and Income Taxation: Theory and an Application." *American Economic Journal: Economic Policy* 2 (1): 31–50.

Cremer, Helmuth, Pierre Pestieau, and Jean Rochet. 2001. "Direct versus Indirect Taxation: The Design of Tax Structure Revisited." *International Economic Review* 42 (3): 781–99.

Deaton, Angus S. 1977. "Equity, Efficiency, and the Structure of Indirect Taxation." *Journal of Public Economics* 8 (3): 299–312.

Devereux, Michael, and Simon Loretz. 2013. "What Do We Know about Corporate Tax Competition?" *National Tax Journal* 66 (3): 745–74.

Devereux, Michael, and John Vella. 2017. "Implications of Digitization for International Corporate Tax Reform." IMF Fiscal Forum 2017: Digital Revolutions in Public Finance, International Monetary Fund, Washington, DC.

Diamond, Peter A. 1998. "Optimal Income Taxation: An Example with a U-Shaped Pattern of Optimal Marginal Tax Rates." *American Economic Review* 88 (1): 83–95.

Diamond, Peter A., and James A. Mirrlees. 1971a. "Optimal Taxation and Public Production I: Production Efficiency." *American Economic Review* 61 (1): 8–27.

———. 1971b. "Optimal Taxation and Public Production II: Tax Rules." *American Economic Review* 61 (3): 261–78.

Diamond, Peter A., and Johannes Spinnewijn. 2011. "Capital Income Taxes with Heterogeneous Discount Rates." *American Economic Journal: Policy* 3 (4): 52–76.

Erosa, Andres, and Martin Gervais. 2002. "Optimal Taxation in Life-Cycle Economies." *Journal of Economic Theory* 105 (2): 338–69.

Fahri, Emmanuel, and Iàn Werning. 2012. "Capital Taxation: Quantitative Explorations of the Inverse Euler Equation." *Journal of Political Economy* 120 (3): 398–446.

———. 2013. "Insurance and Taxation over the Life Cycle." *Review of Economic Studies* 80 (2): 596–635.

Gerritsen, Aart, Bas Jacobs, Alexandra V. Rusu, and Kevin Spiritus. 2017. "Optimal Taxation of Capital Income when Individuals Have Different Returns." Unpublished, MPI Munich/ Erasmus University Rotterdam/KU Leuven.

Golosov, Mikhail, Narayana Kocherlakota, and Aleh Tsyvinski. 2003. "Optimal Indirect and Capital Taxation." *Review of Economic Studies* 70 (3): 569–87.

Golosov, Mikhail, Maxim Troshkin, and Aleh Tsyvinski. 2016. "Redistribution and Social Insurance." *American Economic Review* 106 (2): 359–86.

Golosov, Mikhail, and Aleh Tsyvinski. 2006. "Designing Optimal Disability Insurance. A Case for Asset Testing." *Journal of Political Economy* 114 (2): 257–79.

Golosov, Mikhail, Aleh Tsyvinski, and Iván Werning. 2007. "New Dynamic Public Finance: A User's Guide." *NBER Macroeconomic Annual* 21: 317–63, National Bureau of Economic Research, Cambridge, MA.

Golosov, Mikhail, Aleh Tsyvinski, and Nicolas Werquin. 2014. "A Variational Approach to the Analysis of Tax Systems." Unpublished, Princeton/Yale/Toulouse.

Gordon, Roger H., and Wojciech Kopczuk. 2014. "The Choice of the Personal Income Tax Base." *Journal of Public Economics* 118: 97–110.

Harding, Michelle. 2013. "Taxation of Dividend, Interest, and Capital Gain Income." OECD Taxation Working Paper 19, Organisation for Economic Co-operation and Development, Paris.

International Monetary Fund (IMF). 2016. "Tax Policy, Leverage and Macroeconomic Stability." IMF Policy Paper 16/151, Washington, DC.

Jacobs, Bas. 2013. "From Optimal Tax Theory to Applied Tax Policy." *FinanzArchiv* 69 (3): 338–89.

Jacobs, Bas, and Robin Boadway. 2014. "Optimal Linear Commodity Taxation under Optimal Non-Linear Income Taxation." *Journal of Public Economics* 117 (1): 201–10.

Jacobs, Bas, and A. Lans Bovenberg. 2010. "Human Capital and Optimal Positive Taxation of Capital Income." *International Tax and Public Finance* 17 (5): 451–78.

Jacobs, Bas, and Alexandra V. Rusu. 2017. "Why Is the Long-Run Tax on Capital Income Zero? Explaining the Chamley-Judd Result." Tinbergen Institute Discussion Paper TI 2017–011/VI, Rotterdam, Netherlands.

Jacobs, Bas, and Dirk Schindler. 2012. "On the Desirability of Taxing Capital Income in Optimal Social Insurance." *Journal of Public Economics* 96 (9–10): 853–68.

Judd, Kenneth L. 1985. "Redistributive Taxation in a Simple Perfect Foresight Model." *Journal of Public Economics* 28 (1): 59–83.

Kanbur, Ravi. 2017. "The Digital Revolution and Targeting Public Expenditure for Poverty Reduction." IMF Fiscal Forum 2017: Digital Revolutions in Public Finance, International Monetary Fund, Washington, DC.

Keen, Michael, and Kai Konrad. 2013. "The Theory of International Tax Competition." In *Handbook of Public Economics, Volume 5*, edited by A. J. Auerbach, R. Chetty, M. Feldstein and E. Saez, 257–328.

Keen, Michael, and Joel Slemrod. 2016. "Optimal Tax Administration." NBER Working Paper 22408, National Bureau of Economic Research, Cambridge, MA.

Kleven, Henrik J., Claus T. Kreiner, and Emmanuel Saez. 2009. "The Optimal Income Taxation of Couples." *Econometrica* 77 (2): 537–60.

Kocherlakota, Narayana R. 2005. "Zero Expected Wealth Taxes. A Mirrlees Approach to Dynamic Optimal Taxation." *Econometrica* 73 (5): 1587–621.

———. 2010. *The New Dynamic Public Finance.* Princeton, NJ: Princeton University Press.

Laroque, Guy R. 2005. "Indirect Taxation Is Superfluous under Separability and Taste Homogeneity: A Simple Proof." *Economics Letters* 87 (1): 141–44.

Liebman, Jeffrey B. 2003. "Should Taxes Be Based on Lifetime Income? Vickrey Taxation Revisited." Unpublished, John F. Kennedy School of Government, Harvard University, Cambridge, MA.

Mirrlees, James A. 1971. "An Exploration in the Theory of Optimum Income Taxation." *Review of Economic Studies* 38 (2): 175–208.

———. 1976. "Optimal Tax Theory: A Synthesis." *Journal of Public Economics* 6 (4): 327–58.

———. 1999. "The Theory of Moral Hazard and Unobservable Behaviour: Part I." *Review of Economic Studies* 66 (1): 3–21.

Organisation for Economic Co-operation and Development (OECD). 2011. *Going for Growth.* Paris.

———. 2016a. "Automatic Exchange of Financial Account Information." Background Information Brief, Paris.

———. 2016b. *Pension Outlook 2016.* Paris.

Piketty, Thomas, and Emmanuel Saez. 2013. "A Theory of Optimal Inheritance Taxation." *Econometrica* 81 (5): 1851–86.

Pirttilä, Jukka, and Ilpo Suoniemi. 2014. "Public Provision, Commodity Demand, and Hours of Work: An Empirical Analysis." *Scandinavian Journal of Economics* 116 (4): 1044–67.

Ramsey, Frank P. 1927. "A Contribution to the Theory of Taxation." *Economic Journal* 37 (145): 47–61.

Reis, Catarina. 2011. "Entrepreneurial Labor and Capital Taxation." *Macroeconomic Dynamics* 15 (3): 326–35.

Renes, Sander, and Floris T. Zoutman. 2016a. "As Easy as ABC? Multi-dimensional Screening in Public Finance." Unpublished, Erasmus University Rotterdam/Norwegian School of Economics.

———. 2016b. "When a Price is Enough: Implementation in Optimal Tax Design." Unpublished, Erasmus University Rotterdam/Norwegian School of Economics.

Roberts, Kevin. 1984. "The Theoretical Limits of Redistribution." *Review of Economic Studies* 51 (2): 177–95.

Rogoff, Kenneth S. 2016. *The Curse of Cash.* Princeton, NJ: Princeton University Press.

Saez, Emmanuel. 2001. "Using Elasticities to Derive Optimal Income Tax Rates." *Review of Economic Studies* 68 (1): 205–29.

———. 2002. "The Desirability of Commodity Taxation under Non-Linear Income Taxation and Heterogeneous Tastes." *Journal of Public Economics* 83 (2): 217–30.

Scheuer, Florian, and Iván Werning. 2016. "Mirrlees Meets Diamond-Mirrlees: Simplifying Nonlinear Income Taxation." NBER Working Paper 22076, National Bureau of Economic Research, Cambridge, MA.

Spiritus, Kevin 2017. "Optimal Mixed Taxation with Multidimensional Heterogeneity of Agents." Unpublished, Catholic University Leuven.

Vickrey, William. 1939. "Averaging of Income for Income Tax Purposes." *Journal of Political Economy* 47: 379–97.

———. 1947. *Agenda for Progressive Taxation.* New York: The Ronald Press Company.

Weinzierl, Matthew. 2011. "The Surprising Power of Age-Dependent Taxes." *Review of Economic Studies* 78 (4): 1490–518.

Werning, Iván. 2007. "Optimal Fiscal Policy with Redistribution." *Quarterly Journal of Economics* 122 (3): 925–67.

Zucman, Gabriel. 2015. *The Hidden Wealth of Nations.* Chicago: University of Chicago Press.

CHAPTER 3

Taxation and the Peer-to-Peer Economy

AQIB ASLAM AND ALPA SHAH

INTRODUCTION

As the digital, peer-to-peer (P2P) economy takes off worldwide, it has come under increasing scrutiny and criticism amid the perception that it is far less regulated and taxed than other types of business.[1] Some view this light government touch as distorting competition and giving individuals and businesses in the P2P economy an unfair advantage over competing businesses in the same sectors. Others argue that, by putting beneficial pressure on restrictive practices, it is enhancing efficiency.

If P2P economy users are indeed subject to lower taxation—because of preferential rates or simply underreporting of income—government tax revenues may be at risk, especially if other more tax-rich activities are being displaced. At the same time, it is possible that this new way of doing business is formalizing activities in certain sectors, bringing them within reach of the regulatory and tax authorities.

That the definition and reach of the P2P economy remains open for debate compounds the controversy. Many terms have been coined to describe new digital P2P activities, for example, the "sharing economy" and the "gig economy."[2]

The authors would like to thank Beth Adair, Chelsea Barabas, Sonia Carrera, Francois Chadwick, Peter Coles, Ruud De Mooij, Johannes Degn, Peter Gigante, Sanjeev Gupta, Jonathan Hall, Zach Jones, Michael Keen, Patrick Kallerman, Jed Kolko, Pooja Kondabolu, Jonathan Lieber, Idan Netser, Igor Popov, Lucas Puente, Jennifer Rowland, Joshua Sandler, Mick Thackray, Robert Trotter, Geneviève Verdier, and Travis Woodward for useful comments and discussions and John Damstra for excellent research assistance.

[1]The term "P2P economy" encompasses P2P participants (buyers and sellers) and digital platforms, across all sectors, involved in P2P activities. "P2P businesses" and "P2P sellers" are used interchangeably to describe those entities on the supply side that are providing goods and services over P2P platforms.

[2]"Gig economy" refers to activities centered around a specific job or task (a gig). While this terminology could suggest smaller-scale interactions in the marketplace, importantly larger corpo-

However, these names typically refer to only a subset of the transactions of interest, since P2P businesses can exist in any online market where transactions can be characterized by exchange (sale) or rental (sharing) between two parties—often individuals.

Importantly, the P2P model—the transaction of goods and services between individual buyers and sellers—is not a new way of conducting business (think of bartering). What distinguishes it in recent years are the technological developments that have eliminated various transaction costs associated with running a business, allowing smaller-scale activity to proliferate and collectively challenge incumbent, larger-scale corporate businesses. P2P trading has therefore managed to penetrate an increasing range of sectors, with an increasing range of goods and services sectors boasting P2P provision.

Certain sectors have borne the brunt of the criticism. For instance, the rapid ascension of P2P platforms in the hospitality and tourism sectors has raised questions about whether these new entrants are somehow tax-advantaged compared with traditional businesses, violating the principle of tax neutrality. In the price-setting ridesharing industry, the question of whether drivers are employees or self-employed has been another source of controversy. This issue can have important implications for whom the burden of tax compliance falls on, as well as the level of social insurance and benefits payable.

Governments have become aware of the need to clarify tax obligations for users of the P2P economy with some having already issued specific guidance. They have also recognized the potential benefits of getting access to and using the large amount of information held by digital platforms for enhancing compliance. The role of the platform as a withholding agent has also been identified, raising questions of whether this is feasible for all taxes that P2P users are liable for. Therefore, with increasing numbers of participants and a growing number of markets in which the P2P business model can thrive, interest in the scale, scope, and taxation of the P2P economy is inevitable.

This chapter seeks to address several questions. First and foremost, what are implications of the P2P economy for tax policy and administration? An important part of the answer rests on understanding whether the economic impact of the P2P economy and the P2P business model itself warrants special tax treatment. If the fundamental economic activity of these new businesses is different from existing sectors, are current tax policies sufficient to deal with them? If not, does the current tax structure allow for greater avoidance by participants in the P2P economy? And, if so, can the information which platforms accumulate help to improve compliance with minimal cost? More fundamentally, do the scale and nature of P2P activities suggest an alternative system of taxation—or even a simplification of existing taxes—to ensure that the government can share in the value being created? What this chapter will highlight is that from a tax policy

---

rations also use P2P infrastructure as a supplementary sales channel to reach a broader consumer base. This is often referred to as the business-to-peer channel.

perspective the case for a separate or special tax treatment is not immediately obvious. What appears to be a tax administration issue could be mistaken for a tax policy issue.

The next section defines the P2P economy and reviews the literature on theory and empirics. The chapter then explores features of the P2P economy relevant for tax policy and administration, and, finally, considers design in these two areas in a world where P2P activities are growing.

THE PEER-TO-PEER ECONOMY

The P2P economy can be described as a collection of virtual marketplaces that connect individuals looking to trade goods and services with one another through digital platforms. On one side, you have the buyers, who want specific goods or services and, on the other, the sellers that own the good to be sold (or rented) or control the assets needed to provide the service. Table 3.1 lists examples of P2P platforms in different sectors.

Table 3.1. Examples of Peer-to-Peer Platforms across Sectors	
Industry/Sector Description[1]	**Examples of Peer-to-Peer Platforms[2]**
Couriers and Delivery Services	Deliveroo, Instacart, Postmates
Digital Currencies (financial intermediation, transactions)	Bitcoin, Ethereum, Ripple
Financial Services (crowdfunding, collaborative lending)	Funding Circle, Lending Club, Kickstarter, Prosper, SoFi
Retail Business (online sales, distribution, auctions)	Amazon, Craigslist, eBay, Etsy
Software-, Knowledge-, and Media-Sharing	Apple iTunes, Coursera, Dropbox, Wikipedia
Professional Services	Fiverr, Freelancer, Taskrabbit, Thumbtack, Upwork
Traveler Accommodation	Airbnb, Flipkey, Homeaway
Transit and Ground Passenger Transportation	BlaBlaCar, Careem, Didi Chuxing, Lyft, Ola, Uber

Source: Authors' own classification.
[1]These descriptions span multiple industrial classifications.
[2]Platforms operational at the time of writing.

A defining characteristic of these platforms is the technology and how it helps users interact and manage risk. The technology—much of it developed only recently, with the rest inherited from the first wave of P2P businesses—has allowed individuals to access functions previously too costly and available only to larger-scale businesses with economies of scale and scope.[3] Web-based platforms, such as mobile applications on internet-enabled devices, provide easy access, for example, to payment intermediation functions, which allow rapid exchange of value between users at almost zero marginal cost.

---

[3]Recent P2P businesses have benefited immensely from existing social networks and reputational technology refined over time by the first wave of e-commerce businesses, such as eBay. And now P2P platforms have instigated traditional businesses to adopt these technologies to compete and maintain market share.

Online platforms also provide reputational and feedback mechanisms, transaction histories, and opportunities for advertising and marketing, all improving the provision of information. As information becomes more symmetric, not only is adverse selection reduced, but trust between consumers and sellers also increases, even if they have not previously met. In addition, consumers can access a broader range of goods and services (through ownership or rental) customized to their tastes. Technology therefore provides quality control through user-based reviews and ratings systems, fulfilling roles that tight regulations and even natural monopolies could also play.

P2P platforms exert different degrees of control over their users. On most platforms, sellers are unrestricted in their access and can market themselves and set their own prices. These platforms focus more on improving search, match, marketing, and feedback functions for their users. Other platforms instead screen and select sellers, set the prices for services being offered, determine the matching of buyers and sellers, and impose strict codes of conduct, such as ridesharing platforms, which use semi-automated, algorithmic management systems (Rosenblatt and Stark 2016).

While revenue-generating models also differ from company to company, even within the same sector, Vaughan and Daverio (2016) note that most platforms adopt a fixed or variable commission-based approach, with commissions charged ranging from 1–2 percent for lending to up to 20 percent for transportation network companies, and with more than 85 percent of the value of transactions facilitated received by the seller.

Another feature of P2P markets is that low barriers to entry allow buyers and sellers to switch roles easily and quickly. Such flexibility means that some individuals can engage either regularly (full-time) making it their primary source of income or irregularly at a lower frequency (part-time) to supplement other income. This flexibility to determine when to supply services can be of great value, as it reduces the opportunity cost of working and increases efficiency. Those participants in the labor- and capital-rental sectors typify this freedom for individuals to improve their labor-leisure trade-off. For example, by working a few more hours (or alternatively, renting out an asset for longer), P2P economy participants can loosen their budget constraints, expand their opportunity sets, and raise well-being.

One category of P2P businesses has received a lot of attention and, for many, captures the spirit of the broader P2P economy (Schor and Fitzmaurice 2015). For these businesses, platforms facilitate transactions by matching private individuals and allowing one party to "share" or temporarily rent the use of an underutilized asset to another (such as finance, human capital, labor, and physical capital). Sharing is therefore only one type of activity in the P2P economy and not a synonym for it.[4] This chapter considers all transactions (monetary or in-kind), either through sale or rental, that generate taxable income.

---

[4]When defining the reach of the P2P economy, the chapter does not cover certain P2P business models. For example, we do not consider businesses that provide subscription-based "on-demand"

The next two sections gauge the size and impact of P2P markets, summarizing available data and evaluating research on the effects they have had on competition, efficiency, pricing, and labor opportunities. Understanding these elements will be useful when considering the tax treatment of P2P users later.

The Scale of the Peer-to-Peer Economy

The P2P economy is a global phenomenon with some of the largest platforms operating in Asia (Alibaba and DiDi Chuxing in China). While several platforms operate across multiple countries (Airbnb, Amazon, BlaBlaCar, Uber), the key elements of certain platforms have instead been replicated locally (Casaferias and Zazcar in Brazil, Rappi in Colombia and Mexico, Ola in India, Careem in the Middle East).

Anecdotal evidence suggests that users on some of the largest platforms worldwide can number in the tens of millions (Table 3.2), suggesting that an enormous amount of transactions and income are being intermediated through these platforms. Moreover, results from a Pew Research Center survey suggest that 72 percent of American adults have used at least one of 11 different shared and on-demand services (Smith 2016). What is already clear is that many of the closely held P2P platforms themselves have attracted large amounts of capital and rapidly earned high valuations, which when scaled by the number of employees, exceed many of the largest listed companies, including other listed P2P businesses (Figure 3.1).

Table 3.2. Number of Users on Some of the Largest P2P Platforms

Company	Headquarters	Service	Reported Users (millions)
Airbnb	United States	Tourism	100
Alibaba	China	Commercial marketplaces	440
Amazon	United States	Commercial marketplaces	300
BlaBlaCar	France	Ridesharing	40
DiDi Chuxing	China	Ridesharing	400
eBay	United States	Commercial marketplaces	170
Lyft	United States	Ridesharing	40
Uber	United States	Ridesharing	40

Sources: *Forbes*; *Fortune*; Orbis; Reuters; and *Wall Street Journal*.

However, platforms closely guard data on users and incomes. Short of ordering disclosure, many government agencies are developing other methods to estimate the value added of P2P activity to the economy. For example, the Office of National Statistics in the United Kingdom is considering how to measure the contribution of the P2P economy to GDP more accurately (Office of National Statistics 2016).

---

services, such as, Apple Music, HBO, Netflix, Soundcloud, Spotify, and so on, where assets are not shared by individual owners.

Figure 3.1. Value per Employee of Largest Listed Firms versus Venture-Backed Peer-to-Peer Businesses
(Millions of US dollars per employee)

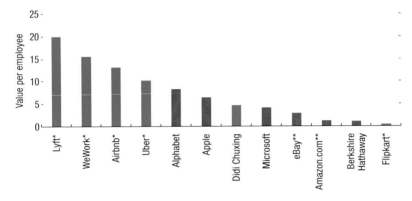

Sources: Dow Jones VentureSource; Orbis; and *Wall Street Journal.*
Note: * denotes closely held, venture-backed peer-to-peer businesses. ** denotes listed peer-to-peer businesses. Red bars denote listed businesses.

Nevertheless, several attempts have been made to ascertain the size and contribution of the P2P economy. Many of these studies have relied on secondary sources or proprietary data. Vaughan and Daverio (2016) examined the size of the P2P economy in five key sectors: accommodation, transportation, household services, professional services, and collaborative finance. Using a review of market, sectoral, and company data at a national, regional, and global level during 2013–15, they estimate that turnover on platforms in five key sectors of the P2P economy reached close to €4 billion (0.03 percent of EU-28 GDP) in Europe in 2015, facilitating about €28 billion (0.2 percent of EU-28 GDP) of transactions.

Three of the five sectors were also found to have expanded sales by several multiples in 2015 compared to 2014. Household services grew fastest, driven by the growing popularity of freelancer platforms and crowdsourced networks offering services such as ready-made food delivery or do-it-yourself tasks. Goudin (2016) examined the economic and social barriers and legislative gaps that could be holding back full implementation of the P2P economy across the European Union. The author estimated that the potential economic gains from employing underutilized capacity through P2P activities is €572 billion in annual consumption (4 percent of EU-28 GDP).

Some Theory and Empirics on the Peer-to-Peer Economy

Shrinking transaction costs

The P2P economy is a reversion to an almost preindustrial mode of organizing activity. Coase (1937) introduced the concept of "transaction costs"—later refined by Williamson (1981)—as the basic unit of analysis for determining how the organization of production developed historically into governance structures or "firms." While the price mechanism efficiently allocates resources in the market, it is costly due to frictions such as search, marketing, and negotiation over contract terms. Firms can economize such costs, for instance, by employing labor in open-ended employment contracts within "islands of conscious power," rather than repeatedly going to the market to negotiate short-term, task-based contracts with labor providers.[5]

Rapid, efficient, arms-length transactions lie at the heart of the P2P economy, and the technology behind the platforms has gone a long way in overcoming costs that previously made many of these transactions too difficult for small businesses to contract and implement. At the same time, technological developments have allowed for ever more precise, flexible, and credible coordination on tasks and services between the two sides of the market. Furthermore, search and matching costs have been reduced to the point where individuals can now transact, including share assets, on a cross-border scale. Therefore, the minimum efficient scale—the level of production at which average cost is minimized and equal to marginal cost—is shrinking relative to demand in the market, encouraging a larger number of smaller businesses to enter.[6]

A short primer on two-sided markets

P2P marketplaces are examples of "two-sided markets," where the decisions of one side affect the outcomes of the other (Caillaud and Jullien 2003; Ellison and Fudenberg 2003; Evans 2003; Rochet and Tirole 2003; Armstrong 2006; Rysman 2009).[7] The interaction between the two sides gives rise to strong complementarities—notably, network and information externalities—where the value in transactions increases for both groups as the numbers on each side increase. While both sides are also typically populated by individuals, this does not preclude businesses from participating in the P2P economy, although they typically do not dominate it.

The academic literature on two-sided markets initially focused on how platforms set prices for both sides to ensure they choose to interact. Rochet and Tirole

---

[5]Coase (1937) quoting Robertson (1923). One can therefore expect the P2P economy to expand rapidly in sectors where contracting costs are already relatively minimal and short-term contracts dominate. In addition, the resource-based view of the firm complements this approach to some extent, by identifying other competitive advantages that firms have over purely market-based interactions, such as intangibles like "corporate culture."

[6]In some sectors, such as natural resources, the minimum efficient scale is large because of the high ratio of fixed to variable costs. In these cases, the sectors are more concentrated and dominated by a handful of major players.

[7]Popular examples of such markets when the literature was first developing include newspaper companies attempting to attract both readers and advertisers; video gaming systems, where the intermediary is the console producer and the two sets of agents are consumers and video game developers; and payment card systems, where both consumers and merchants value each other's participation.

(2003) establish some of the key theoretical results, specifically how prices on both sides of the market depend jointly on the demand elasticities and marginal costs of each side. As Rysman (2009) notes, while prices typically fall as the price elasticity of demand increases in traditional markets, the effects could be magnified in a two-sided market. For instance, consider a market of buyers (side A) and sellers (side B). A lower price on side A will attract demand-elastic consumers, which attracts greater supply or raises prices on side B (or both). By drawing in side B, the value to the platform of having more buyers on side A increases, which leads to an even bigger price decrease and quantity increase on side A, where the price elasticity of demand has increased.

Bolt and Tieman (2008) loosen some of the assumptions in Rochet and Tirole (2003) to show that a skewed pricing result can boost the demand for services supplied over the platform, by using the less elastic side (C) of the market to subsidize the more elastic side (D). Every agent on the high-elasticity low-price side (D) of the market will connect to the platform and the other lower-elasticity higher-price side (C) is therefore also encouraged to join to benefit from the full participation. Since side C is more price inelastic, the platform can charge a higher price to extract greater rents from them. Competition in two-sided markets adds an additional dimension to pricing. With two competing platforms pricing to consumers and sellers, if one lowers the consumer price, it will attract consumers from the competing platform. This reduces the value of the second platform to users, and hence leads to a larger demand for the first platform and eventually a larger supply. Hence, the implications of the joint interaction of pricing in two-sided markets is even more pronounced in competitive markets.

Taxation in two-sided markets has also been examined (see, for example, Kind, Koethenbuerger, and Schjelderup 2008, 2010; Bourreau, Caillaud, and De Nijs, forthcoming). Once again demand complementarities alter the results from traditional one-sided markets. For a monopoly platform, Kind, Koethenbuerger, and Schjelderup (2008) show how an increase in ad valorem tax on one side of the market may result in overproduction (compared to the social optimum), with an increase in output on both sides of the market. For example, an increase in the ad valorem tax on side E may lead the platform to raise sales on side F. To do so, the platform would need to increase output on both sides E and F given their mutual dependence. A specific tax would not have such an effect as it increases marginal cost, decreasing output. To prevent oversupply, positive specific taxes or negative ad valorem taxes should be used in two-sided markets. Therefore, ad valorem taxes, which are traditionally less distortionary, no longer dominate specific taxes and instead the latter may be preferable to the former.[8]

---

[8]Bourreau, Caillaud, and De Nijs (forthcoming) analyze the effects of taxation for a two-sided platform where data collection increases the quality of service to users and the value to advertisers. Their analysis shows that taxes on data collection may reduce the volume of sales and hence lower indirect tax revenues. It may also lead platforms to switch business models and start collecting subscription fees from users. Instead, an ad valorem tax on advertising revenues is superior to a tax on data.

While network externalities remain an essential feature, another important feature of the recent P2P market is that the two sides of the market are no longer distinct. For example, being either an owner or a renter is an endogenous decision that users of the platform make, and more of the former implies fewer of the latter (and vice versa). Therefore, skewing pricing and taxation to one side of the market may no longer be desirable, as it can create an imbalance in the supply and demand for the shared resource. Benjaafar and others (2015) build a stylized model to understand the determinants of ownership and rental. The level of the rental price determines the degree of ownership and usage levels and with a sufficiently high rental price, higher ownership and usage levels are possible even when the cost of ownership is high.

Horton and Zeckhauser (2016) also build a simple framework to understand how P2P markets can develop given the purchase price of the asset to be shared, valuations of owners and renters, the number of owners and renters, and the costs of bringing the asset to market. While durable goods that are expensive, used infrequently, but whose usage can be planned are among the best candidates for rental, P2P rental markets can develop only if prices and valuations are such that there are stocks of both owners and renters.[9] The introduction of P2P rentals is found to decrease ownership but increase utilization with the biggest gains in surplus accruing to renters who gain access to the good.

Some empirical results from the literature

Recent empirical work on P2P markets has produced valuable insights into the impact P2P activities are having on competition, prices, and labor markets. P2P businesses have been found to boost efficiency and supply by reducing transaction costs for search, matching, and overheads. On the demand side, this has translated into lower prices, convenience, and a greater variety. Cullen and Farronato (2016) use data from TaskRabbit to examine how P2P labor markets equilibrate highly variable demand and supply when matches need to be made both rapidly and locally. They find that labor supply is highly elastic, with increases in demand matched by increases in supply per worker with little or no impact on price.[10] The effects of competition are also potentially showing up in service quality: Wallsten (2015) presents suggestive evidence from Chicago that consumer complaints for traditional taxis fell following the entry of Uber.

---

[9]P2P rental activities can therefore also have price effects on durable goods with secondary markets. For example, Fraiberger and Sundararajan (2015) use data from car-sharing company Getaround to calibrate a model of P2P car rental. Their analysis shows both a shift away from asset ownership (by below-median income consumers) and a decline in the price of secondhand assets.

[10]Lower prices also mean that consumers capture greater surpluses. Cohen and others (2016) use big data from Uber's surge pricing algorithm to recover price elasticities of demand to build a short-term demand curve. Using this, the authors calculate that the low-cost portion of the ridesharing service managed to generate an overall consumer surplus of $6.8 billion for consumers in 2015. The estimated consumer surplus is approximately 1.6 times as large as consumer expenditures.

Are P2P businesses therefore displacing and undermining existing businesses? Zervas, Proserpio, and Byers (2017) find that Airbnb is winning customers from hotels that cater to the lower end of the market. Their presence has lowered revenues by about 8–10 percentage points in some segments as incumbents are forced to lower prices. In addition, the gap between high- and low-season prices has narrowed as the P2P platforms can flexibly scale supply during periods of peak demand.

Farronato and Fradkin (2016) use the market for short-term accommodation to study the determinants of Airbnb growth and its effects on the industry. They find that across major US cities, a larger Airbnb presence is associated with low opportunity costs of renting out spare rooms, high investment costs of building hotels, and high demand volatility. Furthermore, a 10 percentage point increase in the size of Airbnb reduces hotel revenue by 0.6 percentage points. Neeser (2015) does not find the same revenue effects, but offers evidence that Airbnb may have pushed down prices in Nordic countries. For ridesharing, there are several signs that Uber is securing market share at the expense of existing taxi firms, such as falling prices of medallions (a city-issued license to operate a taxi) in New York City and notable bankruptcies in recent years, such as Yellow Cab in San Francisco.

However, firms can retain some advantages over P2P sellers. The former can still enjoy economies of scale and expertise in minimizing certain types of transaction costs. For example, Edelman and Geradin (2016) note how a conventional hotel can use a single front desk to process the check-in for hundreds of guests—a common source of friction for property sharing. They also point out that, unsurprisingly, P2P rental platforms are investing heavily to replicate these functions. In addition to these platform-led efforts, a burgeoning industry is now providing complementary services to P2P activities.

The P2P economy has also had a significant impact on labor markets, particularly for lower-skilled jobs. Hall and Krueger (2015) assert that the Uber platform is bringing greater wage-earning opportunities to more people by allowing for much more flexible work arrangements. At the same time, the profile of these drivers is found to be closer to the average employee in the workforce in age and education, as opposed to the profile for more traditional taxi drivers and chauffeurs. Whether these new drivers are displacing existing taxi drivers is still difficult to determine, as is whether these drivers have re-entered the workforce as part of these ridesharing platforms.

Manyika and others (2016) used existing data and workforce surveys to understand the rise of "independent work" in the P2P economy. They estimated that the number of independent earners ranges from 54 million to 68 million in the United States and from 60 million to 94 million in the EU-15. Therefore, between 20–30 percent of the working-age population in the United States and the EU-15 is believed to engage in such independent work. However, the contingent nature of such independent work—notably "zero-hour" contracts—have been blamed for exposing individuals to excessive job insecurity and insufficient benefits and social insurance (Brinkley 2013).[11] The P2P economy could also be weakening worker bargaining power due to both the decentralized nature of interactions and, in some cases, the control exerted by the platform—with implications for wage and inflation pressures. Bernhardt (2014) notes that while it has been hard to find evidence of a strong, unambiguous shift toward nonstandard or contingent forms of work in aggregate data—especially in contrast to the dramatic increase in wage inequality—this is not to say that there have been no changes in the workplace.

KEY TAX-RELEVANT FEATURES OF THE PEER-TO-PEER ECONOMY

This section highlights features of the P2P economy that are particularly relevant for tax policy and administrative design. These relate to both P2P users and the platform.

Growth and Classification of P2P Activities

The previous section noted one of the defining characteristics of the P2P economy, namely the atomistic interactions among a population of highly dispersed users. The ease-of-access and flexibility of the P2P economy means that the number of people transacting over digital platforms has increased substantially over the past few years.

While there is no clear preference *a priori* for how to operate within the P2P economy, the small scale and informality of the engagement means that most individuals carry out P2P activities as self-employed (unincorporated) businesses. However, these activities could just as easily be carried out by individuals that have incorporated their businesses, and tax policy can determine this choice. Data on the number of businesses in the United States with zero employees (nonemployers) provide some confirmation by showing a marked increase in the transportation sector and to a lesser extent in the accommodation sector in the past five years (see Hathaway and Muro 2013; and Figure 3.2). This increase is also significantly larger than the growth in firms with employees.

Business classification has become increasingly controversial for those platforms that manage their users more actively, most notably in the ridesharing sector. The resulting legal challenges have seen sellers demanding employment

---

[11]The issue of adequate social protection is garnering increasing attention from governments. In Europe, principle 12 of the European Commission's "European Pillar on Social Rights" specifies that workers and, under comparable conditions, the self-employed have the right to adequate social protection (European Commission 2017). In the United Kingdom, the "Taylor Review of Modern Work Practices," released in July 2017, reviewed modern employment practices and set out a seven-step national strategy for "good work" in the United Kingdom, calling for equal treatment between those who work through P2P platforms ("Dependent Contractors") and those who do not (Department for Business, Energy & Industrial Strategy 2017).

Figure 3.2. Small Business Trends in the United States

Nonemployer Businesses: Transportation[1]

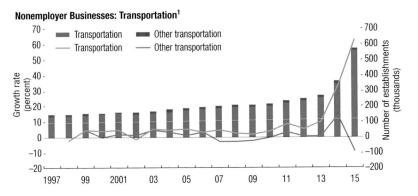

Nonemployer Businesses: Traveler Accommodation[2]

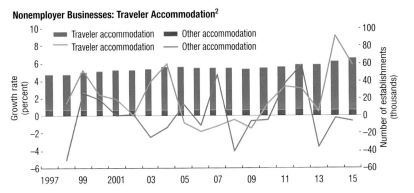

Growth of Employer Firms and Nonemployer Self-Employed Businesses (Percent)

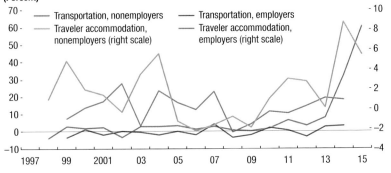

Source: US Census Bureau.
[1]Transportation includes NAICS codes 4853 ("Taxi and Limousine Service") and 4859 ("Other Transit and Ground Passenger Transportation").
[2]Traveler accommodation includes NAICS codes 7211 ("Traveler Accommodation") and 7213 ("Room and Boarding Houses").

rights. From a tax perspective, employment classification has implications for the compliance and reporting obligations of both the platform and the sellers. Tax legislation typically classifies labor into salaried employees or independent contractors (self-employed). Employers withhold payroll taxes and social security contributions on behalf of their employees, while the self-employed are responsible for filing and paying their own taxes and social contributions. Even though mechanisms already exist to address such classification issues in some sectors—for example, in the construction sector, where multi-factor tests are used to determine the appropriate worker classification—the ambiguity in the P2P economy is yet to be resolved. This is clear from the outcomes of recent court rulings across countries.[12]

Transforming all P2P sellers into employees would shift the burden of withholding and reporting to the platform. In some countries, the appropriate classification may also have an impact on direct tax revenues where the effective tax rate on the self-employed differs from that on employees. For indirect taxes, self-employed individuals are required to remit payments when sales income exceeds a certain threshold, and the platform is responsible for remitting taxes on any fees or commission charged for its intermediation services. However, if P2P sellers are restyled as employees, this division of responsibilities would also change and the platform would bear the full indirect tax liability on total sales generated.[13] Even while the debate continues, some labor-intensive platforms are attempting to avoid this issue altogether by offering their sellers the option of participating either as part-time employees or independent contractors.

Low Incomes, Low Rents

The level of engagement in the P2P economy also varies. Sellers can engage irregularly and at low frequency in P2P activity to supplement their income—for example, from low-paid employment—or use it as their primary source.[14] Farrell and Greig (2016a) use anonymized J.P. Morgan bank account data from approximately 260,000 customers in the United States over a three-year period to

---

[12]In February 2017, a Brazilian court recognized P2P ridesharing platforms as employers, while in March 2017, a Paris tribunal dismissed a French request for Uber to make social security payments to drivers. Some US states (California, Florida, Massachusetts) have also ruled in favor of Uber, stating that drivers are independent contractors, not employees. In late 2016, a British employment tribunal ruled in favor of two Uber drivers, entitling them to holiday pay, paid rest breaks, pension contributions, and the national minimum wage. However, this ruling opened the door for P2P sellers to be designated as a third category of "worker" falling between employee and self-employed.

[13]A related case was ongoing in the United Kingdom at the time of writing, where Jolyon Maugham from the Good Law Project is arguing for Uber to provide him a value-added tax (VAT) receipt for the taxi service he was provided. Should the court rule in his favor and classify Uber as a service provider (instead of a third-party platform intermediary for self-employed drivers), the U.K. tax authority would then be able to seek VAT payments for all rides Uber provided during the past four years, which are estimated in the order of hundreds of millions of pounds.

[14]There are also individuals who evolve into "power-sellers" or larger-scale ventures.

explore the degree of engagement. They find that certain groups subject to the greatest income volatility—18–24-year-olds, lower-income individuals, and people residing in the western United States—are most likely to use the P2P economy to smooth earnings. Income earned from labor-intensive P2P activities also helps offset drops in income earned off-platform (non-platform income), while income from capital-intensive P2P activities is used to supplement non-platform income. Individuals providing labor-intensive services are typically from the lower end of the income spectrum, while those providing capital-intensive services have higher average monthly income. At the same time, repeat usage of platforms falls off after the first month by up to one-third for labor-intensive activities and two-thirds for capital-intensive activities, suggesting more regular usage of the former.

While estimates of earnings can vary—for example, some have calculated that it is possible to earn a gross income of up to $50,000 through ridesharing in the United States—it is likely that, for many users, gross incomes earned through P2P activities are low. The average turnover can also vary widely depending on location and local demand. Without concrete data, it is hard to assess at what points along the distribution income is concentrated. However, anecdotal data for three cities from Airbnb suggest that annual incomes from accommodation rental are indeed low (Figure 3.3). Therefore, if we assume that (1) the distribution of income earned is concentrated at the low (left) end and (2) most P2P sellers are self-employed (and earn little other non-P2P economy-related income), then the progressivity of most personal income tax systems will mean that the effective average tax rates of these users will also be low.[15]

Even if gross income is not as low as many suspect, it is unclear whether P2P participants are generating large rents after offsetting costs. New entrants must incur significant fixed capital costs to be able to participate, while those that either rent or use their existing personal assets to provide a service face dramatically lower fixed costs and entry risk. Indeed, the P2P economy has seen its most pronounced growth in sectors in which suppliers make significant use of an otherwise underutilized personal asset for commercial purposes. Sellers do incur variable costs, however, including expenses from adapting their personal assets to commercial use.

Correcting for Externalities

While the success of the P2P economy relies on positive network and information externalities, driven by the technology, externalities also arise from the outcome of the P2P activities themselves. For example, with increased

---

[15]Farrell and Greig (2016b) find evidence that average monthly earnings and participation on online platforms are waning. This could indicate saturation of some parts of the P2P economy, or more generally, cyclicality in its usage. Income from P2P activities might no longer be as lucrative as it was, especially as job growth recovers in some countries and better alternatives with greater benefits and job security materialize.

Figure 3.3. Imputed Income Distribution for Airbnb Hosts

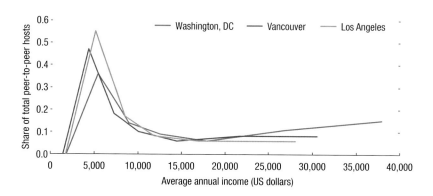

Sources: Airbnb Inc.; and authors' calculations.
Notes: Figure combines binned distributions of nights per listing for three cities (Los Angeles, Vancouver, and Washington, DC). These are combined with data on average incomes per night. These calculations assume zero correlation between (1) price per night and nights per year, and (2) nights and multi-listing host status.

ridesharing, traffic congestion might increase or decrease in cities (Martin, Shaheen, and Lidicker 2010). Property-sharing could boost tourism and spillovers to local economies, and the P2P business model can also bring previously undocumented activity into the formal economy (Box 3.1).

The presence of externalities could call for more direct tax policy intervention in the form of "Pigouvian" taxes or subsidies to discourage or encourage certain P2P activities.[16] However, as discussed in the previous section, the nature of two-sided markets warrants caution in the types of tax instruments used, given the feedback between each side.

P2P Platforms as Data Recorders

Moving on to the P2P platforms themselves, their role as intermediaries means that they maintain a digital footprint of all business income generated by users. The data recorded by platforms allows them to act as third-party reporters and alleviate informational constraints for tax authorities. If direct access to the information held by platforms is not an option, they could instead have the P2P platform withhold taxes on P2P users and then remit these to the exchequer.

If data on income generated from P2P activities by individuals can be combined with income earned from other sources, governments could design better

---

[16]Where certain sectors have emergent natural monopolies or oligopolies (such as ridesharing), the government could even consider nationalizing platforms to administer prices, and regulate congestion. The government could even optimize price-setting to meet some social objective (such as lower prices to subsidize low-income consumers).

tax systems that can ameliorate the equity-efficiency trade-off that results from the inability to perfectly observe individuals' work effort and earnings abilities (see Chapter 2; Dabla-Norris and others 2017). Overall, the potential for alleviating compliance burdens on both users and governments appears significant, and if tax systems tailored to income and consumption patterns are possible, the current system of thresholds—imposed to trade-off revenue gains with compliance losses—may become obsolete.

HOW SHOULD WE TAX THE P2P ECONOMY?

In determining tax policy, governments would need to assess the size and dynamics of P2P activity in their countries and evaluate whether their tax revenue potential and economic impact are sufficiently positive or negative to warrant either special tax structures or modifications to existing features of the tax system.[17] Part of this assessment involves understanding whether activities in the same sector carried out by both P2P and traditional businesses are economically equivalent. Furthermore, issues relevant to cross-border transactions and small businesses more generally—beyond the P2P economy—must be considered.

An important guiding principle is that taxes should have minimal impact on the behavior of economic agents. However, governments may choose to target P2P activities, for example, to correct for externalities. Design considerations might alternatively be driven by the government's desire to ease the burden of compliance and administration for P2P users. This could be achieved by applying simplified tax policies or cooperating with the platform to obtain information from them on income to facilitate audit and verification of tax filing or to have them act as a withholding agent for tax collection.

Neutral or Targeted Treatment of P2P Businesses

Should governments decide to target P2P businesses, they need to consider a number of factors. As noted earlier, evidence on the economic impact of P2P activities remains mixed. In addition, tax revenues raised directly from small businesses in general remain modest compared to the rest of the economy. While countries define their small business segments differently, findings suggest that they commonly account for less than 15 percent of domestic tax collections and often much less in low-income countries (IMF 2015). Assuming most P2P sellers are labor intensive with narrow profit margins and are therefore not generating large rents, it is important not to overstate the potential revenue gains from taxing them or even risks to current revenue. Income misreporting is also more likely, given more irregular, low-frequency, and, therefore, lower-income activity.

---

[17]For example, the revenue authority in the United Kingdom has commissioned a survey of the P2P economy to understand the determinants of its size and growth and whether the tax treatment of income earned is a major deterrent to participating in it.

Revenue potential will therefore depend on exploiting the number of small businesses rather than rents, as well as the responsiveness of reported income to tax rates and thresholds.[18]

As technology continues to eliminate transaction costs, increasingly efficient small businesses may better compete with and displace larger incumbents. Any favorable P2P tax treatment would exacerbate this effect. Where incumbents are being displaced and replacement P2P activity remains below tax thresholds, governments will lose revenue as income and profits are dispersed across many smaller businesses instead of concentrated in large profitable companies. Governments could attempt to recoup this lost revenue by carefully adjusting rates and thresholds. However, if P2P businesses are both more efficient than existing methods of provision and generating positive spillovers, doing so could impose high disproportionate costs and stifle such developments.

Given the relative elasticities of buyers and sellers and their interdependencies, governments should be sensitive to the incidence of taxation. After all, the success of the P2P business model hinges on maintaining a sufficient network of buyers and sellers, that is, exploiting network externalities. A tax on only P2P businesses could shift the tax burden so as to deter participation from either the demand or the supply sides. P2P platforms have been hitherto apprehensive about levying or varying charges on either side, while also demanding equal tax treatment across rival platforms.

These demand complementarities also have the potential to lure previously undocumented merchants—for example, in the household services sector—onto platforms and therefore into the formal economy. Countries would benefit, in that less income would go unrecorded and therefore come into the tax net. Increasing the relative tax burden of P2P sellers risks reversing this positive feedback loop, chasing sellers off the platforms and back into the informal sector.[19] These dynamics may be particularly volatile in emerging market and developing economies with large informal economic sectors.

What have governments tried so far, if anything? As noted earlier, the P2P business model allows alternative provision of goods and services, while the actual goods and services themselves remain unchanged (accommodation, transportation). Recent tax policy measures have therefore focused on leveling the playing field between P2P sellers and traditional businesses, where differences in tax treatment exist (Box 3.2). These differences typically originated from unequal

---

[18]Furthermore, the growth in low-income P2P activities could lead to lower social security contributions, particularly if sellers remain below exemption thresholds. However, many of these sellers could still qualify for social benefits over time where eligibility requirements are minimal, leading to an underfunded social security system. Such problems could also worsen as technological developments continue to threaten employment and polarize the income distribution.

[19]This effect may be less pronounced in markets where demand for such services is high and relatively inelastic—that is, where consumers value the convenience and quality assurances of using the platform rather than individually searching and contracting for services in the informal economy—such that the incidence of taxation falls primarily on consumers.

application of local or sector-specific taxes. Indeed, despite initial claims by ride-sharing and accommodation-rental P2P platforms that they were providing services different to existing taxi and hotel businesses, many governments have recognized their economic equivalence.

For example, occupancy and tourism taxes, which previously applied only to traditional hotels, are now applied to transactions within the P2P accommodation rental sector. In ridesharing, the general sales tax in Australia and the harmonized sales tax in Canada applied previously only to traditional taxi drivers and was viewed as a disadvantage. With its extension to ridesharing, this imbalance has been redressed. However, in most countries, license fees in some parts of the taxi industry currently do not apply to P2P drivers in the ride-sharing industry.

Tax Thresholds

Governments could choose to lower tax thresholds to bring a larger portion of small business activity into the tax system. If so, they need to be sensitive to behavioral impacts and their own administrative costs. Figure 3.4 illustrates how low average annual incomes are in the P2P accommodation rental sector, already falling below current indirect tax thresholds.

The choice of tax threshold can in part be derived as a function of the size distribution of small businesses and the associated revenue-cost trade-off facing governments. An increase in the left portion of the size distribution would eventually alter this balance, leading to a lower threshold that would bring a higher share of self-employed businesses into the tax system. However, lower tax thresholds come with the risk of increasing not only the administrative costs for both governments and small businesses, but also the noncompliance (both legal and illegal) of the latter.

In a world of taxpayers with different compliance preferences, Kanbur and Keen (2014) show that when they are largely honest and compliant, the optimal tax threshold is sensitive to changes in the size distribution of businesses and must be set to ensure that businesses do not choose to avoid taxes by (legally) adjusting their incomes below the threshold. Where, instead, evasion is dominant—for example, in economies with less-developed tax administrations—thresholds should be set higher than would otherwise be optimal to discourage the (illegal) concealment of income.

Keen and Mintz (2004) focus on a special case of thresholds for the value-added tax where compliance is perfect and there are no behavioral responses. This specification implies setting lower thresholds on activities characterized by higher ratios of value-added to sales. Therefore, highly profitable or labor-intensive activities (services), which form an important part of the P2P economy, would be subject to relatively low thresholds. The technology underlying the P2P economy also presents opportunities to alleviate the trade-off between revenue gains and compliance costs by lowering the former.

Figure 3.4. Average Income from Airbnb Inc. by Country versus Indirect Tax Thresholds
(Thousands of US dollars)

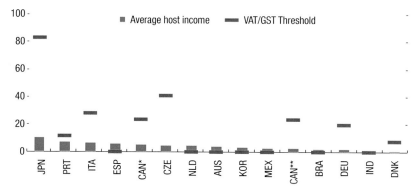

Sources: Airbnb Inc.; and International Bureau of Fiscal Documentation.
Note: (*) Vancouver; (**) Montreal. Data for each country can be either a national average or for a major city. Data labels in the figure use International Organization for Standardization (ISO) country codes.
GST = goods and services tax; VAT = value-added tax.

Cross-Border Taxation of P2P Services

Typically, many P2P transactions are based around local (nontradable) services, such as ridesharing and delivery services. However, some services (and intangibles) are now being increasingly provided across countries, for example, through remote-working platforms. In a cross-border setting, governments must be reminded of the risks of double taxation and unintended non-taxation, for example, arising from inconsistencies in the application of indirect taxes to services. Taxing final consumption in the jurisdiction in which it occurs, according to the destination principle, would not only help overcome such risks, but also benefit local and national governments. To this end, the Organisation for Economic Co-operation and Development has developed international value-added tax (VAT) and goods and services tax (GST) guidelines to minimize irregularities.

Treatment of Capital and Labor

Where capital and labor are combined to deliver a P2P service, the income earned is a mixture of the returns to both inputs. How governments choose to tax labor and capital income has implications for investment and how businesses grow.[20] However, the optimal taxation of capital income, under specific

---

[20]This touches on a foundational and familiar issue in taxation: whether a single rate schedule should apply to the aggregate of different sources of income (a "global" comprehensive income approach) or different schedules should apply to different sources of income (a "schedular"

assumptions, suggests lower rates than on labor (for example, see Atkinson and Stiglitz 1976; Judd 1985; and Chamley 1986). In practice, capital is taxed differently depending on the organizational form (for example, corporate or noncorporate), the difference in present value between the tax depreciation allowance rules and real (economic) depreciation, the source of financing (such as debt or equity), and firm size (in some countries, small firms can expense or immediately write off their capital investments rather than depreciate them over time).

Whether the capital income of P2P businesses is more (or less) punitively taxed than the capital income of competing traditional businesses is difficult to determine given differences in treatment.[21] Furthermore, different asset types face different effective tax rates because tax depreciation rules do not uniformly relate to an asset's economic depreciation. The taxation of capital might therefore be different between different types of capital-intensive P2P businesses, as well as between P2P businesses and existing businesses. These differences would be determined by how investment is financed and capital goods are expensed (such as fully under a cash-flow tax or depreciation over time).

Since P2P businesses can be unincorporated or incorporated, the relationship between capital and labor taxation—expressed through the interplay between corporate and personal income tax rates—becomes important. With more and more self-employed P2P businesses, any pre-existing tax differentials between the corporate and personal income tax schedules become a greater revenue risk should a large swath choose to incorporate. Such differentials are particularly relevant for those P2P users already paying higher marginal personal income tax rates (such as those that engage full-time in the P2P economy or use it to supplement other sources of income).[22]

A Presumptive Tax System for the P2P Economy

We noted earlier how the expansion of atomized P2P sales may give rise to an enforcement challenge for tax authorities. At the same time, even though P2P sellers operate mostly as sole proprietors earning low incomes and profits, they are faced with the same compliance burdens as other self-employed businesses. The nature of many P2P activities involving the use of personal assets for business

---

approach). A global approach has the appeal of eliminating any incentive to artificially transform one kind of income into another, since the taxpayer faces the same marginal tax rate on all types of income. It also satisfies a version of horizontal equity—that is, everyone with the same purchasing power pays the same amount of tax—when tax liability is determined by annual income (rather than lifetime income).

[21] The relative advantage or disadvantage to capital income will also depend on the nature of comparison within and across sectors. For the accommodation rental sector, is the correct comparison a hotel versus a single landlord or a group of properties that generate equivalent income to the hotel?

[22] Within the personal income tax system, some countries even deliberately maintain separate personal income tax schedules for self-employed businesses and employees. Where lower for the latter, this could be motivated by a belief that self-employed businesses are less compliant. Where lower for the former, this could be to incentivize entrepreneurial activity.

purposes adds further complexity in terms of the tracking and allocation of expenses. Indeed, difficulties in complying with tax obligations appear to have proliferated a business of tax advisors targeted at the P2P economy. However, the small amounts of taxable income involved, which may nonetheless be large in aggregate, raise the question of whether it is both efficient for taxpayers to be seeking to comply with and for governments to be enforcing complex legislation.

A *de minimis* tax and reporting threshold for the personal income tax is one option to ease and simplify the tax administration burden. As with the VAT threshold, the precise level of the threshold will depend on administrative costs versus revenue benefits from taxing P2P businesses. The United Kingdom estimates that its new tax-free allowance will impact 700,000 participants in the P2P economy (Box 3.2; Table 3.2.1) with an administrative saving of £20 million per year for individuals who either no longer need to file returns or calculate expenses. With better data from the sector, governments can better calibrate the threshold to balance their administrative costs with revenue objectives.

Introducing a presumptive regime for small businesses below a certain threshold into the general tax system is another option, which is already in place in many countries. This system helps reduce the compliance burden on taxpayers with very low turnover and the corresponding administrative burden of auditing such taxpayers. At its simplest, a low, uniform tax rate is applied to the gross income of P2P sellers. Indeed, in 2016, the Italian government proposed a requirement for platforms to withhold a fixed 10 percent tax on all P2P transactions.

Determining the appropriate flat rate(s) for all P2P businesses is an important choice for governments. They must consider that sellers earn income from both multiple P2P platforms as well as off-platform (for example, through regular employment) as well as their limited knowledge of each sector's typical profitability.

Furthermore, a single rate could be regressive, something which could be alleviated by levying a nonfinal withholding tax and allowing individuals to file a tax return at the end of the year based on their actual income and costs. However, such reconciliation undermines the desired simplification and lower administrative burden. Either introducing a simple basic income exemption or designing a multi-tier rate structure of withholding rates would also introduce some progressivity into the system (Thomas 2017). Then again, the latter would have to be applied separately by each platform, possibly creating incentives for P2P sellers to deliberately spread their activity across several platforms.[23] Furthermore, such a

---

[23]To the extent that income volatility could be higher for P2P businesses, given the irregularity of engagement, another alternative could be to apply a flat rate tax to the average income over a fixed number of years. The average method can provide tax benefits if there are fluctuations in the income from one year to another and the tax system is strongly progressive. In the United States, for example, Schedule J is the Internal Revenue Service form used to average fishing or farming income. Whereas this method is reserved the agriculture and forestry sectors in some countries it may also be an option for small P2P enterprises. However, P2P income can also be used to reduced volatility, given opportunities to earn income across multiple activities.

parallel schedular system for the P2P sector would introduce undesirable complexity and distortions into a country's tax regime.

A presumptive regime can alternatively focus on simplifying the reporting of costs. In a world in which P2P platforms automatically share information on incomes earned by sellers, one possibility would be the introduction of an optional standard business deduction from gross receipts. The United Kingdom has taken this approach through its allowance on trading and property income, targeted at the P2P economy (see Box 3.2). Thomas (2017) suggests an optional standardized deduction for the P2P sectors of 60 percent of the workers' gross receipts to be deducted in lieu of actual business expenses, eliminating the need to track and report business expenses.

Oei and Ring (2016) also suggest the use of safe harbors to define the scope for allowable deductions. Such standardized deductions would ease the compliance burden significantly and would still allow for the appropriate marginal tax rate to apply as per the country's tax schedule, once all sources of an individual's income are considered. In the United Kingdom, the construction industry scheme is designed to minimize tax evasion given the large number of mobile self-employed subcontractors. It allows standardized deductions from payments made by contractors to subcontractors, which count as advanced payments toward the subcontractor's tax and social security contributions.

The difficulty of designing an efficient and equitable method of taxing the income of P2P businesses reinvigorates the debate behind systems such as the Hall-Rabushka "flat tax" for the broader economy (not just small businesses). This scheme works by assessing a flat-rate tax on all businesses (corporate or otherwise), while allowing wages, pension contributions, materials costs, and capital investments to be deducted from the tax base. Individuals (or households) are assessed at the same flat rate on wages and pension benefits above a high basic income exemption. No other income is taxable, and no other deductions are allowed.

Of course, while many countries have enacted special regimes for certain small business sectors, such measures also raise questions about the desirability of a specialized tax regime for the P2P economy or whether such principles should apply more broadly to the small business sector. At the same time, many individuals operate on multiple platforms both within and across different sectors. Therefore, it is important to consider whether special regimes should be applied uniformly across sectors or customized given that individuals earn multiple streams of income from different P2P activities.

Exploiting Technology to Improve Tax Administration

As the onus is on the self-employed individual to report income earned, monitoring a growing number of small-scale P2P participants—with fluid movement in and out of the P2P economy—will become extremely costly for tax authorities.[24] Noncompliance for small businesses is typically very high, and IMF (2015) reports that error rates of over 40 percent are found in small businesses, even in advanced economies. As noted earlier, the use of personal assets for business purposes for P2P activities adds further difficulty in verifying expenses, which can also easily be misreported in error or manipulated.

However, the critical role of the digital platform in facilitating and intermediating P2P transactions presents an important opportunity for tax administrators to authenticate both the incomes reported by P2P sellers. Many countries are now looking to cooperate with platforms to access this information. Others have considered extending the powers of the tax authority to acquire data from platforms, or to require them to automatically report those P2P sellers who have earned income above any tax-free thresholds. For example, the United Kingdom has recently enacted legislation extending the powers of the tax authority to acquire data from digital platforms.

In the United States, all individuals or organizations who pay independent contractors at least $600 during the year must file a Form 1099-MISC to report these payments to the tax authorities. For collaborative finance platforms, any net interest earnings above $10 are reported on Form1099-OID. The contractor will also receive a copy of these forms, providing a definitive record of income earned throughout the year. P2P platforms should, in principle, be fulfilling these reporting requirements, given that they classify their sellers as independent contractors. In doing so, they would also provide the tax authorities with data on turnover which can be cross-checked with the tax filings of those same individuals. However, as Oei and Ring (2016) note, many major platforms have chosen to classify themselves in the United States as "payment facilitators"—a classification originally intended for financial intermediaries—which have obligations to report gross earnings for all US users who earn more than $20,000 and have 200 or more transactions in the calendar year. The vast majority of P2P sellers are unlikely to meet these criteria, reinforcing the importance of appropriately setting reporting thresholds.

However, the willingness of P2P platforms (and participants) to grant such access to information is a function of both institutional and sociopolitical factors. Platforms may be reluctant to provide such information, to protect the privacy of users, or may only do so in exchange for certain concessions. Where trust in government is low or rule of law is weak, information sharing with government may even deter participation in the P2P market.

---

[24]Many governments have recognized the need to issue guidance to clarify the applicable tax regime and Australia, Canada, the United Kingdom, and the United States are examples of countries that have recently issued specific guidance clarifying the tax obligations for users of the P2P economy. Several platforms have also taken responsibility for informing their taxpayers about their responsibilities and tax obligations, with most platforms providing some brief guidance on their website. Airbnb appears to go further, withholding 28 percent of income from US users who do not provide their taxpayer information.

The platform's role in intermediating electronic payments for P2P transactions also highlights the potential for its role as a tax-collection agent. This appears straightforward for indirect taxes on the gross value of the transaction. A handful of platforms have already agreed to collect and remit taxes on behalf of their users. For example, in the accommodation-rental sector, Airbnb now plays the role of tax collector and remitter for hotel and tourist taxes in four countries.

This approach is also being tested for indirect taxes.[25] In 2015, India introduced legislation that requires digital platforms to charge and remit service taxes due on the income of sellers. The possibilities for the platform to act as a collection agent can lower the cost of indirect tax administration, increasing the feasibility of a low or zero threshold. However, several technical issues remain unresolved, including how sellers can claim credits on inputs should the platform withhold indirect tax on their sales on their behalf. A flat rate indirect tax scheme is one way to address this shortcoming. Such a scheme currently operates for farmers in the United Kingdom, who can apply a reduced VAT rate, which reflects a deemed credit on inputs when goods or services are sold to VAT-registered customers.[26] Such a system could be administered by the platform, which would withhold and remit the VAT to the government.

For taxes on income, the situation becomes more complicated. To calculate the correct liability, most tax systems require self-employed individuals to aggregate all income earned and deduct costs before applying the appropriate schedule of exemptions and marginal tax rates. If an individual's entire income were earned on a single platform, platforms could withhold income taxes (as for employees) after deducting an estimate for costs—or if individuals provided a record of expenses to the platform. However, as anecdotal evidence suggests, sellers earn small amounts of income through multiple P2P activities—or are engaged in the same activity across multiple platforms—platforms do not have complete information on sellers' total income and costs and therefore cannot perform such withholding. Without the full income and cost profile for sellers, anything more than a blunt withholding instrument on gross income earned through that platform—either as a final tax or a prepayment—is currently difficult for the platform to administer.

CONCLUSION

The P2P economy continues to grow and gain prominence worldwide as a means of organizing activity and providing services, supported by essential improvements in technology. It has also been proving itself an increasingly

---

[25]India introduced a full-fledged good and services tax in July 2017. This unified national tax replaced multiple cascading indirect taxes levied by the central and state governments.

[26]For turnover of less than £150,000, the United Kingdom applies different flat VAT rates across 54 different types of business, ranging from 4 percent (such as on retailing food, confectionery, tobacco, newspapers, or children's clothing) to 14.5 percent (such as on an architect, civil and structural engineer, or surveyor).

attractive option for users to make a living. As facets of the P2P economy continue to seep into everyday functions—in many cases usurping existing businesses—governments will need to understand and develop opportunities to mobilize revenue from this sector. This chapter attempts to both consolidate and set out issues around the taxation of this range of activities, reviewing the current tax system and the features of the P2P economy that could be a deciding factor in its future tax treatment.

A definitive approach is not immediately obvious, and depends on whether the government wants to minimize differences between traditional and P2P businesses (if any) or differentiate between them through the tax system if one is preferred over the other. However, the chapter has highlighted that several of the issues associated with taxing businesses are familiar, while the presence of platforms presents some important new opportunities. In this sense, the emergence of P2P activities does not seem to be driving a radical rethink of the tax system or the principles upon which it is based. Instead, the P2P economy—should it continue to grow—is forcing tax policy and administration to reconsider old trade-offs in a new light.

With the growth in P2P sellers, the number of unincorporated small businesses is increasing at the lower end of the gross income distribution. These businesses may displace larger firms and reinforce existing well-known challenges for taxing large numbers of small businesses, especially if formalization adds to the influx. Taxes are usually not only more difficult to collect from small businesses, but can be that much more distortionary given the aptitude small businesses can display at avoiding and evading them. The presence of even more small businesses is also altering the revenue-compliance trade-off that has determined the choice of tax thresholds in the past: governments could consider lowering thresholds if distributional shifts suggest revenue gains outweigh administrative burdens. Alternatively, special tax rules for small businesses can help, but the nature of P2P activity (and the dynamics of two-sided markets) could amplify both the behavioral impact as well as their possible benefits and costs. It is unclear how to balance the need for revenue with the distortionary impact of any special tax treatment, and, in time, the P2P economy could grow to such an extent that these special rules might become redundant—or even the norm.

Mercifully, the P2P platforms presents an important opportunity for both tax policy and administration. As online intermediaries, they record data on the myriad of transactions taking place in the virtual markets they oversee. Governments can cooperate with them to access these data, which would undoubtedly alleviate information constraints and strengthen enforcement and allow better quantification of activity that had previously been misreported or undocumented. Access to such data might one day lead to the creation of a connected taxpayer database that could provide a complete profile of the activity and earnings of individuals (for example, linked with employee withholding systems and other taxpayer registers).

While there might still be some way to go before reaching such an environment, platforms can already act as custodians for the tax administration by withholding tax on behalf of sellers, something that seems relatively straightforward for indirect taxes. Such arrangements could help ease compliance and administration while raising revenue, particularly in low-capacity countries, and, again, allow tax authorities to revisit the revenue-compliance trade-off. However, attempting to levy direct taxes through such withholding arrangements is more difficult, as P2P sellers rarely use one platform exclusively and are likely to be mixing many different streams of income from different activities (on- and off-platform, self-employment, and employment). At present, a simplified system of withholding fixed amounts as a prepayment for income tax can partly resolve this difficulty, but any ex post reconciliation mechanism should not impose an unduly high administrative burden on P2P businesses, especially as these activities could be sensitive to high taxes or high compliance costs.

The tax treatment of the P2P economy will ultimately depend on each government's preferences and capacity, and will likely vary by country. Some governments may wish to minimize tax policy differences between P2P sellers and traditional businesses. Others may instead see the rise of the P2P economy as positive and choose to provide tax incentives to encourage it. What is clear is that while the P2P economy has potentially exacerbated the administrative and revenue mobilization challenges associated with small business taxation, the technology behind P2P platforms presents a valuable opportunity to eventually solve them.

Box 3.1. Peer-to-Peer Activities in Developing Economies

The level of economic development can alter how peer-to-peer (P2P) activities evolve and the impact they will have on an economy. While there may be a displacement effect in more advanced economies, the informal provision of personal services (such as by taxi drivers, plumbers, and cleaners) is typically widespread in emerging market and developing countries. In this context, intermediating P2P activities over digital platforms may allow greater access, better organization, and formalization of previously informal economic activity.

Use of these collaborative approaches is already widespread in countries such as Colombia, Kenya, Mexico, and South Africa, both by foreign and locally developed platforms. The P2P economy can increase sources of income quickly and effectively, promote entrepreneurial spirit, and encourage innovations to address constraints faced by these economies, such as ridesharing as a means to alleviate strains on or substitute for public transportation.

The P2P business model is a unique opportunity to help overcome unreliable governance, weak property rights, and binding capital constraints common in emerging market and developing countries. These factors preclude effective regulation or the development of natural monopolies in markets—notably services—where information asymmetry is a serious problem. The decentralized, crowd-based ratings technology that underpins P2P businesses helps mitigate the need for large capital investment or detailed regulation and good governance. It lowers the capital and regulatory bar for the sort of search and match that is required for an effective services industry to flourish. Given that such countries lack the institutional means to overcome such information problems, it is those sectors that lack the ability to have well-functioning regulation or large reputable companies that can benefit most from technology that overcomes information failures in services.

Yet, despite the ingenuity of P2P technology in helping smaller-scale enterprises overcome financial and informational constraints on the supply side, P2P businesses face other demand-side obstacles in many emerging market and developing countries. Biswas, Pahwa, and Sheth (2015) and the Inter-American Development Bank (2016) report on the P2P economy in India and Latin America, respectively, listing various factors that limit its uptake. These include a lack of knowledge and general distrust of these new collaborative business models by customers, and underdeveloped financial mechanisms—for example, secure payments facilities and insurance. Smartphone penetration can also be an important limiting factor.

Low and concentrated asset ownership in emerging market and developing countries means that the emergence of P2P services that rely on a large capital component could also be limited. The concentration of assets in a small part of the population could also have implications for the distribution of benefits from any sharing activities. Of course, the P2P economy has demonstrated its adaptability in overcoming such inequality in the case of ridesharing. For example, drivers in South Africa can use a platform (DriverSelect) to identify available cars that are available for rent for use as a taxi, while in other parts of Africa, some P2P businesses are helping drivers finance the purchase of vehicles. Nevertheless, P2P businesses that are labor-intensive are likely to be more successful in countries with large pool of decentralized and underutilized pools of low-skilled labor and where demand for services from tech-savvy urban middle classes is strong.

Box 3.2. Current Tax Treatment of P2P Businesses

Direct taxes

Peer-to-peer (P2P) sellers worldwide typically register as self-employed businesses and are responsible for self-reporting their income and tax liability to the tax authorities.[1] However, given the irregularity of engagement and small scale of many P2P sellers, they might not always be deemed to be conducting business or commercial activity, removing the legal obligation for P2P sellers to report their income to tax authorities. In Australia, for example, activities deemed a hobby (determined by tests on the activity's intention, frequency, and organization) do not carry any tax or reporting obligations, removing small amounts of casual income from the tax net. Moreover, the resale of secondhand personal items on online marketplace platforms will also typically not be taxable since they are usually sold at a loss. However, many countries, including the United States and Canada, are stricter and require reporting of all P2P income to the tax authorities.

Income exemptions may also apply. For example, for rental income, the US tax authorities allow homeowners to rent out their homes for up to 14 days without having to pay tax on the income. The United Kingdom provides "rent-a-room" relief of up to £7,500 for owner-occupiers or tenants who let out furnished accommodation to a lodger in their home. In April 2017, two new tax allowances for property and trading income targeted at the digital and sharing economy were also introduced. These allowances remove tax reporting and payment obligations where an individual's trading or property income for the tax year before expenses does not exceed £1,000. Individuals with incomes above that amount can also opt to deduct the allowance instead of their actual business expenses.

In calculating their tax liabilities, P2P sellers can make tax deductions from their income like any self-employed business. In most countries, deductible items include bringing-to-market costs (cleaning fees, insurance), and operating costs such as gasoline, as well as financing costs and capital depreciation. Some countries offer specific deductions depending on the sector. For example, if a car is used for both business and personal purposes in the United States, the taxpayer must apportion expenses based on actual mileage and can apply a standard mileage rate ($0.54 per mile beginning 2016) to determine the deduction. For a home used for business, taxpayers can opt to apply a deduction of $5 per square foot for up to 300 square feet.

Indirect taxes

Where such taxes operate, value-added tax (VAT) or a goods and services tax (GST) will apply to the provision of goods and services in the P2P economy. In some VAT/GST systems, certain exemptions could apply to the P2P economy, for example, long-term residential rental income (over one month) on which the tax is not charged.

From an administrative point of view, businesses need to register for VAT only after a certain threshold of gross income is reached. As discussed in the chapter, the rationale for a threshold is usually an administrative practicality, based on the distribution of firm size, costs of administering and complying with the VAT, and the empirical observation that a small number of large firms typically account for a large proportion of VAT revenue. The

---

[1]Many casual P2P participants may not consider themselves as running a regular business and subsequently overlook regulation and taxation. Of course, this does not mean they are free from regulation or taxation, simply that they may or may not understand the need to report their activity (or formalize it as a business).

Box 3.2. Current Tax Treatment of P2P Businesses   (*continued*)

small amounts of income generated by P2P participants would imply that few would be subject to VAT/GST at current thresholds.

While the question over who is liable for transaction taxes has been raised by some authorities and would appear to be closely linked to the worker classification debate, India has already taken a proactive approach. In its 2015 Finance Act, the government introduced provisions under which the platform is liable and therefore required to discharge the tax on services provided by the sellers. However, issues remain, including how sellers can claim credits against this liability.

Other taxes

Some countries apply sector-specific taxes that would extend to P2P business operating in the sector.[2] P2P platforms are moving at different speeds in establishing payment of such taxes. Taxes applicable to hotel guests now extend to users in the P2P accommodation-rental sector, and the largest platform, Airbnb, now collects and remits in certain US states.

In most countries, the operation of taxis and private hire vehicles involves the regular payment of license fees. However, in the ridesharing sector, while the service is most comparable to the taxi sector, the license fees applicable to traditional taxi drivers do not apply. In New York, where taxi drivers must buy a medallion to operate a taxi, the price has fluctuated between about $500,000 to more than $1 million over the past five years. However, some US states have introduced taxes targeted at the ridesharing sector. For example, in 2016, Massachusetts introduced a $0.20 tax on every trip ordered through ride-hailing services earmarked for spending on the traditional taxi sector. In Washington, DC, rides to and from the airport using ridesharing platforms now incur a $4 fee which will be remitted to the airports authority.

---

[2]For example, for the US tax system, see IRS publication 535.

Box 3.2. Current Tax Treatment of P2P Businesses *(continued)*

Table 3.2.1. Selected Recent International Legislative Changes Relating to P2P Businesses (2015–17)

Australia	In 2017, the government removed the goods and services tax threshold for ridesharing companies.
Brazil	In February 2017, a labor court judge in Minas Gerais ruled Uber drivers were employees.
Canada	In January 2017, the government announced plans to redefine ridesharing firms as taxi companies. Lawsuit filed in Ontario seeking US$200 million in damages on behalf of any person who has driven for Uber in Ontario since 2012, arguing that they have been misclassified as contractors.
Caribbean	In February 2017, the Caribbean Tourism Organization reached an agreement with Airbnb, under the terms of which both organizations will share data and studies with policymakers about the impact of the sharing economy in the region.
China	In March 2017, the National Development and Reform Commission disclosed that the government is formulating tax policies and regulations for the sharing economy.
Estonia	As of 2016, the government legalized ridesharing and digitally links drivers' incomes with the revenue authority.
France	Government introduced legislation to increase tax on professional renters using Airbnb. Amounts of more than EUR 23,000 (US$25,200) per year made from renting out homes on P2P economy websites to be considered professional income and subject to income tax. In March 2017, a court ruled against classification of drivers as employees. The French Finance Act for 2016 imposed new reporting obligations on P2P platform users residing, selling products, and providing services in France.
India	In 2015, platforms required to discharge the service tax liability on the services provided by the supplier.
Italy	In 2016, a bill was proposed that requires platforms to act as withholding agents and withhold a fixed 10 percent on all transactions and transfer these amounts to the state.
Kenya	In 2016, Kenya Revenue Authority ruled that Uber drivers are responsible for paying their own taxes.
United Kingdom	In April 2017, government introduced GBP 1,000 tax-free allowance for property and trading income. Finance Act 2016 expanded legislative powers of HM Revenue and Customs to obtain data from digital platforms. In 2016, tribunal deemed Uber driver to be a "worker" rather than an independent contractor.
United States	
Atlanta, Georgia	In 2017, proposal to add a 4 percent sales tax to each ride and each city would add its own taxes.
California	In 2016, following settlement of employee misclassification lawsuit, Uber drivers remain classified as independent contractors.
Hawaii	In 2017, proposal for ridesharing fares to be subject to 4.75 percent excise tax at the point of sale.
Massachusetts	In 2016, state government introduced a US$0.20 tax on every trip ordered through ride-hailing services earmarked for spending on the traditional taxi sector.
New York State	In 2017, proposal for a 4 percent tax on all app-based hails.

Source: Authors' compilation.
Note: P2P = peer-to-peer.

REFERENCES

Armstrong, Mark. 2006. "Competition in Two-Sided Markets." *RAND Journal of Economics* 37 (3): 668–91.

Atkinson, Anthony B., and Joseph E. Stiglitz. 1976. "The Design of Tax Structure: Direct versus Indirect Taxation." *Journal of Public Economics* 6 (1–2): 55–75.

Benjaafar, Saif, Guangwen Kong, Xiang Li, and Costas Courcoubetis. 2015. "Peer-to-Peer Product Sharing: Implications for Ownership, Usage and Social Welfare in the Sharing Economy." Unpublished.

Bernhardt, Anne. 2014. "Labor Standards and the Reorganization of Work: Gaps in Data and Research." IRLE Working Paper 100–14, UC Berkeley, Institute for Research on Labor and Employment, Berkeley, CA.

Biswas, Ranjan, Ankur Pahwa, and Milan Sheth. 2015. "The Rise of the Sharing Economy: The Indian Landscape." Ernst and Young LLP, London.

Bolt, Wilko, and Alexander F. Tieman. 2008. "Heavily Skewed Pricing in Two-Sided Markets." *International Journal of Industrial Organization* 26: 1250–55.

Bourreau, Marc, Bernard Caillaud, and Romain De Nijs. Forthcoming. "Digital Platforms, Advertising and Taxation." *Journal of Public Economic Theory.*

Brinkley, Ian. 2013. "Flexibility or Insecurity? Exploring the Rise in Zero Hours Contracts." The Work Foundation, Lancaster University, Lancaster, United Kingdom.

Caillaud, Bernard, and Bruno Jullien. 2003. "Chicken & Egg: Competition Among Intermediation Service Providers." *RAND Journal of Economics* 34: 309–28.

Chamley, Christophe. 1986. "Optimal Taxation of Capital Income in General Equilibrium with Infinite Lives." *Econometrica* 54 (3): 607–22.

Coase, Ronald H. 1937. "The Nature of the Firm." *Economica,* New Series 4 (16): 386–405.

Cohen, Peter, Robert Hahn, Jonathan Hall, Steven Levitt, and Robert Metcalfe. 2016. "Using Big Data to Estimate Consumer Surplus: The Case of Uber." NBER Working Paper 22627, National Bureau of Economic Research, Cambridge, MA.

Cullen, Zoë B., and Chiara Farronato. 2016. "Outsourcing Tasks Online: Matching Supply and Demand on Peer-to-Peer Internet Platforms." Unpublished.

Dabla-Norris, Era, Florian Misch, Duncan Cleary, and Munawer Khwaja. 2017. "Tax Administration and Firm Performance: New Data and Evidence for Emerging Market and Developing Economies." IMF Working Paper 17/95, International Monetary Fund, Washington, DC.

Department for Business, Energy & Industrial Strategy. 2017. "Good Work: the Taylor Review of Modern Working Practices." London.

Edelman, Benjamin G., and Damien Geradin. 2016. "Efficiencies and Regulatory Shortcuts: How Should We Regulate Companies like Airbnb and Uber?" *Stanford Technology Law Review* 19 (3): 293–328.

Ellison, Glenn, and Drew Fudenberg. 2003. "Knife-Edge or Plateau: When Do Market Models Tip?" *Quarterly Journal of Economics* 118 (4): 1249–78.

European Commission. 2017. "Establishing a European Pillar of Social Rights." Commission Staff Working Document Accompanying the Communication from the Commission to the European Parliament, The Council, The European and Social Committee, and the Committee of the Regions, Brussels.

Evans, David S. 2003. "The Antitrust Economics of Two-Sided Markets." *Yale Journal of Regulation* 20: 325–81.

Farrell, Diana, and Fiona Greig. 2016a. "Paychecks, Paydays, and the Online Platform Economy: Big Data on Income Volatility." J.P. Morgan Chase Institute, New York.

———. 2016b. "The Online Platform Economy: Has Growth Peaked?" J.P. Morgan Chase Institute, New York.

Farronato, Chiara, and Andrey Fradkin. 2016. "Market Structure with the Entry of Peer-to-Peer Platforms: The Case of Hotels and Airbnb." Unpublished.

Fraiberger, Samuel P., and Arun Sundararajan. 2015. "Peer-to-Peer Rental Markets in the Sharing Economy." Research Paper, New York University Stern School of Business, New York.

Goudin, Pierre. 2016. "The Cost of Non-Europe in the Sharing Economy: Economic, Social and Legal Challenges and Opportunities." Study from the European Added Value Unit, European Parliamentary Research Service, Brussels.

Hall, Jonathan V., and Alan B. Krueger. 2015. "An Analysis of the Labor Market for Uber's Driver-Partners in the United States." NBER Working Paper 22843, National Bureau of Economic Research, Cambridge, MA.

Hathaway, Ian, and Mark Muro. 2013. "Tracking the Gig Economy: New Numbers." Brookings Institution, Washington, DC.

Horton, John J., and Richard J. Zeckhauser. 2016. "Owning, Using and Renting: Some Simple Economics of the 'Sharing Economy.'" NBER Working Paper 22029, National Bureau of Economic Research, Cambridge, MA.

Inter-American Development Bank. 2016. "The Sharing Economy in Latin America." School of Business Enterprise Institute, Madrid.

International Monetary Fund (IMF). 2015. "Current Challenges in Revenue Mobilization: Improving Tax Compliance." IMF Staff Report, Washington, DC.

Judd, Kenneth L. 1985. "Redistributive Taxation in a Simple Perfect Foresight Model." *Journal of Public Economics* 28 (1): 59–83.

Kanbur, Ravi, and Michael Keen. 2014. "Thresholds, Informality and Partitions of Compliance." *International Tax and Public Finance* 21 (4): 536–59.

Keen, Michael, and Jack Mintz. 2004. "The Optimal Threshold for a Value-Added Tax." *Journal of Public Economics* 88 (3–4): 559–76

Kind, Hans J., Marko Koethenbuerger, and Guttorm Schjelderup. 2008. "Efficiency Enhancing Taxation in Two-Sided Markets." *Journal of Public Economics* 92 (5–6): 1,531–39.

———. 2010. "Tax Responses in Platform Industries." *Oxford Economic Papers* 62 (4): 764–83.

Manyika, James, Susan Lund, Jacques Bughin, Kelsey Robinson, Jan Mischke, and Deepa Mahajan. 2016. "Independent Work: Choice, Necessity, and the Gig Economy." McKinsey Global Institute, New York.

Martin, Elliot, Susan A. Shaheen, and Jeffrey Lidicker. 2010. "Impact of Carsharing on Household Vehicle Holdings: Results from North American Shared-Use Vehicle Survey." Transportation Research Record 2143, Transportation Research Board of the National Academies, Washington, DC.

Neeser, David. 2015. "Does Airbnb Hurt Hotel Business: Evidence from the Nordic Countries." Unpublished.

Oei, Shu-Yei, and Diane M. Ring. 2016. "Can Sharing Be Taxed?" *Washington University Law Review* 93 (4).

Office of National Statistics. 2016. "The Feasibility of Measuring the Sharing Economy." Article from the Office of National Statistics, London.

Robertson, Dennis. H. 1923. *The Control of Industry*. Hitchin, United Kingdom: Nisbet & Co.

Rochet, Jean-Claude, and Jean Tirole. 2003. "Platform Competition in Two-Sided Markets." *Journal of the European Economic Association* 1 (4): 990–1024.

Rosenblatt, Alex, and Luke Stark. 2016. "Algorithmic Labor and Information Asymmetries: A Case Study of Uber's Drivers." *International Journal of Communication* 10 (2016): 3758–84.

Rysman, Marc. 2009. "The Economics of Two-Sided Markets." *Journal of Economic Perspectives* 23 (3): 125–43.

Schor, Juliet B., and Connor J. Fitzmaurice. 2015. "Collaborating and Connecting: The Emergence of the Sharing Economy." In *Handbook on Research on Sustainable Consumption*, edited by Lucia Reisch and John Thogersen, Cheltenham, United Kingdom: Edward Elgar.

Smith, Aaron. 2016. "Shared, Collaborative and On Demand: The New Digital Economy." Pew Research Center, Washington, DC.

Thomas, Kathleen D. 2017. "Taxing the Gig Economy." UNC Legal Studies Research Paper 2894394, University of North Carolina, School of Law, Chapel Hill, NC.

Vaughan, Robert, and Raphael Daverio. 2016. "Assessing the Size and Presence of the Collaborative Economy in Europe." PricewaterhouseCoopers, London.

Wallsten, Scott. 2015. "The Competitive Effects of the Sharing Economy: How Is Uber Changing Taxis?" Technology Policy Institute, Washington, DC.

Williamson, Oliver E. 1981. "The Economics of Organization: The Transaction Cost Approach." *American Journal of Sociology* 87 (3): 548–77.

Zervas, Georgios, Davide Proserpio, and John W. Byers. 2017. "The Rise of the Sharing Economy: Estimating the Impact of Airbnb on the Hotel Industry." *Journal of Marketing Research* 54 (5): 687–705.

CHAPTER 4

Implications of Digitalization for International Corporate Tax Reform

MICHAEL P. DEVEREUX AND JOHN VELLA

This chapter is concerned with the challenges, but also the opportunities, created by digitalization for the taxation of multinational profit. To cite the European Commission Expert Group on Taxation of the Digital Economy (European Commission 2014):

> The economy is becoming digital. Digitalization is the process of spreading of a general purpose technology. The last similar phenomenon was electrification. Digitalization of products and services shortens distances between people and things. It increases mobility. It makes network effects decisive. It allows the use of specific data to such an extent that it permits the satisfaction of individual customer needs—be it consumers or businesses. It opens up ample opportunities for innovation, investment, and the creation of new businesses and jobs. Going forward it will be one of the main drivers of sustainable growth.

Starting from the same approach as the European Commission Expert Group and the Organisation for Economic Co-operation and Development (OECD) (OECD 2015), we do not believe that it is sensible to attempt to "ring-fence" the digital economy as if it were distinct and separate from the rest of the economy such as, for example, natural resources. All industries are affected by digitalization, in particular for our purposes, in the way it opens up borders. Compared to 20 years ago, individuals can now easily purchase goods and services directly from businesses in other countries, and they can easily purchase shares in businesses in other countries. Even small and medium-sized companies can now operate internationally. So, although digitalization is most pronounced in the *digital* sector, it raises problems for taxation in *all* sectors of the economy.

Clearly, this greater internationalization raises fundamental questions about how national governments can and should tax corporate profit and the extent to which they need to coordinate with each other in doing so. These questions arise

The authors thank Michael Keen for helpful comments on an earlier draft.

against a backdrop of increasing public concern about the taxation of the profits of multinational enterprises, spurred by a general belief that many arrange their affairs to pay minimal taxes with relative ease.

Digital businesses are at the forefront of this concern, as they appear to be particularly adept at shifting profit to tax havens. But these problems are not restricted to such companies. A range of tax-planning techniques to shift profits to tax havens or low-tax jurisdictions are available to all companies.

In response to this widespread concern, the OECD and Group of Twenty launched a reform project in 2013—the Base Erosion and Profit Shifting (BEPS) project. Although hailed at that time as the most ambitious international tax system reform of the past 100 years, it has not ushered in radical change. The BEPS project left the fundamental structure of the international tax system unchanged but proposed a number of actions with the aim of eliminating or narrowing some of the main tax-planning routes available at the time.

Action 1 of the BEPS project dealt with the digital economy (OECD 2015).[1] Its final report identified and discussed the main challenges of the digital economy and discussed targeted measures for dealing with them. However, it did not propose any of these targeted measures itself. Instead, it took into account the specific issues raised by the digital economy when developing its general proposals.. These general proposals were therefore intended to substantially address the issues raised by the digital economy. An update of this report is expected in 2020.

In the meantime, several jurisdictions have unilaterally adopted some targeted measures. India introduced an "equalization levy," and Australia and the United Kingdom both introduced a "diverted profits tax." These measures do not exclusively target digital companies, but those companies were certainly at the forefront of the thinking behind them. Indeed, the United Kingdom's diverted profits tax is widely known as the Google Tax.

For the reasons discussed in this chapter, we do not believe that the international tax system is fit for purpose, even as reformed following the BEPS project. Consequently, we believe that the proliferation of uncoordinated measures implemented within the existing framework is unlikely to provide a satisfactory long-term solution to the challenges digitalization creates for tax systems.

This chapter takes for granted that governments will wish to continue to implement taxes on business profit, and the discussion here focuses on the form of such taxes. Taking a broad view, the chapter compares the existing pattern of such taxation with radical alternatives. It focuses on the radical alternatives, rather than proposals to bring change within the existing framework of the international tax system—on the belief that the framework itself is flawed and cannot provide a long-term solution to the problems at hand. The chapter also does not cover other taxes relevant to businesses such as value-added taxes (VATs), although, as shall be seen, key issues arising under VAT also emerge under some of the reform proposals considered.

---

[1]For a critical evaluation see Olbert and Spengel (2017).

The next section sets out a simple model of a modern multinational company and then briefly describes how the existing system seeks to tax its profit. The following section discusses two radical alternative approaches to coping with the impact of digitalization on the allocation of the tax base among countries. The chapter then considers other models that are more specific to digital businesses.

DIGITALIZATION AND THE EXISTING INTERNATIONAL CORPORATE TAX REGIME

Consider the following example:

- A multinational enterprise has its headquarters and parent company in country P.

- It has shareholders in country S.

- It has a manufacturing subsidiary in country M.

- It owns intangible assets in a subsidiary situated in a low tax jurisdiction, L.

- It sells products to consumers in country C, where it also has a marketing team.

Note that this example is clearly much simplified relative to actual practice, but illustrates the main points of principle.

How does the existing system tax such a company? Essentially, it sets out to avoid "double taxation" by allocating taxing rights between "residence" and "source" countries. Very broadly, the residence country is where a person, natural or legal, who has the right to receive the profits of the activity resides, while the source country is where the economic activity takes place. Broadly again, AND SUBJECT TO EXCEPTIONS, in a 1920s compromise in the League of Nations (Graetz 2001), source countries were allocated primary taxing rights to the active income of the business, and residence countries the primary taxing rights to passive income, such as dividends, royalties, and interest.[2] Crucially, these rules apply, with some modification, to transactions within the multinational enterprise, that is, when an affiliate of a multinational enterprise transacts with another affiliate located in a different jurisdiction. This is of great consequence because multinational enterprises can set up subsidiaries and other affiliates anywhere in the world with relatively minimal effort, and they can dictate the number and kind of transactions among such affiliates.

This compromise is fraught with difficulty; its implementation requires defining and policing the border between residence and source countries and between different types of income. Yet the compromise remains integral to the fundamental structure of the international tax system, and many of the problems afflicting the system ultimately stem from this very structure.

This can be illustrated in the context of our example, in which the company may pay tax on its profit in some or all of countries P, M, L, and C—and

---

[2] For example, see Warren (1994) and Avi-Yonah (1996).

shareholders may pay additional tax in S. In general, a subsidiary is a legal entity in the country in which it is established and therefore liable to tax on its profit in that country. To begin with, therefore, the manufacturing subsidiary would pay tax on the profits that it generates in M. However, suppose that the manufacturing subsidiary paid a royalty to the subsidiary in L owning the intangible asset—this could be for intellectual property (IP) used in production, for example. This would shift profit from M to L, since the royalty would be deductible in M and taxable in L. A system that allows multinational enterprises to shift profits from high- to low-tax jurisdictions by placing IP in the latter is clearly defective.

The extent to which profit is allocated to C depends on the rules for permanent establishments (PEs). As there is no subsidiary in C, the subsidiary in M sells products directly to consumers in C. The question then becomes whether the subsidiary in M is operating in C through a PE, which in turn depends broadly on the physical presence of the company in that country. In our example, if the marketing team constitutes a PE, then part of the profits of the manufacturing subsidiary in M would be allocated to C for tax purposes. Complex rules are in place for defining and attributing profits to a PE.

Finally, if a dividend is paid to the parent company in P, then the parent may also have to pay tax on the receipt of that dividend, usually after receiving a credit for taxes paid elsewhere.[3]

The actual allocation of profit in practice depends on many factors. For example, the extent to which profit can be shifted to L depends on the size of the royalty payment made by the manufacturing company. The multinational enterprise can increase the profit shifted from M to L by inflating this payment. It also depends on how the company was originally able to arrange ownership of the intangible asset in L. If, for example, the IP was developed by another subsidiary located in a high-tax jurisdiction and then transferred to the subsidiary in L, the allocation of profit would also depend on the price paid on the transfer. Complex "transfer pricing" rules are in place to address abuse through the manipulation of such intra-group prices. These rules essentially require intra-group prices to be aligned with the prices that would have been charged by unrelated parties. However, they are problematic for a variety of reasons, and ultimately do not provide a satisfactory solution to the problem at hand.

The Effects of Digitalization

Has digitalization affected this position?

The example presented could exist in the absence of digitalization; it is not intended to be a model of a company in the digital sector. Broadly, digitalization does not affect the nature of the problem. However, digitalization does exacerbate the problem, primarily because it facilitates the internationalization of all aspects

---

[3]Countries that tax such income are commonly designated as having a worldwide tax system; countries that do not are designated as having a territorial system.

of a company's business. In other words, because of digitalization it is easier for a company's shareholders, activities, and customers to be located all over the world.

First, and perhaps most obviously, the setup of multinational firms in many different countries benefits enormously from greater digitalization. In a world of modern communications, it is relatively easy for businesses to be run from many different locations, in increasingly complex supply chains—to the extent that identifying "the" location of a particular activity becomes increasingly difficult. For example, it is increasingly possible for the research and development (R&D), production, and marketing of a product to be undertaken in different countries. Indeed, the production of different components of a product and their assembly may all be undertaken in different countries. Digitalization is a main factor, albeit not the only one, that facilitates this internationalization.

The problem becomes more acute in a purely digital world. Consider the example of a mobile phone application that is collaboratively developed and tested by employees based in a number of countries. As business activities spread across the globe, it becomes even harder for the existing international tax system to allocate their taxable profit coherently and sensibly to the satisfaction of all countries involved.

Second, digitalization allows easier shifting of profits to low-tax jurisdictions. Digitalization has made it easier to set up a subsidiary in L and to make payments to that company, be they royalty, interest, or other payments, which produce valuable deductions in high-tax jurisdictions. In extreme cases, the company in L may simply be a money-collecting box, without any real employees. The BEPS project seeks to address the worse excesses of such strategies, as discussed further below.

A third consequence of digitization is that it is easier for a multinational enterprise to sell its products to consumers in a particular jurisdiction with minimal or no physical presence there. This is evident in cross-border sales of digital products, but it can also arise in more traditional businesses, as seen in our example above. With modern communications, advertising of all forms, including social media and contact with consumers, may be managed by staff located outside the consumers' country, C. Where this happens, C is less likely to be able to tax any part of the profits resulting from the sale because the physical presence necessary to satisfy the PE threshold is missing.

The OECD Commentaries set out the rationale for the traditional PE threshold. They state that the threshold "has a long history and reflects the international consensus that, as a general rule, until an enterprise of one State has a permanent establishment in another State, it should not properly be regarded as participating in the economic life of that other State to such an extent that the other State should have taxing rights on its profits" (OECD 2012). The PE concept thus "effectively acts as a threshold which, by measuring the level of economic presence of a foreign enterprise in a given State through objective criteria, determines the circumstances in which the foreign enterprise can be considered sufficiently integrated into the economy of a state to justify taxation in that state" (OECD 2015). In the context of our example, moving the marketing team to M, for example, would take away the taxing rights previously assigned to C. Arguably, digitalization would then allow companies to generate value more easily in jurisdictions where they make sales (and which are then arguably "source" countries) but which would not have taxing rights because companies' operations there fall short of the PE threshold.

The OECD BEPS Action 1 Final Report discusses this possibility (OECD 2015). It considers expanding the notion of PE by using revenue-based factors, digital factors, and user-based functions. It also considers how to allocate profit to such a PE. The existing profit allocation rules would not work well in this setting; therefore, the OECD considers alternatives, including methods based on fractional apportionment and modified deemed profits methods. However, the discussion in that report illustrates how difficult it is to produce satisfactory rules of this type.

Finally, digitalization has also contributed to the increasing distinction between the location of the parent company and that of its shareholders. There has traditionally been a "home bias" in the investment portfolio decisions of individuals and mutual funds. However, data suggest that this bias has shrunk considerably over time. In addition, the share of personal savings held in tax-exempt accounts has increased. As a result, for example, Rosenthal and Austin (2016) estimate that the share of US corporate stock held in personal taxable accounts fell from 84 percent in 1965 to 24 percent in 2015. For the United Kingdom's more open economy, the share of listed company stock held directly by domestic individuals fell from 54 percent in 1963 to 12 percent in 2014 (ONS 2014). Rosenthal and Austin report that foreigners directly owned about 26 percent of US corporate stock in 2015; the equivalent percentage for the United Kingdom for 2014 is 54 percent, up from 7 percent in 1963 (ONS 2014). Where there is international portfolio investment, the link between the location of shareholders and parent companies breaks down; this link is becoming weaker over time.

This distinction raises the more fundamental question of whether a tax on corporate profit is a reasonable proxy for the taxation of the income due to shareholders. In a world of increasing international portfolio investment, the notion that it is a reasonable proxy is increasingly hard to defend.

The OECD BEPS Project

The OECD BEPS project begun in 2013 produced an extensive set of reports recommending numerous reforms in 2015. The broad thrust of the reforms purport not to be changing the current allocation of taxing rights, but they do depart from it to some extent (Devereux and Vella 2014). This is achieved by adding a qualification to the current allocation rules where abuse is perceived. Specifically, although there is no clear unifying theme, a number of the actions focus on "economic activity," "relevant substance," "substantial activity," or "value creation."[4] The general analysis repeatedly speaks of the need for "a realignment of taxation

---

[4]The four terms appear to be used interchangeably.

and relevant substance . . . to restore the intended effects and benefits of international standards" (OECD 2013). The OECD claim that "no or low taxation is not per se a cause of concern, but it becomes so when it is associated with practices that artificially segregate taxable income from the activities that generate it."[5]

At a general level, then, the OECD BEPS proposals aim to "provide countries with domestic and international instruments that will better align rights to tax with economic activity" (OECD 2013, 11). This principle is reflected in the specific actions. As we have written at length elsewhere (Devereux and Vella 2014), many problems are associated with this new principle. Two central problems are highlighted here.

First, this new principle is simply different from the existing principles inherited from the 1920s. As the basic structure is being kept in place and the new principle is being overlaid on top it, the post-BEPS international tax system is likely to be more incoherent, with taxing rights aligned with economic substance in some cases but not in others. There appears to be no principle for distinguishing between the two sets of cases.

Second, from a conceptual perspective, a system that seeks to align taxing rights over income with the "economic activity" that created it is questionable because it is not at all clear where such economic activity actually takes place. Numerous factors contribute to the creation of income, including finance, research and development, head-office functions, manufacturing, marketing, and sales. All these factors are necessary components of the generation of profit in a multinational enterprise. But they might be spread over several countries, making it impossible—even conceptually—to pinpoint the contribution of each specific location to the overall profit earned.

ALTERNATIVE APPROACHES

The existing system—and in all likelihood the post-BEPS system—has numerous faults. Many commentators are concerned with the effect of avoidance and profit shifting. The BEPS project, which addressed this as its key issue, will likely have some success in limiting the worst excesses of the profit-shifting industry. However, the system's fundamental flaws will remain. Moreover, a lack of any clear principle for where profit should be taxed limits the creation of a good basis for a stable tax system. It is unlikely that the problems of profit shifting have been overcome permanently, and much greater complexity has been introduced.

---

[5]"BEPS relates chiefly to instances where the interaction of different tax rules leads to double non-taxation or less than single taxation. It also relates to arrangements that achieve no or low taxation by shifting profits away from the jurisdictions where the activities creating those profits take place. No or low taxation is not *per se* a cause of concern, *but it becomes so when it is associated with practices that artificially segregate taxable income from the activities that generate it*" (OECD 2013, 10, emphasis added).

Further, as has been well documented, the system also affects the location of real economic activity.[6] Partly as a result, this fragile tax system is further destabilized by competition among states. States compete for investment and company headquarters through their tax rates and bases. For the sake of competition, they are willing to give up parts of their tax bases or knowingly allow them to be eroded (such as by offering generous interest deductibility rules). They are also willing to facilitate the erosion of the base of other jurisdictions. Tax competition among states thus further destabilizes the already fragile international tax system and will continue to do so post-BEPS.

Paradoxically, the BEPS project could enhance tax competitive forces. If a tax system becomes more robust to profit shifting, companies that wish to lower their global tax bill may have to do so by relocating their real activities to low-tax jurisdictions. It seems likely that the outcome of the project will be at least some reduction in the ability of multinational enterprises to use traditional methods to shift their profits to law tax jurisdictions. But if companies have to move their real activities to obtain a favorable tax result, one can then expect states to compete even more intensely through the tax system, since attracting real economic activity (or deterring local companies from moving their real activities abroad) is associated with broader economic benefits than merely attracting (or deterring the outflow of) profit.

A simple example illustrates this point. Action 5 of the BEPS Action Plan addresses harmful tax practices, with a focus on patent box regimes. These regimes offer preferential rates on returns generated by IP. Action 5 seeks to counter situations where IP is produced through R&D activity undertaken in state A, but subsequently transferred to state B, which offers the patent box regime. Very broadly, and subject to qualification, it does so by limiting the income that can benefit from the patent box regime to that generated by IP resulting from R&D undertaken in the country offering the regime. In BEPS terms, this should contribute to the alignment of taxing rights with economic activity (or at least the R&D activity). But this change can lead to greater real economic distortions. Post-BEPS, multinational enterprises will have to move their R&D to the jurisdiction offering the patent box if they are to benefit from it. Given that attracting R&D activity is more beneficial to an economy than merely attracting IP, it follows that states should compete even more intensely over the rates levied on the returns to IP.

A related point on the impact of the BEPS proposals on tax competition follows from the observation that states currently compete through the tax rate and base. The curtailment of profit-shifting opportunities essentially makes it harder for states to compete through the tax base. For example, BEPS Action 4 recommends the introduction of rules limiting the deductibility of interest. This blunts states' ability to offer generous interest deductibility rules, which have the effect

[6]See the literature survey by Voget (2015).

of eroding tax bases in those states. As competition over some aspects of the tax base is curtailed, the pressure to compete over tax rates increases.

From an economic perspective, there is a powerful argument to tax corporate profit in the location of immobile (or relatively immobile) activities. As, by definition, companies cannot easily move the location of these activities, such taxes should have a reduced or even minimal impact on the location of corporate activity. They should also be harder to avoid. In other words, such taxes have attractive economic efficiency properties. It also follows that because companies cannot easily move the location of immobile activities in response to these taxes, states will not have an incentive to compete through their tax system to attract these activities.

The options available for taxing multinational enterprises include four broad locations: the residence of the ultimate shareholders, the residence of the ultimate parent company, the location of subsidiaries and permanent establishments of the multinational enterprise, and the residence of its customers. Each of the activities taking place in these locations might be thought to be necessary, but not sufficient, for the generation of profit (and the "creation of value"): the initial investment by shareholders, management by the parent company, all the activities of the affiliates of the company, and eventually sales to third parties.

The current international tax system for taxing profit is, by and large, based on the third (and partly the second) of the broad locations listed above. As companies can choose where to locate either, the current system distorts these location choices and is thus inefficient.[7]

However, most individuals are relatively immobile. The residences of the ultimate shareholders of a multinational enterprise and of its customers thus offer promising options for corporate tax reform. If the tax liability of an enterprise depends on where its parent company, its intellectual property, its sales teams, or its production are located, it has the ability and the incentive to shift these factors to favorable locations to lower its overall tax liability. But a multinational enterprise cannot easily move the residence of its shareholders (subject to the caveat noted below) or customers and therefore it should choose the location of its activities without the distorting influence of tax considerations.

Each of these two options is discussed in turn.

Location of Shareholders

One radical reform option involves taxing corporate profit as it accrues, but in the hands of the ultimate shareholders. A major advantage of such an approach would be that the location of the tax on profit is identified as the location of the owner of the business. While individuals are not immobile, they are certainly much less mobile than the key elements of a multinational business. Locating the taxation of business profit of a multinational, or a company resident in only one

---

[7]The headline-grabbing company "inversions" out of the United States provide a vivid example of distortions to the location of parent companies.

country in the place of residence of the owner therefore would have a considerable advantage for both profit shifting and the location of real economic activity. It would also align with one of the commonly voiced rationales for a corporation tax—that of acting as a proxy for the taxation of its shareholders.[8]

In the discussion that follows, it should be borne in mind that multinational enterprises are unlikely to be able to shift shareholders to low-tax jurisdictions to lower their overall tax liability if their shares are widely held. However, if the shares are held by a small number of shareholders, there is perhaps a greater likelihood of such a shift. In such cases, corporation taxes levied in the shareholders' residence provide a further incentive—beyond incentives created by personal taxes—for these shareholders to move their residence to low-tax jurisdictions.

Allocating the profits of a company to its shareholders for the purposes of including those profits in the taxable income of the shareholder is generally known as pass-through treatment. Business profit is allocated to shareholders who for tax purposes include their share of profit in their personal income. This is broadly how S corporations are taxed in the United States, and is also common for taxing partnerships.

In principle, there could be several ways in which profit is passed through to the owners of the business. One approach—which is used for S corporations in the United States, for example—would be to allocate all profit to shareholders. Dividend payments from the company to the shareholder, and capital gains on the sale of shares, would then not need also to be taxed.[9] In that case, in principle, in any tax year for the individual, the individual would need to declare in her tax return her share of any profit accrued within companies that she has owned within that year.[10] Note that "her share" would depend on the proportion of each company that she owned during the year. For example, suppose that she began the year owning 10 percent of company X, but after four months she purchased a further 50 percent, and then after eight months she sold 20 percent, meaning that by the end of the year she owned 40 percent. For a precise allocation of profit to this shareholder, the profit accruing in each of these periods would need to be calculated, so that the correct proportion could be allocated to the shareholder for each part of the year.[11] In practice, and as an approximation to this, the sharehold-

---

[8]Note that this rationale does not provide a comprehensive justification for a corporation tax. Consider, for example, a company resident in State A owned by shareholders resident in State B. In such a case, the tax imposed by State A on the company cannot be easily justified as a proxy for State B's taxes on the shareholders.

[9]This tax system differs from an imputation system where profits are taxed at the corporate level but a credit for this tax is given to shareholders when computing the tax to be paid on dividends received.

[10]There is a problem of matching the year-end of the company and the tax year of the shareholder. It is more straightforward to rely on the financial year of the company, and to allocate a share of retained earnings at this point in time to be included in some subsequent tax return of the shareholder.

[11]If the shareholding changed more frequently, then in principle the profit would need to be calculated on a daily basis—or hourly, or minute-by-minute, or even second-by-second.

er could be allocated a share of the total annual profit of the year based on her average shareholding (in this case 36.7 percent) during the year.[12]

A second option would be to tax only the dividends and capital gains received by the shareholder, which could in principle mean that the corporate-level tax could be abolished entirely. Different versions of such an approach have been proposed recently. In a US context, Toder and Viard (2014) propose that non-listed firms be taxed on a pass-through basis as described above. Shareholders of listed firms would be taxed on the dividends and also on the accrued capital again on the value of their shares, on a mark-to-market basis. Grubert and Altshuler (2016) make a similar proposal, also in a US context, with dividends and capital gains taxed as personal income. The main difference is in the determination of the capital gains. Grubert and Altshuler propose to tax capital gains on realization, but to introduce an interest charge to offset the gain from deferral of taxing accrued gains. In this case, there is no need to observe the current market price, and so the system could be applied to all businesses. A problem with both proposals is that—in the US context, at least—they would raise less tax revenue than currently raised under the existing system. Grubert and Altshuler therefore propose to keep the corporation tax, but at a much lower rate, and a later paper of Toder and Viard (2016) proposes the same.

One complication ignored in this discussion so far is how to treat ownership of shares through financial intermediaries such as mutual funds. The principle here is that the tax should be allocated to the ultimate shareholders. But that calls into question the taxation of intermediaries. For example, suppose that pension funds do not pay tax on the accumulation of their returns, as is common. Then should we view the pension fund as being the shareholder, or should we look through the pension fund to identify the beneficiaries, who may not receive their pensions for many decades to come? If there is a deliberate policy of providing a tax advantage to pensions, then looking through the pension fund to tax the beneficiary would undo this advantage. This would suggest treating the pension fund as the shareholder—certainly a simpler approach. It would of course imply that where the pension fund is not taxed on its earnings, then there would be no tax on the profit.

A key question for our analysis, however, is how either of these two broad ways of passing the tax on business profit to the owners of the business deals with the problems afflicting the international tax system, particularly the problems of taxing multinational profit, exacerbated as this is by digitalization. Each is considered in turn.

The first option is to calculate business profit and allocate it to shareholders. This simply does not address the problems of the taxation of multinational

---

[12]For S corporations, where stock is sold midyear, the default rule is that the selling shareholder is allocated a pro-rata share of the annual profit. So, for example, if a shareholder sells a 50 percent share of the business six months into the year, she would be allocated 25 percent of the company's annual profit. But shareholders can also agree to elect that they close the books at date of sale, with a profit allocation made up to that date.

enterprises, since that approach is silent on how to identify and locate profit. The options for identifying that profit are therefore those available more generally—it could be based on the residence of the parent company, the location of the multinational enterprise's affiliates or its customers. In the United States, for example, foreign income of S corporations is taxed in broadly the same way as foreign income of C corporations, that are liable to corporation tax: it is included in the tax base only when it is repatriated.

It might be natural to think of applying this option to the worldwide profit of the business, based on the residence of the parent company, since that is the company in which the ultimate owner directly owns shares. Where the shareholder is resident in the same country as the parent company, this would be an effective way of taxing the worldwide income of the shareholder. But this does not easily deal with international portfolio investment, such as the case when a shareholder in country B owns shares in a company in country A. In principle, the profits accrued in A should be allocated to the shareholder in B, and taxed by the government of B.[13]

There would be one very significant problem with a cross-border implementation of this option: enforcement. The tax authority of the country of residence of the shareholder would require information from all companies (or other businesses) in which a domestic resident has an interest. That might be acquired from the resident shareholder, but then responsibility for information collection is passed to the shareholder, which raises questions of how the information could be audited. Otherwise the tax authority could collect information from the company directly, or from the tax authority in the residence country of the company.

This is potentially where digitalization may offer an advantage. In a pre-digitalization age, it is inconceivable that a tax authority in one country would have the necessary information available to support pass-through treatment to a shareholder in another country. However, digitalization has made this flow of information possible, at least in principle.[14] Of course, creating systems and processes to allow this would be a huge enterprise. Also, and perhaps even more problematically, there must be the necessary political will, commitment, and investment to allow for such information flows. Even here, however, recent events may justify relative optimism. Both the Foreign Account Tax Compliance Act imposed by the United States and the Exchange of Information project led by the Group of Twenty and the OECD have resulted in information exchanges unthinkable just a few years ago. On the other hand, issues would certainly remain even if such systems were put in place. For example, concerns about confidentiality might lead many low-income countries to be refused such information. Nevertheless, it is conceivable that while digitalization helps to create the problem of pass-through

---

[13]This does not happen with US shareholders; they face pass-through treatment only for S corporations resident in the United States, not on corporations resident outside the United States.

[14]This possibility is also discussed in Chapter 2.

treatment in the presence of international portfolio investment, it may also eventually offer a technical solution.

The second option described above bypasses the first of these problems. If we take the approach in its pure form, of abolishing the business-level tax of profit, and relying solely on taxes on dividends and capital gains of the owners, then we no longer have the problem of identifying the relevant profit of a multinational in any particular jurisdiction. In effect, we would be taxing the worldwide profit of any business directly owned, or part-owned, by the individual. That is because, ultimately, it is a share of worldwide profit that is collected by the owner through dividends and capital gains. However, even with this option, the problem remains of dealing with international portfolio investment, when a shareholder in country B directly owns shares in a company in country A.

It is perhaps no coincidence that proposals to rely on taxes on dividends and capital gains have been made in the context of the United States, which has a sophisticated tax system and tax authority. While it is conceivable that the United States might be able to identify and tax all dividends and realized capital gains from the worldwide holdings of US citizens, that seems unlikely for many other countries. In particular, low-income countries tend to rely much more on taxes on business for the administrative reasons that businesses are more likely to have financial records and to be registered with the tax authority. Moving away from taxing the business to taxing the owners of the business would be problematic where tax administrations lack resources.

Finally, note that moving to this system would lead to a fundamental reallocation of tax base across countries. While more work is needed to determine the winners and losers, given that few shareholders in multinational enterprises reside in low-income countries these countries are likely to fall in the latter category.

Location of Consumers

An alternative radical reform would be to identify the location of the opposite end of the spectrum of a multinationals' activities: where it makes sales to third parties. Borrowing from the literature on VAT, we call this the place of "destination."[15]

A key advantage of using the country of destination is similar to that of using the country of residence of the shareholders: consumers are relatively immobile.[16] At least in most cases, we would not expect a consumer to change her location to reduce the tax charge of the multinational from which she buys a product (although this could be possible if the consumer also gains). Thus, under such a system, and unlike a typical tax based on the location of a multinational enter-

---

[15]The US House Ways and Means Committee (2016) recently proposed a tax reform that would move the United States to a destination-based tax along the lines of a destination-based cash flow tax; see Auerbach and others (2017).

[16]Problems may arise when a consumer purchases a good or service in a country in which she is not resident. The OECD has guidelines on VAT "place-of-supply" rules, which address this.

prise's affiliates or the location of the parent company, it is hard for the multinational to affect the location of its tax charge.

In principle, this has significant advantages for economic efficiency and robustness to avoidance and competitive pressures. As noted above, the existing system creates significant distortions to the location of economic activity, and the ownership of assets within a multinational, because these factors determine the location of the tax base. But where a multinational sells its product to a third party depends on the location of that third party. In principle, then, a tax based on the destination of sales could avoid such location distortions. A similar argument applies to profit shifting: if income is taxed in the place of destination, then it is very hard for a multinational to manipulate the source and hence the place of taxation of that income. As a result of these two factors, the likelihood of competition among countries should also be avoided. If country A lowers its tax rate, it should not attract either activity or tax revenue from country B, since the taxable income depends only on sales in A.

While these are powerful reasons for exploring a tax based on the place of destination, it could be argued that having a tax based solely on the destination of sales is rather arbitrary. Under the existing system, as refined by the OECD BEPS project, it has been argued that the return from an activity should be taxed in the place of the activity; thus, the return from undertaking R&D should be taxed in the place where the R&D is undertaken. A system based solely on the destination of sales would not achieve this. And so, arguably, there may be a problem in the fairness of the allocation of the tax base among countries.

Several points can be made in defense of the destination location, however. First, it is not obvious that the return from R&D, say, should accrue to the place in which it was undertaken. Undertaking the R&D may be necessary, but is not sufficient for generating a return. Ultimately, the R&D must be used to produce a good or service that a third party wants to purchase. That requires several other necessary parts of the chain, including production, management, finance, marketing and sales—as well as the ownership of the business. Without all these components, the multinational will not make a profit. It is true that the existing system attempts to identify that part of the profit attributable to the different elements of this chain but certain parts of the chain may be ignored altogether by the existing system; for example, the country of sale if there is no PE. ALSO, it is not at all clear conceptually how much value should be attributed to each part of the chain if each is necessary but not sufficient. The allocation to the different parts inevitably has a somewhat arbitrary nature. Finally, this somewhat arbitrary allocation is further undermined under the existing system, as it is applied inconsistently.

Second, the place of destination can in principle be an important source of profit, even under current rules. The jurisdiction of "the market" is where "customer-based intangibles"—as valuation experts describe them—reside. Such intangibles are an important part of the value of many successful multinational enterprises. For example, in many technology businesses, once a customer has installed a particular company's hardware, software, or both, the company has a competitive advantage for subsequent generations of products and services independent of any technological superiority over other businesses; the value of this advantage amounts to a customer-based intangible asset of the company. Similarly, in many businesses, one successful product—whether based on technology, identification of consumer tastes, or some blend of both—can give a favorable image to a company, which can help sell other products in the future. The intangibles that reflect these elements of value are often described as an "installed customer base" or "customer relations" or even "goodwill." Once developed they can have value far exceeding any specific technology that fueled their initial creation. Arguably, these intangibles are inherently located in the jurisdiction of final purchaser for the product or service, which is the market jurisdiction, because that is where the customer is.

Of course, not all profit is attributable to this type of customer-based intangibles. The development of new products and services, typically protected by patents, trademarks, or copyrights, clearly is an important element in generating such returns. Yet there is also a rationale for sourcing a substantial part of these returns to the market jurisdiction: the value of these products is determined in substantial part by the legal protections offered through patent, trademark, copyright, and other laws in the market jurisdiction itself. A patent-protected drug cannot generate residual returns in a market that readily permits generic products to be sold without regard to patent rights. Similarly, a handbag maker cannot readily earn residual returns if knockoffs are readily available. It is predominantly the law of the market jurisdiction that protects these elements of value.

A tax on profit on a destination basis can therefore be seen in part as a return to several sources of profit related to the country of the consumer. This may justify some taxation based on a charge for publicly provided services, where those services are, for example, the protection of patents, trademarks, and copyrights. But it should be acknowledged that a multinational is also likely to benefit from publicly provided goods and services in other locations, such as the location of production or R&D. So taxing profit solely on a destination basis cannot be justified solely as a way of contributing to the cost of publicly provided goods and services.

A third and more compelling argument for taxing corporate profits on a destination basis is that it might be the only viable option in the long term. As competitive forces continue to drive down source- and residence-based corporate tax rates, countries might simply find that they are unable to meet their revenue targets for corporation tax under the existing system. In this sense, a decision to move to a destination-based corporate tax system reflects an acceptance of the equilibrium toward which countries are being driven by tax competition and a conscious attempt to free themselves from this process. Once a decision is made to tax corporate profit on a destination basis, countries acquire the ability to set their corporate tax rates according to their preferences and free of competitive forces.

A tax based on destination solves many of the problems that affect the existing tax system and that are exacerbated by digitalization. But it also introduces new problems, depending on the system used.[17] One option is a VAT-type approach in which exports are not taxed, but imports are taxed; this is known as a destination-based cash flow tax.[18,19] This means that sales would be taxed in the location of the purchaser, while expenses would receive relief where they were incurred. A country would effectively tax domestic sales less domestic expenses.

Under this option, one issue arising is the taxation of imports for business-to-consumer transactions. For business-to-business transactions, this should not be problematic. Imports by businesses could be taxed, but they would also receive relief. These two tax effects would exactly cancel out. Imports by businesses could, alternatively, simply be ignored. So, challenges for collecting revenue under a destination-based cash flow tax relate primarily to cross-border business-to-consumer transactions, though it would be necessary to identify whether a transaction is business-to-business or business-to-consumer.

The destination-based cash flow tax would tax imports purchased by individual consumers and non-taxable entities. Where a customer purchases a good or service directly from a business in another country, a tax should be levied at the rate of the destination country. Two options open to the destination country are to collect the tax from the exporting company or from the consumer. The former appears to be the more realistic option, although not without difficulties of its own, especially in the absence of fiscal borders, or for digital products, as is clear from the operation of VAT. These are difficulties that already arise under the VAT. In principle, it would be necessary for the exporting company to register for tax in the country into which it is exporting the good or service; this is difficult to administer for relatively small exporters, particularly when the good or service can be downloaded electronically or where there are no customs operations at borders. The exporter must also identify the location of its customer and—depending on the treatment of business imports—whether the customer is a business or a consumer. The tax authority must identify companies from around the world that export to its country, and guard against any opportunities for fraud if, for example, and again depending on the treatment of business imports, final consumers pretend they are businesses.

Once again, however, digitalization may come to the aid of the tax collector. For example, gathering information from intermediaries such as credit card and other payment companies could be an important enforcement tool, for both a destination-based cash flow tax and a VAT.[20]

---

[17]Concerns about the impact of the destination-based cash flow tax on countries with natural resources or other location-specific rents can be addressed by retaining or introducing a tax on the location specific rent alongside the destination-based cash flow tax.

[18]Under a cash flow tax, immediate relief is given to all expenditure, including capital expenditure, and revenues are taxed as they accrue.

[19]A destination-based cash flow tax is equivalent in economic terms to a broad-based, uniform-rate VAT with a payroll subsidy. On the destination-based tax, see Auerbach and others (2017).

[20]See Lamensch (2015).

One innovation in the European Union that could be applied among cooperating countries is a "one-stop shop," as proposed by Devereux and de la Feria (2014) and the European Commission (2014). Under such a system a company selling into several separate countries would need to register in only one; in many cases that is likely to be the origin country from which the company exports. The tax authority in that country would administer the destination-based cash flow tax at the rate of the country to which the good or service is exported. There would be a clearing arrangement at the aggregate level, where payments are made, between tax authorities in recognition of the appropriate recipient of the tax. Such cooperation would clearly create a significant administrative simplicity relative to when the exporter is required to register and pay tax in each country in to which it exports. Again, such a system is helped considerably by the digitalization of tax returns.

SPECIFIC ISSUES FOR DIGITAL COMPANIES

So far, we have considered the implications of digitalization for the taxation of all businesses, on the grounds that digitalization increases the mobility of all elements of multinational companies. This raises increasingly difficult problems for the existing international tax system. But now let us consider two cases that might be thought particularly prone to the problems of digitalization.

Two-Sided Markets

A company has a two-sided market when it provides a platform for bringing together two economic agents that would like to interact with each other. This is not necessarily specific to digital companies, but digitalization makes this considerably easier.[21] There are many examples. For instance, trading platforms such as eBay, Amazon, and Airbnb bring together agents that want to sell their goods or services with consumers who want to purchase them. A common element of such platforms is that the greater the number of people operating on one side of the platform, the more attractive the platform is for participants on the other side. For example, individuals seeking to sell goods or services would find it beneficial if the platform had many potential buyers. Similarly, buyers would find the platform more advantageous if there were many sellers.

This advantage can be developed and exploited by companies operating internationally. Note, however, that this can be achieved without the company itself being multinational in the sense that it operates directly in many countries. In principle, all that is needed is a website that acts as a platform that individuals around the world want to engage with. That could be set up and implemented in a single country. However, a successful company could of course take advantage of digitalization to locate various parts of its activity and resources in different

---

[21]For further discussion, see Chapter 3.

countries: programmers and researchers could be in one location, marketing in another, and the servers customers interact with in yet another.

Most of the issues raised in this case are common to the more general businesses that we have already discussed. However, one question arises when the tax is based on destination, that is, how to identify the place of destination. Where both sides of the market pay for the service provided by the platform, it seems reasonable to consider both parties to be customers of the platform; both represent sales to third parties and hence the location of each can be thought of as a destination.

But what if only one side of the market were required to pay? For example, suppose that the platform was trying to encourage more suppliers to register and hence did not explicitly charge suppliers, but only buyers. Would this mean that since there were sales to only buyers, that only the location of buyers represented a place of destination? On the one hand, this does not seem reasonable. Economic theory suggests that it is likely the cost of paying for the platform would in most cases be effectively shared by the buyer and seller, even if the explicit charge were applied to only the buyer. In that case, it might be reasonable to treat the location of the supplier also as a destination location, even if the supplier had not made an explicit payment. On the other hand, identifying the effective price paid by the seller (through charging a lower price) would be extremely difficult. For practical purposes, it is hard to imagine a tax that sought to impute a tax charge based on the location of the seller. This issue is the subject of the second case, of free usage.

Free Usage

A number of prominent companies in the digital world—such as Google and Facebook—offer their services to one set of customers for "free." They generate revenues through advertising services and employ the users' data to enhance these advertising revenues. Again, this business model is not unique to digital companies—for example, free newspapers financed by advertising are common. But the international scope of these digital companies is clearly now immense. Furthermore, the data collected offer unprecedented opportunities for targeted and tailored advertising, thus enhancing the value of the services. The question then arises as to how the profits of such companies should be allocated to the different countries in which they operate.

A multinational enterprise operating a search engine serves as an example in what follows.

The key issue here is that there is a form of barter. An individual does not pay to make a search on the multinational enterprise's search engine, but in making a search she reveals information valuable to the multinational enterprise in selling advertisements that subsequently appear on her screen. The purchasers of the advertisements may be located in another country.

The appropriate allocation of taxing rights in such cases depends on the principle adopted. Under the existing system, the allocation will primarily depend on the location of employees selling the advertising. Under existing PE rules, rights to tax corporate profit are allocated to the country in which the advertiser resides if the multinational enterprise has a PE in that country. Given that the sales process is inherently digital, the lines defining a PE are somewhat blurred.[22] But the underlying problem here is one of a lack of principle. It is not entirely clear under what principle the existing system is, or should be, operating. If the "source" of income is where the advertiser is located, then this is most naturally associated with the place of residence of the advertiser. But this is not how the OECD model currently works. If profit is allocated to shareholders and taxed in the residence of those shareholders, then the business model is irrelevant to the basis of taxation.

Under a destination-based system, we first have to determine what is the destination country. One obvious answer is that it is the place of residence of the advertiser. That is the person making a purchase. However, it could conceivably be argued that although the income is received from the advertiser, the service of advertising is performed in the country of the user, and that the country of the user should therefore be thought of as the destination country. This issue tests the notion of "destination." To address this, we must return to first principles as to what the aim of the tax is. If the basic aim is to assign taxing rights to an immobile location, then there is some merit in identifying the place the service is performed as the place of destination because this will most often coincide with the place of residence of the (relatively immobile) user. By contrast, if the advertiser is itself a multinational company, then it may have an incentive to locate its purchasing activity in a low-tax jurisdiction to reduce the tax on the seller, and thereby also reduce its own net costs. Note, however, that while this might be an advantage under certain destination-based corporate tax systems such as sales-based formulary apportionment, it would not be an advantage under the destination-based cash flow tax, since the advertiser would ultimately be taxed where it eventually makes a sale—which it presumably hopes will be where the user of the search engine is resident (Auerbach and others 2017).

We also need to consider the barter with the user (in what might be thought of as a different form of a two-sided model). Suppose that the search engine provider is a multinational enterprise that charged a fee for using its search engine, and also paid an equal amount to those using the search engine for the information that they supplied. Then the multinational enterprise's worldwide profit would be unaffected (apart from greater transactions costs); it would have revenue and costs, but no net profit, in the country of the user.

Under existing PE rules, this would not generate any taxable presence in the country of the service provider if the multinational enterprise had no physical presence there. However, under a destination-based tax and based on actual receipts, the multinational enterprise's sales would be partly attributed to the country of the user and partly to the country of the advertiser. However, the destination-based tax would also give relief to the multinational enterprise for the cost associated with purchasing information from the user. The net tax base under a destination-based tax would therefore continue to be zero, as long as the receipts

---

[22]The United Kingdom's diverted profits tax is at least partly intended to address this issue.

and costs were equal. The allocation of taxing rights would therefore depend very much on the value assigned to the search and to the information; identifying the two values would then be of crucial importance.

Another possibility is that the value of the information collected by the search engine exceeds the cost of the provision of the search engine. In this case, the barter is favorable to the multinational enterprise, since it does not pay for the information. In effect, the profit, or economic rent generated by the multinational enterprise, is location-specific since it can be generated only in the place of residence of the user of the search engine. This gives that state an opportunity to impose a tax on the barter transaction, which in principle could be set at a rate that would not have any effect on the underlying activity, but would allow that state to capture a share of the economic rent earned by the multinational enterprise. This would be an attractive option for that state.

However, there remains, of course, the difficulty of determining the profit generated, and hence an efficient level of tax. The difficulty is made worse since there would be no actual transactions, nor, in all probability, any comparable transactions. If the level of tax were too high, then the service provider might not be willing to continue to provide the service. However, this does seem to be an interesting opportunity for countries to levy what could be an efficient tax on the economic rents of digital multinational enterprises. Further work is needed on how such a tax could be constructed and levied in practice.

Another possibility is that the multinational enterprise did not collect any information from users. Suppose instead that it operated more like a free newspaper—its revenues were from advertisers willing to pay for such advertising despite not having any detailed information on the users. Would this make any difference to the position? This is not clear. If the principle is to allocate taxing rights to the country of destination, it could still be argued that the value of the service provided to the user should be taxable. However, this could be thought to effectively overturn the business model, which is to provide a free service financed by advertising.

Finally, the issue of barter comes up under other taxes as well. The country of the user may well consider the user to have purchased an imported service, in which case it should in principle be subject to VAT. At the same time, the notional income from the sale of information would be a benefit in kind for personal income tax. If either tax were collected from individuals the sums involved would likely be so small as to be dominated by the costs of collection. However, the scale of the large digital companies is so great—that is, they have so many individual participants —that collecting revenue from the company is more feasible.

CONCLUSION

We have considered a number of ways in which greater digitalization has increased the internationalization of business. For example, shareholders and customers may be located in different countries, and the company itself can organize itself in complex supply chains also covering many countries. These factors pose significant problems for the national taxation of such international businesses. These problems have been reflected in increasing public and political concern over the strategies used by multinational companies to exploit the existing international tax system to reduce their tax liabilities.

In our view, the existing system does not provide a good basis for taxation. It is based on arbitrary distinctions: those between countries (residence versus source) and between types of income (active versus passive). Closing loopholes generally increases complexity, and is unlikely to generate a more sensible and stable system. Rather, fundamental reform is required, and the tax base should be based on relatively immobile factors, either where shareholders are located or where consumers are located. Both types of reform have a significant advantage in that the conceptual basis of the system would be clear. But they also both raise practical difficulties. A tax on shareholders would need to associate corporate profit in one country with a shareholder in another. A tax in the place of sale would need to tax imports, possibly exported by a small company in another country. However, both problems might in principle be helped by digitalization. To the extent that tax records are digitized, and possibly combined with other data, for example, from banks, then the problems of information for these systems might eventually be overcome.

Other issues also emerge, particularly in digital companies—for example, in which cash sales are made to advertisers in one country and the advertisements appear on the screens of users in another. This may be combined with the use of information provided freely by those users. At the moment, little attempt is made to levy a tax in the country of the users, typically because no money changes hands in these locations. There is a case to be made in principle for tax to be levied in the country of the user, but doing so presents significant practical and conceptual difficulties.

REFERENCES

Auerbach, A.J., Michael Devereux, Michael Keen, and John Vella. 2017. "Destination Based Cash Flow Taxation." Centre for Business Taxation Working Paper 17/01, Oxford University, Oxford.

Avi-Yonah, S. Reuven. 1995. "The Rise and Fall of Arm's Length: A Study in the Evolution of U.S. International Taxation." *Virginia Tax Review* 15 (1): 85–159.

———. 1996. "The Structure of International Taxation: A Proposal for Simplification." *Texas Law Review* 74: 1301–59.

———, and Ilan Benshalom. 2011. "Formulary Apportionment: Myths and Prospects—Promoting Better International Policy and Utilizing the Misunderstood and Under-Theorized Formulary Alternative." *World Tax Journal* 3 (3): 371–98.

Devereux, Michael, and R. de la Feria. 2014. "Defining and Implementing a Destination-Based Corporate Tax." Centre for Business Taxation Working Paper 14/07 Oxford University, Oxford.

Devereux, Michael P., and John Vella. 2014. "Are We Heading for a Corporation Tax Fit for the 21st Century?" *Fiscal Studies* 35 (4): 449–75.

European Commission. 2014. "Expert Group on Taxation of the Digital Economy." Report of the Commission High Level Expert Group on Taxation of the Digital Economy, Brussels.

Graetz, Michael J. 2001. "Taxing International Income: Inadequate Principles, Outdated Concepts, and Unsatisfactory Policies." *Tax Law Review* 54: 261–336.

Grubert, Harry, and Rutgers Altshuler. 2016. "Shifting the Burden of Taxation from the Corporate to the Personal Level and Getting the Corporate Tax Rate Down to 15 Percent." *National Tax Journal* 69 (3): 643–76.

Lamensch, Marie. 2015. *European Value Added Tax in the Digital Era*. Amsterdam: IBFD.

Office for National Statistics (ONS). 2014. *Ownership of UK Shares, 2014 Dataset*. London.

Olbert, Marcel, and Christoph Spengel. 2017. "International Taxation in the Digital Economy: Challenge Accepted?" *World Tax Journal* 9 (1): 3–46.

Organisation for Economic Co-operation and Development (OECD). 2012. *Model Tax Convention on Income and Capital 2010*. Paris: OECD Publishing.

———. 2013. *Base Erosion and Profit Shifting Action Plan*. Paris: OECD Publishing.

———. 2015. *Addressing the Tax Challenges of the Digital Economy, Action 1—2015 Final Report*. Paris: OECD Publishing.

Rosenthal, Steven, and Lydia S. Austin. 2016. "The Dwindling Taxable Share of U.S. Corporate Stock." *Tax Notes* 151 (6).

Toder, Eric, and Alan D. Viard. 2014. "Major Surgery Needed: A Call for Structural Reform of the US Corporate Income Tax." Peter G. Peterson Foundation, New York.

———. 2016. "A Proposal to Reform the Taxation of Corporate Income." Report of the Tax Policy Center, Washington, DC.

US House Ways and Means Committee. 2016. "A Better Way Forward on Tax Reform." Washington, DC.

Voget, Johannes. 2015. "The Effect of Taxes on Foreign Direct Investment: A Survey of the Empirical Evidence." ETPF Policy Paper 3, European Tax Policy Forum, London.

Warren, Alvin C. 1994. "Alternatives for International Corporate Tax Reform." *Tax Law Review* 49: 599–614.

CHAPTER 5

Testing and Implementing Digital Tax Administration

JINGNAN (CECILIA) CHEN, SHAUN GRIMSHAW, AND GARETH D. MYLES

The benefits of digital technology are well documented, leaving no doubt that it can also ease tax compliance, reduce tax collection costs, and increase administrative efficiency.[1] Yet detailed analysis of consequences is crucial to these efforts.

Behavioral economics has shown that even small changes, or "nudges," can significantly affect actions.[2] This is particularly true of taxation, in which compliance is determined by a complex mixture of financial, social, moral, and psychological factors. The behavioral implications of any implementation of digital technology for tax administration need to be scrutinized to avoid unintended consequences. Innovations that initially appear innocuous and beneficial may well introduce nudge behavior in detrimental directions.

Pre-population of tax returns is a leading and current digital innovation, pioneered by the Danish revenue service in 1988 and followed in a number of countries.[3] Pre-population is often accepted without question as a way to significantly reduce transaction costs in tax payment, but it is also a significant nudge that, psychologically, transfers "ownership" of errors from the taxpayer to the revenue agency. Tax administrations are also encouraging online submission of tax returns. Evidence shows the consequences of onscreen prompts, but little research is directly related to the tax environment.[4] Taxation is complex, and individuals

The authors thank Andy Morrison, Floria Hau, Andrea Scott, and Tim Bryant at the National Audit Office (United Kingdom) for their help, in particular, their guidance and expertise on the relevant tax issues and efforts to produce the profile used. They also thank Michael Keen for his extensive comments on an earlier draft.

[1]The experiment reviewed in the section "Taxpayer Guidance: Popup or Paper?" was financed by a contract with the U.K. National Audit Office. The description of the results in this chapter are the authors' own and do not necessarily reflect those of the audit office.

[2]Sunstein and Thaler (2009).

[3]A tax return is pre-populated when the tax administration enters data into the return before sending it to the taxpayer. Tax returns are now pre-populated to varying degrees in more than 10 European Union countries, as well as in Australia and California (OECD 2008).

[4]Shu and others (2012) report the outcome of an experiment designed to reduce cheating on exams.

filing online may make errors. The service must always be designed to minimize errors. Unlike participants in most online activities, those in tax payment are unwilling, and compelling evidence suggests that a significant percentage are prepared to cheat if they perceive it to be beneficial. Digital developments must be designed to ensure that they do not provide additional incentive or motivation for cheating.

Digital technology in tax administration not only offers lower transaction costs, but also allows innovation in tax policy. A tax system will not function effectively if it imposes requirements that administration cannot meet. For example, the marginal rate of income tax cannot be determined by family income if the administrative system records only individual income. Nor can a consumption tax depend on the quantity of consumption if the system does not record purchaser identity. The policy implications of digitalization are inherently linked with advances in other areas of science and technology. What we can do with digital technology depends on the level of our understanding of what creates individual differences. As this knowledge progresses, our perspective on the foundations of tax policy will also have to change. Where this may lead is currently unknown, but speculative ideas are presented in the following discussion.

The United Kingdom provides an example of advancing digitalization. In its March Budget of 2015 the government outlined a vision for a digitized and online tax system, dubbed "Making Tax Digital" by HM Revenue and Customs (HMRC). It looks forward to simplification of tax payment for individuals and firms with information from third parties used to pre-populate returns, and ultimately envisages real-time taxation, eliminating the need for annual tax returns.

HMRC has used information technology to store and process tax data for a considerable time, and online submission of returns is gradually becoming the norm. However, the online submission system is little more than a digitized version of the paper return, with little or no added functionality. It produces an automatic tax calculation, but has no interaction with the taxpayer. The step remaining is the full exploitation of interactive online systems that integrate reporting, recording, advising, submission, and payment.

The reluctance of many revenue agencies to advance digitalization is clearly understandable given the potential costs of mistakes. Foremost among these are the risk to revenue, damage to reputation, and potential reduction of tax morale. The digitalization of tax administration is technically complex given the volume of activity the system will have to accommodate and the importance of security and absence of errors. The required quality standards will be achieved only through extensive technical and functional testing. Any system inadequately tested will quickly fall into disrepute, with potentially significant financial and reputational costs.[5]

---

[5]A list of systems that either failed, ran over budget, or have not yet been delivered is available at https://en.wikipedia.org/wiki/List_of_failed_and_overbudget_custom_software_projects.

The necessity for technical testing seems self-evident. What this chapter argues is that a system needs an accompanying and equally intensive program of behavioral testing. This is because any system carries with it behavioral implications, and the design will determine how taxpayers react. These reactions will include whether the system was intuitive to use or attractive to look at, as well as the extent to which taxpayers are compliant with the tax code and their attitudes to tax collection.

Clearly, compliance is affected by a complex set of economic, psychological, and social factors, and behavioral economics has demonstrated how small nudges can lead to large behavioral change.[6] And a move from traditional paper-based filing to an online system, with pre-population and real-time activity, as rather more than a small nudge, could significantly impact compliance. This is why a digitized system needs behavioral testing, which is based on the idea that small details can matter. The methodology of experimental economics described in Box 5.1 is perfect for this.[7]

The results of two experiments undertaken at the United Kingdom's Tax Administration Research Centre that investigated different aspects of making taxation electronic form a major part of the chapter.[8] The first experiment was designed to explore taxpayer response to incorrect or incomplete pre-population. The results of the experiment are described alongside other research investigating pre-population.

The second experiment considered the impact of online assistance during completion of a tax return relative to traditional paper or phone assistance. Providing guidance to taxpayers in paper form is the long-established standard, and it is not known how behavior will change if paper guidance is transferred to online guidance or what effect online "pop-up" boxes offering assistance will have. As a byproduct, the experiment also provided insight into the nature of errors in tax returns. Moving beyond this, the online environment permits greater interaction with the taxpayer during return completion, which can allow inclusion of nudges and prompts in the return. Experimental methods can be used to maximize the effectiveness of these.

The introduction of pre-population and integrated online tax services are small steps at the start of the digital revolution in tax administration, and many countries have already gone much further than the United Kingdom. What

[6]The chapter focus narrowly on how administrative systems directly affect compliance. Many more factors can affect compliance (see IMF 2015).

[7]Tax compliance experiments have examined the effects of several policies: amnesties (Alm, McKee, and Beck 1990), audit schemes (Collins and Plumlee 1991; Alm, Cronshaw, and McKee 1993; Alm and McKee 2004; Tan and Yim 2014), publicizing information about audits and those audited (Coricelli and others 2010; Fortin, Lacroix, and Villeval 2007; Alm, Bloomquist, and McKee 2015), and positive inducements to encourage tax filing and compliance (Alm and others 2012; Bazart and Pickhardt 2011).

[8]The center is operated in partnership with the University of Exeter and the Institute for Fiscal Studies. More information is available at https://tarc.exeter.ac.uk/.

impact will these innovations have on tax policy? In particular, will they open the possibility for refinement of existing tax instruments or introduction of new instruments?

The economic theory of taxation was developed amid pre-digital tax administration. The chapter takes the implications of the experiments as a starting point from which to explore the extent to which extant theory must be updated given new technology. The conclusion—based on speculation about technologies that may be developed—sees the elimination of one of the most basic tenets of tax theory.

The next section reviews the key principles and the methodology of experiments in economics, followed by a review of experiments on the consequences of the pre-population of tax returns. The chapter then considers how completion of returns is affected by the form of customer service, reflects on how economists conceptualize tax theory, and speculates on the consequences of digitalization and technology.

PRE-POPULATION

An important component of digital innovation is the use of third-party data to pre-populate the tax return. This is a first step to eliminating the need for an annual return. Under the U.K. system (and those of many other countries) taxpayers are required to enter data obtained from third parties into the tax return. Examples of such data include income from employment, income from property, and eligible expenses such as private pension contributions.

HMRC receives much of this information directly from the third party, so that the taxpayer is providing information that HMRC already holds. This might have some strategic advantage for the revenue service as an indicator of potential noncompliance, but it unnecessarily burdens taxpayers, who are required to store information and may need to seek information to complete the return. HMRC's intention is to use the information they already hold to pre-populate the tax return so the taxpayer will not need to re-enter the data when filing.

Pre-population is appealing because it reduces the compliance costs of taxpayers and has potential to reduce errors and omissions. It saves the revenue agency time, because pre-populated data will not need checking against the records from third parties. Moving to pre-population is a small task relative to moving to real time, and the benefits to doing so are identifiable. But experiments have also revealed potential costs: if the pre-populated data are not correct, how do taxpayers respond?

The fundamental problem with pre-population is that it is possible for the revenue agency to include incorrect or incomplete information. The latter could arise, for example, when a taxpayer has multiple sources of income and the revenue agency does not receive reports from all third parties. How a taxpayer responds to a pre-populated form on which the information is not entirely correct then becomes a question in behavioral economics. The most positive outcome

Box 5.1. Economic Experiments

Only a few years ago economics could, without risk of dissent, be labeled a nonexperimental science. A leading textbook noted that "It is rarely, if ever, possible to conduct controlled experiments with the economy. Thus, economics must be a non-laboratory science."

This situation has changed completely and experiments are now accepted as part of the standard methodology of investigation in economics (Starmer 1999).

Experiments permit investigation of complex behavioral phenomena that may be hidden within economic data by the multiplicity of simultaneous environmental changes. Experiments can be deliberately designed for implementation in an experimental laboratory or in the field. Others, called natural experiments, are derived from exogenous changes in policy or situations that create treated and control groups whose behaviors can be contrasted. The ability to precisely control the environment is a key benefit of designed experiments. Replication is also possible, to compare results across time and cultures (such as the public good games discussed by Ledyard 1995). Natural experiments do not permit control or replication, but have the advantage of natural behavior and large sample size.

Experimental economists are generally agreed on a set of principles that govern the conduct of experiments: (1) salient financial incentives for experimental subjects to encourage considered participation, (2) absence of deception in the design and execution of the experiment, and (3) random assignment of subjects to treatment conditions to provide statistical validity.

A typical experiment lasts between 30 minutes and 2 hours and involves completion of one or more tasks and sometimes repetition of the same task. It may also involve pre- and post-testing of attitudes and opinions. The sample size is usually 60–300 participants depending on the task and the number of treatments. A treatment is a specific set of values for the experimental parameters, and experimenters are interested in how a change in parameters affects behavior. The number of subjects has to be large enough to ensure sufficient participation in each treatment to obtain statistical significance. The level of subject payments is set to reflect the opportunity cost of the time spent in the experimental session by subjects. All monetary amounts within an experiment are expressed in experimental currency units, the exchange rate of which to US dollars is set according to duration and number of repetitions or rounds.

Laboratory experiments permit "clean" comparison of the consequences of different treatments, but the laboratory is always an unnatural environment for experimental subjects and a simplified setup will always appear artificial. External validity requires results that hold for the general population facing a real decision problem in their natural environment. This makes the use of university students as subjects questionable for tax experiments (Choo, Fonseca, and Myles 2016; and Alm, Bloomquist, and McKee 2015). Using an appropriate subject pool (such as taxpayers for a tax compliance experiment) and moving the experiment online enhance external validity. It can be improved further by taking the laboratory into the field (a framed field experiment), but the control of the experimenter is reduced and the experiment will be context heavy.

Experimental investigations of tax compliance share common features (Alm 2012). Each experimental subject is given or earns income and then decides the amount to declare to the tax authority, which is subject to tax at a given rate. Meanwhile, there is a given probability of being audited. A subject who is audited and has unpaid tax will be fined proportionally to the level of unpaid tax. The results of experimental investigations into tax compliance to date suggest that there is no single design that is the best fit for all purposes, and that designs should be constructed in line with the research question under investigation.

from the perspective of the revenue service is that the taxpayer will simply correct the information. It might be thought that this would definitely be the outcome if the revenue service had overstated the true level of income.

However, as reported in the following paragraphs, a different behavior sometimes emerges in experiments. There are also two potential negative reactions to incorrect or incomplete pre-population. The taxpayer may accept the pre-populated values without comment, perhaps through having more faith in the revenue agency than in their own records, so the pre-populated value becomes established as the truth. In behavioral terms, this is a form of status quo bias or behavioral inertia. It can arise whether the pre-populated value is above or below the true value. The alternative negative reaction is more strategic. The pre-population of the tax return can be interpreted as a signal of the information held by the tax agency and, correspondingly, of what it does not know. Pre-populated values below the true level indicate the limited information of the revenue agency and can encourage deliberate evasion (by knowingly accepting an incorrect value) since they signal reduced likelihood of evasion being accepted.

The economic analysis of tax compliance has focused on explaining how taxpayers react to changes in the audit rate, level of punishment, and tax rate. Substantial theoretical literature models the decision process (see Hashimzade, Myles, and Tran-Nam 2013) and experimental literature tests these models. However, the effectiveness (or lack thereof) of pre-population of tax returns has not been a significant topic. This is possibly because pre-population has only recently become important to administration. The limited evidence is now reviewed.

Bruner and others (2015) studied the effect of pre-populating tax returns using undergraduate students at two US universities as experimental subjects. The experiment involved subjects earning income and making reports. The level of income for each subject was determined by undertaking a task at the start of the experiment and then remained constant for the subject throughout the experiment. The tax liability depended on earned income and claimed deductions. Tax returns could be audited and a punishment imposed for noncompliance.

The subjects had to make three entries into the tax return. Income was separated into "on-the-record" and "off-the-record" components. On-the-record income was known to the revenue agency through reports from third parties. Income "off the record" was not subject to third party reporting, so was unknown by the revenue agency (and this was known by the subject). Subjects could also make tax deductions that could be standard (such as deductions for spouses or children) or itemized. In some of the treatments, lines on the tax return were pre-populated, but were not in other treatments.

Subjects filed multiple tax returns in a sequence, each of which corresponded to a different profile of deductible expenses. In some cases, it was advantageous to file an itemized deduction, and in others it was not. A number of audit rates were also used, and fixed for each treatment and so did not respond to reported incomes. The baseline treatment had no pre-population, certainty of deductions, and the subjects received no off-the-record incomes. This was compared to a treatment with pre-population, certainty, and no off-the-record income. Further treatments introduced off-the-record income, uncertainty of deductions, and higher levels of off-the-record income for some subjects.

The results showed that compliance was extremely high for matched income. Most of the noncompliance that arose was from underreporting off-the-record income (only 81 percent of this income was reported) and from overstating deductions (claimed deductions were 112 percent of the allowable amount). Pre-population caused underreporting of off-the-record income to increase, and this effect was strongest when the pre-populated deduction exceeded the allowable amount. Furthermore, if the pre-populated amount incorrectly understated tax liability, then underreporting increased. This final result illustrates the danger revenue agencies face when using pre-population, and that it can signal the limited information of the agency.

Kotakorpi and Laamanen (2016) used data from a "natural experiment" in the mid-1990s in Finland. In the experiment, a subset of taxpayers had their tax forms partially pre-populated with data from third parties. These taxpayers were only required to file a return if the pre-populated information was incorrect or incomplete. They had the option to file if they wished to claim eligible deductions. All other taxpayers had to complete a standard tax return that was not pre-populated. The analysis explored how pre-population affected filing for five types of items: (1) pre-populated income (from primary and secondary employment), (2) non-pre-populated income (other earned income and capital income), (3) pre-populated deductions (mortgage interest deduction in 1997), (4) non-pre-populated deductions, and (5) reported wealth.

The most significant impact of pre-population was observed for non-pre-populated deductions: a partially pre-populated return led to a reduction in filed deductions compared to the control group. Overall, about 25 percent fewer taxpayers claimed non-pre-populated deductions. In contrast, claims for the pre-populated deductions increased. The reported level of non-pre-populated income and reported wealth also declined. The reporting of pre-populated items was not affected, nor was total taxable income. Kotakorpi and Laamanen (2016) observed that receiving a partially pre-populated tax return creates a tendency to report fewer of the items not pre-populated but more of those that are.

Fonseca and Grimshaw (2017) tested the effects of pre-population using a one-shot decision quasi-field experiment using U.K. taxpayers as subjects (because it is questionable whether students act in the same way as taxpayers in experiments).[9] That is, the evidence is mixed on the extent to which results from student samples can be generalized to the wider population, with indication that students are more noncompliant than experienced taxpayers in an experimental setting (Alm, Bloomquist, and McKee 2015; Choo, Fonseca, and Myles 2016). Experimental subjects played the role of a fictitious taxpayer with two income

---

[9]A quasi-field experiment engages a relevant population (in this case, taxpayers) in a laboratory or online experiment.

streams (not subject to withholding) and tax-deductible expenses. Using two income streams allowed modeling of a revenue service with limited information, in which case the return was pre-populated with only one of the two streams.

Various forms of pre-population were assessed against a baseline treatment without pre-population. Pre-population was also combined with onscreen prompts intended to create barriers to noncompliance. The prompts included the need to click on a checkbox to unlock entries and warning messages about the audit probability. The experiment also included an expense item determined by the roll of a dice by the experimental subject. Experimenters did not observe the value of the roll, giving an unverifiable component to the experiment. The subjects were told they could be audited, but were not informed of the audit rule.[10]

The experiment used seven separate treatments:

- BASE: The tax form was not pre-populated.
- CORR: The two income streams were correctly pre-populated and the tax form revealed that the revenue agency held the correct information.
- OVER: The revenue agency is shown as having information on three income streams (the form is pre-populated with one of the actual streams double-counted).
- UNDER: Pre-populated with data on only one of the two income streams and this is the only stream known to the revenue agency.

Three variations of UNDER were also used:

- UNDERGENERIC: Featured a checkbox that had to be clicked to unlock the pre-populated income field and clicked again to confirm any new value entered.
- UNDERALWAYS: Featured the message: "Most people in your circumstances enter an income value of more than 40,000. Values below this amount are more likely to be audited. Click the tick box to confirm you wish to proceed."
- UNDERTRIGGER: The same message as UNDERALWAYS if the participant inputted a total self-employment income amount lower than 40,000.

Figure 5.1 illustrates the results: it displays the verifiable compliance rate for the experimental treatments. Part always remained unverifiable because the dice roll was not observed. The BASE treatment had a very high compliance rate, but only 70 percent of subjects fully reported income.

The CORR treatment had a higher average compliance rate and a higher proportion of fully compliant subjects than BASE, though neither difference was statistically significant. The OVER treatment was slightly lower than BASE in both dimensions. A marked difference occurs with the UNDER treatment, which

---

[10]The precise rule relating the probability of audit (denoted p) to the declared liability (denoted X) was: $p = 10$ percent for $X \leq 22{,}600$ ECU, $p = 6.6$ percent for $22{,}600$ ECU $< X < 42{,}500$ ECU, $p = 3.3$ percent for $42{,}500$ ECU $\leq X$.

Figure 5.1. Average Verifiable Compliance Ratio, by Treatment

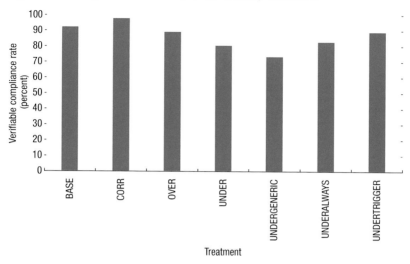

Source: Fonseca and Grimshaw 2017, p. 33.

led to a large and significant fall in average compliance and in fully compliant subjects. There was a further fall for the UNDERGENERIC treatment. The latter two treatments show that subjects were willing to accept false low reports but unwilling to engage in a process (checking a box) to make a correction. The nudges used in UNDERALWAYS and UNDERTRIGGER restored some of the compliance.

Figure 5.2 details the results by showing separate compliance rates for each class of income. When self-employment income is correctly pre-populated the rate of compliance is high. This reveals that pre-population is successful for the revenue agency if it holds correct information.

An unexpected finding in the OVER treatment is that it is compliance with expenses that responds to the incorrect pre-population. What seems to be happening is that subjects realized the overstatement of income, but were reluctant to change the pre-populated value. Instead, they engaged in compensating behavior through over-claiming for expenses. Compliance for self-employment income in the UNDER treatments declined significantly. The results emphasize the willingness of subjects to accept mistakenly low pre-populated values and the benefit of nudges to restore some degree of compliance. It is perhaps not surprising that the triggered nudge was most effective since, psychologically, this creates an impression of monitoring of actions.

A surprising finding of this experiment was that pre-population with over-estimated income levels had little effect on behavior. The values were corrected in some cases, but in others the subjects accepted the incorrect values even

Figure 5.2. Propensity for Verifiable Compliance, by Treatment

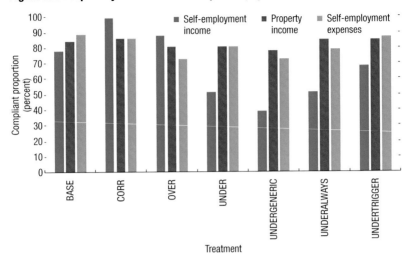

Source: Fonseca and Grimshaw 2017, p. 34.

though this resulted in an excessive tax payment. This behavior reflects an acceptance of the authority of the revenue agency, with the thought process "if they say this is correct then I have to believe it."

In contrast, pre-populated values that understated correct income had a significant impact. This arose because subjects were happy to accept the incorrectly low values. As discussed earlier, this can be explained in that low values were seen as a sign of revenue agency ignorance, which subjects were willing to exploit. The introduction of barriers to editing pre-populated fields may worsen noncompliance if the pre-populated values are incorrect. Finally, behavioral prompts help overcome incorrect pre-population only if they are responsive to behavior in the filing process. The appearance of a pop-up box in response to a lower-than-expected income report conveys the impression that the system is taking notice and encourages increased compliance.

The focus of Fonseca and Grimshaw (2017) is slightly different to that of Bruner and others (2015), so the two studies are complementary. Fonseca and Grimshaw study a one-shot decision with one set of parameters, where only the pre-populated value in one of the entries is varied, whereas Bruner and others look at a wider set of parameters and a more complex filing decision. Bruner and others consider several audit rates, which are invariant to behavior and known with certainty, while Fonseca and Grimshaw consider an unknown audit rate, which depends on filing behavior. Bruner and others consider a more complex environment with itemized and non-itemized deductions, as well as on-the-record and off-the-record incomes. That both studies find that pre-populating tax returns with values that underestimate taxpayers' liabilities leads to higher non-compliance lends greater robustness to both sets of results.

These investigations into pre-population are informative of the consequences of further digitalization of the tax process. We know there are taxpayers who are noncompliant under the current system. Pre-population may help reduce some of the noncompliance that arises from error. But even this is not guaranteed, because the experiments reveal a reluctance to change incorrect pre-population.

Only if the revenue agency is correct are errors sure to be reduced. OECD (2008) reports apparently high accuracy of pre-populated returns (about 70 percent in Denmark and Sweden needing no adjustment). But, critically, it also observes "these reporting arrangements do not include details of income from self-employment and rental properties" (OECD 2008, 8). This is important because these are the income sources that are open to noncompliance and the hardest to pre-populate. Some of the deliberate noncompliance may be deterred by the pre-populated value acting as a minimum which a noncompliant taxpayer will not wish to correct downward for fear of signaling their noncompliance. However, taxpayers with a propensity to be noncompliant will take the pre-populated information as a signal and use it to refine their noncompliance strategy. Pre-population with an incorrect value acts as a signal of the limited information of the revenue agency which a noncompliant taxpayer will wish to exploit. The experiments agree that revenue agencies run a significant compliance risk from understated entries.

On the other hand, the results provide clear encouragement for strategic behavior by the revenue agency. The following comments should be prefaced by saying that it is not expected that any revenue agency should ever adopt these strategies. But, the strategic implications of pre-population cannot be ignored. Because understating increases noncompliance and some taxpayers are reluctant to reduce overstated entries, there is a strategic incentive for the government to overstate. Clearly, this would be counter to all rules of good governance, and if a revenue agency were discovered to have acted in this way, it would reduce trust.

Even more sinister is the nature of the motive a revenue agency has to deliberately understate. The revenue service could understate an item about which it is certain to test the willingness of the taxpayer to make the required correction. A failure to correct could then be used as an indicator that an audit is required. More disturbingly, understatement in pre-populated values could be used to lure a taxpayer into noncompliance—with punishment to follow.

The experiments give valuable information on how taxpayers will respond to mistakes in pre-population. The revenue service could act strategically, but if it is simply trying to be as straightforward as possible, then pre-population should be undertaken to the best of the agency's ability using all available information. The potential noncompliance implications will have to be accepted as the price paid for easing the tax affairs of compliant taxpayers. Behavioral prompts can work, but have to be carefully designed and tested. Implementation should also account for the evident reluctance of taxpayers to correct errors in pre-populated entries.

What is not clear is whether pre-population with imperfect information will ultimately increase or reduce tax revenues received; none of the experiments is sufficiently precise to answer that question. A fair expectation is that refinement of the system over time by increased integration of systems would improve accuracy and ultimately eliminate the noncompliance effects.

TAXPAYER GUIDANCE: POP-UP OR PAPER?

National Audit Office (2016) scrutinizes the impact of HMRC customer service on personal taxpayers.[11] The office estimated that 17.5 million taxpayers used HMRC's information and advice services in 2015. The report found that the quality of service of taxpayers may affect tax compliance. The move to online tax accounts will shift the emphasis of service from traditional paper to online guidance. The experiment investigates whether HMRC tax guidance affects tax compliance and, if it does, by how much. The effect of a support line handled by tax advisors on tax compliance is also explored. In addition, as a by-product, the experiment gives insight into the possibility of errors when completing a return.

Revenue service tax guidance is often the starting point of the taxpayer journey. The contents, as well as the delivery form of the contents, largely determine the ease of comprehension and thereby the need for additional help. Consequently, the quality of the tax guidance (such as the ease of comprehension) may affect demand for further contact with the revenue service and ultimately influence the overall tax compliance level. If the cost of seeking help exceeds the benefits of completing a fully compliant tax return, taxpayers may simply resort to their own best endeavors to complete a compliant tax return or potentially even behave in a deliberately noncompliant manner (for example, see Graetz and Wilde 1985; Clotfelter 1983).[12] Many reforms in tax administration strive for better service quality to attain greater compliance.

Traditionally, enforcement effort, intensity of audits, and fines and penalties have been the tax authority's primary tools to promote voluntary tax compliance. More recently—and lagging the actions of revenue services—academic research has begun to focus on the impact of the provision of tax information and assistance services on overall tax morale and compliance. Alm and others (2010) demonstrated that taxpayers respond positively to service programs in an experimental setting. Specifically, customer-friendly tax administration increased average compliance by 27 percent.[13]

---

[11]This section describes an experiment on tax compliance behavior undertaken online and at the Finance and Economics Experiments Laboratory at Exeter at the University of Exeter between January and April 2016. The research was funded under contract by the National Audit Office.

[12]The costs and benefits here refer to not only the monetary costs and benefits taxpayers may incur when seeking help from HMRC, but also to psychological costs and benefits.

[13]The experimental design left subjects uncertain about the correct value of a tax deduction and a tax credit. In the basic treatment, decisions had to be taken with this uncertainty unresolved.

Two main reasons were proposed to account for the results. First, by relieving the burden of complying with tax regulations, the tax authority can affect "soft" tax compliance factors, such as the perception of fairness and trust. Secondly, the tax authority is able to reduce "hard" tax compliance factors, such as the actual compliance costs of the taxpayers. Another experiment, by McKee, Siladke, and Vossler (2011), found additional evidence in support of the arguments above by showing that a helpful information service drastically reduced tax evasion. A further experiment, by Vossler and McKee (2013), looked into the effectiveness of a taxpayer service program in enhancing tax reporting, with the emphasis on the accuracy of tax filing. They found that even an imperfect service helped increase the likelihood of filing and filing accuracy.

Finding appropriate tax filing information and applying it costs taxpayers in time and effort. There may be barriers to the degree of cost subjects are willing to bear to find an appropriate rule, and factors that reduce search costs may therefore lead to greater compliance.

Based on this line of reasoning, we predict that holding the delivery form constant, people are less likely to make mistakes when tax guidance is succinct and precise rather than long and detailed. On the other hand, holding the contents of the guidance constant, people may be less likely to make filing mistakes when the guidance is provided as an online pop-up. As such, relevant information is immediately at hand, requiring no searching through pages of printed materials.

Combining these observations, precise guidance delivered in an online pop-up may be more customer-friendly and may encourage greater tax compliance than the long and detailed guidance printed on paper. The experiment we report is designed to test these observations to enhance the online filing experience.

Experimental Design

The experiment features a one-shot tax filing decision. The primary focus of the research was the investigation of the effect of various treatments on the values reported in a tax return for a moderately complicated taxpayer profile. Typically, there are benefits of experimental designs with repeated actions as they allow for learning by subjects. However, such benefits are typically greatest when time allowed for decisions is short. The design presented here does not have such advantages as there is a requirement for the decision to be complex to force subjects to examine the tax materials they are presented with to be able to file a compliant return. This is different than many other laboratory tax experiments in which the filing decision is very simple.

In the experiment, subjects were given the profile—receipts and expenditures—of a particular taxpayer. The experiment focused on whether the expenditures were allowable business expenses. Uncertainty arose in whether an item in the profile was allowable, what proportion of a particular expenditure was allowable,

---

The treatment with a "customer-friendly" revenue service introduced an information service that resolved this uncertainty.

and into which field in the tax return the subject should enter a value deemed allowable. The information services were provided to remove these uncertainties for subjects who wished to be compliant.

Self-employment was chosen as the basis for the experimental tax profile due to the level of relevance to the self-assessment population as a whole.[14] Given the complex nature of the tax return that needs to be completed (SA100), it can be assumed that many self-employed need some level of support. The number of accountants and tax advisors offering assistance suggests that many self-employed seek professional help.

Table 5.1 details the profile used throughout the experiments, with the profile itself shown in Annex 5.1. Values are given in experimental currency units (ECU), as is typical in experimental economics. This is primarily to preserve framing effects over different subject pools, as the exchange rate for ECUs to actual cash can be varied to allow for different levels of compensation, but also to frame the experiment with real-world values.

Table 5.1. Tax Profile Details and Correct Allowance

Category	Detail	Amount	Correct Allowance
Income	Fitness classes	25,200	Not applicable
Expenses	Car purchase	1,500	0
	Running car (8,000 business miles out of 10,000 total miles) to/from place of work	2,500	0
	Church hall hire	5,760	5,760
	Advertising flyers	175	175
	Gym membership	1,200	0
	Annual household bills (one day a month working from home)	7,500	246.58
	Mobile phone (15 percent of total usage was for business purposes)	420	63
Total	Expenses	19,055	6,244.58

Source: Authors' calculations.

From Table 5.1, net income (income less total expenses) is 6,145 ECU (subjects were informed of this figure as part of the system). The compliant level of deductions is 6,244.58 ECU, leaving a taxable income of 18,955.42 ECU. The payment of the subject for participation in the experiment was based on the subjects' post-tax balance (net income less tax payment). The experiment used a tax rate of 20 percent so the compliant tax payment was 3,791.08 ECU and a post-tax balance of 2,353.92 ECU.[15] This value of the post-tax balance corresponded to the subject earning £7.06 for the completion of a compliant return (for a total of £12.06 once the show-up fee was included). The maximum earnings possible from the task, obtained by an over-declaration of expenses to give a taxable liability of zero, was £18.43 (£23.43 with the inclusion of the show-up

---

[14]Approximately 15 percent of the U.K. workforce are self-employed.

[15]2,353.92 = 6,145.00 – 3,791.08.

fee). The minimum level of earnings, from over-declaration of expenses leading to a large fine, is £0 (£5 with the inclusion of the show-up fee).

The focus of the experiment was to examine the effect of guidance on those who file for themselves. The experimental treatments vary the contents of the guidance as well as the delivery form of the guidance to examine compliance behavior. All the guidance contents were direct from HMRC materials. In the experiment, the long form of guidance (LONG) refers to the set of downloadable and printable PDF help sheets available on the U.K. government website.[16] The short form of guidance (SHORT) refers to the information contained in the pop-up boxes on the HMRC online tax return. The items covered in both forms of guidance are mostly identical. However, there are notable differences in the information provided and the delivery form between the paper and the online guidance. First, for the same item, the long-form guidance is generally more detailed than the short. Second, how the information is delivered also differs. The short-form guidance appears as pop-up information boxes right next to the item in the tax form. With the exogenous variation implemented in the experiment, we are able to disentangle the differential effects of guidance contents and delivery form on voluntary tax compliance.

The first component of the experimental software was a set of instructions that explained the task. The instructions included details of the calculation of tax payable as 20 percent of the tax liability defined as the difference between declared income and expenses, and of the random chance of audit (set at 50 percent) and the calculation of fines for unpaid taxes, based on payment of the unpaid tax plus an additional 100 percent of the unpaid tax. Numerical details were presented for a number of examples of different filing decisions, based on a simple profile rather than the actual profile presented to subjects. The instructions detailed the incentive scheme to participants, in particular, the payment of a fixed £5 show-up fee and the conversion of any balance in the experimental system at the end of the session to pounds at a rate of 1,000 ECU to £3. The instructions also detailed the presence of assistance with the tax-filing decision based on the treatment.

The tax filing components consisted of three screens. The first screen allowed subjects to enter values for a number of expense fields. The value of the subject's income, as shown on the profile, was pre-populated and un-editable. The second, the tax filing screen, showed participants their tax calculation based on the value of expenses they had entered and the default income level. Subjects were invited to either alter their tax declaration, which would return them to the previous submitted screen, or to submit their tax return. Upon submission of the tax return, subjects were shown the third and final page of the tax filing component of the system. On this page subjects were informed of their tax payment, whether they had been selected for audit, and in the case of any audit, what the result of the audit was and any additional taxes or penalties to be paid. Finally, subjects

---

[16]See https://www.gov.uk/self-assessment-forms-and-helpsheets.

were directed to complete an online questionnaire as part of the software that asked them questions about their motivations for choices in the experiment as well as gathering demographic details.

Experimental Treatments

Original treatments

The initial set of experiments focused on three treatments in terms of the effect on compliance of assistance materials without the use of phone or online help. The treatments were decomposed into two parts. The first part addressed the content of the materials, in terms of the form of guidance: LONG used HMRC printed materials, while SHORT used HMRC guidance from the self-assessment tax filing website. The second component addressed the delivery form of the assistance. Assistance was either provided to subjects in print, referred to as PAPER, or provided through the pop-up information box, referred to as ONLINE. The three treatments detailed in Table 5.2 were undertaken in the first stage.

From Table 5.2, it can be seen that no SHORT_PAPER treatment was conducted. Although it was felt that while this treatment may have added some insight, the results that would have been obtained would probably not be worth the cost of running the treatment. A further comment on this omission is presented after the results.

Table 5.2. Stage 1 Treatments

Treatment Name	Description
LONG_PAPER	HMRC long form guidance delivered on paper
LONG_ONLINE	HMRC long form guidance delivered as online pop-up box
SHORT_ONLINE	HMRC short form guidance delivered as online pop-up box

Source: Authors' calculations.
Note: HMRC = Her Majesty's Revenue and Customs.

Additional treatments with a support line

Two additional treatments were run in which subjects were offered the opportunity for additional guidance through a support line. In all cases, the SHORT_ONLINE guidance was used. In one set of treatments the laboratory computers were preinstalled with Skype and with a link to call a tax advisor. Subjects were told in the instructions and on the tax form that they could call through Skype if they required assistance. In a further set of sessions, telephones were installed in the laboratory with a fixed number to dial. Subjects were told they could use the phone to gain additional guidance on the instructions and on the tax form. They were also given a note with the direct number to call in case they were unfamiliar with the direct call mechanism.

Students who had previously undertaken the experiment in the first round of experiments were asked if they would wish to serve as paid advisors in the experiment. Ten advisors were recruited and attended a training session where they were given a document detailing the process of how to handle a call from a subject. Having worked through the process, advisors then undertook a series of practice calls with one another to complete their testing. The advisors were then recruited for each of the sessions requiring advisors ready to respond to calls for guidance. The advisors followed scripts with standard answers.

Experimental sessions

Sessions were conducted in the experimental laboratory at the University of Exeter. For the majority of the experiment, participants were undergraduate students at the university. A final session with advisors available was run using professional services staff recruited from the university. In a typical session, there were on average 20 (for original treatments) or 10 (for the additional treatments) subjects per session. In total, 266 subjects participated.

Results

Table 5.3 summarizes the overall tax filing error rate by different treatments for stage 1. The error rate here is calculated as the percentage of the population who fail to declare the correct amount of allowable expenses (the correct amounts of allowable expenses for each of the items are outlined in Table 5.1). We include both underpayment of taxes (claiming more expenses or making positive errors) and overpayment of taxes (claiming lower expenses or making negative errors) in calculating the overall error rate. Across all treatments, around 98 percent of the population make errors in their tax filing. And most people made an error on the positive side, that is, they over-claim expenses and underpay taxes. However, still about 9 percent under-claim expenses and overpay taxes. Tables 4.4 and 4.5 detail the magnitude of those errors.

Table 5.3. Overall Error Rate by Treatment			
Treatment	**Observations**	**Overall Error Rate (percent)**	**Population Overpaying Taxes (percent)**
SHORT_ONLINE	79	97	10
LONG_PAPER	78	100	12
LONG_ONLINE	79	97	6

Source: Authors' calculations.

Table 5.4 shows that the average amount of underpayment accounts for about 27 percent of the total taxes to pay. In comparison, the average overpayment (Table 5.5) amounts to about 17 percent of total taxes to pay. While some subjects (9.5 percent of the sample) under-claim on the amount of expenses they are entitled to (and thereby overpay their tax due), the majority of subjects over-claim in that amount, leading to underpayment of tax due on average.

Figure 5.3. Average Underpayment of Taxes by Treatment

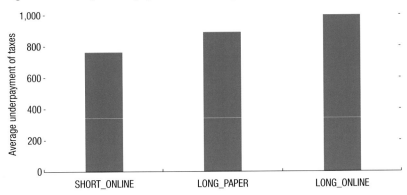

Source: Authors' calculations.

Table 5.4. Underpayment by Treatment			
Treatment	**Observations**	**Average Underpayment**	**As Percent Tax to Pay**
SHORT_ONLINE	69	937.9	24.7
LONG_PAPER	69	1113.9	29.4
LONG_ONLINE	72	1138.6	30

Source: Authors' calculations.

Table 5.5. Overpayment by Treatment			
Treatment	**Observations**	**Average Overpayment**	**As Percent Tax to Pay**
SHORT_ONLINE	8	554.5	14.6
LONG_PAPER	9	795.1	21
LONG_ONLINE	5	560.6	14.8

Source: Authors' calculations.

Next, we compare the average tax underpayment among the three treatments. As Figure 5.3 shows, people tend to underpay by the least amount in the SHORT_ONLINE treatment and by the largest amount in the LONG_ONLINE treatment. The difference between these two values is statistically significant. This suggests that it is the content of the short-form guidance that causes a higher level of compliance, since we are holding the delivery form constant. Although on average people underpay taxes less in the LONG_PAPER than in the LONG_ONLINE treatment, the difference is not statistically significant. This implies the surprising conclusion that whether the information of the guidance is delivered using the pop-up information boxes or printed paper does not seem to cause a significant change in compliance behavior. Ordinary least squares regression analysis also confirms the above findings.

Table 5.6 reports the regression results. The dependent variable is the tax filing error (the difference between the subjects' correct allowance and claimed allowance, which can be positive or negative). The control group for the regressions is the LONG_ONLINE. The regressor SHORT_ONLINE is a dummy variable, equal to 1 if it is the SHORT_ONLINE treatment and 0 otherwise. Likewise, LONG_PAPER is also a dummy variable, equal to 1 if it is the LONG_PAPER treatment and 0 otherwise. From (1), we can see that people in the SHORT_ONLINE treatment claim 239 ECU (or 6 percent) less than people in the LONG_ONLINE treatment. This is a rather large effect, especially considering the number of people in the treatment. In comparison, how the information is delivered also has positive impact on tax compliance, but the effect is fairly small and insignificant. From (2), the SHORT_ONLINE treatment effect persists while controlling for gender and age of the subjects. We observe no effect of gender or age on filing errors.

Table 5.6. Ordinary Least Squares on Tax Filing Errors with Treatment Effects

	(1)	(2)
SHORT_ONLINE	239.177*	283.604**
	(140.63)	(140.96)
LONG_PAPER	108.613	96.203
	(155.07)	(159.47)
Male		−48.739
		(121.963)
Age		44.485
		(30.35)
Constant	−1002.215***	−1819.429***
	(103.10)	(624.25)
Number of Observations	236	229

Source: Authors' calculations.
Note: Robust standard errors are reported in parentheses. * indicates significance level at 10 percent, ** at 5 percent, *** at 1 percent.

We conducted similar analyses on the data from the additional treatments with either Skype or telephone support. We find that people in SHORT_ONLINE treatment with support behave similar to the original SHORT_ONLINE treatment. The main explanation is that only 10 percent (3 out of 30) subjects used the support line. From the post experimental survey, over 65 percent of subjects attributed their reason for not calling to the provision of sufficient information.

Our result, that appropriate guidance can increase the degree of tax compliance, is in line with previous studies into the effect of tax assistance on compliance behavior. As noted, many of these studies were conducted using students as subjects, so the subjects typically have little experience of the taxation system. This has raised questions about generalizability. The results from the student sample used in this study could, therefore, be best considered as applying to a set of taxpayers new to the self-assessment system, though only 34 percent of the sample responded positively to a question asking how likely they thought they would be self-employed in the future.

Our study differs from other investigations of the effect of customer service on tax compliance in that previous studies have been based on abstract settings, with a focus on the effect of simple information, revealing either a single correct value or a narrowing of the correct values appropriate for a specific field. In the experiment presented here, the goal was to investigate the effect of customer service using real-world examples of complexity in filing and the associated actual tax guidance. This design allows us to better examine our subjects' decisions in the context of the real materials, but comes at the cost of the loss of some degree of environmental control.

The main result, based on comparison of the SHORT_ONLINE and LONG_ONLINE treatments, may overlook an important effect arising from the design of the experiment. The SHORT_ONLINE treatment reflects an operational reality: we used text from the HMRC online system so the information had been tailored for each of the fields in the online tax return. This design may lead to low search costs for tax filers for simple issues, in particular, questions of positive inclusion such as whether an expense should be filed in that particular field. The LONG_ONLINE treatment is artificial, however, in that the long-form guidance was simply pasted into the online pop-up. There is no such tailoring, therefore, and the tax filer was left to search through the full information.

On the other hand, such searching may have led the tax filer to discover issues of negative inclusion. For example, looking to see if an expense should be included in a particular field it might lead to the discovery that it should be filed in a different field. The results are consistent, nonetheless, with a reduction in search cost through guidance items with positive inclusion.

A fourth treatment using the short-form guidance on chapter materials may have shed further light on the issues by allowing further comparisons. But such a design again would have been artificial in that there is no such current operational reality. It was not clear how the linking of the short form guidance in chapter format to the tax form could best be performed to match that inherent in the SHORT_ONLINE treatment.

The post-experimental survey provides subjective evidence about the unintentional tax evasion. Among subjects, asked how they approached this experiment, 58 percent indicated that "I want to get my return right." Another 30 percent suggested that "I don't mind small errors." Only 12 percent said "I did not mind having errors on my form if it benefited me financially." A closer look at the error patterns suggests that the majority of subjects made an effort to determine the correct declaration values (Annex 4.2 provides detailed analysis of the error pattern). However, despite their efforts, they failed to get the tax return right.

More than 65 percent of the sample, meanwhile, indicated that the guidance provided sufficient information for them to complete the task (from the additional treatments). It may be of interest to further examine the gap between the high error rate and the level of overconfidence among taxpayers. Additionally, questions remain as to the characteristics of the contents that are the driving force of the behavior change and more detailed studies should be carried out with those questions in mind.

Digitalization and Tax Policy

The focus of the discussion here has been the impact of digitalization on tax administration in the near future. This is a necessary prelude to an analysis of policy, because administration determines what is possible, and practical value is limited in constructing a policy that is not administratively feasible.[17] Furthermore, if administrative limitations result in a distorted version of a policy being implemented, then the outcome may be worse than from using a less desirable but implementable policy. The key observation is that technology does not just affect administration, but can transform what is possible in tax policy and, eventually, perhaps will even change how to conceptualize tax theory.

The first part of this section considers what policy innovations are possible in the near future as taxation moves online. The second takes a more fundamental perspective on tax policy and technology and speculates on what may ultimately occur.[18]

Policy Innovation

The focus of HMRC's Making Tax Digital for individual taxation is the personal tax account that will provide real-time data on incomes, deductible expenses, tax payments, and tax credits. The simplest implication is that this moves the burden of the tax calculation from the individual (or the employer under pay-as-you-earn (PAYE) onto the revenue agency. It also removes the need for the current PAYE system, because the personal tax account could be linked directly to the individual's bank account for regular payment of taxes. This would reduce the administrative burden on employers, but may not be advantageous for the revenue agency.[19] A more significant advance from automating the calculation at the revenue agency is to permit greater complexity in the structure of marginal tax rates. Present systems that use a limited number of bands and marginal rates have no justification in tax theory, but reflect only computational convenience. They cannot provide the targeted incentives that many tax analysts consider justified (Mirrlees and others 2011) and can also create perverse incentives when combined with other features of the tax and benefit system.

If the system approaches anywhere close to using real-time data collection, then it becomes possible to extend a PAYE-like system to all taxpayers, including the self-employed. This can be implemented provided receipts of the self-employed can be matched to payments from third parties to confirm their tax status. This would remove the need for *ex post* payment of large sums of tax, easing the burden of payment and smoothing cash flow for the individual. Default would be less

---

[17]A detailed development of this argument into a system-based perspective on taxation can be found in Slemrod and Gillitzer (2013).

[18]See also the discussion of these issues in Chapter 2.

[19]Under the present U.K. system of PAYE, employers provide an unpaid tax collection and enforcement service.

likely, which would reduce the need for the revenue agency to engage in chasing defaulters and in debt collection.

In addition, a system that tracked incomes and expenditures would ensure correct treatment of allowable expenses and, consequently, reduce errors. As revealed by the experiment reported in the previous section, such errors are commonplace in the completion of returns. For the United Kingdom, the latest figures for 2014–15 show that errors (£3.2 billion) and failure to take reasonable care (£5.5 billion) constituted almost a quarter of the £36 billion tax gap (HMRC 2016). This illustrates the potential benefits of an intelligent system that removes the possibility of error or ability not to take care. A truly advanced system could adjust tax charges according to the flow and the timing of income in recognition of the lumpiness of income for many self-employed.

The discussion of the experimental evidence made frequent reference to the compliance impact of pre-population and customer service. Noncompliance is a significant issue for all tax agencies, so it is important to consider if digitalization might prove beneficial in this respect. The noncompliant population (for income tax, similar comments apply to other taxes) can be broken broadly into deliberate cheats who report a false income level, moonlighters who report income from one or more jobs legitimately but have other income from additional employment that is not reported, and "ghosts" who simply do not appear in the system.[20] Our discussion has mostly focused on the impact of pre-population and customer service upon the first two groups. If digitalization increases the information received by the revenue agency from third parties, then it will necessarily lead to an eventual reduction in noncompliance. We say "eventual" because the experiments have revealed that pre-population that is incomplete or incorrect can act as a signal of limited information and encourage noncompliance.

Ghosts are the most difficult group for a tax agency to monitor and control. HMRC is unlikely to be the only tax agency that has very limited data on the extent of the ghost problem. Since they are, by definition, outside the official system, there is no tax record to even form the basis of an investigation. It is with this group that digitalization holds the most promise for increasing compliance. The growth of digital records coupled with the linking of records will ensure that it becomes increasingly difficult to avoid leaving a digital fingerprint somewhere in the system. There may be no tax records, but it is hard to avoid a birth, school, medical, or welfare record, or in some cases a criminal record. If all systems were linked then the absence of a tax record for an individual could be easily flagged by the system and act as a marker for investigation. This may not directly affect the motivation behind becoming a ghost, but it reduces the probability that a ghost can continue unobserved.

The discussion so far has identified some minor revisions to the operation of the U.K. system. We now explore the potential for digitalization to permit fundamental changes to the way in which individuals are taxed.

---

[20]This discussion does not cover groups engaged in criminal fraud.

Before proceeding to this, it is worth noting that the first impact of successful digitalization may be implementation of the current system as intended. Noncompliance coupled with auditing and punishment result in the effective tax system being significantly different from the intended system. Hashimzade and others (2015) show that the effect of noncompliance is to create a group of taxpayers who pay very low effective rates of tax (the noncompliant who are not detected), a group who pay the correct rate of tax (the compliant), and a final group who pay high effective rates of tax (the noncompliant who are caught and eventually pay the correct tax plus a fine). It is very difficult to conceive of any scenario in which this would be the intended outcome of tax policy design. Hence, digitalization which reduces noncompliance can ensure the intended system is more closely implemented.

The significant issues of whether digitalization can support any major changes in tax policy and whether policy can be improved by fundamental change are now addressed. Linking currently separate data systems can allow for policy innovation in addition to the better administration already noted. Under current arrangements a revenue service receives a flow of data about a taxpayer's income that is simply stored until the time at which the annual tax return is compiled. The revenue service may hold other data—such as residential address, or sex—but this is can be of limited value for tax design. What we have in mind here are potentially valid reasons for differentiating personal taxes according to individual characteristics. Arguments have been advanced that a lower marginal rate of tax on people aged over 65 will encourage them to remain productive in the workforce, and that lower average rates can help overcome disincentives to labor force participation for females with young children or others who face high fixed costs of work.[21] Both variations from the standard tax schedule are possible without digitalization, but would be administratively easier if operated through a personal tax account using data that are already held in administrative databases that could be linked to tax data. The benefits of digitalization for capital taxes, corporate taxes, and value-added tax are explored in Chapter 2.

A further benefit of linking datasets is that it makes possible the seamless integration of taxation and benefits. Many examples have been presented of how the interaction of the tax system and the benefit system can result in the creation of perverse incentives. This is particularly a problem in systems, such as in the United Kingdom, that apply tax at the individual level but allocate benefits at the family level. The benefit of digitalization and linking of datasets is that the system can be administered in close to real time with an online environment easing the input of updated information.[22] This cannot remove all the conflicts caused by individual/family distinctions but can lead to some alleviation. Pushing this fur-

---

[21]See Mirrlees and others (2012).

[22]The U.K. Child Tax Credit and Working Tax Credit introduced in April 2003 were based on annual assessment. A change in family circumstances over the year could result in overpayment and a consequent demand from HMRC for repayment. In the first year of operation, approximately one-third of claimants were overpaid a total of £1.9 billion.

ther, the current system of tax credits could be developed into a fully fledged negative income tax system, with all benefits collapsed into a negative income tax that was fully and automatically responsive to changes in circumstances. As examples, linking tax data with educational data could deliver a reduction in tax in the month before a child starts senior school to assist a family with related school expenditures, while linking with health data could automatically adjust the tax level without further eligibility testing. In brief, linkage would make possible the automatic implementation of a range of targeted assistance without the need for testing of eligibility.

The argument that a consumption tax is preferable to an income tax because it does not distort the saving decision has a long history in public finance. Meade (1978) was a forceful proponent of the idea and the arguments were reinforced in Mirrlees and others (2012). A flat consumption tax can be implemented by a uniform and comprehensive value-added tax.[23] A non-uniform value-added tax permits some progression in the consumption tax if budget shares for commodities are correlated with individual characteristics. However, if the correlation is weak the progression will be poorly targeted. Meade (1978) demonstrated that a progressive consumption tax could be implemented if income and contributions to eligible saving instruments were recorded. The consumption tax could then be levied on the difference between income and eligible savings with, potentially, any chosen degree of progressivity. The drawback with this approach is that it requires annual assessment to determine the tax base, and so runs into the problems of payment difficulty and default that withholding schemes such UK PAYE are designed to avoid.

The limits to what can be achieved by digitalization are met when the implementation of a consumption tax is considered. For people in employment, the flow of income is fairly smooth and predictable so a consumption tax can be implemented (approximately) using a withholding tax based on either actual saving in recorded assets (accepting the lumpiness in tax payments this may cause) or a presumptive level of saving (which would smooth tax payment). An annual adjustment would be required unless actual saving was sufficiently smooth (or equal to presumptive saving if this method were used), so annual interaction with the revenue service would remain necessary.

Further progress meets with a fundamental difficulty even if comprehensive data on purchases were linked to income data. This difficulty is that many significant household purchases are very lumpy (such as the purchase of a house or car) even when the resulting flow of consumption is smooth. Implementing a consumption tax based on observed purchases would tax expenditures but not the flow of consumption. This is why the arguments made in Chapter 2 applied only to perishable consumption goods. To tax the latter would require imputation of the flow of consumption since it is not directly observed. The housing services tax proposed in Mirrlees and others (2011) proposed using housing rents to measure

---

[23]Flat here meaning the same marginal tax rate on all consumption with no exemption.

consumption flow, and similar methods could be used for other goods, so the problems are not insurmountable. The main point is that digitalization in itself does little to assist with this practical difficulty.

The Foundations of Tax Policy

The fundamental question for tax policy is *why* do we want to tax? The answer determines *what* we would want to tax if there were no limitations on the design of the system. This determines the nature of the ideal tax system. How we are *able* to tax is determined by the available technology for tax administration. The theory of optimal tax design studies the nature of the tax system that emerges as the best attainable approximation of the ideal tax system.[24] The underlying premise of the economic theory of tax policy is that individuals have unalterable personal characteristics, some of which are unobservable, but make observable market transactions. The ideal tax system for equity purposes would be based on the immutable personal characteristics that generate differences in economic potential between people. Remarkably, using these characteristics as the tax base is also the most efficient way to tax: there is no change in behavior that can reduce the tax burden and, hence, there is no deadweight loss.

By definition, an unobservable personal characteristic cannot be used directly as the tax base. The imperfect tax system that is implemented has instead to be based on the observable personal characteristics—some of which may not be relevant for determining economic potential—and observable market transactions. Using transactions for the tax base causes two sources of deviation from the ideal. First, the observed transactions may be imperfectly correlated with unobservable personal characteristics. Second, an incentive can be created to change transactions to reduce tax liability, giving rise to a deadweight loss. These ideas were first clearly expressed by Mirrlees (1971) in his seminal study of income taxation and have become the foundation of tax theory. The models of tax theory focus on differences in endowments and preferences and explore the nature of the optimum tax systems that emerge. One general conclusion of the theory is that we should compensate for differences in endowments but not in choices.[25] Another way to express this is that the role of the tax system is to achieve the equalization of economic potential. What people choose to do with their economic potential should not affect the design of the tax system. For example, if two individuals have the same level of labor market skill, but one chooses to work while the other does not, then there is no justification for redistributing income between the two. Hence, it is argued that it is economic potential that matters, not choices.

When this view of the world is pushed into a practical interpretation some difficulties start to emerge. The model assumes that economic potential is a

---

[24]The following discussion does not consider equality of opportunity. This could also be a motive for a tax-transfer scheme, but a direct solution would always be preferable.

[25]Banks and Diamond (2010) explores this argument.

fundamental and unalterable characteristic. This cannot be the case since potential reflects both ability and training, so it seems natural to search for something deeper that determines ability.[26] It is here that we currently run into difficulties because of our incomplete understanding of what makes one person a talented musician and another a talented swimmer. Superficially, it is possible to point at various physical traits but the real question is what determines these traits. At present our conceptualization of the unobservable personal characteristics as an endowment of "ability" reflects our current ignorance. Only when we reach a position where the true underlying source of differences are understood can we proceed with the implementation of an ideal tax.

The Future

Current modeling in tax design is founded on the assumption that there are unalterable personal characteristics that determine economic potential. When some, or all, of these characteristics are unobservable the tax system has to tax observed market transactions as a proxy. The question is, will technological advances make currently unobservable characteristics observable and, hence, allow the implementation of novel taxes?

To implement the ideal tax system we need to determine *what* the relevant characteristics are and *how* these characteristics determine economic potential. These two requirements are equally important, and the first alone is not sufficient. For example, suppose we conclude that what matters for economic potential is an individual's genetic code. Current technology allows us to read the genetic code at reasonably modest cost. What we must also possess for this reading to be of any value for tax purposes is knowledge of the link between the genetic code and economic potential. Such knowledge—with the possible exception of some weak correlations—is almost entirely absent at present. Without it we cannot use our current knowledge of the genetic code to progress any deeper with our tax theory.

Putting aside current limits on knowledge and technology, it is interesting to engage in speculation about potential consequences of technology. For the sake of argument assume individual economic potential is determined by genetics alone.[27] It is possible that research will eventually unlock the genetic code and identify the mapping from genetics to economic potential. In the context of the discussion of tax theory above, this will make genetic makeup the personal characteristic on which the ideal tax system should be based. The interpretation of this reasoning is that behind the veil of ignorance all individuals are a genetic blank canvas. We know what outcome will be achieved by each set of genetics and this determines how we should redistribute. Crossing the veil of ignorance then

---

[26]Extensive literature debates whether "genius" stems from natural ability or from hard work. It seems natural to believe it takes both.

[27]Considerable literature on genius debates the relative importance of ability and training in explaining exceptional performers. By focusing on potential, it is possible to sidestep this debate.

assigns a genetic structure of each individual and the tax policy is then implemented. As observed in Logue and Slemrod (2008), the tax system will then impose redistribution from those with genetics linked to economic success to those with less successful genetics to a degree that is merited by social perceptions of equity.[28] This may be extreme but it is where we are led by following our existing representation of the optimal tax problem.

However, we have not reached the end of the story. The difficulty for the application of tax theory is that—even with current technology—genetics can be changed. The development of CRISPR and other gene splicing techniques already allows the replacement of sections of the genetic code. There can be no doubt that these techniques will advance in the future and become more accurate, even to the point where the genetic code is entirely a matter of choice. Although the legal system in the United States and many other countries does not currently allow the modification of the human genome, this is a position that will prove very difficult to sustain. It might seem an extreme claim, but if the human genome can be modified, then it is no longer an unchangeable characteristic. We can conceive of parents selecting the genetics of children based on a range of factors from among which tax implications cannot be excluded. Basing the tax system on genetics in a situation in which genetics can be modified then creates a new and disturbing direction in which tax policy can have a distortionary impact on behavior. We would lose any notion of there being an ideal and non-distortionary tax system and have to face the consequences of taxation potentially influencing the genetic mix of the population.

The conclusion of this discussion is that technological advance may fundamentally impact our conception of how tax policy is formulated. We may reach a point at which there are no unalterable characteristics that determine economic potential. Instead, economic potential may be a matter of choice through genetic design. If this position is ever achieved the current foundations for optimal tax theory no longer apply. There will be no unchangeable characteristics, so there will be no ideal and non-distortionary tax system. The achievement of technology may just be to push the margin at which taxation is distortionary to another level.

CONCLUSION

The implementation of digital technology for tax administration has proceeded at different rates across countries. Some countries have been quick to adopt new technologies and others, including the United Kingdom and the United States, have been more cautious. Consequently, in these countries digital technology has had little to no impact on tax policy beyond the possibilities opened up

---

[28]There are obviously many practical issues being glossed over. But it should be noted that we are not necessarily discussing a one-off lifetime transfer that would require knowledge of the future value of alternative genetics. Instead, the taxes could be annual and matched each year with the current value of genetics.

for data mining to improve management information. The reluctance is understandable given the impact that unforeseen consequences may have on compliance and revenues.

The chapter has described how economic experiments can be used to test the impact of new digital platforms. The results of the experiments are not always as expected, but can be understood when interpreted using behavioral economics. The revenue service is an embodiment of authority, which explains the reluctance of experimental subjects to alter pre-populated values; but a conception of fairness will lead those same subjects to obtain compensation by exaggerating expenses. Digital systems should of course be tested exhaustively for technical functioning before implementation. We believe the results of the experiments provide strong grounds for advocating that digital systems also be thoroughly tested for behavioral impacts.

We have also looked ahead to speculate on how digitalization may impact tax policy. Digitalization has considerable promise for allowing the implementation of tax systems that would not be possible without it. This is particularly true when administrative data sets can be linked to fully exploit the potential of the information that is held. When we explore what future developments in technology can achieve, it becomes clear that some fundamental questions concerning the foundations of tax policy have to be resolved. Our current theory is based on current constraints on policy. In particular, existing tax theory judges potential tax systems by how they perform relative to the ideal system that would be used in the absence of constraints on the observation of economic potential. How we might want to tax if technology can relax these constraints requires a significant re-imagining of the theory.

REFERENCES

Alm, J. 2012. "Measuring, Explaining, and Controlling Tax Evasion: Lessons from Theory, Experiments, and Field Studies." *International Tax and Public Finance* 19 (1): 54–77.

Alm, J., K. M. Bloomquist, and M. McKee. 2015. "On the External Validity of Laboratory Tax Compliance Experiments." *Economic Inquiry* 53 (2): 1170–86.

Alm, J., T. L. Cherry, M. Jones, and M. McKee. 2010. "Taxpayer Information Assistance Services and Tax Compliance Behaviour." *Journal of Economic Psychology* 31 (4): 577–86.

———. 2012. "Social Programs as Positive Inducements for Tax Participation." *Journal of Economic Behaviour and Organization* 84 (1): 85–96.

Alm, J., M. B. Cronshaw, and M. McKee. 1993. "Tax Compliance with Endogenous Audit Selection Rules." *KYKLOS* 46 (1): 27–45.

Alm, J., B. R. Jackson, and M. McKee. 1993. "Fiscal Exchange, Collective Decision Institutions, and Tax Compliance." *Journal of Economic Behaviour and Organization* 22 (3): 285–303.

Alm, J., and M. McKee. 2004. "Tax Compliance as a Coordination Game." *Journal of Economic Behaviour and Organization* 54: 297–312.

Alm, J., M. McKee, and W. Beck. 1990. "Amazing Grace: Tax Amnesties and Compliance." *National Tax Journal* 43 (1): 23–37.

Banks, J., and P. A. Diamond. 2010. "The Base for Direct Taxation." In *Dimensions of Tax Design*. Oxford: University Press.

Bazart, C., and M. Pickhardt. 2011. "Fighting Income Tax Evasion with Positive Rewards." *Public Finance Review* 39 (1): 124–49.

Bruner, D., M. Jones, M. McKee, and C. A. Vossler. 2015. "Tax Reporting Behavior: Underreporting Opportunities and Prepopulated Tax Returns." Working Paper 15–11, Department of Economics, Appalachian State University, Boone, NC.

Choo, C. Y. L., M. A. Fonseca, and G. D. Myles. 2016. "Do Students Behave Like Real Taxpayers in the Lab? Evidence from a Real Effort Tax Compliance Experiment." *Journal of Economic Behaviour and Organisation* 124: 102–14.

Clotfelter, C. T. 1983. "Tax Evasion and Tax Rates: An Analysis of Individual Returns." *The Review of Economics and Statistics* 65 (3): 363–73.

Collins, J. H., and D. R. Plumlee. 1991. "The Taxpayer's Labor and Reporting Decision: The Effect of Audit Schemes." *The Accounting Review* 66 (3): 559–76.

Coricelli, G., M. Joffily, C. Montmarquette, and M.-C. Villeval. 2010. "Cheating, Emotions, and Rationality: An Experiment on Tax Evasion." *Experimental Economics* 13 (2): 226–47.

Fonseca, M. A., and S. B. Grimshaw. Forthcoming. "Do Behavioral Nudges in Pre-Populated Tax Forms Affect Compliance? Experimental Evidence with Real Taxpayers." *Journal of Public Policy and Marketing*.

Fortin, B., G. Lacroix, and M. C. Villeval. 2007. "Tax Evasion and Social Interactions." *Journal of Public Economics* 91 (8): 2089–112.

Graetz, M. J., and L. L. Wilde. 1985. "The Economics of Tax Compliance: Fact and Fantasy." *National Tax Journal* 38: 355–63.

Hashimzade, N., G. D. Myles, F. H. Page, and M. Rablen. 2015. "The Use of Agent-Based Modelling to Investigate Tax Compliance." *Economics of Governance* 16 (2): 143–64.

Hashimzade, N., G. D. Myles, and B. Tran-Nam. 2013. "Applications of Behavioural Economics to Tax Evasion." *Journal of Economic Surveys* 27 (5): 941–77.

HM Revenue Commission (HMRC). 2016. "Measuring Tax Gaps 2016 Edition: Tax Gap Estimates." London.

International Monetary Fund (IMF). 2015. "Current Challenges in Revenue Mobilization: Improving Tax Compliance." IMF Staff Report, Washington, DC.

Kotakorpi, K., and J. P. Laamanen. 2016. "Prefilled Income Tax Returns and Tax Compliance: Evidence from a Natural Experiment." Tampere Economic Working Paper, School of Management, University of Tampere, Finland.

Ledyard, J. O. 1995. "Public Goods: A Survey of Experimental Research." In *Handbook of Experimental Economics*, edited by J. Kagel and A. Roth. Princeton, NJ: Princeton University Press.

Lipsey, R. G. 1979. *An Introduction to Positive Economics*. London: Weidenfeld and Nicholson.

Logue, K., and J. Slemrod. 2008. "Genes as Tags: The Tax Implications of Widely Available Genetic Information." *National Tax Journal* 61 (4): 843–63.

McKee, M., C. Siladke, and C. A. Vossler. 2011. "Behavioural Dynamics of Tax Compliance Under an Information Services Initiative." MPRA Working Paper 38865, University Library of Munich, Munich.

Meade, J. E. 1978. *The Structure and Reform of Direct Taxation*. London: George Allen & Unwin.

Mirrlees, J. A. 1971. "An Exploration in the Theory of Optimum Income Taxation." *Review of Economic Studies* 38 (2): 175–208.

Mirrlees, J., S. Adam, T. Besley, R. Blundell, S. Bond, R. Chote, M. Gammie, P. Johnson, G. Myles, and J. Poterba. 2011. *Tax by Design*. Oxford: Oxford University Press for the Institute for Fiscal Studies.

———. 2012. "The Mirrlees Review: A Proposal for Systematic Tax Reform." *National Tax Journal* 65 (3): 655–84.

National Audit Office. 2016. *The Quality of Service for Personal Taxpayers*. London: National Audit Office.

Organisation for Economic Co-operation and Development (OECD). 2008. "Third Party Reporting Arrangements and Pre-Filled Tax Returns: The Danish and Swedish Approaches." Paris.

Shu, L. L., N. Mazar, F. Gino, D. Ariely, and M. H. Bazerman. 2012. "Signing at the Beginning Makes Ethics Salient and Decreases Dishonest Self-Reports in Comparison to Signing at the End." Proceedings of the National Academy of Sciences 109 (38): 15197–200.

Slemrod, J., and C. Gillitzer. 2013. *Tax Systems*. Cambridge, MA: MIT Press.

Starmer, C. 1999. "Experiments in Economics: Should We Trust the Dismal Scientists in White Coats?" *Journal of Economic Methodology* 6 (1): 1–30.

Sunstein, C. R., and R. H. Thaler. 2009. *Nudge: Improving Decisions about Health, Wealth and Happiness*. New York: Penguin.

Tan, F., and A. Yim. 2014., "Can Strategic Uncertainty Help Deter Tax Evasion? An Experiment on Auditing Rules." *Journal of Economic Psychology* 40: 161–74.

Vossler, C. A., and M. McKee. 2013. "Efficient Tax Reporting: The Effects of Taxpayer Information Services." Working Paper 13–24, Department of Economics, Appalachian State University, Boone, NC.

ANNEX 5.1

Tax Profile for the Experiment

In this experiment, you will take the role of Tom, a self-employed fitness instructor. During this tax year, you have earned ECU 25,200 of income from running fitness classes. You are in the process of completing your tax return form, and need to decide what expenses to claim as tax allowances.

Your files show the following for this tax year.

Secondhand car sales receipt			Year 2014–15	
	06-Apr-2014			
XXX	xxx			
XXX	xxx		Personal journeys	2,000
XXX	xxx			
XXX	xxx		Travel between home and class	8,000
CO_2 emission	165g/km			
Total	ECU 1,500			

1. You bought a secondhand car to help you get to and from your classes.

2. Here is the receipt for the purchase of your car and a summary of mileage, fuel, servicing expenses, and insurance costs.

3. You run your fitness classes every evening in a local church hall, which you paid ECU 5,760 to hire.

4. You paid ECU 175 for printing flyers to advertise your fitness classes.

5. You paid ECU 1,200 for a gym membership to stay fit.

6. Your household bills amounted to ECU 7,500 for annual rent, gas, electricity, water rates, and council tax. You spend about one day a month (12 days a year) working from your home (a studio flat) designing posters and leaflets about

Figure 5.2.1. Subjects Entering Particular Values for Phone Costs

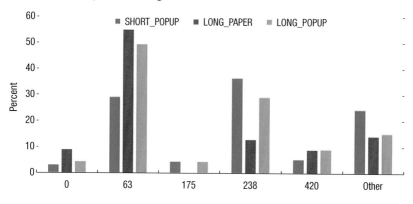

Source: Authors' calculations.

the classes, calling new members and dealing with the finances and administration.

7. Your mobile phone bills were ECU 420; only 15 percent of total usage was for business purposes.

ANNEX 5.2

Analysis of Errors

Analysis of specific fields yields interesting results. Subjects appear to have taken time to complete the information given to them in the profile and the tax guidance, but not fully able to file a correct tax report. As a first example, the correct value to enter for phone costs was 238 ECU, because the flyer costs of 175 were appropriate for this category as was 15 percent of the 420 ECU mobile phone bill (63 ECU). Figure 5.2.1 shows that the majority of values entered reflect these numbers in some way.

More subjects put 63 as the value in the LONG guidance-based treatments than in the SHORT guidance based treatment, where the response 238 was more popular suggesting that the correct field to enter the flyer costs into was more clear in the SHORT guidance. An offsetting value of 175 for the flyers can clearly be seen in the filings made for Other Expenses, shown in Figure 5.2.2.

A third example can be seen for values filed under rent. The correct value for this category was 6,007 ECU, comprised of 5,760 ECU for hire of the church hall and (12/365)*7,500 (247) as the appropriate value for use of the home for business purposes. Figure 5.2.3 shows the proportions of subjects filing particular values for rent by treatment.

Figure 5.2.2. Proportion of Subjects Entering Particular Values for Other Expenses

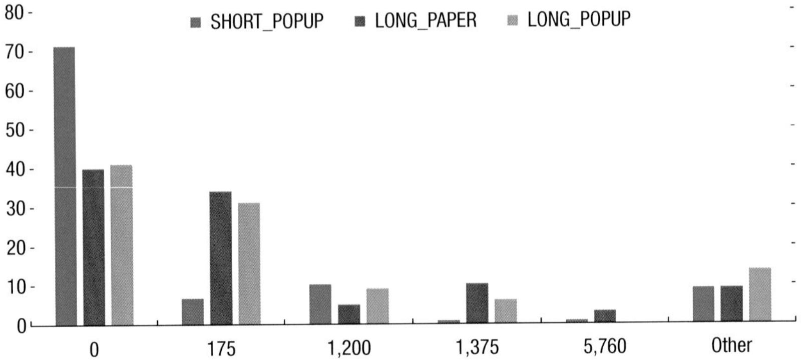

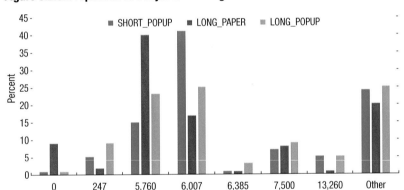

Source: Authors' calculations.

Figure 5.2.3. Proportion of Subjects Entering Particular Values for Rent

Source: Authors' calculations.

The pattern in Figure 5.2.3 for rent is similar to that shown in Figure 5.2.1 for phone costs in that the majority of values entered reflect a combination of the raw values and calculations, though some are wildly wrong, such as the value 13,260, which simply sums the value for church hall hire with the household rent bill. The higher proportion filing the correct value 6,007 in the SHORT guidance based treatment than for the LONG guidance treatment suggests that the mechanism for handling household rent was more apparent in the SHORT guidance. The figure of 6,385 arises as subjects (incorrectly) divide the household rent (7,500) by 12 and add that to the 5,760 figure for church hall hire.

Figure 5.2.4. Proportion of Subjects Entering Particular Values for Travel Expenses

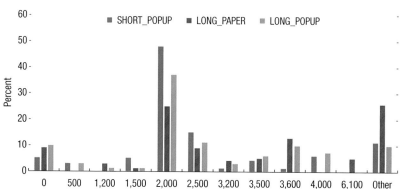

Source: Authors' calculations.

A final example is shown in Figure 5.2.4 for travel expenses. The actual correct value of travel expenses was zero as the use of the car to drive to and from the same place of work does not qualify as a taxable expense. The values reported in this field are, however, informative of subject behavior. Subjects were informed of a purchase of a car for 1,500 ECU and running costs of 2,500 ECU, 80 percent of which were for business purposed. The range of values filed includes 2,000 ECU (80 percent of running costs); 2,500 (the full running costs); 3,500 (80 percent of running costs plus purchase cost); 3,600 from application of simplified costs; 4,000 (total cost of car); and 6,100 from simplified costs plus running costs.

Once again, the figure suggests that subjects were working with the profile and the tax guidance but not quite able to get to the correct result. Notably, in all cases, the values used typically skew to over-claiming on expenses, as reflected in the previous results. It should also be noted however that this is designed into the profile, as there are items that subjects are required to exclude and therefore we cannot say from the results here that such over-claiming would apply more generally.

PART II

Innovations in
Fiscal Management

CHAPTER 6

Nowcashing

Using Daily Fiscal Data for Real-Time Macroeconomic Analysis

FLORIAN MISCH, BRIAN OLDEN, MARCOS POPLAWSKI-RIBEIRO, AND LAMYA KEJJI

Increasingly, countries at all levels of income are consolidating their government banking arrangements and implementing information technology (IT) systems designed to automate the management of public finances. These systems record information on thousands, and frequently millions, of government transactions, allowing construction of daily data series in a range of fiscal aggregates and indicators. This chapter shows how these data can complement conventional data and statistics for governments and researchers, in particular by enabling real-time macroeconomic analysis, which is not feasible using conventional fiscal statistics.

Fiscal data include information on revenue aggregates, such as revenue collected by tax type (such as income taxes, indirect taxes, and excises); public expenditure aggregates (such as the government wage bill, goods and services, and capital expenditure); and financing items (such as debt issuance and use of financial assets). Traditionally, analysis based on fiscal data is carried out using official fiscal statistics (monthly, quarterly, or even annual, depending on the country). These are frequently published with a significant lag. Even in those economies that produce monthly fiscal reports, publication delays can be long enough that it limits use for signaling imminent fiscal events or other macroeconomic shocks.

By contrast, using information from transactions processed through government financial management IT systems, fiscal data can be produced daily, and potentially even more frequently. In addition, reliability and accuracy of such

The authors thank Aqib Aslam, Samya Beidas-Strom, Cibelle Cesar Brasil, Oya Celasun, Alfredo Cuevas, Era Dabla-Norris, Leodelma de Marilac Félix, Vitor Gaspar, Sanjeev Gupta, Leandro Santos Gonçalves, Richard Hughes, Roberto Kodama, Otavio de Castro Neves, Eduardo Soares de Paiva, Andrea Pescatori, Mario Pessoa, Ruth Goodwin-Groen, Barbara Viana, Giovanni Bogea Viana, and Geneviève Verdier for helpful comments.

high frequency data are typically very high when measured in terms of ex post revisions (which tend to be small, at least in cash terms).

To date, this data source has largely been underexplored and underexploited, despite the seemingly obvious value that it can provide for a variety of stakeholders, including governments and multilateral organizations. For example, trends in daily fiscal data can mirror a large array of macroeconomic developments in real time. However, usage hinges on data availability and on whether useful information can be extracted and aggregated, given that daily fiscal data are inevitably subject to significant noise and complex seasonal patterns, and sometimes come in a highly disaggregated format.

The chapter makes two contributions to the public finance and relevant macroeconomic literature. First, it shows that due to the digitalization of public finances daily fiscal data are available and relatively easily accessible for a diverse range of countries. For some countries, daily cash flow data are even public (such as the United States and Brazil). Second, the chapter provides evidence that procedures to remove noise and seasonality from daily fiscal data are relatively easy to apply. As demonstrated through case studies, those procedures make such data useful for a variety of purposes, including (1) fiscal surveillance and management; (2) prediction of economic activity for the present, the near future, or the recent past, often referred to as *nowcasting*;[1] and (3) key analytical macro-fiscal work, such as research estimating the size of fiscal multipliers.

Taken together, the revolution in the use of IT systems over the past 20 years has created an opportunity to take advantage of high frequency and reliable fiscal data. Availability will only increase in the future, as the digitalization of public finances progresses and as more countries automate the recording and reporting of their fiscal activities. Ongoing improvements in technology and accounting and reporting standards will also improve the quality of high-frequency fiscal data. Finally, increasing demand for greater transparency in government operations is leading a push for more daily data.

This chapter first provides background information on the information technology generating daily fiscal data and broad characteristics of the data, then examines the characteristics of the data set. It follows with case studies, and finishes with a look at the future.

GENERATION OF DAILY FISCAL DATA

Two significant innovations in public financial management that have taken place largely over the past 20 years have changed the landscape for the availability of high-frequency fiscal data. First, the introduction of Financial Management

---

[1]As discussed in Banbura and others (2013), nowcasting relies on real-time updating of economic series, providing forecasting gains, particularly for very short time horizons. By contrast, *nowcashing* refers to the use of daily fiscal data that are mostly cash-based for various types of real-time macroeconomic analyses, including nowcasting.

Information Systems (FMIS) has significantly advanced the automation of government financial management processes. FMIS systems are used to manage public finances at each stage of the budget process, including formulation, execution, government payment systems, and accounting and financial reporting.

Second, increasing efforts to consolidate government banking arrangements have accompanied these advances. The centralization of government cash balances and accounts through the establishment of a treasury single account (TSA) system—used to pool all available cash resources—has also been an important element of public financial management reform programs. Without such consolidation of government banking arrangements, the ability to introduce IT systems and processes such as FMIS would undoubtedly have been much more complex and likely unsuccessful in many instances.

Financial Management Information Systems

The backbone of most FMIS is the general ledger, which records details of all government financial transactions for preparing financial and fiscal reports on operations. FMIS solutions typically allow for automatic posting of all revenue, expenditure, and financing transactions flowing through the FMIS to the general ledger, making the quality of the data reliable (at least for cash-based transactions) and frequency extremely high. For most FMIS, daily reporting is likely to be feasible. And, dependent on the level of coverage of transactions flowing through the FMIS, the capacity to produce data on the fiscal position is achievable.

While not yet ubiquitous, many countries have now introduced FMIS. A World Bank survey (Dener and Min 2013) indicates the availability of 176 FMIS platforms across the globe, suggesting that the usage of such systems is now widespread. The degree to which many of these systems are fully operational and the breadth of coverage is less clear. As of January 2017, however, a World Bank FMIS database indicated that of 133 projects at least partially funded by the World Bank since 1984, and which included the implementation of an FMIS as a component, 97 have been completed, while 29 are still active and seven are pending. This means that daily fiscal data could be available to a greater or lesser degree in at least 97 economies.[2]

The level of investment in these systems has also been high. World Bank–funded projects alone have cost more than $2.2 billion during this period (Dener, Watkins, and Dorotinsky 2011), not counting projects funded by other donors and by national governments themselves.

The coverage of government by FMIS can be a constraining factor, especially in emerging markets and developing economies. Initially, many FMIS were limited in coverage to little beyond the central state budget and occasionally only to central ministries and agencies. However, increasingly, coverage is being extended to the entire central government and in some cases beyond. Central government,

---

[2]The number is likely higher, as it does not include those systems that have been developed without World Bank assistance, including in the majority of advanced economies.

in addition to the state budget, can include extra-budgetary funds such as social security funds and subordinate agencies of line ministries (such as educational or health institutions). In some limited cases, the coverage of the systems has been extended to the general government and includes subnational government trans-actions (such as France or Kosovo).[3]

Another constraint of FMIS revenue and expenditure data is that, in many countries, they are cash-based and take little account of noncash-based transac-tions, especially if public accounting standards are cash rather than accrual based.[4] This can be an issue in getting a full picture of government operations. These omissions could include details on accounts payable and receivables, the stocks of financial and nonfinancial assets and liabilities, and other stock and flow adjust-ments that could impact the overall picture of the government's finances.

However, despite the absence of balance sheet information (which is also often absent in formal fiscal reports for countries that use a cash basis for public accounting), access to immediate and reliable cash-based data offers many bene-fits, including real-time information on major fiscal aggregates. In addition, many governments are transitioning from cash- to accruals-based accounting standards, facilitated by the availability of FMIS that have full accruals-based accounting systems.[5] It is therefore likely that over time the ability to track all stocks and flows, more or less in real time, will steadily improve as this transition takes hold.[6]

Consolidation of Government Bank Accounts

A TSA is a unified structure of government bank accounts through which the government transacts all its receipts and payments, allowing for a consolidated overview of its cash position in real time or at least daily. This enables the govern-ment to manage its cash efficiently and ensure it has the resources to finance ongoing government operations (Gardner and Olden 2013). It also offers the opportunity to de-link control over expenditures from cash management opera-tions. In most advanced economies, and increasingly in emerging market and developing economies, nearly all revenues are consolidated daily in a TSA.

---

[3]However, most countries do not include subnational governments within the coverage of their FMIS, for reasons of both over-complexity and, in many cases, the difficulty of includ-ing what are frequently autonomous entities within the remit of a centrally controlled financial management system.

[4]For a definition of the different types and scopes of public accounting systems as well as their advantages and disadvantages, see Irwin (2015), for example.

[5]Most countries continue to use cash-based accounting or some modified version for reporting rather than full accruals, although the number of countries adopting accrual standards is increasing. According to IMF 2016a, in 2015, 41 governments completed the transition to accrual accounting, while 16 governments account on a modified accrual basis, 28 governments are operating on a modified cash basis, and 114 governments still use pure cash accounting.

[6]Unexpected accumulation of expenditure arrears may also distort information on government activities using cash data (Flynn and Pessoa 2014). However, as discussed later, daily fiscal data can in fact help to identify patterns of arrears accumulation and even help the government improve its mapping of fiscal activities.

Typically, the main treasury account of the TSA system of accounts is held at the central bank and is used for receiving all government revenues and making government payments.[7]

Revenues and payments can be either centrally managed by a treasury or decentralized to individual agencies and line ministries. However, in both cases, all government financial resources are managed through a single account structure. Most advanced economies include all or most of the central government account within coverage of the TSA and the trend in other countries has been to continue to broaden the coverage. It has become international good practice to include government-controlled trust funds and extra-budgetary funds within the TSA (Pattanayak and Fainboim 2010).

CHARACTERISTICS OF DAILY FISCAL DATA

Daily fiscal data as defined for the purposes of this chapter include transaction-based data on various aggregates and indicators of revenue collected, government spending, financing flows (such as borrowing and debt repayment), and government cash balances for each business day.

Advantages

Relative to official fiscal statistics published either monthly, quarterly, or even annually, daily fiscal data have several advantages.

- *Relatively low accessibility costs:* The significant investment that has already taken place in developing FMIS and consolidating government banking arrangements means that the infrastructure to provide high-frequency fiscal data is already in place. Most FMIS can transfer the data easily into common data formats or into databases and portals that can be configured for analytical purposes at little or no cost. As outlined above, many countries already post significant volumes of data on their fiscal activities on their websites and some include daily data (such as the United States).

- *Timeliness:* At present, most formal fiscal statistics are published with a significant lag, which limits their usefulness even in economies that produce monthly fiscal reports, especially in periods of rapid economic change and imminent fiscal events. Access to timely and accurate data can better inform policy decisions needed to react quickly to unfolding events (Box 6.1).

---

[7]While a full survey of country TSA coverage has yet to be carried out, regional studies have demonstrated that the implementation of TSAs is widespread. For example, IADB (2015) indicates that 13 out of 17 Latin American countries studied have legislated for a TSA. A similar situation exists in Europe, where the majority of advanced and emerging economies now operate a TSA of various levels of coverage. In Africa, except Nigeria and South Africa, while TSAs are nominally in place, the presence of multiple bank accounts outside the coverage of TSAs is widespread. Nevertheless, the situation is continually improving.

- *Accuracy:* Because the data are transaction-based, and generated from accounting systems, they can be relied upon as an accurate picture of government activities in real time. Once the coverage of the FMIS is complete, there should be no ambiguity as to the accuracy of the data (at least in cash terms).
- *Fiscal Transparency:* Daily fiscal data also enhance fiscal transparency, thereby increasing the credibility of public finances (for example, see IMF 2007; Félix 2011; Poplawski-Ribeiro and Ruelke 2011; and Wang, Irwin, and Murara 2015). Making daily fiscal data publicly available is not technically challenging and governments are coming under increased scrutiny and face ongoing demands for greater transparency (for example, see Stiglitz 2001 and Darbishire 2009), which in turn lead to an increase in the number of countries where high-frequency fiscal data are published online.

Data Access and Data Collected

Table 6.1 shows the daily fiscal data collected for this chapter, which have been sourced from four countries including Brazil, Kosovo, Slovenia, and the United States. Each of these has distinct characteristics. Except for Brazil and the United States, the data cover only relatively short and recent time series, which probably reflects (at least in part) the time when governments acquired the relevant technical capacity (such as relevant IT systems). Although many governments now have IT systems in place that collect high-quality, transactional-level data, most countries do not make the data publicly available. Brazil and the United States are exceptions and provide online and unrestricted access to daily fiscal data.

Table 6.1. Overview of Data Sources

Country	Series Coverage	Access	Level of Disaggregation	Classification of Line Items	Coverage of Government
Brazil	Since 2013	Public	Highly disaggregated, requires calculating relevant aggregates	Economic	Central government
Kosovo	Since 2011	Non-public	Aggregated (most relevant fiscal aggregates contained in data)	Economic	General government
Slovenia	Since 2013	Non-public	Aggregated (most relevant fiscal aggregates contained in data)	Economic	Central government
United States	Since 1989	Public	Aggregated, but some aggregates are based on an institutional classification	Some economic, some institutional	Central government

Sources: Brazilian Ministry of Transparency, Supervision and Control; Republic of Kosovo Ministry of Finance; Slovenian Ministry of Finance; US Treasury Department; and authors' compilations.

Box 6.1. Advantages of Daily Fiscal Data for Timeliness: The VAT Revenue Case

The advantage of daily fiscal data revenue can be illustrated by observing how differences in the frequency of value-added tax (VAT) revenue data can lead to different conclusions.

Consider a hypothetical scenario where VAT revenue underperforms expectations within a given quarter. Assume that all VAT revenue comes in on the due date—the 15th of each month—and that monthly and quarterly fiscal data are published one month after the end of the reporting period. The time it takes for signs of fiscal stress to first emerge under daily, monthly, and quarterly fiscal reporting can be quite striking.

Figure 6.1.1 illustrates the simulated "perceived" level of fiscal stress depending on the frequency of revenue data that are available. With daily data, the first warning signs appear immediately after the 15th of each month, suggesting that offsetting measures could be necessary. With monthly data, instead, the first warning signs take six weeks to materialize (that is, it takes two weeks to complete the month, and the publication delay is approximately another four weeks). After 10 weeks, that is, before the completion of the quarter, examining daily data already provides full certainty that VAT revenue performance within that particular quarter was poor and that offsetting measures are required. With monthly and quarterly data, the same insights and the same level of certainty are available only after 16 weeks.

Figure 6.1.1. Perceived Level of Fiscal Stress

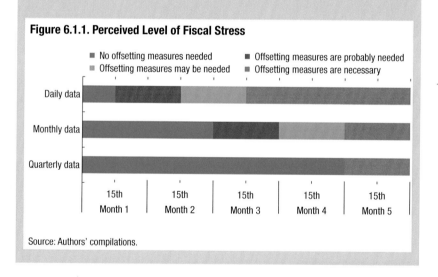

Source: Authors' compilations.

In most cases, daily fiscal data come in a reasonably aggregated format, in that they contain a fairly limited number of line items that already sum up individual transactions from different government bodies and line ministries. Brazil is an exception, with data made public online through the *Transparency Portal*. These data are highly disaggregated and contain line items for each governmental body collecting or spending public money or by the classification of the revenue and spending item (Box 6.2). However, the availability of the data in aggregated form does not mean that they cannot be further disaggregated. The data have for the most part been generated from FMIS that contain transactional-based data that theoretically could be reported on an individual basis. The level of aggregation is, in principle, a user choice in determining the level of detail they wish to publish.

The classification of the line items differs across countries. For Kosovo and Slovenia, fiscal aggregates included in the data follow economic classification, which are broadly in accordance with international standards (such as the IMF's *Government Finance Statistics Manual 2014*), allowing for international comparison. For the United States, some of the aggregates included in the data follow an institutional classification that complicates international comparisons. In the case of Brazil, for more aggregate categories of revenues and spending, the format is also in accordance with international standards.

In most cases, daily fiscal data are not available for subnational governments (or at least not provided by central governments), implying that coverage is here restricted to central government. In this respect, Kosovo is a notable exception in the sense that the central government has IT systems in place that also generate daily fiscal data for general government (which encompasses both central and subnational governments).

Volatility and Noise

As with any high-frequency data, daily fiscal data are inevitably subject to substantial noise and complex seasonal patterns. Noise in the data results from a variety of factors. On the revenue side, large one-off items such as dividends of state-owned enterprises, tax returns of particularly large taxpayers (for example, the Brazilian oil company Petrobras), and the idiosyncratic time pattern of refunds paid to taxpayers often lead to significant day-to-day fluctuations in revenue collected. On the expenditure side, noise often results from public spending on large capital projects (such as one payment may represent a significant share of capital expenditure) or large purchases of goods and services.

Seasonal patterns reflect the institutional features of fiscal policy, such as due dates of tax returns; payment dates for social transfers, including unemployment benefits and pensions; and public wages. In addition, common features of budgetary management can exacerbate seasonality. For instance, capital expenditure is often heavily skewed toward the last month or even last days of the fiscal year. This is especially the case in countries in economies where there are restrictions on carryovers of budget appropriations to the next fiscal year, incentivizing a rush to spend so as not to forfeit allocated budget resources.

The primary budget balance, which represents the difference between total revenue and the sum of all expenditure (except for interest spending), reflects this seasonality and noise. For example, Figure 6.1 plots the cumulative primary balance for each business day (which is the difference between cumulative revenue minus cumulative expenditure up to that day) in percent of annual GDP for Kosovo in 2015. While Kosovo faced a primary deficit in 2015 based on annual data (that is, there was a primary deficit on December 31, 2015), the figure shows

Box 6.2. Daily Fiscal Data and Fiscal Transparency: Brazil

The Brazilian government provides daily fiscal data publicly through the internet website *Transparency Portal*,[1] which is managed by the Ministry of Transparency, Supervision and Control and was launched in 2004 to increase the transparency of Brazilian public financial management.[2] It publishes a myriad of information about Brazilian central government public finances, federal civil servants (including organograms), and contractual companies working for the federal government, among others. In particular, the portal provides daily fiscal data series on:

- **Revenues**: budgeted, authorized, and realized daily nominal revenues organized by: (1) the *collecting unit*, categorized at three different hierarchical levels (that is, from the office level such as tax administration, government foundation, public federal universities, and so on, up to the ministerial level of the collecting office); and (2) the *revenue category*, classified at six distinct levels (that is, from the specific revenue items such as different royalties, taxes, fees, and up to the broad economic category of *current* and *capital* revenues).

- **Direct spending**: realized daily spending organized by: (1) *spending unit*, categorized into three distinct hierarchical levels (that is, from the entity level, including public federal universities and federal offices, and up to the ministerial level of the spending office); and (2) *spending category*, classified by six distinct levels (that is, from the specific action items and up to the broad economic classification of *financial investment*, *public investment*, and *other (current) spending*). The data also provide the names of companies and individuals receiving the payment.

- **Transfers**: public transfers to states and municipalities and other programs not managed by the federal government. It again provides the names of public bodies, private companies, and individuals receiving the federal transfers.

Revenue data series are available for consultation from 2004 onward and for download from 2013 onward, whereas the series for expenditure are available for consultation from 2009 and for download from 2011. They can be downloaded in a common data format. A single file, detailing revenue collected (non-cumulative), is created each business day. The information is uploaded to the site with a one-day lag and is highly disaggregated. As an example, the June 20, 2016, file contains 3,718 entries (rows). For expenditures, a single monthly file is created, which includes daily noncumulative data, again, highly disaggregated. For example, the December 2015 file contains 1,563,737 entries (rows). Data on previous months are maintained on the site.

Finally, the website includes several user-friendly snapshots of the data by different categories, themes, and programs for public consultation (such as public spending related to the Bolsa-Familia pro-poor spending program or details of spending on the 2014 World Cup and the 2016 Rio de Janeiro Olympics).

---

[1]www.transparencia.gov.br.

[2]For more information on fiscal transparency in Brazil see Félix (2011). For information about the Brazilian public financial management and fiscal framework see Celasun and others 2015.

Figure 6.1. Primary Deficit, 2015

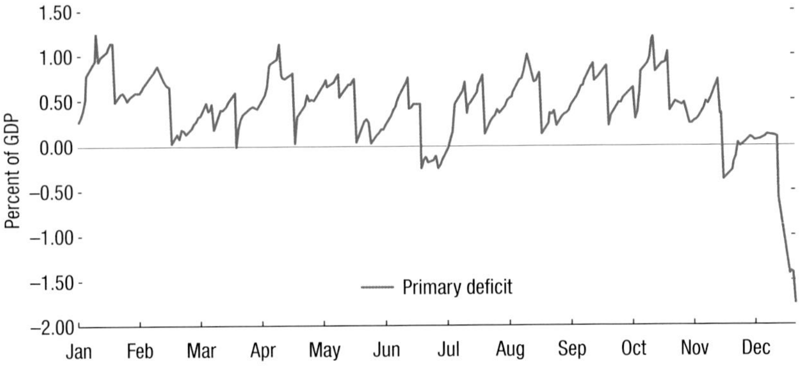

Sources: Republic of Kosovo Ministry of Finance; and authors' calculations.

that for many months during that year, Kosovo was actually running a surplus. This seasonal pattern of the budget balance is fairly standard and driven by the disconnect between revenue collection—which is to some extent concentrated in the first couple of months of the fiscal year (when annual tax returns are due)—and expenditure, which is either spread relatively equally throughout the year (most types of current spending) are concentrated at the end of the fiscal year (capital spending).

Processing and Smoothing

In this chapter, we adopt a fairly simple method to remove noise and seasonality in the main revenue and expenditure items (see the section on "Applications of Daily Fiscal Data" and references therein for other statistical methods). Here, we consider only *year-over-year changes (growth rates)* in the *cumulative* sum of the values of a particular series (say, total expenditures in local currency) over a longer period (such as the rolling sum over the past few months, or sum from the beginning of the year).

If the period is sufficiently long, *cumulative* and *rolling* sums are less affected by idiosyncratic day-to-day differences in the amount of revenue collected or money spent by governments (also see Lachowska 2016, which uses moving averages to smooth a different type of daily data which is a similar approach). Computing year-over-year changes is a common, albeit fairly basic, way of removing seasonality from macroeconomic data (see FED-Dallas 2014; and IMF 2014a). Here, it is important that data from a specific day are related to the same day in the previous year. The caveat of compiling year-over-year growth rates is that there are inevitably missing observations for some days if the same day of the previous year was not a business day, implying that no daily fiscal data in the

Figure 6.2. Fiscal Data at Daily and Monthly Frequencies[1]
(Growth rates, percent, unless stated otherwise)

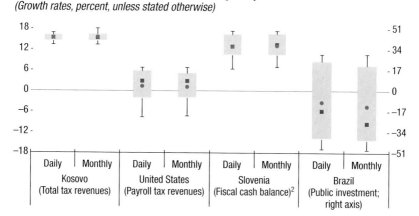

Sources: Brazilian Ministry of Transparency, Supervision and Control; Republic of Kosovo Ministry of Finance; Slovenian Ministry of Finance; U.S. Treasury Department; and authors' calculations.
[1]Percentiles of the distribution: 10th, bottom line; 25th, bottom of box; 75th, top of box; 90th, top line. Blue circle reports the mean, and red box reports the median.
[2]Cash balance is denoted in levels and as a percentage of GDP.

previous year for that day are available. For this chapter, this smoothing technique is applied to the different case studies investigated, generating the following:

- Kosovo—the year-over-year change in cumulative central government tax revenue since the beginning of the fiscal year.

- Brazil—the year-over-year change in cumulative public investment over a three-month rolling window.

- United States—the year-over-year change in cumulative payroll tax revenue over rolling windows of 60 and 180 business days.

In the latter case, a 10-day moving average filter is used to further smooth the growth rates. Finally, the daily cash balances in percent of annual GDP in Slovenia are considered, but in this case, smoothing is not necessary, as explained below. The annex provides descriptive statistics for those series, including more details on time span of the data. Figure 6.2 displays the box plots of the distribution of each of those series.

Importantly, once these techniques have been used, daily data are not significantly noisier than the same series at monthly frequency.

Figure 6.2 further compares the standard deviation of the same series discussed above using monthly data (also see annex table). Those series contain only observations of the last day of the month. The comparison shows that the standard deviation and the distribution for both monthly and daily data are of a similar order of magnitude. This again indicates that the approach used in the paper ensures that the level of noise in daily data is not higher than in monthly data.

APPLICATIONS OF DAILY FISCAL DATA

Fiscal Surveillance and Management

This section presents several case studies that show how daily fiscal data can enhance fiscal surveillance and management. The benefits of using daily fiscal as opposed to lower-frequency data for monitoring key revenue and expenditure aggregates as part of fiscal surveillance include, but are not limited to, the timeliness of the data.[8]

Tax revenue monitoring and forecasting

In the first case study, we demonstrate that the availability of daily fiscal data considerably improves the relevance and immediacy of the tax revenue trend and the end-of-year forecast analysis, using Kosovo as an example. The obvious benefit of daily fiscal data in this context is the gain in greater timeliness (Box 6.1).

Another, less obvious, benefit concerns the increase in accuracy of tax revenue trends calculated using daily fiscal data. Revenue is typically recorded only on business days, which matters if (contrary to the current year), the last day of a given month in the previous year was not a business day. In this case, year-over-year growth rates of cumulative revenue (which is our measure of interest, see the section on "Processing and Smoothing") based on monthly data essentially compare revenue collected for the full month of year t with revenue collected for the full month less one business day in year $t − 1$. This can significantly distort revenue performance measures using monthly data (particularly if no data are available for the last couple of days in either year t or year $t − 1$, for instance due to holidays). By contrast, with daily data, this effect does not arise, as we calculate year-over-year growth rates only for the exact same calendar days in year t and $t − 1$.

Figure 6.3 compares changes in year-over-year tax revenue constructed using daily data with those using official monthly data, which are assumed to become available with a delay of one month.[9] The focus is on the last three quarters of the year, given that: (1) revenue trends in the first weeks and months of the year are generally volatile (as the cumulative sums encompass only data from a relatively small number of days); and (2) the authorities did not produce daily data for each business day during the first quarter of 2016. Since daily data are essentially avail-

---

[8]At present, fiscal surveillance mechanisms do not even make use of quarterly fiscal data. Onorante and others (2010) and Asimakopoulos, Paredes, and Warmedinger (2013), for instance, discuss how quarterly or monthly fiscal indicators are already used by European policymakers but note that, even though these indicators represent one of the main sources of publicly available intra-annual fiscal information in the European Union, they are not formally included in the European multilateral fiscal surveillance process. The authors then make the case for formal inclusion of Europe's surveillance process through either a mixed-frequency state-space econometric model (Onorante and others 2010) or through the employment of MIDAS (Asimakopoulos, Paredes, and Warmedinger 2013).

[9]In some cases, the publication lag has deviated from that, but for consistency and simplicity, the assumption is that it has always been one month.

Figure 6.3. Kosovo: Monitoring Tax Revenue—March 30, 2016– December 31, 2016

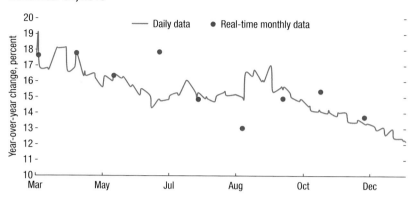

Sources: Republic of Kosovo Ministry of Finance; and authors' calculations.

able in real time, for monthly data, we also chose a real-time representation with the x-axis referring to the release date of the monthly data (and not to the period the data refer to). In other words, each observation of the monthly series represents the latest data point available at that time.

At particularly crucial months in the year, daily and monthly series significantly differ. That is the case, for instance, during the period when the budget was being prepared in September 2016. The latest monthly observations released in early September refer to July, showing a nominal revenue growth of 13 percent. This monthly revenue growth value was subsequently updated only a month later, when August data became available. On the other hand, daily data, showed a more accurate 15 percent growth rate for September 2016, significantly higher than the monthly estimates. These differences can be explained by factors discussed above, namely the publication lag of monthly relative to daily data; and the possibility that monthly year-over-year revenue growth rates can be distorted by differences in business days at the end of the month between the two years (t and $t-1$). These differences could result in significantly distinct policy responses from authorities, particularly in times of fiscal stress.

Another benefit concerns the increase in precision of revenue forecasts at the end of the fiscal year. With so many more data points, revenue forecasts can be updated and revised daily. This can improve the quality of the forecasts, which is particularly relevant for countries like Kosovo, where revenue trends calculated using monthly data significantly deviate from actual outturns. Moreover, by employing daily data, the number of forecasts also rises significantly. This, in turn, helps the forecaster to assess the reliability of the projection, allowing the variation or the trend in forecast errors to be considered more frequently, and thereby facilitates monitoring of fiscal policy implementation (Ley and Misch 2013; Lledó and Poplawski-Ribeiro 2013).

Monitoring government expenditures during fiscal adjustment

Daily fiscal data also add value for monitoring changes in government expenditure patterns during fiscal consolidation. Daily fiscal data allow quicker detection of changes in the size and composition of public expenditure than conventional fiscal statistics. Despite long lags in implementation of policy measures, daily fiscal data can be useful in monitoring when such measures translate into changes in actual expenditure, that is, when policy decisions to adjust the composition of expenditure begin to have an impact so that there are turning points in actual spending trends. While fiscal adjustment measures based on cuts in current expenditures (such as wages or social benefits) become effective more quickly, thereby showing more immediate results, cuts in current expenditure are also often the most difficult measures to implement politically, implying that current expenditure is therefore often more rigid in times of fiscal crisis.

Consequently, governments typically turn to capital expenditures as the first port of call when looking for consolidation measures in times of economic hardship (for example, see Baldacci, Gupta, and Mulas-Granados 2012; or IMF 2014b). However, there can be significant lags in the timing between policy decisions to reduce the level of public investment and the effective implementation or impact of these policies on the fiscal position. These lags can be longer than in the case of current expenditure, which is primarily the result of the existence of contractual commitments that can be wound down only over time. While this would suggest that daily fiscal data are less useful in monitoring the immediate impact of changes in fiscal policies surrounding capital expenditures, use of these data can support analysis as to when these policy changes begin to bite and when the effectiveness of consolidation measures materializes over time.

For example, Figure 6.4 reports the evolution of public investment as well as overall economic activity using publicly available data for Brazil described in the section on "Data Access and Data Collected" and Box 6.2. The years 2014 and 2015 were periods of economic downturn in Brazil. This prompted the government to embark on a program of fiscal consolidation, some of which included policies to reduce capital expenditure. By deflating daily data on public investment and the monthly series of the Brazilian general price index, and cumulating that data using a three-month rolling window,[10] this new series can be represented by

$$\sum_{d-90}^{d} i$$

where d is a specific business day; and i is the aggregate public investment for that day. The *year-over-year* change of that series is then computed and smoothed by

---

[10]The Brazilian General Price Index (*Índice Geral de Preços do Mercado—IGP-M*) from the Fundação Getulio Vargas in Brazil is also used as a deflator. This is a hybrid index composed of the producer price index (*IPA*, weighting 60 percent of the total IGP-M), the consumer price index (*IPC*, weighting 30 percent of the total IGP-M), and the construction price index (*INCC*, weighting 10 percent of the index). The results are similar if we deflate the public investment by the CPI series (*Índice de Preços ao Consumidor Amplo—IPCA*).

Figure 6.4. Brazil: Public Investment and Economic Activity, April 4, 2014–December 31, 2015

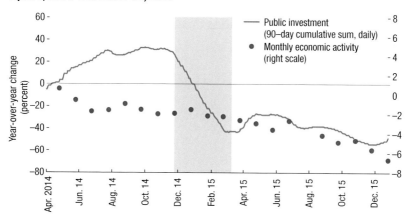

Sources: Brazilian Ministry of Transparency, Supervision and Control; and authors' calculations.

using the moving average over 90 days to remove seasonality and noise in the data as discussed in the section on "Processing and Smoothing." To measure economic activity, we use the year-over-year change of the Brazilian Central Bank's monthly economic activity index, a leading indicator of economic activity.[11]

Figure 6.4 plots the two series between April 2014 through December 2015, where the right-hand x-axis contains the scale for the year-over-year change in economic activity.[12] In 2015, when economic activity plummeted, public investment also declined significantly, suggesting that the government cut capital expenditure in the wake of lower revenue (see shaded area, which represents a turning point for capital expenditure trends). However, that decline came with a lag, as public investment was still increasing in 2014, even though economic activity was already falling. This again suggests that public investment growth in Brazil seems to follow economic activity with some lag, which has also been indicated by other studies (Celasun and others 2015; IMF 2016b).

Monitoring government cash balances

Monitoring aggregate daily government cash balances data can offer insights into the government's level of available liquidity, its ability to meet its obligations on an ongoing basis, and, more generally, the potential fiscal vulnerability faced

---

[11]This monthly and seasonally adjusted index was created in 2010, but has retroactive information since 2003. It includes activity estimates for the agriculture, industry, and services sectors, as well as an estimation of indirect (products) taxation. Other indicators of economic activity in Brazil were also used, but did not produce qualitatively different results.

[12]We exclude the first three months of 2014 given the still high volatility in the public investment series for those months even after applying the smoothing techniques discussed above.

Figure 6.5. Slovenia: Cash Balances, January 1, 2013–September 30, 2016

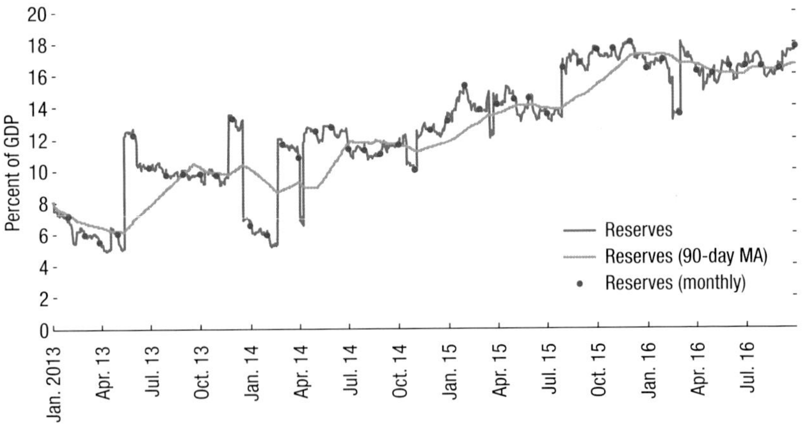

[handwritten margin note: ? monthly doesn't look bad (?)]

Sources: Slovenian Ministry of Finance; and authors' calculations.
Note: MA = moving average.

by individual economies. Most governments make efforts to smooth out the balances on the TSA to ensure sufficient resources to meet ongoing obligations, implying that changes in the cash balance can also offer signaling information. Sharp reductions in liquidity buffers may also be a sign that the government is beginning to experience signs of fiscal stress and warrants further analysis (see Baldacci and others 2011; and IMF 2016a). Having access to daily data can allow more rapid response than reliance on monthly or quarterly reports, as is often currently the case.

Equally, gradual increases in the level of cash on deposit imply that the government is starting to hoard cash. This could be an indication that policymakers are anticipating possible fiscal stress in the future and attempt to build up buffers. This was witnessed in many countries in the lead up to and during the great recession when cash levels in many advanced economies increased dramatically. In more recent years, countries such as Slovenia (Figure 6.5) have seen their cash balances drift up over time. This could possibly signal an expectation of fiscal stress or at least a great degree of uncertainty as to the direction of the economy.[13] Having access to this information daily can better inform policymakers and multilateral institutions such as the IMF during their ongoing surveillance discussions.

---

[13]However, this is not necessarily the explanation for the upward drift witnessed in the case of Slovenia since 2013. The upward drift should only be regarded as an indicator that warrants further analysis.

Improving cash planning

Access to daily data on government cash balances can also help countries develop cash management and analysis capacities. As discussed, many countries tend to smooth their cash flows and to reduce the amount of cash lying idle in the TSA. They do this to increase the efficiency of asset and liability management, helping reduce debt and debt service levels and maximizing the efficiency of management of liquid assets—the less cash you need the less you need to borrow.

Having access to high-frequency data on historical cash balances helps in two ways. First, daily data can be used to assess the true volatility on cash balances, which is a measure of how sophisticated cash management is, whereas monthly data can potentially hide much of the volatility. Second, historical daily data on cash balances are a significant input to efforts to develop accurate cash forecasts. The more accurate the forecasts the less cash needed to ensure the government can meet ongoing commitments.

While many advanced economies have now developed sophisticated cash planning systems, that is not the case in some emerging market economies and most low-income developing countries. Advanced economies, such as those in the euro area, have information on their daily cash balances and can use this to determine with a high degree of accuracy how much cash they need daily. This allows them to maintain relatively low levels of cash (the great recession being an exception in which threats to the banking systems in many advanced economies and fears about lack of availability of market access led many countries to hoard cash, notably Ireland and France). However, in some emerging market economies and many low-income developing countries over-borrowing and a lack of understanding of the true level of government liquidity are still common.

Ongoing TSA and FMIS reforms are gradually addressing these issues and with the help of ongoing capacity building, consolidated data may become available and help improve cash management in low-income developing countries.

Monitoring and Forecasting Real Economic Activity

Background

This section illustrates that daily tax revenue data can enhance efforts to *nowcast* economic activity. As Banbura and others (2013) discusses, nowcasting (or real-time updating) can be defined as the prediction of output (GDP) in the present, the near future, or the recent past. This technique has been used for a long time in meteorology and is becoming more common in economics (Giannone, Reichlin, and Small 2008). It relies on real-time updating, providing forecasting gains, particularly for very short time horizons, and becomes progressively more accurate as the end of the forecasting horizon approaches and relevant information accumulates (Banbura and others 2013). Mixed-frequency data, another tool for forecasting and surveillance in real time, rely on different techniques such as Kalman filters or MIDAS (Mi(xed) Da(ta) S(ampling)) regressions.

Using tax revenue for nowcasting

The main hypothesis is that changes in the tax base of major taxes broadly reflect economic activity and trigger changes in tax revenue, which in turn can be observed. Obviously, changes in tax revenue may also reflect changes in tax policy, which may need to be corrected for if they have important revenue implications in the context of nowcasting.

Value-added tax (VAT) and payroll taxes are particularly suitable for such exercises as they are often filed at a higher frequency, implying a small lag between, say, changes in tax revenue trends and changes in the tax base. They can also be expected to mirror private consumption (for VAT) and economic activity more broadly (payroll tax). Hence, this is especially useful in countries where daily fiscal data are available but national accounts statistics are poor—that is, quarterly GDP data are either unavailable, unreliable, or significantly delayed, and other monthly indicators of economic activity (such as industrial production) are likewise not provided by the authorities.

To illustrate how to use daily fiscal data for nowcasting, we use year-over-year growth rates of cumulative payroll tax revenues constructed using daily data from the United States. Here, payroll tax in the United States has desirable features as its payment frequency is very high (some employers have to file once every fortnight); and because the due dates for payroll tax differ significantly across firms (on many days in a given month, there are significant amounts of revenue collected even if most taxpayers pay exactly on the due date).

Figure 6.6 shows three smoothed series of daily data on payroll tax revenue, differing in the length of the rolling window considered for the construction of cumulative sums (60 and 180 days). The series also diverge on the moving average filter applied (five or 10 days) on the year-over-year changes to further smooth the series. Considering a longer rolling window results in a smoother but also more backward-looking series, which picks up changes in economic conditions with a longer lag.[14]

The example shows that daily fiscal indicators relatively accurately mirrored key features of the US business cycle before, during, and after the global financial crisis. Figure 6.6 includes a seasonally adjusted indicator of industrial production, providing a proxy for the business cycle in the United States. Importantly, the

---

[14]Statutory personal income tax rates remained unchanged during 2003–12, and the tax rebates sent out to individuals under the Economic Stimulus Act of 2008, described in greater detail in Broda and Parker (2014), did not affect gross payroll tax revenue, which is used here. By contrast the American Recovery and Reinvestment Act of 2009 increased tax credits and deductions, which had an impact on gross payroll tax revenue in 2009 and in subsequent years, implying that year-over-year changes in tax revenue were not solely driven by changes in economic conditions. However, the magnitude of the changes in the payroll revenue-based indicators in 2009 and 2010, and the fact that most of the revenue losses were ex ante estimated to occur in 2010 when the indicators were showing significant year-over-year growth, imply that this tax reform is unlikely to distort our analysis (see https://www.jct.gov, publication JCX-19–09, for details on the ex ante estimated revenue effects).

Figure 6.6. United States: Nowcasting Economic Activity, January 1, 2007–December 31, 2011

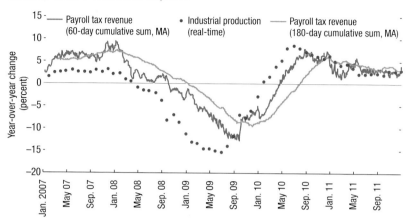

Sources: U.S. Treasury Department; and authors' calculations.
Note: MA = moving average.

peak of the recession in 2009 is picked up by the 60-day payroll tax indicator with a lag of only a few weeks relative to the industrial production benchmark.[15]

Other Applications for Macro-Fiscal Analytical Work

Recently, offering further support to the important role that high-frequency fiscal data can play, economic literature has begun to examine different research questions related to fiscal policy using daily fiscal data. For example, Auerbach and Gorodnichenko (2015) constructed two daily series of government spending to analyze their effects on exchange rates. One of the daily fiscal series refer to payments to defense contractors reported in the daily US fiscal data discussed above. The other series compiles the announced volume of contracts awarded daily by the US Department of Defense. They show that announcements about future spending cause a significant and real-time appreciation of the US dollar. They claim that this contrasting result with the previous literature is due to the use of daily data, which allows for a much finer precision in the timing of fiscal shocks and other economic variables' responses.[16]

---

[15]Note that the real-time representation of industrial production is not shown and the indicator of industrial production is subject to a publication lag normally of at least one month.

[16]As Auerbach and Gorodnichenko (2015) argue, such a response of exchange rates to fiscal spending is important to policymakers and researchers, given their implications to (1) the size of fiscal multipliers (Ilzetzki, Mendoza, and Végh 2013; Mineshima, Poplawski-Ribeiro, and Weber 2014), (2) the degree of fiscal spillovers (Beetsma, Giuliodori, and Klaassen 2006), and (3) the potential benefit of fiscal policy coordination (Beetsma, Debrun, and Klaassen 2001).

Hebous and Zimmermann (2016) study of the effects of US federal purchases on firms' investment and use daily fiscal data from US federal procurement contracts, combined with key financial firm-level information. Several restrictions were included to ensure that firms did not anticipate the fiscal demand shock, and they found that $1 of US federal spending increased firms' capital investment by 7–11 cents, but with significant variation around this average.[17] Effects are stronger for firms that face financing constraints, while they are close to zero for unconstrained firms. In line with the financial accelerator model, their findings indicate that the effect of government purchases works through easing firms' access to external borrowing (see also IMF 2015; and Correa-Caro and others forthcoming). Furthermore, industry-level analysis suggests that the increase in investment at the firm level translates into an industry-wide effect without crowding out capital investment of other firms in the same industry.

Rahal (2016), in turn, analyzes disaggregated daily public payments data from the UK, constructing a database of almost 25 million local government payments. With these data, the author examines several types of public spending, such as (1) which third-sector organizations in the UK receive local government funding, (2) which schools receive most public money, (3) what types of public body receive funding, and (4) which sports are funded at an amateur level in the United Kingdom.

Finally, Hoopes and others (2016) study the heterogeneity in investors' propensity to sell stocks during the global financial crisis using a unique daily data set of sales of stocks and mutual fund shares in the population of US taxable individual investors. The data are extracted from the universe of (anonymized) tax returns filed with the Internal Revenue Service, allowing them to match asset sales reported for capital gains taxation purposes with some demographic information on each taxpayer. While the authors do not observe asset purchases in these tax records, they present indirect evidence from dividend receipts and a supplementary brokerage account data set, suggesting that individuals with high levels of gross sales are also, to a substantial extent, net sellers of stocks.[18]

---

[17]Hebous and Zimmermann (2016) include restrictions in the contracts investigated to enable them to filter out potential anticipation effects, focusing only on unexpected changes to a firm's future cash flows.

[18]The papers discussed in this section only illustrate some areas in which daily fiscal data could be employed. There are many areas of use, though. For example, daily fiscal data could facilitate comparisons of the levels of cash reserves held by countries. Information on the cash reserves would also allow government cash and debt management activities to be benchmarked, an area that has gained much traction outside the IMF recently (see Faraglia, Marcet, and Scott 2010; and Greenwood and others 2015). Several other papers recently have started using other types of daily data (not fiscal) to analyze economic questions. For example, Lachowska (2016) employs daily data to understand what can be learned about the dynamics of consumer confidence and spending, finding that the estimated relationship between daily consumer confidence and daily spending is weak. This indicates that on a day-to-day basis, consumers are rationally inattentive and do not react to small and temporary fluctuations in consumer confidence. In turn, Hoopes and others (2016) study the heterogeneity in investors' propensity to sell stocks during the global financial crisis using a unique daily data set of sales of stocks and mutual fund shares in the population of US taxable individual

CONCLUSION

This chapter makes two contributions. First, it addresses a common prejudice, namely that analysis based on fiscal data is essentially slow moving and heavily backward looking, compared to, say, analyses involving monetary or financial markets data, because higher frequency data are unavailable. Given recent technological advances, daily fiscal data are now indeed widely available and easily sourced, even though the data are not published in most countries and some (modest) upfront investment is necessary to convert it into a useable format. Second, it demonstrates that noise and seasonality inherently present in daily fiscal data can be removed relatively easily to make them useful. The chapter argues that daily fiscal data have significant advantages relative to conventional monthly or quarterly fiscal statistics in the areas of fiscal surveillance and management, nowcasting economic activity, and macro-fiscal analytical work.

Despite these benefits, many countries make inadequate use of daily fiscal data as an input for policy-relevant analysis, implying that such data remain heavily underutilized. Addressing this underutilization could be of benefit both to fiscal authorities and multilateral organizations in their surveillance and advisory roles. So far, there is only limited evidence that authorities are beginning to see the benefits and opportunities offered through greater utilization of this rich data source (see Félix 2011), in part because potential caveats need to be taken into account when operationalizing working with daily fiscal data.

First, care needs to be taken that this high-frequency and largely unaudited data are fully understood, and that steps are taken to ensure that noise and seasonality in the data are adequately addressed and taken account of, including safeguards that ensure false alarms are not triggered through misinterpretation of short-term data glitches or volatility in the data. This concern could be addressed through capacity building with technical assistance from bilateral and multilateral institutions including the IMF. This, in turn, would help countries to build their data analytics capacity in order to ensure that high-frequency data can be interpreted correctly, thereby allowing them to reap tangible and significant benefits.

Second, daily fiscal data reflect for the most part only cash-based transactions and may therefore not capture all government operations, especially accumulations of payment or revenue arrears to meet their cash targets. The increased use of daily fiscal data may also result in a reversion to an emphasis on cash-based analysis at a time when governments are being encouraged to move to a richer and more informative balance sheet approach to fiscal policymaking. As indicated in the section on "Characteristics of Daily Fiscal Data," these concerns should decline as governments begin to implement reforms that focus on accruals-based accounting standards, but this is still some time off in the majority of countries.

---

investors. With data extracted from the universe of (anonymized) tax returns filed with the Internal Revenue Service, they present indirect evidence that individuals with high gross sales are also, to a substantial extent, net sellers of stocks.

Taken together, there is a strong business case for much wider use and exploitation of daily fiscal data in governments and multilateral institutions alike. This will most likely disrupt the way surveillance operations are carried out, but that is not a reason to slow down this juggernaut. Instead, authorities and multilateral institutions need to consider how best to leverage this opportunity to better serve their citizens and member states, respectively. That could be done by adopting increasingly nimble responses to fiscal shocks and other unexpected events and to better inform their discussions with stakeholders.

REFERENCES

Asimakopoulos, Stylianos, Joan Paredes, and Thomas Warmedinger. 2013. "Forecasting Fiscal Time Series Using Mixed Frequency Data." ECB Working Paper 1550, European Central Bank, Frankfurt.

Auerbach, Alan J., and Yuriy Gorodnichenko. 2015. "Effects of Fiscal Shocks in a Globalized World." NBER Working Paper 21100, National Bureau of Economic Research, Cambridge, MA.

Baldacci, Emanuele, Sanjeev Gupta, and Carlos Mulas-Granados. 2012. "How to Cut Debt." *Economic Policy* 27 (71): 365–406.

Baldacci, Emanuele, Iva Petrova, Nazim Belhocine, Gabriela Dobrescu, and Samah Mazraani. 2011. "Assessing Fiscal Stress." IMF Working Paper 11/100, International Monetary Fund, Washington, DC.

Banbura, Marta, Domenico Giannone, Michele Modugno, and Lucrezia Reichlin. 2013. "Now-Casting and the Real-Time Data Flow." In *Handbook of Economic Forecasting*, edited by Graham Elliott, Clive Granger, and Allan Timmermann. Amsterdam: Elsevier.

Beetsma, Roel, Xavier Debrun, and Frank Klaassen. 2001. "Is Fiscal Policy Coordination in EMU Desirable?" CESifo Working Paper Series 599, CESifo Group, Munich.

Beetsma, Roel, Massimo Giuliodori, and Franc Klaassen. 2006. "Trade Spill-Overs of Fiscal Policy in the European Union: A Panel Analysis." *Economic Policy* 21 (48): 639–87.

Broda, Christian, and Jonathan A. Parker. 2014. "The Economic Stimulus Payments of 2008 and the Aggregate Demand for Consumption." *Journal of Monetary Economics* 68: S20–S36.

Celasun, Oya, Francesco Grigoli, Keiko Honjo, Javier Kapsoli, Alexander Klemm, Bogdan Lissovolik, Jan Luksic, Marialuz Moreno-Badia, Joana Pereira, Marcos Poplawski-Ribeiro, Baoping Shang, and Yulia Ustyugova. 2015. "Fiscal Policy in Latin America: Lessons and Legacies of the Global Financial Crisis." IMF Staff Discussion Note 15/06, International Monetary Fund, Washington, DC.

Correa-Caro, Carolina, Leandro Medina, Marcos Poplawski-Ribeiro, and Bennett Sutton. Forthcoming. "Fiscal Stimulus Impact on Firms' Profitability during the Global Financial Crisis." IMF Working Paper, International Monetary Fund, Washington, DC.

Darbishire, Helen. 2009. "Proactive Transparency: The Future of the Right to Information?" Governance Working Paper Series, World Bank Institute, Washington, DC.

Dener, Cem, and Saw Young Min. 2013. "Financial Management Information Systems and Open Budget Data: Do Governments Report on Where the Money Goes?" World Bank, Washington, DC.

Dener, Cem, Joanna Alexandra Watkins, and William Leslie Dorotinsky. 2011. "Financial Management Information Systems: 25 Years of World Bank Experience on What Works and What Doesn't." World Bank, Washington, DC.

Faraglia, Elisa, Albert Marcet, and Andrew Scott. 2010. "In Search of a Theory of Debt Management." *Journal of Monetary Economics* 57 (7): 821–36.

Federal Reserve Bank of Dallas (FED-Dallas). 2014. "Seasonally Adjusting Data." Databasics.

Félix, Leodelma de Marilac. 2011. "Proactive Transparency: What Has Been Done in Brazil." Minerva Program, The George Washington University, Washington, DC.

Flynn, Suzanne, and Mario Pessoa. 2014. "Prevention and Management of Government Expenditure Arrears." IMF Technical Notes and Manual, Fiscal Affairs Department, International Monetary Fund, Washington, DC.

Gardner, John, and Brian Olden. 2013. "Cash Management and Debt Management: Two Sides of the Same Coin." In *Public Financial Management and Its Emerging Architecture*, edited by Marco Cangiano, Teresa Curristine, and Michel Lazare. Washington, DC: International Monetary Fund.

Giannone, Domenico, Lucrezia Reichlin, and David Small. 2008. "Nowcasting: The Real-Time Informational Content of Macroeconomic Data." *Journal of Monetary Economics* 55 (4): 665–76.

Greenwood, Robin, Samuel G. Hanson, Joshua S. Rudolph, and Lawrence H. Summers. 2015. "The Optimal Maturity of Government Debt." In *The $13 Trillion Question. How America Manages its Debt*, edited by David Wessel. Washington DC: Brookings Institution Press.

Hebous, Shafik, and Tom Zimmermann. 2016. "Can Government Demand Stimulate Private Investment? Evidence from U.S. Federal Procurement." IMF Working Paper 16/60, International Monetary Fund, Washington, DC.

Hoopes, Jeffrey, Patrick Langetieg, Stefan Nagel, Daniel Reck, Joel Slemrod, and Bryan Stuart. 2016. "Who Sold During the Crash of 2008–9? Evidence from Tax-Return Data on Daily Sales of Stock." NBER Working Paper 22209, National Bureau of Economic Research, Cambridge, MA.

Ilzetzki, Ethan, Enrique Mendoza, and Carlos Végh. 2013. "How Big (Small?) Are Fiscal Multipliers?" *Journal of Monetary Economics* 60 (2): 239–54.

Inter-American Development Bank (IADB). 2015. *The Treasury Single Account in Latin America: An Essential Tool for Efficient Treasury Management*, edited by Mario Pimenta and Carlos Pessoa. Washington, DC.

International Monetary Fund (IMF). 2007. "Manual on Fiscal Transparency." Fiscal Affairs Department, Washington, DC.

———. 2014a. "Seasonal Adjustment." In *Update of the Quarterly National Accounts Manual: Concepts, Data Sources, and Compilation*. Washington, DC.

———. 2014b. "Public Expenditure Reform, Making Difficult Choices." *IMF Fiscal Monitor.* Washington, DC.

———. 2015. "Private Investment: What's the Holdup?" *World Economic Outlook*, Chapter 4. Washington, DC.

———. 2016a. "Analyzing and Managing Fiscal Risks—Best Practices." IMF Policy Paper, Washington, DC.

———. 2016b. "Brazil: 2016 Article IV Consultation." IMF Country Report 16/348, Washington, DC.

Irwin, Timothy C. 2015. "The Whole Elephant: A Proposal for Integrating Cash, Accrual, and Sustainability-Gap Accounts." IMF Working Paper 15/261, International Monetary Fund, Washington, DC.

Lachowska, Marta. 2016. "Expenditure and Confidence: Using Daily Data to Identify Shocks to Consumer Confidence." *Oxford Economic Papers* 68 (4): 920–44.

Ley, Eduardo, and Florian Misch. 2013. "Real-Time Macro Monitoring and Fiscal Policy." World Bank Policy Research Working Paper 6303, World Bank, Washington, DC.

Lledó, Victor, and Marcos Poplawski-Ribeiro. 2013. "Fiscal Policy Implementation in Sub-Saharan Africa." *World Development* 46 (C): 79–91.

Mineshima, Aiko, Marcos Poplawski-Ribeiro, and Anke Weber. 2014. "Size of Fiscal Multipliers." In *Post-Crisis Fiscal Policy*, edited by Carlo Cottarelli, Phill Gerson, and Abdelhak Senhadji. Cambridge, MA: MIT Press.

Onorante, Luca, Diego J. Pedregal, Javier J. Pérez, and Sara Signorini. 2010. "The Usefulness of Infra-Annual Government Cash Budgetary Data for Fiscal Forecasting in the Euro Area." *Journal of Policy Modeling* 32 (1): 98–119.

Pattanayak, Sailendra, and Israel Fainboim. 2010. "Treasury Single Account: Concept, Design and Implementation Issues." IMF Working Paper 10/143, International Monetary Fund, Washington, DC.

Poplawski-Ribeiro, Marcos, and Jan-Christoph Ruelke. 2011. "Fiscal Expectations under the Stability and Growth Pact: Evidence from Survey Data." IMF Working Paper 11/48, International Monetary Fund, Washington, DC.

Rahal, Charles. 2016. "Unlocking Public Payments Data." Unpublished, University of Oxford.

Stiglitz, Joseph. 2001. "On Liberty, the Right to Know and Public Discourse: The Role of Transparency in Public Life." In *The Rebel Within*, edited by Ha-Joon Chang. London: Anthem.

Wang, Rachel F., Timothy C. Irwin, and Lewis K. Murara. 2015. "Trends in Fiscal Transparency: Evidence from a New Database of the Coverage of Fiscal Reporting." IMF Working Paper 15/188, International Monetary Fund, Washington, DC.

ANNEX: DESCRIPTIVE STATISTICS

Annex Table 6.1. Descriptive Statistics

(Percent; unless otherwise shown)

Country	Series	Period	Frequency	10th	90th	Median	Mean	Standard Deviation
Kosovo	Tax revenue (year-over-year change of cumulative sum since beginning of fiscal year)	03/25/2016 to 12/31/2016	Daily	13.3	16.8	15.1	15.2	2.0
			Monthly	13.2	17.9	15.1	15.3	1.4
United States	Payroll tax revenue (year-over-year change of 60-business day cumulative sum, 5-day MA applied)	01/01/2007 to 12/31/2011	Daily	−7.8	6.7	2.7	1.1	5.6
			Monthly	−7.4	6.7	2.7	1.0	5.5
Brazil	Public investment (year-over-year change of 90-business day cumulative sum, 90-day MA applied)	04/04/2014 to 12/31/2015	Daily	−47.9	29.7	−16.9	−10.1	30.9
			Monthly	−48.9	29.6	−27.3	−13.6	31.8
Slovenia	Cash balance (percent of GDP)	01/01/2013 to 09/30/2016	Daily	6.4	17.2	12.8	12.7	3.6
			Monthly	6.9	17.2	13.3	12.9	3.7

Sources: Brazilian Ministry of Transparency, Supervision and Control; Republic of Kosovo Ministry of Finance; Slovenian Ministry of Finance; US Treasury Department; and authors' calculations.

Note: 10th = 10th percentile; 90th = 90th percentile; MA = moving average.

CHAPTER 7

Instilling Digital Trust

Blockchain and Cognitive Computing for Government

ARVIND KRISHNA, MARTIN FLEMING, AND SOLOMON ASSEFA

INTRODUCTION

Despite broad technological progress, modern transaction systems remain heavily burdened by antiquated practices, creating "friction" that slows international commerce and inhibits service delivery of all kinds. For example, banks still issue letters of credit to importers, a practice that has remained virtually unchanged for 700 years since its origin in medieval Italy. The practice requires the costly and time-consuming entry of a banking intermediary for many transactions.

Likewise, cross-border regulations, customs delays, fraud, corruption, and graft are frictions that add a significant layer of costs, delays, and complexity to global trade and business flows. An IBM test determined, for example, that paperwork alone accounted for 15 percent of the cost of a shipment of produce from Africa to Europe.

The emerging digital technologies called "blockchain" and "cognitive computing" can help reduce or eliminate these frictions.[1]

Friction inhibits not only trade and business flows, but also people. Small farmers, evaluating the costs of shipping produce overseas—from bank fees to paperwork to bribes—may decide it is simply not worth the time and money to try to sell outside of local markets.

The authors thank Rob Lewis, Michael Donnelly, Alan Thurlow, Ramesh Gopinath, and Terry Lutes for their contributions, reviews, and editing.

[1]Blockchain is a shared, immutable digital ledger for recording the history of transactions. As each transaction occurs, it is put into a block. Each block is connected to the one before and after it. Transactions are linked together and each block is added to the next in an irreversible chain. Cognitive computing employs key artificial intelligence technologies to augment human capabilities and expertise.

To be sure, successful economic transactions are based on trust. And digital technologies and other innovations can disrupt economic order, thereby undermining trust by disturbing the status quo and inviting unfamiliar or risky conditions.

Nonetheless, many technological advances have significantly expanded trust throughout history. Innovations such as paper money, banking systems, the printing press, and electronic payment systems have all done so. The internet, which initially fueled access to new ways of buying and selling without a host of guarantees and safeguards, quickly introduced consumers to secure e-commerce.

Each of these advances spurred economic activity by creating systems that enhanced trust so that parties could more freely engage with one another. If seemingly disruptive digital technologies engender greater trust, they can stimulate economic improvements while providing distinct advantages to those who adopt them.

Digital disruption replaces large, capital investment with cloud-based technologies that grow as needed to handle increasingly larger workloads.[2] They are "disruptive" in that they often upend traditional business and service delivery models, while offering new value to consumers. The business models of companies like Amazon, Airbnb, and Uber offer powerful examples (Chapter 3). Using more efficient digital interfaces between consumers and the providers of goods and services, they have revolutionized the retail, hospitality, and transportation industries, respectively.

This chapter looks closely at how blockchain and cognitive computing can help government become more transparent, accurate, and efficient in its activities. Indeed, these technologies are already being applied to tax collection, delivery of public benefits, digital citizen identity, land registry management, and public records.

Governments may not think of themselves as employing "business models." They exist to serve their citizens. But here, too, digital disruption can radically alter both the way governments meet this mandate and their speed and effectiveness in doing so. Blockchain and cognitive computing are digital disrupters that will help accomplish this goal while instilling greater trust, security, and enhanced risk management across government operations.

HOW BLOCKCHAIN AND COGNITIVE COMPUTING WORK

As noted, digital technologies can reduce friction and increase trust in transaction systems. Blockchain accomplishes this by putting data into shared,

---

[2]Cloud computing, often referred to as simply "the cloud," is the delivery of computing resources—everything from applications to data centers—over the internet on an as-needed, pay-for-use basis.

distributed ledgers[3] that allow every participant access to the system of record for a transaction, using a "permissioned" network—one that can distinguish who has permission to see what. Only parties involved in the transaction can see and make alterations to it. A transaction, once executed, cannot be changed. And because it is distributed, no malicious actor can make harmful changes without others knowing about it.

And because they can process and analyze massive quantities of both structured and unstructured data, *cognitive systems*, in turn, can use this blockchain data to gain valuable insights and detect patterns in nearly-real time from multiple data streams.[4]

Digital technologies can also remove barriers to economic participation by lowering costs and simplifying administrative processes. For example, blockchain can eliminate the costs of verifying transaction information, which currently takes place at various points in time throughout the transaction. Since every party has access to the same information at the same time, verification costs may be reduced or eliminated. This lowers the price of auditing transaction information, reducing the barrier for entry for new participants into the marketplace (Catalini and Gans 2016).

To understand blockchain and cognitive computing, it is first useful to view them in the context of information technology's longstanding role in helping governments and financial systems.

The Tabulating Era (1900–70)

The earliest computers involved single-purpose, mechanical systems that counted. These tabulation machines supported the progress of both business and society, helping governments and businesses understand and manage major challenges from population growth to the advance of global capitalism.

For example, in 1937 punch-card systems pioneered by IBM enabled the US government to implement a sweeping new program of social security for nearly 30 million citizens.

The Programmable Era (1950s–present)

Counting, though, was insufficient for the major societal challenges that emerged. Computers that could follow detailed instructions—often using if/then logic—combined with rapidly advancing telecommunications, helped create cross-border payment systems, electronic payments systems, a system of international bank settlements, and transactional websites for internet banking, to name just a few. Advances in this era have also led to billions of connected people with

---

[3]A distributed ledger is a database that is consensually shared and synchronized across participants in a business network that can span multiple sites, institutions, or geographies.

[4]Computers easily understand and work with structured data, which is organized in columns, tables, databases, and the like. Unstructured data—such as the words in this book or the information contained in a video—has traditionally required humans to understand. Cognitive systems can process both kinds of data.

mobile phones, making knowledge and services dramatically more accessible and cheaper.

The Cognitive Era and Blockchain (2011–present)

Today's advances, particularly in applying artificial intelligence technologies to augment human cognition, are beginning to introduce an easier way to interact with computing systems. This method uses natural language, accesses information in images and audio files, and collaborates with systems that learn from human expertise and continue to increase in knowledge. Today, the volume, complexity, and unpredictability of world data are unprecedented. Cognitive computing's greatest strength is its ability to handle enormous loads of complex data, extract meaning from them, and propose ways to act on newfound insights.

But how data are collected, stored, and maintained can be critical to their effective use, and no more so than in complex transactions involving multiple parties from various jurisdictions. Integrating a rigorous, trustworthy method of ensuring accurate transaction data like blockchain with cognitive computing capabilities will help people and governments solve practical problems, find new opportunities, boost productivity, and foster new discoveries. The combination of blockchain and cognitive systems offer further opportunities to transform business and financial transactions of many kinds.

How Blockchain Works

A blockchain is a distributed ledger that allows records (blocks) to be added and securely maintained in a way that prevents tampering or revision. It emerged as the core technology underpinning the digital currency known as Bitcoin. However, its uses go far beyond payments and have the potential to touch all aspects of the real economy.

Blockchain technology can be used to share a digital ledger of transactions across a business network without being controlled by any single entity, making it simpler to establish cost-efficient trusted relationships. It establishes trust and integrity without relying on third-party intermediaries.

In a private blockchain network, cryptography ensures that participants can view only information in the ledger they are authorized to see. This is an important distinction from public blockchains, such as Bitcoin, that are accessible to anyone. The permissioned feature of private blockchain networks is critical to establishing adequate levels of privacy and data integrity. Once committed to a blockchain, transactions can never be changed since no node can unilaterally alter its copy of the ledger. In effect, participants cannot rewrite history or deny past transactions.

Blockchain's business-rule feature (also known as "smart contracts") enables certain conditions to be imposed automatically on transactions, such as that two or more parties must endorse them, or that another transaction must be completed first. For example, instead of obtaining a letter of credit from a bank, an importer of goods could utilize a smart contract on a blockchain stating that when goods cross a specific point and customs authorities approve it, money flows back from the receiver's bank to the sender's bank immediately, without a waiting period.

The blockchain ledger can record every sequence of a transaction from beginning to end, whether it involves hundreds of steps in a supply chain or a single online payment. As will be explained, because of the transparency made possible by blockchain, government agencies can gain a better understanding of what is occurring within financial and commercial systems and identify potential problems before they become critical.

In 2015, IBM and 16 other cross-industry leaders formed Hyperledger, a Linux Foundation project that is using an open source approach to advance cross-industry blockchain technologies. Open source methods provide the transparency, interoperability, and support required to bring emerging technologies forward to mainstream commercial adoption. Participants can freely license, use, copy, and adapt related software for specific applications. The source code is openly shared among members so that software design can be voluntarily improved, though in a consistent, controlled manner.

This approach ensures that blockchain development proceeds with uniform standards and applications in mind, an important goal given the potential application of the technology to a wide range of industries. The open source process, combined with liberal licensing terms and strict governance by multiple organizations, will enable the broadest adoption of blockchain by regulated industries (US Congress 2016).

How Cognitive Computing Works

Cognitive computing describes systems that apply artificial intelligence technologies to learn at scale, reason with purpose, and interact with humans naturally. These systems perform functions that resemble what people do when acquiring knowledge, understanding and learning from it, reasoning on it, and then sharing what is known. Cognitive systems offer evidence-based decisions, continuing to refine them based on new information and results, so that humans can make better decisions and choose better actions.

Cognitive computing systems differ in significant ways from the information systems that preceded them. They are probabilistic, as opposed to deterministic, meaning they do not follow a lengthy, but finite, set of directions that end in a single solution to a question or problem. They use statistical reasoning—such as analyzing the likelihood of two word phrases being related, or how often they appear together—to begin to make hypotheses about potential meaning and answers. They generate hypotheses, piece together reasoned arguments, and make recommendations for action with an associated probability or confidence measure.

Unlike conventional computing systems, cognitive systems can also process and derive insight from the 80 percent of the world's data classified as unstructured (Kelly 2015). This is fast becoming an essential function given the exponential growth of such data and the pressing need to exploit value as quickly as possible for business and societal gain.

Generally, cognitive systems are:

- *Adaptive:* They learn as information changes, and as goals and requirements evolve. They help resolve ambiguity and tolerate unpredictability. They can process dynamic data in real time or near real time.

- *Interactive:* They interact more naturally with and adapt to people using them. They may also interact with other processors, devices, and cloud services, as well as with people, and can make use of more traditional programmable systems to complete a task.

- *Iterative:* When faced with incomplete or ambiguous problem statements, they can ask questions or find additional input to further define the problem. They can "remember" previous interactions in a process and return information that is suitable for the specific application at that point in time.

- *Contextual:* They understand, identify, and extract contextual elements such as meaning, syntax, time, location, appropriate domain (relevant business sector) and regulations, the task at hand, and its goal. They draw on multiple sources of information, including both structured and unstructured digital information, as well as sensory inputs such as visual, gestural, auditory, or sensor-provided.

IBM's Watson is perhaps the most widely known example of a cognitive computing system that reflects the above features today. It combined innovations in more than a dozen disciplines of advanced computer science to defeat the top human champions on the quiz game show *Jeopardy!* in 2011 by understanding and answering spoken language questions faster than its opponents.

Since then, Watson has been trained to analyze increasingly complex data sets from specific business domains and to reason, draw insights, and learn from them. Consider, for instance, health care fields such as oncology.

The amount of research and data available to help inform cancer treatments is growing exponentially. Medical professionals cannot possibly keep up with all of it on their own. Watson for Oncology helps care teams identify key information in a patient's medical record, surface relevant articles, and explore treatment options to reduce unwanted variation of care. The system was trained for 15,000 hours by specialists at Memorial Sloan Kettering Cancer Center in New York. It has ingested nearly 15 million pages from relevant journals and textbooks and continues to expand its knowledge.

Watson combines understanding of the longitudinal medical record and its oncology training to quickly recommend options to physicians for each unique patient case. This capacity has been made available to healthcare providers around the world. For example, in trials at the University of North Carolina's Lineberger Comprehensive Cancer Center, in one-third of the cases Watson suggested potential treatment options that the hospital's tumor board had not considered. Manipal Hospitals in Bangalore, India, found that Watson agreed with its tumor board recommendations in 90 percent of cases of breast cancer.

Watson's potential is not limited to health care. It is also being used to assist local and national governments with various core activities such as customer service.

The US Census Bureau has enlisted IBM to support its Census 2020 Program with cognitive technologies to help answer respondent questions. Anyone filling out the 2020 Census will be able to call an 800 number where the Watson system will answer natural language questions. It is expected that increasing self-service with the help of virtual agents will lead to significant cost reductions.

Similarly, Miami-Dade County, Florida, has enlisted IBM to enhance customer self-service for the Water and Sewer Department through Watson and IBM Cognitive Solutions. With the help of a cognitive advisor, customers of the department can engage with Watson on an array of questions about water services and payments. The goals of the new system are to increase first call resolution, provide customer advocacy, billing information, and payment options. The service is expected to reduce cost per contact as well as provide around-the-clock answers and support to customers.

BLOCKCHAIN AND COGNITIVE COMPUTING APPLICATIONS TO PUBLIC FINANCE

Blockchain Potential Benefits

While blockchain's potential benefits touch almost all industries, its potential for government is particularly promising, because it has the capacity to provide far greater levels of transparency, accuracy, and efficiency in government activities. As noted, it is already being applied to a wide range of functions including tax collection, the delivery of public benefits, digital citizen identity, land registry management, and public records, to name just a few.

Blockchain's business rules feature could be adapted to perform a regulatory function, perhaps even at no cost to outside parties involved in government transactions. Government policies and terms could be digitally enshrined in the "smart contracts" that underpin a blockchain, ensuring that those policies are executed faithfully across all transactions conducted on that blockchain.

Blockchain offers governments the possibility of establishing permanent, immutable records of identity, for citizens and businesses, that cannot be lost or stolen. This, in turn, establishes the access to data required for enhanced service delivery and the distribution of public benefits. Nearly 2.5 billion people in the world today lack official identification, including children up to age 14 whose birth has never been registered, as well as many women in poor rural areas of Africa and Asia. This is a major impediment to accessing welfare benefits, education, and broadening financial inclusion (Daha and Gelb 2015).

For example, Estonia, well-known for its early adoption of digital technologies, is the first nation to offer its citizens a digital identity card based on blockchain. Citizens can use it to access public, financial, and medical and emergency services; pay taxes online; e-vote; provide digital signatures; and travel within the European Union without a passport (Shen 2016). Through another program called e-Residence, Estonia provides a transnational digital identity for non-Estonians and nonresidents of the country. It can be used to establish a location-independent online business registered in Estonia and to utilize digital services like those accessible by Estonian citizens and Estonia-based businesses.

Finally, blockchain, in tandem with cognitive systems, can help governments and industry alike ensure provenance, the chronology of the ownership, and custody or location of an asset or object, as the example below demonstrates.

Well-documented provenance demonstrates that an item is authentic. This has enormous implications for everything from food safety, to the integrity of life-saving drugs, to the health and well-being of consumers. Provenance creates an auditable record of transport of all physical products. It can prevent the sale of counterfeit goods as well as the problem of "double spending" of certifications present in current systems.

A relevant industry example is IBM Research's work with Everledger, a company that tracks and protects diamonds and other valuables. Diamonds depend on certificates of authenticity and origin that are still largely paper-based. As a result, this information is more vulnerable to tampering. It also poses a major challenge to regulators trying to prevent the flow of "conflict diamonds" into the market, which have been tied to funding for armed insurgencies.

Everledger has built a digital business network using IBM Blockchain to underpin its global certification system. The platform holds digital information on 1 million diamonds, including industry certifications and key data points with links to laser inscriptions inside each stone. A cognitive computing system ensures that these diamonds are authentic and compliant with thousands of regulations, including those imposed by the United Nations to prevent the sale of conflict diamonds.

For the first time under this system, cognitive analytics can be performed directly on data within the blockchain, where it resides. This prevents the need for the data to be extracted for analysis, which makes it more susceptible to fraud. The system can cross-check all relevant regulations and records as well as supply chain and Internet of Things data, including time and date stamps and geospatial information, in a fraction of the time it takes humans to do this.[5]

Everledger believes this system can eventually be applied to a whole range of high-value goods—everything from priceless works of art, to rare wines, to automobiles. In a similar way, IBM believes blockchain can benefit certain key government activities as highlighted in Table 7.1.

---

[5]The Internet of Things refers to the growing range of connected devices that send data across the internet. A "thing" is any object with embedded electronics that can transfer data over a network without any human interaction. Examples are wearable devices, environmental sensors, machinery in factories, devices in homes and buildings, or components in a vehicle.

Table 7.1. Blockchain Benefits to Government

Benefit	Challenge	How Blockchain Can Help
Revenue Collection	• Diverse taxpayer base of companies and individuals • Legacy processes • Complex financial obligations • Auditability	• Smart contracts automate transactions under specific legal agreements • Immutable record of financial obligations and transactions • Increased transparency • Outside auditing and regulatory reviews are made easier
Expenditure Accountability	• Auditability and regulatory oversight • Confidentiality of sensitive personal information • Budget priorities	• Security is enhanced through encryption and cryptology • Consensus required for changes to the ledger improves data integrity • Immutable chain of transactions establish provenance
Anticorruption	• Opaque governance models • Complex financial systems • Corrupt financial practices	• Network architecture can meet predefined governance models • Regulator participation supports automated compliance • Single version of truth for all permissioned parties in the network • Increased visibility between parties in the network • Supports data encryption and the management and enforcement of complex permission settings for participants and third parties

Source: IBM Research.

Applications of Blockchain and Cognitive Computing to Revenue Collection

Government revenue collection also offers a helpful lens through which to view the potential impact of blockchain and cognitive computing.

Revenue collection is currently a separate process from the commercial transactions on which it depends. It happens periodically and is contingent upon the trustworthiness of the parties involved to record transactions correctly. The government collects tax when an invoice is settled with a supplier. This might occur on a quarterly basis, for instance, and require the completion of a tax return. With blockchain, companies would not be required to submit a return as their tax account could be continuously maintained and settlement could be automated.

The existing separation between the commercial transactions and their tax component also encourages both deliberate and accidental under-reporting. Cognitive systems can spot this under-reporting by looking at the patterns of commercial transactions and their relative tax generation.

This integration of cognitive analytics with blockchain technology can considerably reduce the risk of error in the taxation of commercial transactions. Blockchain's security and immutability help ensure that the provenance of the sequence of transactions is established, reducing the possibility of fraud and error. The tax transaction on the blockchain can be automatically generated from the commercial transaction. Smart contracts can be employed to implement current tax policy, enabling tax authorities to deploy any amendments quickly and effectively. And cognitive systems can continually scour the blockchain data to look for anomalous behavior and other exceptions that might signal noncompliance or fraud.

With tax transactions and key elements of the commercial transaction on blockchain, government can execute compliance activities continuously at no additional cost to commercial entities. The tax owed by each taxpayer could be stored on the blockchain as a digital currency (US dollars) and backed by the central bank. This digital currency could be used to settle tax due and to net tax allowances, for example when processing value-added tax. In this way, taxpayers would no longer need to submit filings, as the net tax account would be maintained continuously on the blockchain.

IMPLEMENTING DIGITAL TECHNOLOGIES: KEY CONSIDERATIONS FOR GOVERNMENT

Costs and Challenges

Any form of technology acquisition requires financial investment that will vary according to each potential adopter's existing infrastructure and needs. It is therefore difficult to generalize about the cost of digital technologies such as cognitive computing and blockchain to government. This must be determined on a case-by-case basis. Cost will also moderate as these technologies mature and scale up with wider use.

Despite these unknowns, certain core assumptions can be made about the relative affordability and overall value of blockchain and cognitive-computing-based solutions.

As noted previously, these solutions can now be delivered through cloud computing. While initial access may require certain upgrades to existing computer hardware and software, cloud-enabled services largely preclude the need for large, capital-intensive technology investments. Based on private sector projects IBM is currently involved in, an investment in the single-digit millions of US dollars is sufficient to get digital technology projects up and running on a relatively large scale. Viewed against total government spending, this is not a prohibitive cost, even in developing countries. For example, the government of Kenya announced that overall government spending would amount to more than $22 billion in fiscal year 2017/18 (Njini and Changole 2017).

It is also true that countries in developing regions may be at a distinct advantage when it comes to digital technology adoption owing to their relative lack of existing technology infrastructure. They do not have to maintain older "legacy" systems common to much of the developed world. They can choose to build out a modern infrastructure, underpinned by blockchain and cognitive computing, rather than retrofit equipment that may be several decades old.

A more urgent challenge, and one that government is uniquely positioned to address, lies in the process changes that are required for digital adoption. Taking the example of blockchain, the technology is expressly designed to facilitate multi-party business interactions. Its adoption requires cooperation and participation from private sector entities, which must agree to a new set of policies on transactions and data sharing built around blockchain. This necessitates changes in policies, which government can facilitate, as opposed to a technical solution, which it cannot.

While the combination of cognitive systems and blockchain is inherently secure, security and technical challenges will likely develop. Drawn by the increasing numbers of users of these new technologies, computer hackers and cyber-criminals will attempt to find and exploit new vulnerabilities. The large volume of trusted information that can be shared on a blockchain could also increase the risk of participants compromising some part of the system.

But the primary challenge to security will remain people that are part of the system, as opposed to the technologies themselves: blockchain cannot prevent data from being corrupted at the source by a human, such as if an official were bribed to submit a phony transaction. Various security innovations are now taking place at the "edge" of the network, near the source of the data, to complement blockchain technology and address this challenge. These include promising work on cryptographic, tamper-proof anchors and tiny computers that can securely link a physical product with its digital representation in a blockchain system and help eliminate fraud in complex, global supply chains.

Despite the potential challenges, blockchain will still make it far harder for malicious actors to commit transactional fraud because of the following three core capabilities:

1. Every transaction is digitally signed making it non-repudiable.

2. Every transaction is vetted by two or more parties via a consensus mechanism (one cannot unilaterally enter information into the blockchain).

3. Data on the blockchain are immutable because multiple copies of it are managed by independent parties. It is also grouped into blocks and transactions are chained cryptographically, making it virtually impossible for anyone to tamper with information once entered.

Finally, there is the longer-term challenge of how to manage the indefinite growth of data on a blockchain, given that it is an append-only log of all transactions. While not insurmountable, this is an important technical consideration and work is under way to understand how it can best be resolved.

Legal Framework

IBM's experience has been that a significant number of the advantages of digital technology adoption can be realized without the need to change existing legal and regulatory frameworks. Many years helping thousands of public and private sector clients adopt digital technologies make clear that most advantages can be realized within current law. This has proven true in financial services, supply chain and logistics, health care, and other industries. Given the proximity of these industries to government services and oversight, it will likely hold true for government adoption as well.

Yet it is also true that by definition, innovation precedes regulation. As digital technologies like blockchain and cognitive computing spur a reimagination of many business processes, need will likely emerge for new legal and regulatory modifications to maximize their potential and guide their use. For example, certain digital documents (such as a digital bill of lading in shipping) are not considered legally admissible in some jurisdictions. In such cases, blockchain-based systems for managing secure document approval workflows may not be feasible until such laws are modified.

Privacy

Blockchain's central promise is to deliver trusted data and business processes to users by enabling permissioned and selective visibility into data. Its security features can be configured to comply with existing privacy laws (such as the European Union's General Data Protection Regulations and others), and its privacy controls are a function of policy decisions, not technology limitations. Viewed in this light, a blockchain can be made to mirror the strength of the laws themselves. The technology can also be configured to generate supporting documents such as automated audit compliance reports, increasing trust in the audit process.

A private blockchain network's permissioned feature prevents anonymous entities from taking part in a transaction, which minimizes the potential for criminal use. This is in sharp contrast to well-publicized uses of Bitcoin's public blockchain ledger for alleged criminal purposes.

Sequencing

Successful government technology projects must be undertaken with an optimal order of steps or "sequences" in mind. These sequencing steps should include legal assessments, determination of impact, and capacity development.

Certain lessons can be drawn from IBM's work in Kenya to improve that country's business environment to attract more foreign direct investment and strengthen domestic firms. Above all, this effort requires enhancing the efficiency of government services and the underlying regulatory framework. In IBM's experience, these are essential precursors for successful technology adoption.

The key sequencing steps in IBM's Ease of Doing Business project in Kenya included the following:

- Data collection from various agencies to determine the root cause of the observed inefficiencies

- Data analysis to develop recommendations for reforms (process, legal, and technology)

Figure 7.1. Reforms in Kenya's Ease of Doing Business Project

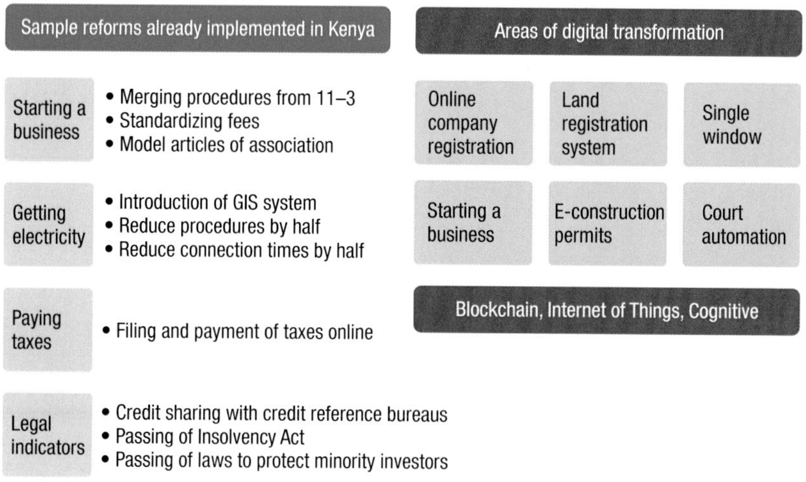

Source: IBM Research.

- Development of an action plan to aid implementation
- Implementation of technology to transform governance
- Implementation monitoring
- Communication to stakeholders of implemented reforms

Figure 7.1 illustrates reforms and technology recommendations that have already been implemented in Kenya based on this methodology.

As one indication of the success of this approach, Kenya has dramatically improved its World Bank Ease of Doing Business ranking, used by countries throughout the developing world to gauge reform success. Kenya's ranking rose a total of 44 places in the past two years and in both years, it was rated the third most reformed country in the world. IBM Research is now expanding the focus of this project by developing cognitive technologies to help government officials make more informed decisions about policymaking, revenue, and expenditure.

OTHER GOVERNMENT AND INDUSTRY APPLICATIONS

Governments and industries worldwide are actively experimenting with blockchain and cognitive computing. Applications include welfare payments distribution, government customer service and call centers, digital currencies, electronic records, land titles, citizen identity, fraud prevention, global supply chain security, and many more. The following discusses specific projects.

Currency and Payments

African nations have advanced national payment systems to rival and exceed those in many western countries. Examples include M-Pesa in Kenya (Chapter 10), a mobile phone-based money transfer, financing, and microfinancing service, as well as the beginnings of the world's first blockchain-based digital currencies in Tunisia and Senegal.

In Tunisia, more than 3 million citizens have no banking relationship (DCE 2015). The Tunisian government aims to use digital currency to improve this through blockchain technology. Using a smartphone application offered by the Tunisian National Post Office, which provides bank accounts and has a 45 percent share of the country's banking market, clients can have nationwide access to instant, secure, and affordable merchant payments and remittances. They can use the digital currency, known as eDinar, to make instant mobile money transfers, pay for goods and services in person and online, pay bills, and manage government identification documents (Parker 2015).

Senegal has also announced plans to use a blockchain-based digital currency in 2017 called eCFA. The currency would be legal tender with the same status as the existing currency, the *Communaute Financiere Africaine* (CFA) franc. Unlike other forms of digital currency, supply of eCFA would be controlled by the Senegalese central bank in the same way as physical currency (Douglas 2017).

Welfare Disbursement

In the United Kingdom, the government's Department of Work and Pensions, the country's largest public service department, is engaged in a pilot project to employ blockchain's distributed ledger technology to improve the payment of welfare benefits. It is aimed in part at reducing the £3.1 billion that is overpaid in benefits in the United Kingdom each year (National Audit Office 2016). Claimants use a mobile phone application to receive and spend their benefit payments. With their consent, their transactions are recorded on a distributed ledger to support their financial management.

Bond Issuance

The retailer Overstock is using blockchain technology for the global issuance, settlement, and trading of corporate bonds. The private bonds Overstock has issued this way offer same-day settlement, instead of the two or three days it typically takes. In 2016, Overstock became the first publicly traded company to issue stock over the internet, distributing more than 126,000 company shares through technology based on blockchain (Metz 2016).

Global Financing

IBM Global Financing is the world's largest technology financier. Yearly, it facilitates credit among 4,000-plus suppliers and partners worldwide and handles nearly 3 million invoices and 25,000 disputes. The unit created a blockchain platform to reduce dispute times from more than 40 days to under 10, freeing up about $100 million in capital that is otherwise tied up at any time (Krishna 2016). With blockchain, participants in the transaction share a single platform with permissioned and secure access. They receive a full view of the process and can easily track transactions from purchase order to product delivery. They are also able to see every step in a transaction and identify the exact moment of a delay or error. This enables parties to the transaction to resolve problems more easily without filing a dispute.

Global Supply Chain

Maersk, the world's largest shipping company, has collaborated with IBM to build the first industrywide cross-border supply chain solution on blockchain. The solution will help manage and track the paper trail of tens of millions of shipping containers across the world by digitalizing the supply chain process from start to finish. By enhancing transparency and the secure sharing of information, the platform can reduce the amount of paperwork currently required to ship goods, thereby lowering transaction costs. Blockchain's immutable and transparent audit trail will also begin to address the approximately $600 billion lost every year to maritime fraud, when goods are illegally removed from ships during transactions (WIRED 2017).

Dubai Customs is working with IBM to explore the use of blockchain for the import and re-export process of goods in and out of Dubai. The blockchain solution transmits shipment data through a cloud computing delivery system, so that key stakeholders will be able to receive instantaneous information about the condition of goods and shipment status. Taking the example of the journey of a shipment of fruit, parties in the transaction will receive timely updates as the fruit is exported from India to Dubai by sea, then manufactured into juice in Dubai, and exported as juice from Dubai to Spain by air. The solution aims to replace paper-based contracts with smart contracts. It uses data from sensor devices to update or validate smart contracts (including the condition of fruit). And it integrates all key trade process stakeholders from the ordering stage, in which the importer obtains a letter of credit from its bank, through the intermediary stages of freight and shipping, ending with customs and payment.

A SIMULATION OF HOW BLOCKCHAIN ADOPTION COULD BENEFIT GOVERNMENTS

The emerging nature of digital technologies and their early stages of adoption in most instances makes existing data about impact on national economies scarce. Therefore, we examine the potential effect of blockchain use on three developing economies with the help of the Oxford Economic Global Model.[6]

As an exercise, the scenario focuses on three countries: South Africa, Kenya, and Nigeria. Because South Africa offers a more robust set of baseline statistics, it is used here as the primary example in presenting the methodology and results.

To see the benefit of blockchain, we imagine the government of South Africa decides to take a different policy path to accelerate digitalization of the economy.[7] Perhaps even more importantly, the government commits to establishing nationally mandated standards that allow businesses to participate seamlessly in a new and simplified transactional world by leveraging blockchain technology.

Blockchain, as noted, is designed to remove the friction of global commerce, that is, the many additional transactions that complicate the flow of goods and services and drive up overall cost. These include everything from excessive processing times to numerous fees charged by intermediaries, multiple inspections of goods at border checkpoints, administrative paperwork, corruption, and other inhibitors. IBM estimates that more than $300 billion in the underlying costs of global commerce can be optimized with digital technologies like cognitive computing and blockchain (Krishna 2016).

BASELINE ECONOMIC ASSUMPTIONS FOR TRANSPORTATION AND HANDLING EXPENSES

Before presenting the results of the macroeconomic model, it is important to understand the key underlying assumption of how revenue is allocated in the typical transaction. Generally, revenue is parsed across several cost categories: labor costs, operating costs, transportation and handling expenses (TE), and profits.

---

[6]Oxford Economics has developed a fully integrated global macroeconomic model. The model is Keynesian demand driven over the short term, combined with monetarist concepts driving the longer term. The combination allows for shocks to demand that can generate recessions, with economies responding to monetary and fiscal policies. However, output over the long term is determined by supply-side factors, such as investment, demographics, labor participation, and productivity. This quarterly model covers 80 countries and the remaining smaller nations are aggregated into six regional blocs and the euro area. All countries covered are linked to each other through trade flows, world prices, interest rates, exchange rates and other factors. Nations vary in coverage, with the United States and the United Kingdom leading the model, with over 850 variables, and Iraq the smallest coverage, with just over 170 concepts covered. See Oxford Economics for more information: http://www.oxfordeconomics.com/about-us.

[7]The focus here is on measuring benefits. Of course, there are costs as well, including acquisition and deployment costs and transition and transformation costs. The former is a small part of the total costs, while the latter reflects the need to change organizational processes and procedures, retrain workers and managers, and engage with third parties in new and different ways. As is well known, organizations often resist such change, making transition and transformation costs high. These costs are captured by spreading the implementation of the new technology over four years, forgoing the full benefit during implementation.

Labor costs include wages, salaries, benefits, training, recruiting, hiring, and all other costs related to labor. Operating costs include costs of materials, plant and facility operations, taxes, and all other costs of producing a good. TE includes all expenses required to ship and move a good through its supply chain to the buyer. Profits include earnings, depreciation, interest, and all other returns to capital. Ratios vary, but the generally accepted equation is as follows:

Revenue = Profits + Labor Cost + Operating Cost + Transportation Expense
          10%   70%   15%   5%

Our scenario focuses on using blockchain adoption to reduce the cost of TE. We assume that 5 percent of revenue for transportation and handling expense is reasonable.

Worldwide, the transport and storage industry accounts for 4.1 percent of total industrial output, not including any of the output involved in the retail and wholesale sectors.[8] In the trade and transportation sectors, the TE ratio rises to 15.9 percent (NACE 2008).

Transport costs typically consume 10 percent of total revenue of a product (Rodrigue and Notteboom 2017). Transportation costs within the US mining sector typically run 4–5 percent of total revenue (Eurostat 2008).

We assume that 20 percent of TE, or 1 percent of total revenue, falls as a result of the cost reduction in our scenario. This is based on three examples:

1. Within the airline industry, passenger services, ticketing, station and ground, and administrative costs are a combined 23 percent of the total (Leinbach 2005).

2. In container shipping, more than 40 percent of the total logistics costs are indirectly due to delays that include additional inventory demurrage costs and bribes paid at a wide variety of police checkpoints and weighing stations. Overland shipping in Africa is characterized by significant lost time in regulatory delays. For example, transporting goods from Mombasa to Nairobi takes an average of 30 hours, with 10 hours spent at security checkpoints and six hours at regulatory weigh stations (Rodrigue and Notteboom 2017). This added time requires an additional 11 hours of driver rest and meals. In contrast, a similar distance traveled across the North America Free Trade Agreement trade zone takes only six hours. Unreliable transportation shipping times not only add costs, they can also make a perishable shipment worthless. In addition, each stop along the way opens the supply chain to graft. At best, consumers bear the added cost; at worst, such friction restricts trade among potential partners.

3. In carrying out a test case using a shipment of avocados from Mombasa to Rotterdam, IBM calculated the cost of moving the shipping container itself to

---

[8]The transport and storage industry is defined in Eurostat (2008, 76). The 4.1 percent estimate can be found at Oxford Economics aggregates, using data from national statistical offices http://www.oxfordeconomics.com/.

be approximately $2,000. The cost of the paperwork associated with it comes to $300, 15 percent of the total (Allison 2017). By removing much of the processing time for paperwork and other inefficiencies through digitalization with blockchain, IBM showed vast cost and time savings.

Under this assumption, our scenario lowers the rate of increase of the consumer price index (CPI) by 20 percent. Consider the following:

$$\text{CPI}(t) = \text{CPI}(t-1) * (1 + \text{Rate of Inflation}(t)) * (1 - (\text{TE percent} * \text{Change in TE percent}))$$

If the CPI($t - 1$) is 100 with a rate of inflation of 5 percent, then a 20 percent reduction in TE costs (assuming TE costs 5 percent of revenue) results in a CPI(t) of 104. The apparent rate of inflation will be reduced to 4 percent. An array of factors determines the rate of inflation, including the actions of the nation's central bank, while the reduction in TE costs is a result of the introduction of the newly available technology.

SIMULATION OF COST REDUCTION ASSUMPTIONS IN THREE AFRICAN ECONOMIES

Employing the Oxford Economic Model, the exercise simulates the impact of the introduction of the new technology as a one-time supply shock. Because of the transition and transformation costs, four years are required to realize the full benefit of the new technology. While the cost reduction is permanent, it is a one-time event. Future benefits would require the introduction of additional technology improvements or other positive supply shocks.

To achieve consistent results, the same methodology is applied in the model to blockchain adoption in Kenya, Nigeria, and South Africa. However, only annual data are available for the model for Kenya and Nigeria, whereas the South African model is quarterly. This has implications for the scenario. For South Africa, the changeover to prices occurs over the course of a year, while in the annual models the result occurs at once. In the scenarios, prices change dramatically in the annual models and considerably more slowly in the quarterly model.

In broad terms, the lower rate of inflation flows through to all the appropriate price metrics including CPI, producer price index, import and export prices, wage costs, and the GDP deflator.[9] These changes have immediate impacts on all nominal data series. Figure 7.2 presents a change from the baseline and not absolute growth rates. For example, in 2018 the Kenyan GDP deflator, economywide

---

[9] The 1 percent cost improvement contributes to a reverse wage-price spiral lowering wage-price expectations and producing a 2.1 percent price level decline over four years in South Africa, a 2.7 percent price level decline over four years in Nigeria, and a 3.0 percent price level decline over four years in Kenya.

Figure 7.2. Change in GDP Deflator
(Percentage point reduction from baseline)

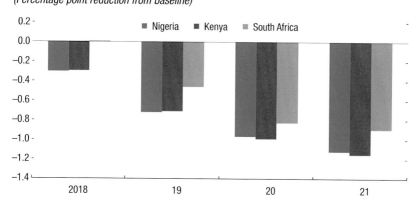

Source: Authors' calculations with Oxford Economics model.

inflation, rises 5.4 percent in the baseline and 5.1 percent in the IBM scenario. The resulting 0.3 percentage point reduced inflation is shown in the chart.

Generally, lower inflation is very positive in the three simulated cases. Real GDP responds in this scenario. For example, Kenya's real GDP rises 6.4 percent in 2018 in the baseline and 6.9 percent in the scenario, or 0.5 percentage point of additional GDP growth.

In both cases shown in Figure 7.3, the Nigerian and Kenyan economies encounter supply constraints as they are unable to sustain expansion at such rapid rates. The technology cannot remove all growth constraints faced by these nations. For these economies, strong growth in 2018 and 2019 leads to slower growth relative to the baseline in 2020 and 2021. However, on balance real GDP is higher in all four years than it would be in the absence of the technology. It is unlikely that all the benefits will vanish.

Compared to the baseline, the Kenyan economy realizes 0.9 percent additional real GDP. By 2021, the real GDP in Kenya is nearly a percentage point higher than it would be in the absence of the technology. The Nigerian economy adds 0.4 percent of real GDP.

The improving economy slows government expenditures and raises revenues, reducing the government deficit. Figure 7.4 shows the improvement as a percentage of GDP. For example, the current baseline projection for South Africa in 2021 is a rand (R) 194 billion (US$14.9 billion) deficit. Under the simulation with digital adoption, the deficit is R158 billion, or an improvement of R35.6 billion. As a result, the South African deficit as a percent of GDP is improved from 3.1 percent to 2.6 percent, an improvement of 0.5 percentage point.

In the scenario, South Africa stands out for its comparatively large fiscal balance improvement. There are two reasons for this result.

Figure 7.3. Real GDP
(Percent improvement from baseline)

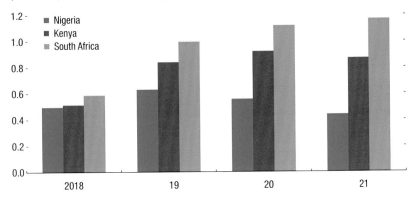

Source: Authors' calculations with Oxford Economics model.

Figure 7.4. Reduction in the Government Deficit
(Percentage point reduction, as percent of GDP from baseline)

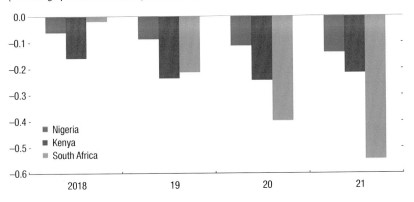

Source: Authors' calculations with Oxford Economics model.

First, as shown in Figure 7.5, South African real GDP relative to the baseline in 2021 is 1.2 percent larger compared to 0.4 percent for Kenya, or nearly three times the improvement. Therefore, the impact to the deficit will be much larger.

Second, and not as obvious, the econometric model for South Africa is more complex. South African government spending data include more detail, notably about interest payments and interest rates. The data for Kenya and Nigeria do not have a comparable level of detail.

For South Africa, as inflation and interest payments fall, the model simulates the fiscal balance response. With lower nominal interest rates, the government can allocate more spending to pay down principal, which in turn generates lower

Figure 7.5. Simulation Highlights 2021 Impact

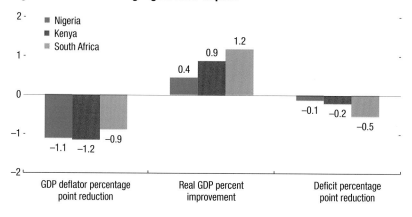

Source: Authors' calculations with Oxford Economics model.

future interest payments. The resulting virtuous cycle quickly produces long-standing and permanent gains. The assumption that there are no sudden tax cuts or additional spending is critical to the improved fiscal outcome. These options could both be very tempting to implement given the improved fiscal position.

Cost savings slowly filter through the economies of Kenya, Nigeria, and South Africa over four years. On average, removing the transaction friction involved in transportation, handling, and inventory reduces inflation by 1 percentage point from the baseline forecast. In the scenario, real GDP expands by 0.85 percentage point. The improvement in the real economy feeds into higher government revenue and lower government expenditure, resulting in an 0.3 percentage point reduction of the deficit as a percent of GDP.

While this exercise using formal modeling cannot guarantee real-world results, it does demonstrate the potential power of blockchain adoption using tools that are accessible to government planners.

RECOMMENDATIONS FOR GOVERNMENT

As discussed throughout this chapter, blockchain and cognitive computing can be transformational for many facets of governmental operations. But to realize their full potential, governments must ensure that certain preconditions are in place.

Standardize Data Models Nationally and Globally

For cognitive systems to learn continuously and provide decision support capabilities, they must have access to large-scale, high-quality data sets. It is therefore essential for governments to have standardized data models, starting at a national level and broadening internationally to the extent possible. Standardization improves the quality of data to be acted upon by minimizing "noise" (extraneous or misleading data) and facilitating information sharing across different sectors and countries. The adoption of standardized models will enable rapid, high-volume, high-quality data collection, which is a core requirement for cognitive systems and blockchain.

Standardize Process Models

While tax laws vary from nation to nation, the basic processes that apply to public finance are very similar. These include work flow, document management, authentication and certification, case management, and others that are ripe for improvement. These processes could be made even more efficient with the help of standardized process models. Such models could streamline data flow and drastically reduce required investment in resources (hardware, software, and human). Moreover, they would enhance the ability of cognitive systems to extract key insights from government data.

Invest in Human Skill Development

Human labor is a finite resource, as are the budgets that support them. The key to success in adopting disruptive technologies is to update human skills rapidly to harness the potential of the new technology. Higher-value jobs that require human judgment, domain expertise, goal setting, relationship building, and creativity are the perfect partners for cognitive systems that support them. They will drive the success of collaborations between people and systems in areas such as counter-fraud, compliance, and citizen-customer engagements, among others. One way to do this is by improving the quality and quantity of the data that fuels digital technologies like cognitive computing and blockchain. Highly skilled humans are the key to overcoming barriers to data sharing and collection. As human skills are updated, lower-value repetitive tasks can be standardized and automated, allowing more efficient use of revenue resources.

Engage in Digital Experimentation

For governments to transform core functions with digital technologies, it will be important for them to develop a flexible, iterative approach to experimentation. Revenue services and treasuries, for example, will need to develop "sandboxes" where they can experiment with specific applications of emerging technologies, such as cognitive and blockchain, in isolation from existing systems. This will enable them to assess the value of these applications and improve them continuously based on the analysis of data outcomes before moving to full-scale implementation. It will also give governments the opportunity to develop the right policy framework to accompany any new applications being introduced.

Such an approach could provide a valuable opportunity to update the skills of government workers by placing them within an innovation ecosystem that includes start-ups and private companies.

CONCLUSION

This chapter argues that the growth and widespread adoption of disruptive digital technologies like blockchain and cognitive computing are both inevitable and essential because of the powerful benefits they provide to users. They are poised to transform the business processes of many industries that are now actively experimenting with them. They can also be used to transform key government public finance activities.

Indeed, it has been said that blockchain is poised to do for transactions what the internet did for information. Blockchain's distributed ledger technology has the potential to build trust into every transaction and remove barriers to doing business globally.

For governments, adoption of these technologies is also a responsibility. Countries everywhere are struggling to deliver sustainable economic growth, adequate social benefits, and efficient public services to their citizens. They face extraordinary budgetary pressures arising from events and vulnerabilities that are extremely difficult to factor into planning using conventional computer systems. These factors include economic downturns, revenue declines and leaks, potential shocks to financial systems, and demographic shifts that impact welfare disbursement. To manage these and other challenges more effectively, governments can utilize blockchain and cognitive computing to help them navigate complexity in operational environments and improve their engagement with constituents.

One way to do this is by using these technologies to understand and interpret fast-growing and complex bodies of data. Ginni Rometty, the IBM chief executive, has referred to data as the "next natural resource," due to its abundance and value to society (Rometty 2013).

But much of these data are messy, unstructured, and unreadable to conventional computing systems. Cognitive computing systems, in contrast, are designed to ingest and interpret massive quantities of unstructured and structured data and discern valuable patterns and insights from both. In a global economy, where time is of the essence in managing crises and value increasingly comes from information, this is a vital capacity for governments and industries to possess.

In a similar way, trusted information, as provided by blockchain, can serve as the foundation for an expansion of the global marketplace by allowing new entrants to participate who otherwise might be shut out—everyone from small farmers to small business owners. Blockchain can help achieve this in large part through the costless verification of transaction data. Blockchain removes the prospect that a trading partner will have to engage in an expensive and time-consuming audit should a transaction with a smaller, lesser-known party go wrong. With a single version of transaction data on a ledger, all the required information to settle a dispute may be evident and visible to everyone who has permission to see it on the blockchain. The audit trail is laid out in one place and there is no need to involve costly intermediaries.

Governments can also draw assurance from the relatively low cost of adopting blockchain and cognitive computing solutions by implementing their delivery through the internet and cloud computing. Moreover, the benefits of these technologies have been shown so far to require few changes to legal and regulatory frameworks. However, their effectiveness can be greatly improved by changes in key data gathering and sharing processes that governments must have the means and the will to implement.

Like all technology, cognitive computing and blockchain will change the way people work. The vast majority of new technologies have broadly benefited human populations over time. They have dramatically improved industrial output, leading to far fewer grueling jobs. But such disruptive improvements are always associated with periods of training and adjustment.

Inevitably, people adapt best by finding higher value in new skills. Technologies that are easiest to integrate will be those that improve human productivity and are easy to interact with. But they cannot replace human judgment. Blockchain and cognitive computing were designed from the beginning to work in concert with human expertise. Governments can help lead the way in developing that expertise for a new technology era and in realizing the full potential of these emerging technologies for all of society.

REFERENCES

Allison, Ian. 2017. "Maersk and IBM Want 10 Million Shipping Containers on the Global Supply Blockchain by Year-End." *International Business Times*, March 8.

Catalini, Christian, and Joshua S. Gans. 2016. "Some Simple Economics of the Blockchain." NBER Working Paper 22952, National Bureau of Economic Research, Cambridge, MA.

Daha, Mariana, and Alan Gelb. 2015. "The Identity Target in the Post-2015 Development Agenda." Note 19, World Bank Transport and ICT Global Practice Connections Series. World Bank, Washington, DC.

Digital Currency Executive (DCE). 2015. "Tunisia Becomes First Nation to Put Nation's Currency on a Blockchain." DCE Brief, December 28.

Douglas, Kate. 2017. "What Makes Senegal's Digital Currency Different? How We Made It in Africa." January 25.

Eurostat. 2008. "NACE Rev. 2: Statistical Classification of Economic Activities in the European Community." Methodologies and Working Papers, Office for Official Publications of the European Communities, Luxembourg.

Kelly, John. 2015. *Computing, Cognition and the Future of Knowing: How Humans and Machines are Forging a New Age of Understanding.* New York: Somers.

Krishna, Arvind. 2016. "IBM Investor Briefing 2016: Blockchain." Presentation at IBM Investor Day, IBM, New York.

Leinbach, Thomas R. 2005. "Transport Costs, Factors and Issues." PowerPoint presentation, University of Kentucky, Lexington, KY.

Metz, Cade. 2016. "Overstock Begins Trading Its Shares via the Bitcoin Blockchain." *WIRED*, December 15.

National Audit Office. 2016. "Fraud and Error in Benefit Expenditure." Report by the Comptroller and Auditor General, London.

Njini, Felix, and Adelaide Changole. 2017. "Kenya Budgets Increased Spending Ahead of General Elections." *Bloomberg Markets*, March 30.

Parker, Luke. 2015. "Tunisian Post Tests African Digital Currency Market." *Brave New Coin*, December 29.

Rodrigue, Jean Paul, and Theo Notteboom. 2017. "Transport Costs and Rates." In *The Geography of Transport Systems*. New York: Routledge.

Rometty, Virginia. 2013. "A Conversation with Ginny Rometty." Interview by James Owens. Council on Foreign Relations Corporate Program. New York, March 7.

Shen, Joyce. 2016. "e-Estonia: The Power and Potential of Digital Identity." Thomson Reuters, December 20.

US Congress House Subcommittee on Energy and Commerce. 2016. Hearing on How to Capitalize on Blockchain, 114th Congregation 2nd Session. Statement by Gennaro Cuomo, Government Publishing Office, Washington, DC.

US Department of Transportation. 2015. "Industry Snapshots, Uses of Transportation 2015." Bureau of Transportation Statistics, Washington, DC.

WIRED. 2017. "The Blockchain Will Save Healthcare and Shipping Billions of Pounds." May 18.

PART III

Modernizing Public Service Delivery and Spending

CHAPTER 8

Using Digital Technology for Public Service Provision in Developing Countries

Potential and Pitfalls

JENNY C. AKER

Public services are important to a country's productivity, growth, and development.[1] Yet the quantity and quality of public services varies widely, in part due to information asymmetries, high transaction costs, and weak institutions.

As such, one promising trend over the past two decades has been growth in the coverage and adoption of digital technologies, particularly information and communication technologies, especially in remote rural areas (Aker and Mbiti 2010; Aker 2011; Nakasone, Torero, and Minten 2014; Aker and Blumenstock 2014; Aker, Ghosh, and Burrell 2016).

In particular, the spread of mobile phone technology offers new opportunities for rural households to realize a variety of broader development goals. In public service provision, digital technology has the potential to increase citizens' access to public and private information, improve coordination among citizens, facilitate data collection to better allocate public goods, and improve access to financial services, especially through mobile money. In addition, by using digital technology to improve tax design and enforcement, this might increase public funds available for financing public services (Chapters 2 and 13).

Over the past decade, numerous digital public service initiatives have been developed and disseminated by both the public and private sector, with an estimated 400 initiatives deployed worldwide as of 2017.[2] While these initiatives span a variety of countries, sectors, and digital technologies, the majority of these initiatives in developing and emerging countries have been in the agriculture,

---

[1]Public service provision is defined as the provision of services to promote economic, social, and environmental sustainability.

[2]For prior reviews in economics on digital agricultural services, see Nakasone, Torero, and Minten (2014); Aker (2011); and Aker, Ghosh, and Burrell (2016); in computer science see Parikh, Patel, and Schwartzman (2007).

education, and health sectors (Nakasone, Torero, and Minten 2014; Aker 2011), as well as the social protection and civic education spheres.

A small but growing number of economic studies of these initiatives suggests that impact is mixed. In particular, the research suggests that such initiatives are primarily successful in improving the efficiency of public service provision—in other words, providing a public service of a given quality and quantity at a lower cost—especially in the area of social protection. However, such systems often require substantial fixed costs to build the necessary digital infrastructure, provide the technology to citizens, and develop the necessary platforms.

In other sectors, such as education and civic education, digital public service provision seems to improve the effectiveness of such interventions—that is, ensuring that these programs meet their stated goals, such as improving educational outcomes and increasing voter participation. The results are more mixed, however, in agriculture and health, despite the relatively large number of initiatives in these areas. In addition, much of the research does not seem to focus on whether digital public service provision is improving the coverage of these services or whether public funds are being put to best use. These initiatives also seem to be most successful when they address key information asymmetries and high transaction costs in that market and sector.

What is less often considered in economic research of these initiatives are basic questions of digital technology access and usability. Digital technologies encompass different types of infrastructure, technologies, and platforms, each of which has unique features, as well as different rates of access and usage, especially in remote areas of developing countries. While research in the computer science discipline focuses heavily on how technology can be used and manipulated by poor and low-literate populations (Medhi, Ratan, and Toyama 2009; Patel and others 2010; Wyche and Steinfield 2015; Aker, Ghosh, and Burrell 2016), these factors are less often considered in economics studies of the subject. Yet low uptake or usage of digital public service initiatives could, in part, explain some of the observed null results in economics studies of their impact.

This chapter first reviews the challenges in public service provision, focusing on different types of market failures. It then looks at ways digital technologies can overcome these failures and discusses the types of digital public services disseminated in the past decade, updating recent economics reviews in this area (Aker 2011; Aker and Blumenstock 2014; Nakasone, Torero, and Minten 2014; Aker, Aker, Ghosh, and Burrell). The chapter then reviews existing research of the impact of digital public services on the effectiveness and efficiency of such services, focusing primarily on the agriculture, civic engagement, education, health, and social protection sectors. It closes with a look at the gaps in the design and implementation of these initiatives, before providing suggestions for future research and policy.

This review focuses primarily on lower- and middle-income countries and does not include digital public service provision in high-income countries. Notably, it also does not include the so-called Digital Five—a network of leading digital governments that seek to strengthen the digital economy and the government's relationship with technology.[3] Also excluded are key digital services such as tax design, collection and enforcement, as well as national identification schemes. These are covered in other chapters of this book. In addition, while this chapter covers the use of digital technology in social protection programs and for salary payments, it focuses on only those programs with rigorous economic research evaluating their impact. Other examples of the use of digital payments are included in Chapter 13.

PUBLIC SERVICE PROVISION AND ECONOMIC DEVELOPMENT

The Challenge of Public Service Provision

Public service provision is broadly defined as the provision of goods and services to promote economic, social, and environmental sustainability (World Bank 2005). These goods and services include, among others, electricity, education, emergency services, environmental protection, financial services, health care, postal services, public security, transport, social welfare, and water.[4] Public service provision is often associated with a social consensus that certain services should be available to all, regardless of income. These services can either be provided directly by the public sector or financed by the public sector and outsourced to other service providers (World Bank 2005).[5] Even where public services are not publicly provided or financed, they are often subject to regulation.

Significant economic literature measures the relationship between public services and economic development, showing a positive correlation between the two (Bartik 1991; Wasylenko 1991; Munnell 1992; Fox and Murray 1993). A majority of these studies focus on the impacts of particular public services, such as infrastructure, education and public safety, and show that "some public services . . . have a positive effect on some measures of economic development in some contexts" (Fisher 1997). Of the public services examined, transportation and infrastructure services show the strongest positive relationship with economic growth (Fisher 1997; Donaldson, forthcoming; Dinkelman 2011; Michaels 2008; Duflo and Pande 2007; Jensen 2007; Aker 2010). At the same time, many of these studies focus on a single partial equilibrium result.

---

[3]The Digital Five include New Zealand, Estonia, United Kingdom, Israel, and Korea.

[4]While access to financial services is required for economic and social development, it is often not directly provided by the public sector, but access and usage is usually regulated or enabled by the public sector.

[5]A number of models can be used in providing public services. These include, but are not limited to, "government provision; managing, funding, and regulating external providers through grants and the purchase of services, including where a market or quasi-market for public services is created (that is, purchaser); subsidizing users to purchase services from external providers; imposing community service obligations on public and private providers; and encouraging individuals and communities to be responsible for their public services and to use mutual aid and philanthropic resources to supplement government funding" (World Bank 2005).

Despite the potential importance of public services for economic growth, stability, and development, the quantity and quality of public services remain limited worldwide, especially in countries with limited resources and weak institutions (Batley, McCourt, and Mcloughlin 2012; World Bank 2005).

In infrastructure, for example, the density of road networks—a key public good for the flow of goods and services—varies widely across and within countries. The lowest density of paved roads in the world is in sub-Saharan Africa, for example; out of 2 million kilometers of roads, only 29 percent are paved (Aker and Mbiti 2010). While it is estimated that 85 percent of the world population has access to electricity, this hides wide disparities across and within countries, ranging from 20 to 80 percent (World Bank n.d.).[6] In sub-Saharan Africa and Southeast Asia, it is estimated that 48 and 32 percent of people do not have access to electricity, respectively (McKinsey & Company 2015).

In education, pupil-teacher ratios—a common indicator of human resource capacity in this sector—have either remained stable or increased considerably in certain regions. In South and West Asia, pupil-teacher ratios have reached 41:1 and 44:1 in sub-Saharan Africa, compared with an average of less than 25:1 in other regions (UNESCO 2014). Yet even in those areas where teachers are present, teacher absenteeism remains a problem. Transparency International (2013) estimated that absenteeism, across 21 developing countries, ranged from 11 to 30 percent. Not only is teacher absenteeism correlated with lower educational outcomes (Duflo, Hanna, and Ryan 2012; Muralidharan and others 2017), but it also accounts for the loss of up to one-quarter of primary school spending in some countries. This amounts to $16 million in Ecuador and $2 billion in India annually, representing 10–24 percent of recurring primary education expenditures in those countries (Transparency International 2013).

In social protection programs worldwide, implementation bottlenecks reduce their effectiveness, but developing countries face particularly high costs (Banerjee and others 2016; Finan, Olken, and Pande 2015).[7] Social assistance programs often represent a significant portion of government spending, between 1 percent and 2 percent of GDP on average, according to the World Bank ASPIRE database. Yet, despite their importance in government spending, these programs are often subject to challenges in targeting, that is, reaching the intended beneficiaries (World Bank 2005; Pritchett 2005). In India, for example, only 15 percent of spending actually reaches the intended beneficiaries by some measures, even though the country spends about 2 percent of GDP on social protection pro-

[6]The World Bank Sustainable Energy for All database is from the Sustainable Energy for All Global Tracking Framework led jointly by the World Bank, International Energy Agency, and Energy Sector Management Assistance Program.

[7]While definitions of social protection programs vary widely, the World Bank's Atlas of Social Protection program (ASPIRE) defines them as publicly funded programs that aim to improve the well-being of targeted populations, especially of the poor, including, but not limited to, conditional and unconditional cash transfers, social pensions, school feeding, in-kind transfers, food and fuel subsidies, fee waivers, and public works (ASPIRE: Indicators of Resilience and Equity).

grams (IPA 2016). Focusing on a subsidized rice distribution program in Indonesia (*Operasi Pasar Khusus*), Olken (2006) found that 18 percent of rice disappeared. In a separate study of a rice subsidy program in Indonesia (*Raskin*, or "Rice for the Poor"), beneficiaries received only about one-third of their intended subsidy (Banerjee and others 2016).

Beyond transfers in-kind—which may seem especially vulnerable to corruption and leakage—cash transfer programs can also be subject to inefficiencies. In India, the Mahatma Gandhi National Rural Employment Guarantee Scheme is one of the largest social protection programs in the world, reaching almost 50 million households in 2013 (Banerjee, Duflo, and others 2016; Muralidharan, Niehaus, and Sukhtankar 2016). The scheme guarantees households 100 days of work per year, typically in unskilled manual labor on infrastructure projects (Banerjee, Hanna, and others 2016). However, a recent study estimated that at least 20 percent of official employment under the scheme was not accounted for in household surveys (Banerjee and others 2016).[8]

The constraints related to access to and quality of public service provision seem to disproportionately affect the poor. For example, Chaudhury and others (2006) found that 19 percent of public primary school teachers and 35 percent of public health care workers were absent in six developing countries, with lower absenteeism in poorer countries and in poorer states. In addition, Olken (2006) found that ethnically heterogeneous and more sparsely populated areas seemed to be disproportionately missing rice.

Market Failures in Public Service Provision

Politics, poor governance, and weak institutions have become central to explanations of the under-provision and low quality of public services in developing countries (Batley, McCourt, and Mcloughlin 2012). While much of the economics literature on public service provision focuses on the importance of good governance and strong institutions (Batley, McCourt, and Mcloughlin 2012; Finan, Olken, and Pande 2015), it has historically paid less attention to the internal workings of the state and the individuals who provide the public services (Finan, Olken, and Pande 2015). While institutions and personnel economics are crucial in understanding the provision of public services, they are also set within the context of other market failures.

As some public services are pure public goods, the market will fail to provide these goods at optimal levels. This is, in part, due to the non-rivalry and non-excludability of these goods, and hence the free-rider problem. In the context of weak institutions, it is difficult for governments to identify citizens' preferences and willingness to pay for, monitor the provision of, or enforce

---

[8]Furthermore, demand for employment is often greater than supply: in Bihar, an estimated 77 percent of households wanted but could not find Mahatma Gandhi National Rural Employment Guarantee Scheme work in 2009–10.

taxation to raise funds for these goods, which, in turn, undermines their efficient allocation.

Even if a public service is not a pure public good, some public services may have public goods properties, such as health, education, and some infrastructure, and therefore generate positive and network externalities (Besley and Ghatak 2006).[9] If these externalities are not internalized by the market, then, similar to the public goods problem, these services will not be provided at optimal levels.

In theory, public services can be provided by the public or private sector, as long as there are no transaction costs and strong informational assumptions are met (Coase 1960). Yet public service provision is often plagued by imperfect information. For example, given long distances to remote rural areas, limited budgets, and poor infrastructure, governments often have a difficult time monitoring public sector employees, which can lead to corruption, absenteeism, and poor performance. These problems may, in fact, be further exacerbated by the nature of public sector employment contracts, which may make it difficult to provide incentives to or sanction employees who are consistently underperforming (Finan, Olken, and Pande 2015).

These information constraints also affect citizens' knowledge about the location of public services and their quality, where to find these services, whether they are eligible to receive such services, and how best to use them. This can further affect the efficient provision of public services, as well as citizens' ability to provide feedback on their allocation and quality (World Bank 2016).

Yet, imperfect information can also affect governments' ability to finance the provision of public services. As mentioned above, if governments are unable to identify consumers' preferences and willingness to pay for such services, it can be difficult to determine their optimal provision. This, in turn, makes it more challenging to design tax schemes to fund public goods. Even if consumers' preferences could be revealed, an additional question is whether tax schemes could be effectively enforced, thus further reducing the financing mechanisms available to finance public goods.

Finally, some public services may have few service providers, either in the public or private sector. While this may be optimal in markets with economies of scale or high entry costs, in the absence of appropriate regulation, this can also lead to higher prices, lower quantities, and lower-quality services.

The next section outlines some of the ways in which digital technology can address some of these market failures and the mechanisms through which it may improve the provision of public services.

---

[9] Only some parts of the health, education, and infrastructure sectors have substantial public goods components. For example, the distribution of electricity may have important network externalities, whereas electricity generation may not necessarily be a public good. Interventions such as clean water and vaccination have much stronger public goods components than some curative treatments (Besley and Ghatak 2006).

THE POTENTIAL FOR DIGITAL IN PUBLIC SERVICE PROVISION

Digital Coverage and Adoption

Despite constraints in public service provision worldwide, digital infrastructure—including the internet, mobile phones, and other tools that can be used to collect, store, analyze, and share information digitally—has increased substantially over the past 15 years (World Bank 2016). Between 1999 and 2014, the percentage of people with access to mobile phone coverage grew from 10 percent to 90 percent (ITU 2014; GSMA 2013). Mobile phone coverage has expanded rapidly in Africa, Asia, and Latin America, from largely non-existent networks at the turn of the century to a point where over 70 percent of the population of sub-Saharan Africa is covered by the mobile network (GSMA 2013; Aker and Blumenstock 2014).[10]

This expansion in mobile network coverage has corresponded with increases in mobile phone adoption and usage (Aker and Mbiti 2010; Aker and Blumenstock 2014). According to the World Bank's 2016 *World Development Report*, more households in certain regions own a mobile phone than have access to electricity or clean water, and approximately 70 percent of the poorest populations in developing countries own a mobile phone (World Bank 2016).[11] In sub-Saharan Africa alone, approximately one-third of the population has an active mobile phone subscription (GSMA 2013). In addition, over half of the world's mobile-broadband subscriptions are based in developing countries, with coverage rates in Africa reaching close to 20 percent in 2014 (ITU 2014; Aker and Blumenstock 2014).

In addition to mobile phone coverage, the number of internet users has increased significantly, from 1 billion users in 2005 to an estimated 3.2 billion users at the end of 2015 (World Bank 2016). Nevertheless, while internet access and smartphone penetration have grown substantially in many developing countries, disparity remains wide across and within countries. Smartphone usage is still primarily concentrated in urban, wealthier, and more highly educated populations in these countries.

---

[10]As the growth of mobile telephony has been driven largely by the private sector, this growth has not been uniformly accessible to all segments of society, and was initially skewed toward a wealthier, educated, urban, and predominantly male population (Aker and Mbiti 2010; Aker and Blumenstock 2014).

[11]Growth of the worldwide subscriber base is fastest in developing countries, with "four out of five new connections being made in the developing world, and 880 million unique developing-market subscribers estimated to register new accounts by 2020" (GSMA 2013). As of 2009, over two-thirds of the population of Asia and three-quarters of the population of Latin America had access to mobile phone coverage (Aker and Blumenstock 2014). Roughly 55 percent of the world's 2.3 billion mobile-broadband subscriptions are also based in developing countries, with coverage rates in Africa reaching close to 20 percent in 2014, as compared with 2 percent in 2010 (ITU 2014; Aker and Blumenstock 2014).

The Potential for Digital in Public Service Provision

In remote rural areas, digital technology—primarily mobile phone networks—has often represented the first access to digital infrastructure (Aker and Mbiti 2010; Aker and Blumenstock 2014). While each type of digital technology has unique features, this section focuses on one type of digital technology: simple mobile phones. This is primarily because simple mobile phones are still the most ubiquitous digital technology by coverage and adoption, especially in rural areas of developing countries, which often have the lowest access to public services.[12]

Broadly speaking, simple mobile phone technology has two primary functions: for communication (voice, messaging) and for money transfers. As a communication device, mobile phone technology reduces the cost of communicating, improving the circulation of information within a person's social networks ("private" information) (Aker and Mbiti 2010; Aker and Blumenstock 2014; Aker, Ghosh, and Burrell 2016). It also facilitates the dissemination of "public" information (that is, information that is provided through the government, non-governmental organizations, and firms). With the introduction of mobile money and other digital financial services, mobile phones can also allow consumers and firms to more easily access financial services, such as money transfers, input vouchers, commitment savings, and credit (Aker and Mbiti 2010; Aker and Blumenstock 2014; Aker, Ghosh and Burrell 2016).

As communication devices, simple mobile phones have greatly reduced the cost of communicating over long distances, allowing individuals to communicate with each other more frequently (Aker and Mbiti 2010). Relative to personal travel, the transport and opportunity costs of using a mobile phone are significantly cheaper (Aker 2010; Aker and Mbiti 2010; Aker and Blumenstock 2014; Aker, Ghosh, and Burrell 2016). From the government's perspective, mobile phone technology can reduce the cost of disseminating crucial information.[13] In Niger, for example, replacing an extension agent's field visit with one digital interaction (that is, an SMS or a phone call) reduced the communication costs by half (Aker 2010).

In addition, simple digital technology can reduce the cost of collecting, processing, and disseminating information, especially compared with traditional survey methods used by government agencies (Aker 2010; Aker and Blumenstock 2014; Aker, Ghosh, and Burrell 2016). This can take the form of simple phone or SMS surveys, as well as "big data" on voice, SMS, and mobile money transactions (Blumenstock 2016).

The launch of mobile money services—which allows individuals to transfer stored value on their phone—significantly reduces the cost of transferring money

---

[12]In theory, more advanced digital technologies—such as computers, laptops, and smartphones, which have access to the internet and other features—would offer additional possibilities for addressing some of these market failures.

[13]If information is shared by a public or private sector "clearinghouse," this can, in turn, allow governments to share information more widely and more quickly.

compared with other means (Aker and Mbiti 2010; Aker and Blumenstock 2014). This cost reduction can, in turn, allow individuals to transfer money more easily, potentially increasing the frequency and amount of transfers received and allowing households to smooth consumption in the face of shocks (Jack and Suri 2014; Aker and Blumenstock 2014; Blumenstock and others 2016). As discussed in other chapters of this book, mobile money can therefore reduce the costs associated with implementing public transfer programs or salaries, as well as encourage new financial providers to enter the public service space, especially as the costs of providing these services can be cheaper.

Mobile money can also potentially be used as a secure place to save (Mas and Mayer 2012; Aker and Wilson 2013; Aker and Blumenstock 2014). Since the mobile money "account" is protected by a user password, m-money might offer greater security than at-home savings mechanisms, improving access to emergency savings or encouraging individuals to save for particular objectives (Aker and Blumenstock 2014).

How can these features of digital technology—even the simple mobile phone—address market failures in public service provision?

In *information*, these cost reductions can improve citizens' access to public and private information (Aker and Blumenstock 2014; Aker, Ghosh, and Burrell 2016), which can make markets more efficient and lead to net welfare gains. This reduction in search costs should, in theory, allow market actors to search more quickly and over a broader geographic area, in a wide variety of domains—education, health, and agricultural prices (Aker and Blumenstock 2014). These cost reductions also facilitate increased and more timely contact with members of one's social network, as well as promote better access to both public and private information (Aker 2010; Aker and Blumenstock 2014; Aker, Ghosh, and Burrell 2016).

Mobile phones also offer a promising and cost-effective method for the dissemination of public or quasi-public information, such as a public or private sector "clearinghouse," which can, in turn, allow governments to share information on public goods (Aker 2010; Aker and Blumenstock 2014; Aker, Ghosh, and Burrell 2016). This can also help to address the moral hazard problem associated with monitoring public sector agents, by allowing governments to more easily contact employees or collect data on absenteeism. In addition, digital technology can provide educational services for public sector employees and citizens at lower cost and greater outreach than traditional programs (Aker and Blumenstock 2014).

In public goods provision, digital data collection can allow governments to get better access to citizens' preferences for public goods—such as through digital surveys, which can allow automation of routine activities (World Bank 2016, 2017). At the same time, it can also improve citizens' involvement in and engagement with those public goods, potentially improving provider accountability (Aker and Blumenstock 2014; World Bank 2017).

Increased access to digital services and information-sharing can also increase citizens' social learning from their peers, which could speed up the adoption process of other public services.

And finally, with public-private partnerships, as well as the involvement of the private sector in public service provision, digital technology can encourage new service providers to come into this space, potentially addressing imperfect competition.

Thus, even simple digital technology could improve public service provision by (World Bank 2016):

- "Enabling governments to replace some factors used for producing services through the automation of routine activities, particularly discretionary tasks vulnerable to rent-seeking, such as social protection programs" (World Bank 2016); and

- Overcoming information barriers, which can improve monitoring (both by citizens through regular feedback on service quality and by governments through better management of government workers) and citizen coordination (World Bank 2016).

In particular, digital technology could improve the effectiveness of such services by allowing public service programs to better meet their stated goals and improve the efficiency of such services by ensuring that they are being delivered in a least-cost manner for a given quantity and quality. It could also improve coverage of such services by ensuring that they are being expanded with appropriate partnership or contractual relationships within and beyond government as well as ensure that they are providing "money's worth" by helping to assess whether the public funds are being put to best use. These potential impacts are, of course, affected by the existing market failures associated with public service provision and the strength of institutions within a given context.

DIGITAL PUBLIC SERVICE PROVISION: PRACTICE AND EVIDENCE

Overall, it is estimated that there are more than 400 digital public service programs worldwide, in a variety of contexts, digital forms, and sectors (GSMA m-Agri deployment tracker; GSMA m-Health deployment tracker; Aker, Ghosh, and Burrell 2016).[14] These are implemented by governments, non-governmental organizations, the private sector, and public-private partnerships. These programs span public services in sectors including agriculture, civic education, education, environment, health, financial services, social protection, and utilities. In addition, they use a variety of digital technologies, from computers to mobile phones to radios to smartphones (Aker, Ghosh, and Burrell 2016).[15]

---

[14]These estimates are based upon GSMA's database of m-agriculture, m-health, and mobile money deployments, as well as the author's own research on specific digital initiatives and economic research in this area.

[15]More broadly, "Digital government is defined as the optimal use of electronic channels of communication and engagement to improve citizen satisfaction in service delivery, enhance economic competitiveness, forge new levels of engagement and trust, and increase productiv-

Figure 8.1. Number of Research Studies on Digital Public Services, by Region and Sector

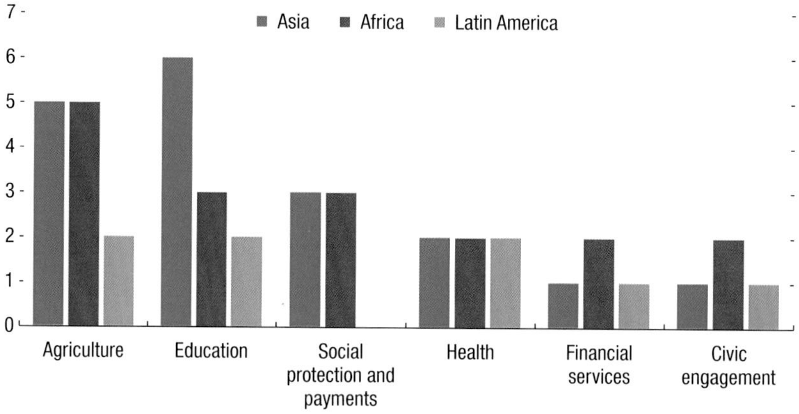

Source: Author's calculations.

Despite the proliferation of digital public service programs, only a fraction of these are being researched. For this chapter, we identified 44 studies across 17 countries, primarily focusing on studies in developing countries or emerging markets and those using rigorous impact evaluation methodologies.[16] A majority of studies take place in Asia and Africa, with many in Asia focusing on India. Across all different types of public services, the studies are primarily focused on certain sectors, namely, agriculture, education, health, social protection, and civic education (Figure 8.1).

While the impacts of these initiatives depend upon the sector, the technology, and the context, in general, digital service provision seems to have a positive impact on the effectiveness of certain public services, such as education, social protection, and civic education. In social protection, studies have shown that digital systems are often more efficient, as they have lower costs of implementation, despite high initial fixed costs. Few studies are designed to measure the impacts of digital technology on the coverage of these public services or "money's worth"—that is, whether public spending should be spent in another sector or area.

---

ity of public services. A digital government encompasses the full range of digitalization—from the core digitalization of public services to the digital infrastructure, governance and processes, including both front- and back-office transformation needed to deliver the new service paradigm" (Accenture 2014).

[16]This includes impact evaluation studies that use both experimental and non-experimental approaches. The 44 studies discussed in this chapter may not be representative of all academic or other studies in this field. This review excludes key studies in other areas, such as tax collection and national identification schemes covered in other chapters of this book.

Education[17]

In education, digital technology has primarily been used for one of two purposes: as a pedagogical tool in the classroom and as a tool for monitoring teacher attendance. Overall, most studies of the impact of digital technology as a pedagogical tool suggest that digital technology improves student learning in the short term, but that these impacts diminish in the medium term. Studies in digital monitoring suggest that these programs improve teacher attendance and improve learning outcomes, where they are measured.

Substantial literature assesses the impact of digital technology on learning outcomes, with most of these studies focusing on computers and laptops in primary and secondary schools. While a majority of these studies find that computers have positive effect on student learning outcomes (Banerjee, Cole, and others 2007; Linden 2008; Lai and others 2015; Yang and others 2013; Lai, Khaddage, and Knezek 2013; Mo and others 2014), some find no effects (Barrera-Osario and Linden 2009; Beuermann and others 2015) or negative effects (Linden 2008; Malamud and Pop-Eleches 2011). Yet, few of these studies measure the impacts upon learning outcomes in the longer term, except Banerjee and others (2007).[18]

Focusing on mobile phones as a pedagogical tool for adults, Aker, Ksoll, and Lybbert (2012) conducted a randomized control trial (RCT) in Niger, where a mobile-phone-based component was added to an otherwise standard adult education program. Overall, the authors found that the mobile phone technology substantially improved adults' writing and math scores in the short and medium term, and led to other improvements in household well-being (Aker, Ksoll, and Lybbert 2012; Aker and Ksoll 2017). While the digital approach was not more efficient, as it was more expensive than the traditional program, it was more cost-effective. Aker and others (2014) found similar results for a mobile-phone-administered adult education program in Los Angeles.

In digital monitoring, Duflo, Hanna, and Ryan (2012) find that interventions that use cameras and financial incentives reduce teacher absenteeism and increase children's test scores. In Uganda, Cilliers and others (2016) find that mobile phone monitoring and financial incentives in Uganda improve teacher attendance, primarily when there are financial incentives; however, they do not measure impacts on learning outcomes. And finally, using mobile phones to monitor adult education teachers in Niger (without financial incentives), Aker and Ksoll (2017) find that monitoring increases students' learning outcomes, but primarily in the short term.

---

[17]This section excludes many of the studies included in paper by Escueta and others 2017, which focuses on the use of digital in education for developed countries and which was released in August 2017.

[18]These include Linden (2008); Barrera-Osario and Linden (2009); Banerjee and others (2007); Barrow and others (2009); Malamud and Pop-Eleches (2011); Lai, Khaddage, and Knezek (2013); Beuermann and others (2013); Fairlie and Robinson (2013); and Carrillo, Onofa, and Ponce (2010).

Social Protection

In general, digital technology has been used in social protection in one of two ways: as a mechanism for implementing such programs, either through digital national identification schemes or electronic income transfers; or as an alternative means for targeting potential beneficiaries of such programs, primarily through big data. While there are a number of initiatives in this area, existing studies suggest that digital can reduce the costs associated with implementing these programs, allowing the public sector to provide these transfers at a lower cost.

In one of the first studies of a digital social protection program, Aker and others (2016) used an RCT to measure the impact of using mobile money to distribute cash transfers in Niger. They found that mobile money reduced the implementing agency's costs of disbursing the transfers and program recipients' costs of obtaining those transfers as compared with the manual cash transfer program. In addition, program recipients who received the transfer through m-money used the transfer to purchase more diverse food items and had higher diet diversity. Nevertheless, there were substantial fixed costs to setting up the digital transfer distribution system and there were no impacts on leakage, which has been a primary justification for many of these programs.

Using a different digital technology—biometrically authenticated payments infrastructure ("Smartcards")—Muralidharan, Niehaus, and Sukhtankar (2016) measured the impact of this digital infrastructure on two social protection programs in India. Using an RCT, they found that the new system delivered faster and less corrupt payments without adversely affecting access to the program (Muralidharan, Niehaus, and Sukhtankar 2016). The investment was cost-effective as well, as beneficiaries' time was equal to the cost of the intervention. There was also a significant reduction in leakage.

Finally, Banerjee and others (2016) assessed the impact of a digital program that linked the flow of funds to expenditures in the context of a social protection program in India. They found that the new system reduced program expenditures without a concurrent decrease in employment or wages, suggesting that increased transparency reduced leakage (JPAL 2016). The policy did not have an impact on beneficiaries' employment or wages (JPAL 2016).

Outside of the use of digital technology to implement social protection programs, digital data—such as mobile phone records—have been used as an alternative means of targeting the poor (Blumenstock and others 2015; Blumenstock 2017). While these studies have not been used for targeting in an existing social protection program, Blumenstock and others (2015) and Blumenstock (2016) show that an individual's mobile phone use can be used to infer socioeconomic status, and a population's mobile phone data can be used to reconstruct the distribution of wealth within a nation.

Yet beyond the use of big data for targeting, mobile phones can also be used to collect remote and more frequent data for social protection or other development programs (Dillon 2012; Aker 2011). For example, mobile phones can be used to collect more frequent data from households, either as a complement or substitute for in-person surveys, which often occur annually (Dillon 2012).

Civic Education

In civic education, digital technology has been primarily used in one of three ways: (1) providing more frequent transmission of information between citizens and the state, often during elections; (2) verifying polling results digitally during elections; and (3) digitalizing electoral ballots. Overall, these studies have found that digital approaches have effectively increased voter participation during elections and reduced fraud.

While numerous studies assess the impact of the provision of civic information on voter participation and electoral outcomes (Gine and Mansuri 2011; Banerjee and others 2011; Chong and others 2015; Humphreys and Weinstein 2012), studies on the provision of civic information digitally—especially in developing countries—are more recent (Dale and Strauss 2009). Using an RCT during the 2009 elections in Mozambique, Aker, Collier, and Vicente (2017) found that the provision of civic education through SMS, as well as a mobile phone hotline to report electoral fraud, increased voter turnout and reduced voter fraud.

In electoral monitoring, an RCT that introduced a simple camera-phone-based intervention that photographed election return forms at polling centers in Afghanistan substantially reduced fraud (Callen and Long 2015; World Bank 2016). A similar experiment during the 2012 elections in Uganda decreased the vote share for the incumbent, the candidate most likely to benefit from voter fraud, and decreased other measures of fraud (Callen and others 2016; World Bank 2016). In Brazil, the introduction of the digital ballot in the 1990s increased voter participation—especially for low-literate populations—and reduced voter fraud (Fujiwara 2015; World Bank 2016).

Agriculture[19]

Digital technology in the agricultural sector has primarily been used in three ways: (1) to provide information to farmers about agricultural techniques, prices or weather; (2) to provide agricultural extension advice; and (3) to monitor agricultural extension agents (Aker, Ghosh, and Burrell 2016). Overall, studies on digital agriculture initiatives suggest that such services increase farmers'

---

[19]This section draws heavily on Aker, Ghosh, and Burrell (2016). It excludes research on the impact of information technology on the private provision of information, that is, in which farmers, traders, and other actors share information privately through digital technologies, rather than an external platform. Overall, that body of evidence suggests that access to mobile phone coverage and usage can improve farmers' and traders' access to information and market performance. Several studies have found that mobile phone coverage is associated with improved agricultural market efficiency, as defined as a reduction in price dispersion across markets (Jensen 2007; Aker 2010; Mittal and others, 2010; Aker and Fafchamps 2015), but with mixed impacts on farm-gate prices (Aker and Fafchamps 2015; Mitra and others 2015; Futch and McIntosh 2009).

knowledge in particular areas—such as prices and cropping systems—but have little to no impact on agricultural practices, production, or farm-gate prices.

In digital agricultural information, there is a significant body of research in sub-Saharan Africa, India, and Latin America. In Uganda, an RCT that assessed the impact of providing market prices through the radio found that the intervention increased farmers' prices and maize sold (Svensson and Yanagizawa 2009; Aker, Ghosh, and Burrell 2016). Yet other studies on the impact of digital market price information and weather systems were more mixed: while two studies found that digital information systems increased prices, others found no effects (Aker, Ghosh, and Burrell 2016; Courtois and Subervie 2015; Hildebrant and others 2014; Nakasone 2013; Mitra and others 2015; Camacho and Conover 2011; Fafchamps and Minten 2012). Yet the introduction of internet kiosks that provided price information and quality testing in India had a positive effect on soybean prices and production (Goyal 2010).

In digital agricultural extension advice, using a RCT in India, Cole and Fernando (2016) found that mobile-phone-based agricultural extension information encouraged farmers to invest more in recommended agricultural inputs and increased cumin and cotton yields (Aker, Ghosh, and Burrell 2016). In Kenya, an RCT of an SMS-based extension information system found that the system increased sugar cane yields, but these results were not sustained beyond the first year (Casaburi and others 2014).

In digital monitoring, Jones and Kondylis (2014) used an RCT to test the impact of different feedback mechanisms for agricultural extension providers (Aker, Ghosh, and Burrell 2016). While both in-person and digital monitoring interventions were equally effective, the digital services were substantially cheaper, suggesting it is a more cost-effective way to obtain such feedback.

Health

While digital technology in the health sector has been used in a variety of ways—for medical devices, recordkeeping, and providing information and reminders—the majority of studies in developing countries has been in the latter area. Similar to digital agriculture interventions, these studies have found that digital technology is associated with improvements in knowledge, with mixed evidence on behavioral change and other health outcomes.

The use of SMS to provide health-related information has increased substantially over the past decade (Akerlof 1991; O'Donoghue and Rabin 1999, 2001; Frederick, Loewenstein, and O'Donoghue 2002; Banerjee and Mullainathan 2008, 2010; Bandiera, Barankay, and Rasul 2005; Duflo 2012). While some studies found that sending mothers SMS improved breastfeeding practices (Jiang and others 2014; Flax and others 2014), a systematic review of interventions that used SMS to encourage drug adherence found mixed results (Nglazi and others 2013). In sexual and reproductive health, several studies have found that the provision of reproductive health information in public schools led to behavioral change, lower sexually transmitted disease prevalence, and lower self-reported pregnancy rates (Chong and others 2013; Rokicki and others 2017).

Putting It All Together

While the studies included above include only a subset of digital public service initiatives, particularly those in developing countries and emerging markets, there are several key findings. Across all sectors and countries, digital service provision seems to improve the effectiveness of these interventions, defined as the likelihood that a particular intervention helps to meet a stated goal.

This is particularly the case in the education, social protection, and civic education sectors. For example, in education, digital technology has helped to improve educational outcomes, at least in the shorter term. In social protection, digital technology increased the likelihood that program recipients received their transfers in a timely manner.

Finally, in civic education, digital technology increased voter participation and reduced voter fraud in elections. However, in the health and agriculture sectors, while digital technology often improved beneficiaries' access to information, impacts upon other outcomes—in terms of either behavioral change or welfare—were more mixed.

In the area of efficiency—defined in this chapter as providing a public service at a lower cost than the status quo—the impact of digital technology is also more mixed. While the provision of information digitally in the agriculture, health, and civic education sectors is, on average, less expensive than traditional means of providing this information, these initiatives are not necessarily always more cost-effective, with the exception of the civic education sector. In education, digital approaches are often more expensive than the traditional means of providing educational services. But they are also more cost-effective, as they result in better outcomes for the same cost. And for social protection programs, there are large efficiency gains: of the three digital social protection programs studied, the variable costs of providing such programs were lower than the alternative, although this often meant large fixed costs for setting up the systems.

Two other criteria often used to assess public service provision are coverage and value for money; in other words, whether public services are provided to the broader population, even in remote rural areas, and whether public funds are being put to their best use. For these two criteria, the evidence is less informative, as most of the studies included in this chapter do not explicitly assess either of these measures.

THE POTENTIAL PITFALLS OF THE DIGITAL PROVISION OF PUBLIC SERVICES

Despite the potential of digital technology to improve the effectiveness, efficiency, and coverage of digital services in developing countries, there are potential pitfalls in the use of digital for public service provision.

A primary consideration is the type of the digital technology that can be used; that is, the infrastructure, the device (that is, computer, smart phone, mobile phone), the platform (SMS, voice, USSD), and the interfaces (Aker, Ghosh, and Burrell 2016). While smartphones offer new opportunities in many countries, they also add new challenges and costs, and are not yet widely adopted in most rural areas (Aker, Ghosh, and Burrell 2016). Simple mobile phones are widely adopted, but SMS holds limited information and requires some ability to read, and voice platforms can be costly. While digital public service provision can rely upon higher-tech options, understanding the costs associated with building such infrastructure, as well as the constraints to adoption and usage by the targeted populations, is important.

A key assumption of using digital for public service provision is that it will help to overcome key market failures for poor rural populations—namely, imperfect information and high transaction costs (Aker, Ghosh, and Burrell 2016; Aker and Blumenstock 2014). While these are relevant assumptions in most contexts and for most public services, digital technology will only be successful in increasing knowledge, lowering transaction costs, changing behavior, and improving outcomes if a number of necessary conditions exist.

Focusing on information asymmetries, for digital technology to have an impact on knowledge, behavioral change, and other welfare outcomes, information must be a constraint in a given market context. One potential explanation for the weak and mixed results of digital for agriculture and health initiatives may be that such initiatives are not providing relevant, high-quality, and timely information for the intended users (Aker, Ghosh, and Burrell 2016).

Even if digital technology addresses the key market failures of imperfect information and high transaction costs, citizens still need access to other public goods, financial services, and institutions to translate those cost reductions into action. For example, in the area of agriculture, several research papers have noted farmers' limited bargaining power, which limits the potential effectiveness of providing information (Nakasone, Torero, and Minten 2014). Similarly, if farmers do not have access to credit markets, this can limit their capacity to meaningfully use any information provided digitally (Srinivasan and Burrell 2013; Casaburi and Reed 2014; Aker, Ghosh, and Burrell 2016). And finally, if digital technology is used to monitor public service agents, but there are no incentives or sanctions associated with that monitoring, this can limit their effectiveness.

Clearly, a number of digital deployments exist worldwide, yet economic research on these initiatives remains relatively limited and concentrated in particular areas. While such programs may lead to net welfare improvements, it is not always clear that they will improve the welfare of targeted populations. Additional research into these initiatives is needed, using a combination of experimental and non-experimental techniques, comparing the digital intervention with the standard approach (Aker 2011; Aker, Ghosh, and Burrell 2016). As part of this research, it will also be important to think about the cost-effectiveness and efficiency of such interventions, both from the institutional (government) and beneficiary perspective. This is particularly important for low-income users; although the service may be provided more cheaply using information technology, it may also result in additional expenses costs.

THE WAY FORWARD

Overall, digital technology offers opportunities to increase access to information, reduce transfer costs, and automate certain tasks, with multiple programs being piloted worldwide. While existing evidence suggests that digital technology can improve efficiency and effectiveness, especially in particular sectors, this is a fraction of what we need to know in this area, and many of these results are often partial equilibrium results. In addition, while digital technologies can improve the effectiveness and efficiency of public service provision, this may not necessarily translate into macroeconomic growth or stronger institutions. And finally, as these technologies are used, understanding the existing market failures—as well as the existing digital technology infrastructure and usage—is key to thinking through their potential impacts and pitfalls.

REFERENCES

Abdul Latif Jameel Poverty Action Lab. 2011. "The Price Is Wrong: Charging Small Fees Dramatically Reduces Access to Important Products for the Poor." *J-PAL Bulletin* (April), Poverty Action Lab, Cambridge, MA.

Accenture. 2014. "Digital Government: Pathways to Delivering Services for the Future."

Aker, Jenny. 2010. "Information from Markets Near and Far: Mobile Phones and Agricultural Markets in Niger." *American Economic Journal: Applied Economics* 2 (3): 46–59.

Aker, Jenny C. 2011. "Dial A for Agriculture: A Review of ICTs for Agricultural Extension in Developing Countries." *Agricultural Economics* 42 (6): 631–47.

Aker, Jenny C., and Joshua Blumenstock. 2014. "The Economics of New Technologies in Africa." In *Handbook of Africa and Economics.* New York: Oxford University Press.

Aker, Jenny, Rachid Boumnijel, Amanda McClelland, and Niall Tierney. 2016. "Payment Mechanisms and Anti-Poverty Programs: Evidence from a Mobile Money Cash Transfer Experiment in Niger." *Economic Development and Cultural Change* 65 (1): 1–37.

Aker, Jenny C., Paul Collier, and Pedro C. Vicente. 2017. "Is Information Power? Using Mobile Phones and Free Newspapers during an Election in Mozambique." *Review of Economics and Statistics* XCIX (2).

Aker, J. C., and M. Fafchamps. 2015. Mobile Phone Coverage and Producer Markets: Evidence from West Africa. *The World Bank Economic Review* 29 (2): 262–92.

Aker, Jenny C., Ishida Ghosh, and Jenna Burrell. 2016. "The Promise (and Pitfalls) of ICT for Agriculture Initiatives." *Agricultural Economics* 47 (S1).

Aker, Jenny C., and Christopher Ksoll. 2016. "Can Mobile Phones Improve Agricultural Outcomes? Evidence from a Randomized Experiment in Niger." *Food Policy* 60 (Issue C): 44–51.

———. 2017. "Call Me Educated: Evidence from a Mobile Monitoring Experiment in Niger." Center for Global Development Working Paper 406, Washington, DC.

———, and Travis J. Lybbert. 2012. "Can Mobile Phones Improve Learning? Evidence from a Field Experiment in Niger." *American Economic Journal: Applied Economics* 4 (4): 94–120.

Aker, Jenny C., Christopher Ksoll, Karla Perez, Danielle Miller, and Susan Smalley. 2014. "Learning without Teachers? Evidence from a Randomized Evaluation of a Mobile

Phone-Based Adult Education Program in Los Angeles." CGD Working Paper 368, Center for Global Development, Washington, DC.

Aker, Jenny C., and Isaac M. Mbiti. 2010. "Mobile Phones and Economic Development in Africa." *Journal of Economic Perspectives* 24 (3): 207–32.

Aker, Jenny, and Kim Wilson. 2013. "Can Mobile Money Be Used to Promote Savings? Evidence from Northern Ghana." SWIFT Institute Working Paper 2012–003, London, SWIFT Institute.

Akerlof, George A. 1991. "Procrastination and Obedience." *American Economic Review Papers and Proceedings* 81 (2): 1–19.

Bandiera, Oriana, Iwan Barankay, and Imran Rasul. 2005. "Social Preferences and the Response to Incentives: Evidence from Personnel Data." *Quarterly Journal of Economics* 120 (3): 917–62.

Banerjee, Abhijit V., Shawn Cole, Esther Duflo, and Leigh Linden. 2007. "Remedying Education: Evidence from Two Randomized Experiments in India." *The Quarterly Journal of Economics* 122 (3): 1235–64.

Banerjee, Abhijit V., Esther Duflo, Clement Imbert, Santhosh Mathew, and Rohini Pande. 2016. "E-Governance, Accountability, and Leakage in Public Programs: Experimental Evidence from a Financial Management Reform in India." NBER Working Paper 22803, National Bureau of Economic Research, Cambridge, MA.

Banerjee, Abhijit V., Rachel Glennerster, and Esther Duflo. 2008. "Putting a Band-Aid on a Corpse: Incentives for Nurses in the Indian Public Health Care System." *Journal of the European Economic Association* 6 (2–3): 487–500.

Banerjee, Abhijit V., Rema Hanna, Jordan Kyle, Benjamin A. Olken, and Sudarno Sumarto. 2016. "Tangible Information and Citizen Empowerment: Identification Cards and Food Subsidy Programs in Indonesia." Working Paper, Massachusetts Institute of Technology, Cambridge, MA.

Banerjee, Abhijit V., and Sendhil Mullainathan. 2008. "Limited Attention and Income Distribution." *American Economic Review* 98 (2): 489–93.

———. 2010. "The Shape of Temptation: Implications for the Economic Lives of the Poor." MIT Working Paper 10–9, National Bureau of Economic Research, Cambridge, MA.

Barrera-Osorio, Felipe, and Leigh Linden. 2009. "The Use and Misuse of Computers in Education: Evidence from a Randomized Experiment in Colombia." Policy Research Working Paper 4836, Impact Evaluation Series 29, World Bank, Washington, DC.

Bartik, Timothy J. 1991. *Who Benefits from State and Local Economic Development Policies?* W.E. Upjohn Institute for Employment Research, Kalamazoo, MI.

Batley, R., W. McCourt, and C. Mcloughlin. 2012. "The Politics and Governance of Public Services in Developing Countries." *Public Management Review* 14(2): 131–45.

Besley, Timothy, and Maitreesh Ghatak. 2006. "Public Goods and Economic Development." In *Understanding Poverty*, edited by Abhijit Vinayak Banerjee, Roland Bénabou, and Dilip Mookherjee. Oxford Scholarship Online.

Beuermann, Diether, Christopher McKelvey, and Carlos Sotelo-Lopez. 2012. "The Effects of Mobile Phone Infrastructure: Evidence from Rural Peru." Working Paper, Banco Central de Reserva Perú, Lima.

Beuermann, Diether, Julian Cristia, Santiago Cueto, Ofer Malamud, and Yyannu Cruz-Aguayo. 2015. "One Laptop per Child at Home: Short-Term Impacts from a Randomized Experiment in Peru." *American Economic Journal: Applied Econometrics* 7 (2): 53–80.

Blumenstock, Joshua E. 2016. "Fighting Poverty with Data." *Science* 353 (6301): 753–54.

Blumenstock, Joshua E., Gabriel Cadamuro, and Robert On. 2015. "Predicting Poverty and Wealth from Mobile Phone Metadata." *Science* 350 (6264): 1073–76.

Blumenstock, Joshua E., Michael C. Callen, Tarek Ghani, and Lucas Koepke. 2015. "Promises and Pitfalls of Mobile Money in Afghanistan: Evidence from a Randomized Control Trial." Paper in *Proceedings of the 7th IEEE/ACM International Conference on Information and Communication Technologies and Development (ICTD 2015)*.

Blumenstock, J. E., N. Eagle, and M. Fafchamps. 2016. Airtime Transfers and Mobile Communications: Evidence in the Aftermath of Natural Disasters. *Journal of Development Economics* 120: 157–81.

Blumenstock, Joshua, Jessica E. Steele, Pal Roe Sundsøy, Carla Pezzulo, Victor A. Alegana, Tomas J. Bird, Johannes Bjelland, Kenth Engø-Monsen, Yves-Alexandre de Montjoye, Asif M. Iqbal, Khandakar N. Hadiuzzaman, Xin Lu, Erik Wetter, Andrew J. Tatem, and Linus Bengtsson. 2017. "Mapping Poverty Using Mobile Phone and Satellite Data." *Journal of the Royal Society Interface.*

Brown, Alan W., Jerry Fishenden, and Mark Thompson. 2014. "Revolutionising Digital Public Service Delivery: A UK Government Perspective." Paper.

Cadena, Ximena, and Antoinette Schoar. 2011. "Remembering to Pay? Reminders vs. Financial Incentives for Loan Payments." NBER Working Paper 17020, National Bureau of Economic Research, Cambridge, MA.

Callen, Michael, Clark C. Gibson, Danielle F. Jung, and James D. Long. 2016. "Improving Electoral Integrity with Information and Communications Technology." *Journal of Experimental Political Science* 3 (1): 4–17.

Callen, Michael, and James D. Long. 2015. "Institutional Corruption and Election Fraud: Evidence from a Field Experiment in Afghanistan." *American Economic Review* 105 (1): 354–81.

Camacho, Adriana, and Emily Conover. 2011. "The Impact of Receiving Price and Climate Information in the Agricultural Sector." Working Paper, Centro de Estudios sobre Desarrollo Economico Universidad de los Andes, Bogota, Colombia.

Carrillo, P., M. Onofa, and J. Ponce. 2010. "Information Technology and Student Achievement: Evidence from a Randomized Experiment in Ecuador." Working Paper, Inter-American Development Bank, Washington, DC.

Casaburi, L., and M. Kremer. 2016. "Management Information Systems and Firm Performance: Experimental Evidence from a Large Agribusiness Company in Kenya." PEDL Research Note, .

Casaburi, Lorenzo, Michael Kremer, and Sendhil Mullainathan. 2016. "Contract Farming and Agricultural Productivity in Western Kenya." In *NBER African Successes.* Cambridge, MA: National Bureau of Economic Research.

Casaburi, L., M. Kremer, S. Mullainathan, and R. Ramrattan. 2014. "Harnessing ICT to Increase Agricultural Production: Evidence from Kenya," Harvard University, Cambridge, MA.

Casaburi, L., and T. Reed 2014. "Interlinked Transactions and Pass-Through: Experimental Evidence from Sierra Leone," Harvard University, Cambridge, MA.

Castellano, Antonio, Adam Kendall, Mikhail Nikomarov, and Tarryn Swemmer. 2015. "Brighter Africa: The Growth Potential of the Sub-Saharan Electricity Sector." McKinsey Report, McKinsey & Company, New York.

Chaudhury, Nazmul, Jeffrey Hammer, Michael Kremer, Karthik Muralidharan, and F. Halsey Rogers. 2006. "Missing in Action: Teacher and Health Worker Absence in Developing Countries." *Journal of Economic Perspectives* 20 (1): 91–116.

Chong, Alberto, Marco Gonzalez-Navarro, Dean Karlan, and Martin Valdivia. 2013. "Effectiveness and Spillovers of Online Sex Education: Evidence from a Randomized Evaluation in Colombian Public Schools." NBER Working Paper 18776, National Bureau of Economic Research, Cambridge, MA.

Chong, Alberto, Ana L. De La O, Dean Karlan, and Leonard Wantchekon. 2015. "Does Corruption Information Inspire the Fight or Quash the Hope? A Field Experiment in Mexico on Voter Turnout, Choice, and Party Identification." *The Journal of Politics* 77 (1): 55–71.

Cilliers, Jacobus, Ibrahim Kasirye, Clare Leaver, Pieter Serneels, and Andrew Zeitlin. 2016. "Pay for Locally Monitored Performance? A Welfare Analysis for Teacher Attendance in Ugandan Primary Schools." Occasional Paper 244098, Economic Policy Research Centre, Kampala, Uganda.

Coase, Ronald H. 1960. "The Problem of Social Cost." *The Journal of Law and Economics* 3: 1–44.

Cole, S. A., and N. A. Fernando. 2016. "The Value of Advice: Evidence from the Adoption of Agricultural Practices." HBS Working Group Paper, Harvard University, Cambridge, MA.

Courtois, P., and J. Subervie. 2015. "Farmer Bargaining Power and Market Information Services." *American Journal of Agricultural Economics* 1–25.

Dale, Allison, and Aaron Strauss. 2009. "Don't Forget to Vote: Text Message Reminders as a Mobilization Tool." *American Journal of Political Science* 53 (4): 787–804.

Dillon, Brian. 2012. "Using Mobile Phones to Collect Panel Data in Developing Countries." *Journal of International Development* 24 (4): 518–27.

Dinkelman, Taryn. 2011. "The Effects of Rural Electrification on Employment: New Evidence from South Africa." *American Economic Review* 101 (7): 3078–108.

Donaldson, Dave. Forthcoming. "Railroads of the Raj: Estimating the Impact of Transportation Infrastructure." *American Economic Review.*

———, and Richard Hornbeck. 2016. "Railroads and American Economic Growth: A 'Market Access' Approach." *The Quarterly Journal of Economics* 131 (2): 799–858.

Duflo, Esther. 2012. "Human Values and the Design of the Fight Against Poverty." Tanner Lectures, Harvard University, Cambridge, MA, May 4.

Duflo, Esther, Rema Hanna, and Stephen P. Ryan. 2012. "Incentives Work: Getting Teachers to Come to School." *American Economic Review* 102 (4): 1241–78.

Duflo, Esther, and Rohini Pande. 2007. "Dams." *Quarterly Journal of Economics* 122 (2): 601–46.

Escueta, Maya, Vincent Quan, Andre Joshua Nickow, and Philip Oreopoulos. 2017. "Education Technology: An Evidence-Based Review." NBER Working Paper 23744, National Bureau of Economic Research, Cambridge, MA.

Fafchamps, Marcel, and Bart Minten. 2012. "Impact of SMS-Based Agricultural Information on Indian Farmers." *World Bank Economic Review* 26 (3): 1–32.

Fairlie, Robert W., and Jonathan Robinson. 2013. "Experimental Evidence on the Effects of Home Computers on Academic Achievement among Schoolchildre." *American Economic Journal: Applied Economics, American Economic Association* 5 (3): 211–40.

Farrell, Diana, and Andrew Goodman. 2013. "Government by Design: Four Principles for a Better Public Sector." McKinsey & Company.

Finan, Frederico, Benjamin A. Olken, and Rohini Pande. 2015. "The Personnel Economics of the State." NBER Working Paper 21825, National Bureau of Economic Research, Cambridge, MA.

Fisher, Ronald C. 1997. "The Effects of State and Local Public Services on Economic Development." *New England Economic Review* (Mar/Apr): 53–82.

Flax, Valerie, Mekebob Negerie, Alawiyatu Usman Ibrahim, Sheila Letherman, Erica J. Daza, and Margaret E. Bentley. 2014. "Integrating Group Counselling, Cell Phone Messaging, and Participant-Generating Songs and Dramas into a Microcredit Program Increases Nigerian Women's Adherence to International Breastfeeding Recommendations." *The Journal of Nutrition* 144 (7): 1120–24.

Food and Agriculture Organization (FAO). 2015. *FAO Statistical Pocketbook: World Food and Agriculture,* Rome.

Fox, William F., and Matthew N. Murray. 1993. "State and Local Government Policies." In *Economic Adaptation: Alternatives for Rural America,* edited by David Barkley. Boulder, CO: Westview Press, Inc.

Frederick, Shane, George Loewenstein, and Ted O'Donoghue. 2002. "Time Discounting and Time Preference: A Critical Review." *Journal of Economic Literature* 40 (2): 351–401.

Futch, M. D., and C. T. McIntosh. 2009. "Tracking the Introduction of the Village Phone Product in Rwanda." *Information Technologies & International Development* 5 (3): 54.

Fujiwara, Thomas. 2015. "Voting Technology, Political Responsiveness, and Infant Health: Evidence from Brazil." *Econometrica* 83 (2): 423–64.

Gine, Xavier, and Ghazala Mansuri. 2011. "Together We Will: Experimental Evidence on Female Voting Behavior in Pakistan." Policy Research Working Paper 5692, The World Bank.

GSMA. 2013. "The Mobile Economy 2013."

Goyal, Aparajita. 2010. "Information, Direct Access to Farmers, and Rural Market Performance in Central India." *American Economic Journal: Applied Economics* 2 (3): 22–45.

Hildebrandt, N., Y. Nyarko, G. Romagnoli, and E. Soldani. 2014. *Information is Power? Impact of an SMS-based Market Information System on Farmers in Ghana.*

Humphreys, Macartan, and Jeremy M. Weinstein. 2012. "Policing Politicians: Citizen Empowerment and Political Accountability in Uganda - Preliminary Analysis." Working Paper of the International Growth Center.

Innovations for Poverty Action (IPA). 2016. "The Impact of Smartcard Electronic Transfers on Public Distribution." Study Summary, New Haven, CT.

International Telecommunications Union (ITU). 2014. "Measuring the Information Society Report."

Jack, William, and Tavneet Suri. 2014. "Risk Sharing and Transaction Costs: Evidence from Kenya's Mobile Money Revolution." *The American Economic Review* 104 (1): 183–223.

Abdul Latif Jameel Poverty Action Lab (JPAL). 2016. *Evaluation Summary.*

Jensen, Robert. 2007. "The Digital Provide: Information (Technology) Market Performance, and Welfare in the Southern Indian Fisheries Sector." *The Quarterly Journal of Economics* 122 (3): 879–924.

Jiang, Hong, Mu Li, Li Ming Wen, Qiaozhen Hu, Dongling Yang, Gengsheng He, Louise A. Baur, Michael J. Dibley, and Xu Qian. 2014. "Effect of Short Message Service on Infant Feeding Practice Findings from a Community-Based Study in Shanghai, China." *JAMA Pediatric* 168 (5): 471–78.

Karlan, Dean, Alberto Chong, Jeremy Shapiro, and Jonathan Zinman. 2015. "(Ineffective) Messages to Encourage Recycling Evidence from a Randomized Evaluation in Peru." *The World Bank Economic Review* 29 (1): 180–206.

Karlan, Dean, Margaret McConnell, Sendhil Mullainathan, and Jonathan Zinman. 2016. "Getting to the Top of Mind: How Reminders Increase Saving." *Management Science* 62 (12): 3393–411.

Karlan, Dean, Melanie Morten, and Jonathan Zinman. 2012. "A Personal Touch: Text Messaging for Loan Repayment." NBER Working Paper 17952, National Bureau of Economic Research, Cambridge, MA.

Kearney, Melissa S., and Phillip B. Levine. 2015. "Media Influences on Social Outcomes: The Impact of MTV's 16 and Pregnant on Teen Childbearing." *The American Economic Review* 105 (12): 3597–632.

Jones, Maria, and Florence Kondylis. 2014. *Your Feedback Matters, To You: Evidence from Extension Services.*

La Ferrera, Eliana, Alberto Chong, and Suzanne Duryea. 2012. "Soap Operas and Fertility: Evidence from Brazil." *American Economic Journal: Applied Economics* 4 (4): 1–31.

Lai, K. W. 2011. "Digital Technology and the Culture of Teaching and Learning in Higher Education." *Australasian Journal of Educational Technology* 27 (8): 1263–75.

Lai, K. W., F. Khaddage, and G. Knezek. 2013. "Blending Student Technology Experiences in Formal and Informal Learning." *Journal of Computer Assisted Learning* 29 (5): 414–25.

Lai, Fang, Renfu Luo, Linxiu Zhang, Xinzhe Huang, and Scott Rozelle. 2015. "Does Computer-Assisted Learning Improve Learning Outcomes? Evidence from a Randomized Experiment in Migrant Schools in Beijing." *Economics of Education Review* 47: 34–48.

Linden, Leigh L. 2008. "Complement or Substitute? The Effect of Technology on Student Achievement in India." InfoDev Working Paper 17, World Bank, Washington, DC.

Liu, Xiaoqiu, James J. Lewis, Hui Zhang, Wei Lu, Shun Zhang, Guilan Zheng, Liqiong Bai, Jun Li, Xue Li, Hongguang Chen, Mingming Liu, Rong Chen, Junying Chi, Jian Lu, Shitong Huan, Shiming Cheng, Lixia Wang, Shiwen Jiang, Daniel P. Chin, and Katherine L. Fielding. 2015. "Effectiveness of Electronic Reminders to Improve Medicaiton Adherencein Tuberculosis Patients: A Cluster-Randomised Trial," *PLOS Medicine*.

Malamud, Ofer, and Cristian Pop-Eleches. 2011. "Home Computer Use and the Development of Human Capital." *Quarterly Journal of Economics* 126 (2): 987–1027.

Mas, Ignacio, and Colin Mayer. 2012. "Savings as Forward Payments: Innovations on Mobile Money Platforms." GSMA.

Mbiti, Isaac, and David N. Weil. 2011. "Mobile Banking: The Impact of M-Pesa in Kenya." NBER Working Paper 17129, National Bureau of Economic Research, Cambridge, MA.

McKinsey & Company. February 2015. *Brighter Africa: The Growth Potential of the Sub-Saharan Electricity Sector.*

Medhi, Idrani, Aiswarya Ratan, and Kentaro Toyama. 2009. "Mobile-Banking Adoption and Usage by Low-Literate, Low-Income Users in the Developing World." In *Internationalization, Design and Global Development*, edited by N. Aykin. Berlin, Springer.

Michaels, Guy. 2008. "The Effect of Trade on the Demand for Skill: Evidence from the Interstate Highway System." *The Review of Economics and Statistics* 90 (4): 683–701.

Mitra, S., D. Mookherjee, M. Torero, and S. Visaria. 2015. *Asymmetric Information and Middleman Margins: An Experiment with West Bengal Potato Farmers.*

Mo, Di, Linxiu Zhang, Renfu Luo, Qinghe Qu, Weiming Huang, and Jiafu Wang. 2014. "Integrating Computer-Assisted Learning into a Regular Curriculum: Evidence from a Randomized Experiment in Rural Schools in Shaanxi." *Journal of Development Effectiveness* 6 (3): 300–23.

Munnell, Alicia H. 1992. "Infrastructure Investment and Economic Growth." *Journal of Economic Perspectives* 6: 189–98.

Muralidharan, Karthik, Jishnu Das, Alaka Holla, and Aakash Mohpal. 2017. "The Fiscal Costs of Weak Governance: Evidence from Teacher Absence in India." *Journal of Public Economics* 145: 116–35.

Muralidharan, Karthik, Paul Niehaus, and Sandip Sukhtankar. 2016. "Building State Capacity: Evidence from Biometric Smartcards in India." *American Economic Review* 106 (10): 2895–929.

Nakasone, Eduardo. 2013. "The Role of Price Information in Agricultural Markets: Experimental Evidence from Rural Peru." Agricultural and Applied Economics Association. 2013 Annual Meeting No. 150418.

Nakasone, Eduardo, Maximo Torero, and Bart Minten. 2014. "The Power of Information: The ICT Revolution in Agricultural Development." *Annual Review of Resource Economics* 6: 533–50.

Nglazi, Mweere, Linda-Gail Bekker, Robin Wood, Gregory D. Huddey, and Charles S. Wiysonge. 2013. "Mobile Phone Text Messaging for Promoting Adherence to Anti-Tuberculosis Treatment: A Systematic Review." *BMC Infectious Diseases* 13 (566).

O'Donoghue, Ted, and Matthew Rabin. 1999. "Doing it Now or Later." *American Economic Review* 89 (1): 103–24.

———. 2001. "Choice and Procrastination." *Quarterly Journal of Economics* 116 (1): 121–60.

Olken Benjamin A. 2006 "Corruption and the Costs of Redistribution: Micro Evidence from Indonesia." *Journal of Public Economics* 90 (May): 853–70.

Parikh, Tapan S., Neil Patel, and Yael Schwartzman. 2007. "A Survey of Information Systems Reaching Small Producers in Global Agricultural Value Chains." Proceedings of the International Conference on Information and Communication Technologies and Development 2007 ICTD. 334–44.

Patel, Neil, Deepti Chittamuru, Anupam Jain, Paresh Dave, and Tapan S. Parikh. 2010. "Avaaj otalo—A Field Study of an Interactive Voice Forum for Small Farmers in Rural India." Proceedings of ACM Conference on Human Factors in Computing Systems.

Pop-Eleches, Cristian, Harsha Thirumurthy, James P. Habyarimana, Joshua G. Zivin, Markus P. Goldstein, Damien de Walque, Leslie MacKeen, Jessica Haberer, Sylvester Kimaiyo, John Sidlek, Duncan Ngarem, and David R. Bangsbergn. 2011. "Mobile Phone Technologies

Improve Adherence to Antiretroviral Treatment in a Resource Limited Setting: A Randomized Controlled Trial of Text Message Reminders." *AIDS* 25 (6): 825–34.

Pritchett, Lant. 2005. "The Political Economy of Targeted Safety Nets." World Bank Social Protection Unit Discussion Paper Series, World Bank, Washington, DC.

Rokicki, Slawa, Jessica Cohen, Joshua A. Salomon, and Gunther Fink. 2017. "Impact of a Text Messaging Program on Adolescent Reproductive Health: A Cluster-Randomized Trial in Ghana." *American Journal of Public Health,* American Public Health Association (February).

Shah, Anwar, ed. 2005. *Public Services Delivery. Public Sector Governance and Accountability.* Washington, DC: World Bank.

Srinivasan, J., and Jenna Burrell. 2013. Revisiting the Fishers of Kerala, India. Proceedings of the International Conference on Information and Communication Technologies and Development, 56–66.

Svensson, Jakob, and David Yanagizawa. 2009. "Getting Prices Right: The Impact of the Market Information Service in Uganda." *Journal of the European Economic Association* 7 (2–3): 435–45.

Transparency International. 2013. *Global Corruption Report: Education.* Routledge: New York.

UN Educational, Scientific and Cultural Organization (UNESCO) Institute for Statistics. 2006. *Teachers and Education Quality: Monitoring Global Needs for 2015.* Montreal.

UNESCO Institute for Statistics. 2014. Data on Pupil-Teacher Ratios. World Bank Indicators.

Wasylenko, Michael J. 1991. "Empirical Evidence on Interregional Business Location Decisions and the Role of Fiscal Incentives in Economic Development." In *Industry Location and Public Policy,* edited by Henry Herzog and Alan Schlottman. Knoxville, TN: University of Tennessee Press.

World Bank. 2005. *Public Sector Governance and Accountability Series: Public Services Delivery.* Washington, DC.

———. 2015. *World Development Report 2015: Mind, Society, and Behavior.* Washington, DC.

———. 2016. *World Development Report 2016: Digital Dividends.* Washington, DC.

———. 2017. *World Development Report 2017: Governance and the Law.* Washington, DC.

———. n.d. Database. *ASPIRE: The Atlas of Social Protection—Indicators of Resilience and Equity.*

Wyche, Susan, and Charles Steinfield. 2015. "Why Don't Farmers Use Cell Phones to Access Market Prices? Technology Affordances and Barriers to Market Information Services Adoption in Rural Kenya." *Information Technology for Development* 22 (2): 320–33.

Yang, Yihua, Linxiu Zhang, Junxia Zeng, Xiaopeng Pang, Fang Lai, and Scott Rozelle. 2013. "Computers and the Academic Performance of Elementary School-Aged Girls in China's Poorest Communities." *Computers & Education: An International Journal* 6 (1): 335–46.

CHAPTER 9

The Digital Revolution and Targeting Public Expenditure for Poverty Reduction

Ravi Kanbur

Former Indian Prime Minister Rajiv Gandhi famously commented that only 15 percent of every rupee spent on the public food distribution system reached the poor. Indeed, the widespread view is that anti-poverty programs, and not only those in India, are badly targeted, with massive "leakage" to the nonpoor. Yet the move to cash-transfer programs alongside a burgeoning use of digital technology in recent years is being hailed in India and elsewhere as the solution to this problem of leakage. New digital technologies such as biometrics, goes the reasoning, will improve identification of the poor, and electronic banking will facilitate the transfer of resources to them.

The entrenched problems of so-called leakage notwithstanding, discussions as to the benefits of the digital revolution are prone to hype—perhaps nowhere more so than in policymaking, wherein new information technologies are meant to provide innovative solutions for problems once seen as intractable.

This chapter, taking a contrarian though not a Luddite stance, recognizes the benefits of new technology. But it nonetheless urges caution and a deeper examination of the fundamental trade-offs, as well as the advantages and disadvantages of "fine targeting," for poverty reduction.[1] These trade-offs fall into three major categories: information costs, high marginal tax rates, and political economy. The impact of digitalization on the trade-offs needs to be scrutinized with due reference to the institutions and social norms that structure society.

The chapter begins by setting down the fundamental principles of targeting transfers to minimize poverty, setting the costs of fine targeting against its undoubted benefits.[2] It then examines the likely impact of digitalization and new technology on these costs and benefits. And it argues that in some dimensions the trade-offs are quite independent of the use or otherwise of new technology. In

---

[1]Fine targeting refers to the targeting of benefits to the poor and only to the poor.

[2]While the chapter focuses on poverty reduction as the objective, it should be clear that the issues raised apply as much to more general objectives as well.

other cases the benefits are clear, and in still others the use of technology may worsen the trade-offs.

THE FUNDAMENTALS OF TARGETING

We start by specifying the measurement of poverty. Consider a distribution of income, with incomes y_i ranging from lowest to highest as $i = 1, 2, \ldots n$:

$$y_1 \leq y_2 \leq \ldots \ldots \ldots y_q < z < y_{q+1} \leq \ldots \ldots \ldots \leq y_n \tag{1}$$

Also shown is the poverty line z, with q individuals below the poverty line. The fraction of individuals below the poverty line is thus q/n. The Foster-Greer-Thorbecke class of poverty indices (Foster, Greer, and Thorbecke 1984) P_α is given by

$$P_\alpha = \frac{1}{n} \sum_{i=1}^{q} \left[\frac{z - y_i}{z} \right]^\alpha \tag{2}$$

Thus, the proportional poverty gap $[z - y_i]/z$ for each person is raised to a power α and summed across the q poor individuals. The parameter α measures the degree of "poverty aversion." When $\alpha = 0$, we get the standard head count ratio measure of poverty, also known as the incidence of poverty:

$$P_0 = (q/n) \tag{3}$$

When $\alpha = 1$ we get the poverty gap measure

$$P_1 = \frac{1}{n} \sum_{i=1}^{q} \left[\frac{z - y_i}{z} \right] \tag{4}$$

When $\alpha = 2$ the squared poverty gap measure weights the larger shortfalls from the poverty line more severely.

Suppose now that a poverty reduction budget, B, becomes available to the policymaker. Start with a model in which the transfers have no impact on individual incentives to earn income. Further, assume that making transfers has no information or administrative cost. What is then the most effective way of using this budget to reduce poverty? The answer depends on the value of α (Bourguignon and Fields 1990). If $\alpha = 0$, then the most effective transfer rule is to start with the individual closest to the poverty line, make sufficient transfers to move this individual over the poverty line, then move to the next poorest individual, and so on until the budget is exhausted. If $\alpha = 1$, then transfer to any individual below the poverty line, so long as the transfer is not so large as to take the individual above the poverty line, is equally effective in reducing poverty P_1. But if $\alpha = 2$, then the effective strategy is the following: start with the poorest individual and make transfers to this individual to bring income up to the next poorest individual, then make transfers to these two individuals until they are brought up to the next highest income, and so on until the budget is exhausted.

The above exercise highlights the key feature of "perfect targeting"—the transfer to each individual is just enough to bring income up to the poverty line, no more and no less. There is no leakage whatsoever to those who are above the poverty line to begin with, and those who were below the poverty line are not given more than is necessary. With this scenario, if the budget available was

$$B = nzP_1 \qquad (5)$$

then poverty would be eliminated. With imperfect targeting and inadequate budget, poverty would be reduced only partially. For the P_1 measure, it can be shown (Fiszbein, Kanbur, and Yemtsov 2014) that the reduction in poverty resulting from the transfers is given by

$$\frac{\Delta P_1}{P_1} = [\frac{T_p}{B}][\frac{B}{nzP_1}] \qquad (6)$$

in which ΔP_1 is the reduction in poverty and T_p is the sum of the transfers reaching the poor. The impact of the program on poverty is thus composed of two effects. The first term measures targeting efficiency—the fraction of transfers reaching the poor—while the second term quantifies budgetary adequacy, that is, the ratio of the budget to the poverty gap. The two together produce the poverty reduction we observe. With perfect targeting, the first term is 1. In contrast, an untargeted universal benefit would give an equal amount to everybody in the population, making the first term equal to the incidence of poverty in the population less than one. Fiszbein, Kanbur, and Yemtsov (2014) presents targeting efficiency and budgetary adequacy measures for nearly 50 countries.

It is the scenario of fine targeting, even perfect targeting, which people implicitly have in mind as a benchmark when they criticize a program for being inefficient in reducing poverty. They see individuals above the poverty line, sometimes well above, receiving transfers while payments to the poor are insufficient, and they argue either that poverty could be reduced more with the same budget or that the same poverty reduction could be achieved with a lower budget if targeting could only be finer. Indeed, this is the start of many a discussion between the international financial institutions and ministries of finance on food and fuel subsidy programs, for example.

Fine targeting, if costless, is clearly better than weak targeting or non-targeting if the objective is to minimize poverty with a fixed resource budget. But fine targeting is not costless. As noted, three major categories of issues arise— information costs, high marginal tax rates, and political economy.[3]

Fine targeting requires "fine" information on individual incomes. In principle, every single income in the economy needs to be assessed and verified, since someone with a high income could still claim to have income below the poverty line. The administrative costs of running such programs, with very detailed participation criteria, have been well discussed in the literature (see Coady, Grosh, and Hoddinott 2004; Grosh and others 2008). This has led to the significant literature on mitigating these informational costs by using easily observable indicators

---

[3] These categorizations were formulated in Besley and Kanbur (1993).

that are correlated with income to undertake contingent targeting. The idea is that income within these categories cannot be distinguished, but statistical properties of the distributions within these groups can be used to design transfer strategies that will be more efficient at poverty reduction than no targeting at all. Thus, for example, in an early exercise, Kanbur (1987) showed that if the objective is to minimize national P_α then transfers should be in proportion to each group's $P_{\alpha-1}$ (for $\alpha \geq 1$). An application to food subsidies was provided by Besley and Kanbur (1988) and to land-holding-based targeting by Chao and Ravallion (1989). The literature is now extensive and the basic analytical issues are reasonably well understood.[4]

One important type of targeting that addresses the information issues is known as "self-targeting." It does not rely on external assessment and validation to identify the poor and the nonpoor. Rather, it sets up an incentive system such that only those people whose incomes are sufficiently low would come forward to claim the benefit. The best-known example of this is a transfer contingent on employment at a public works site. The employment is guaranteed for all those who present themselves, but clearly only those for whom the opportunity cost is less than the wage at the public works site will show up. If the hourly wage at the public works site is 100, why should someone with an alternative wage rate of 200 elsewhere work at the public site? If the opportunity cost is in turn correlated (negatively) with poverty status, the targeting objective is achieved. An early assessment and validation of this argument is presented in Ravallion (1991). Kanbur (2010) provides a recent application of the argument in the context of the global financial crisis. And analogous reasoning leads to the case for subsidizing coarse rather than fine grains in food subsidies (the nonpoor are more likely to prefer the latter).

Employment guarantee schemes are a type of conditional cash transfer—transfers conditioned on some behavioral response—in this case upon employment at the public works site. However, not all conditional transfers are self-targeting in the same progressive direction (Rodriguez-Castelan 2017). Consider the very popular policy intervention of a cash transfer conditional on keeping children in school. But if education is a normal good, the well-off will keep their children in school in any case—for them the transfer will be a pure inframarginal transfer. For poorer households, who are being incentivized to change their behavior, the value of the transfer will be less than the cash value. Indeed, it may not be worthwhile for the poorest households to participate in the program at all. As Rodriguez-Castelan (2017) shows, the more efficient use of a given budget to reduce poverty may in fact be to provide an unconditional rather than a conditional cash transfer. No doubt the debate on conditional cash transfers will continue, touching also on the issue of cash versus in-kind transfers (Fiszbein and others 2009).

[4]For a recent theoretical exploration see Kanbur and Tuomala (2016); for a policy-based application, see Nazara and Rahayu (2013).

The informational costs of fine targeting, and ways of addressing them, are thus well understood and assessed in the literature. However, a far less-well understood implication of fine targeting exists. Recall once again the description of perfect targeting—every individual gets just enough to rise to the poverty line. Thus, higher-income poor individuals get less transfers. In fact, with perfect targeting the reduction is one for one: for every unit increase in pre-transfer individual income, government transfer declines by one unit (the sum of the pre-transfer income and the transfer is equal to the poverty line). What we have described, in effect, is an effective tax and transfer schedule with a marginal tax rate of 100 percent! In any normal context, the incentive effects of this would be prominently discussed but not, seemingly, in the context of anti-poverty programs.

In any sort of standard labor supply model, a 100 percent marginal tax rate over an extended range could lead to zero labor supply. If this happened and pre-transfer incomes below the poverty line fell to zero, the cost of the transfer would rise significantly to

$$qz > \sum_{i=1}^{q} [z - y_i] \tag{7}$$

Thus, in a setting in which incentives for earning income are important, the incentive effects of high marginal tax rates implicit in fine targeting will have to be balanced against the targeting gains. Kanbur and Keen (1989) and Kanbur, Keen, and Tuomala (1994) present early analyses of this issue, showing the extent to which fine targeting will have to be mitigated in the face of these incentive issues. More recently, Banerjee and others 2015 brings up-to-date quantification of the labor supply effects of transfer programs.

This discussion of incentives relates to the earlier discussion of informational costs and the use of easily observable indicators. The tension between fine targeting and high marginal tax rates can be mitigated if we are allowed to use easily observable characteristics to design different transfer schedules for different groups. The extra instrument of "categorical" targeting allows better use of resources, as shown by Immonen and others (1998).

The third dimension of the costs of fine targeting is perhaps most elusive—political economy. Fine targeting means, by definition, confining transfers to the poor. But this means a separation of the interests of the poor from middle-income groups. As the political economy of this plays out, such separation could mean lower overall budgets for poverty reduction transfers. In the words of Gelbach and Pritchett (2002), more for the poor could end up being less for the poor. In an early allusion to these forces, Anand and Kanbur (1991) referred to the reform of the Sri Lankan rice subsidy in the late 1970s, which went from a universal subsidy to one targeted to those below the poverty line. But the real value of the subsidy then fell over subsequent years, with little in the way of political repercussions. Kanbur (2010) also alludes to these forces in discussing the efficacy of employment guarantee schemes as vehicles for rapid response to macro shocks—while their targeting properties are beneficial, political support at the local level may be problematic for this very reason. Gelbach and Pritchett (2002) present a formal model of the forces in play.

IMPLICATIONS OF THE DIGITAL REVOLUTION

Thus, fine targeting, while obviously a good thing if it can be implemented costlessly, is not in fact costless. As noted, trade-offs exist in information, incentives, and political economy. This section assesses whether the digital revolution can enhance the benefits of targeting while reducing the costs.

Digitalization and Anti-Poverty Programs

What does the digital revolution mean in the specific context of targeting anti-poverty transfer programs, as opposed to the general implications for state capacity? Digitalization is thought to be helpful in at least three ways. The first is ease of payment of cash. Radcliff (2016, 2017) provides a specific example:

> The link between payment access and fuel subsidy reform was powerfully demonstrated by Iran's reform efforts in 2010–11. Then, the Iranian government was spending $70 billion per year on fuel subsidies—a clearly unsustainable subsidy bill. But the government couldn't raise fuel prices without offering citizens something in return, lest it face a political backlash. So, it decided to replace fuel subsidies with cash transfers, setting aside $30 billion to deliver $40 per month to every citizen. ... To make the reform possible, the Iranian Government had to deliver monthly payments to every Iranian household. Today, 67 percent of Iranian adults receive a government payment—higher than any country in the world—and 92 percent of these payments are delivered digitally into an account.

The second is biometric identification, as Gelb and Diofasi (2015, p. 61) discuss for South Africa:

> Provincial governments in South Africa have used fingerprint-based biometric ATMs and smartcards since the mid-1990s to deliver pensions and social grants, including in locations with limited connectivity. ... Biometric re-registration of over 20 million social grant recipients was completed in 2013 by the South African Social Security Agency in an effort to streamline the recently centralized system. Even though the system had been able to draw on an extensive identity infrastructure initiated during the apartheid period re-registration enabled SASSA [South African Social Security Agency] to remove 650,000 social grants going to non-eligible individuals which resulted in savings of over $65 million annually. ... The new system also ensures that payments cease once a beneficiary has died without having to rely on death registration records: all grant recipients must present a "proof of life" once a month by scanning their fingerprints or through voice recognition.

The third is keeping track of payments at the next level up, in the government system itself. Here is how Banerjee and others (2016, 2011) reported the results of a recent study in India:

In collaboration with the Government of Bihar, India, we conducted a large-scale experiment to evaluate whether transparency in fiscal transfer systems can increase accountability and reduce corruption in the implementation of a workfare program. The reforms introduced electronic fund-flow, cut out administrative tiers, and switched the basis of transfer amounts from forecasts to documented expenditures. Treatment reduced leakages along three measures: expenditures and hours claimed dropped while an independent household survey found no impact on actual employment and wages received; a matching exercise reveals a reduction in fake households on payrolls; and local program officials' self-reported median personal assets fell.

Digital technologies thus hold clear benefits for social programs and, as the costs of digitalization decline, the benefit-to-cost ratio will continue to improve along these dimensions. But notice that the three examples are all somewhat independent of the issue of anti-poverty targeting as presented in the previous section, ensuring that transfers flow *only* to people living below the poverty line. The Iran example is one where a poorly targeted fuel subsidy program was replaced with a completely untargeted cash transfer program. The problem in the reform was how to make the cash transfer to every household, not how to restrict the transfer only to poor households. The issue in South Africa is how to identify those who meet pension eligibility requirements (basically, age and gender), not how to target flows to the poor. And in the Indian case, targeting to the poor is being taken care of by the self-targeting nature of the public works programs; the issue addressed by digitalization is the standard one of public sector corruption.

So, we return to the fundamentals of targeting, with its issues of (1) the need for information on income or consumption of individuals for fine targeting, (2) the incentive effects of fine targeting, and (3) the political economy of fine targeting. How, if at all, can the digital revolution help ease the trade-offs identified?

Information Costs

Clearly, the most obvious entry point is the potential of the digital revolution to reduce information costs in targeting. Biometrics and identification of individuals is often put forward as the solution to the information problem in targeting. However, what fine targeting needs is not just unique identification of individuals, but detailed information allowing computation of income or consumption and, thus, identification as poor. Further, this computation needs to be updated annually if the program is to continue to be finely targeted. In small, developed, and highly formalized economies, such as Finland's, such income information is already digitized and linked in to other national databases, and the use of such information is not a problem.[5] But in a developing country with a large informal

---

[5]An amusing account of this phenomenon is to be found in this report of a speeding fine in Finland: "The fines are calculated based on half an offender's daily net income, with some consideration for the number of children under his or her roof and a deduction deemed to be enough to cover basic living expenses, currently 255 euros per month. ... Then, that figure is multiplied by the number of days of income the offender should lose, according to the severity of the offense. ... In

untaxed sector it is not clear how exactly digitalization can help, at least not for many years to come. And it does not seem that informality is declining sharply or at all in many developing countries (Kanbur 2015).

In the absence of detailed income or consumption data for individuals or households, correlates derived from household surveys can be used to fashion a "proxy means test," as described in the previous section. This provides ground-level implementers of the transfer program with a formula that weights several observable characteristics, and a cut-off value of this weighted sum to identify households to whom the transfer should be made. But this then requires information on these observable characteristics for each household (and in some cases individuals within the household) to be obtained, maintained, and updated at the local level. Clearly, digitalization can help enormously in maintaining and updating these data sets. Yet, verification and validation of some of this information, going beyond births and deaths where digitalization of vital statistics is a complementary input, is not a simple, straightforward technical exercise. Quality of housing is often an element in proxy means tests—whether the house has a tin roof, for example. But this is a subjective assessment—how is a tin roof with holes in it to be counted? Whether the man in a household is employed is another typical criterion, an ambiguous one in rural and agricultural settings, and so on. These issues are not amenable to easy resolution by digitalization.

Marginal Tax Rates

Let us turn now to the basic tension between fine targeting and the high implicit marginal tax rates that fine targeting entails. The tension arises in the attempt to make sure that no poor person gets more than needed to reach the poverty line, which is an important element of fine targeting. The tension can be resolved by giving up on this requirement and going for a universal benefit, but then we are at the other extreme of fine targeting—no targeting at all.

However, with a universal benefit there is leakage to those above the poverty line. This leakage can be reduced by conditioning the transfer on individual characteristics through a proxy means test, as has been discussed. But everyone with the same value of the proxy is treated identically—there is "universalism" among those in the same observable category. So, some of these are getting more than they need to reach the poverty line. There is leakage, but since all incomes within a category receive the same transfer, not conditioned on income, there is not an implicit marginal tax rate. Thus, to the extent that new information technology helps manage differential transfers to several groups differentiated by observable characteristics, universalism within each group avoids the high marginal tax rate issue, while proliferation and optimal use of group information allows better targeting.

---

today's digital age, however, a few seconds is all it takes for the police, using mobile devices, to get information directly from the Finnish tax office" (Daley 2015).

Political Economy, Norms, and Institutions

Consider now the political economy dimension. The central issue posed in the previous section is that of the separation of the interests of the poor from the middle-income groups. The resources needed for poverty reduction, even with fine targeting, will have to come from somewhere. The question then is at what income level does the switch between net recipient and net contributor occur? With perfect targeting, the answer is obvious—it occurs at the poverty line. Those above the poverty line must pay for transfers to those below the poverty line. With no targeting at all, everybody gets an equal amount, but this has to be paid for. The switch point depends on the exact nature of the tax schedule and the income distribution. But if the universal transfer is z, enough to make even the lowest income come up to the poverty line, then the switch point will be above the poverty line. Thus, with a high enough universal benefit, the poor and the lower-middle classes have a common cause.

How is the above argument affected by digitalization? On the face of it, not at all. The issue is where the switch point between net gainers and net losers occurs, and it is not clear why digitalization should affect this in general. However, suppose now that over and above the costs of the transfer there are operational costs, and that somehow the costs of the whole transfer operation are lowered by digitalization—the leaky buckets are plugged better, so that fewer resources need to be extracted from the net payers. Then the switch point will rise and more of the middle-income groups will be brought into solidarity with the poor. But such political economy analysis, and the implications of digitalization, is in its infancy and needs to be explored further in a complete model that solves simultaneously for the parameters of the tax-transfer schedule as part of the political economy equilibrium, following on from the work of Gelbach and Pritchett (2002).

Suppose now that we are in the realm of proxy means tests, where transfers are conditioned not on income but on observable characteristics. A political economy framework would now see advantage in a coalition of those with common observable characteristics, combined with agitation by this coalition for increased transfers to those characteristics. The politics of caste coalitions, and the demands for reservations of government posts and state transfers, are of this nature in India.[6] A theoretical analysis of community-based targeting is provided in Dasgupta and Kanbur (2005). Thus, while the new information technology makes it easier to develop ever more sophisticated proxy means tests, it may at the same time introduce new and perhaps unintended elements to the political economy of a country by intensifying the logic of group coalitions, fueled now by the prospect of transfers to the group from anti-poverty programs. Such political economy models also need further development and exploration.

Finally, another aspect of the political economy dimension of fine targeting is perhaps less well understood in the analytical economics literature (it was not

---

[6]The literature on this topic is vast. For an article targeted toward the generalist see *The Economist*. "Affirmative Action: Indian Reservations." June 29, 2013.

addressed, for example, by Besley and Kanbur 1993), although it is well recognized by those with ground-level implementation experience. This aspect, the use of proxy indicators in targeting, links directly to the informational aspects of targeting and the use of proxy indicators in targeting. A well-developed methodology now exists for deriving these proxies, as weighted sums of observable indicators, and the methodology is being implemented in many parts of the world (see, for example, Nazara and Rahayu 2013). But, by definition, these proxy methods will have inclusion and exclusion errors. These are weighted appropriately in a loss function in deriving the optimal proxy, but outcomes on the ground are a different matter.

The complicated proxies, derived by technocrats, are not easy to explain to ordinary people, who put the non-receipt or receipt of a transfer across households down to political and ethnic connections, thereby undermining solidarity at the local level. Adato (2011) notes in a discussion of conditional cash transfers in Nicaragua how purely quantitative analysis can lead policymakers astray:

> The survey found that the program was well targeted, with under-coverage rates of 3 to 10 percent. The qualitative research found, however, that people saw themselves as "all poor" and did not understand why households were selected into or out of the program, resulting in several types of stress and tension in the communities.

Such experiences are found in many qualitative studies. Thus, one female recipient of the Program Keluarga Harapan transfer program in Indonesia is reported in Reality Check Analysis (2015, 29) as follows:

> ... she was originally selected via a household survey where she was asked her name, house condition, how much land she owned and her employment. However, she said others got bigger allowances, some as much as 1 million [rupiah], "*because it was unfairly decided by the last* kepala desa—*you had to be connected to him.*" The last elections she has voted for a family member to ensure that she will benefit in the future.[7]

Thus, if new technology drives implementation of ever more complicated proxy means tests they may end up worsening tensions at the local level even as they satisfy "better targeting" from a technocratic perspective. More generally, the fineness of the targeting may be unrelated to local conceptions and norms of those who deserve the transfer and those who do not, leading to a disconnect between technocrats believing they are doing well while the local political economy suffers. At the very least, then, qualitative analysis will be needed to identify these ground-level repercussions of fine targeting.

A broader type of institutional issue emerged on a field trip the author made a decade ago to Adilabad district in what was then the state of Andhra Pradesh in India. In discussions on the newly introduced National Rural Employment Guarantee Act, we were told about the virtues of the new electronic system of payment. In "the bad old days," the muster rolls were used to make physical

---

[7]*Kepala desa* is village head. IDR 1.0 million is about $75.0.

payment to workers at the public works site. It was alleged, no doubt correctly, that this led to a lot of corruption, with only a part of the payment being handed over, the rest being kept by powerful local interests—their henchmen being the ones who were handing out the payments. But now each worker was required to open an account at a local financial institution and the payment would be made directly into the account electronically, thereby circumventing opportunities for corruption at the public works site. Thus, all seemed well. But further inquiries and private conversations with the workers revealed that, in fact, the henchmen now gathered outside the post office or local bank to collect their take and the counter staff of the financial institutions also took their share before handing the cash to the workers.

This anecdotal evidence is not inconsistent with the rigorous experimental evidence provided by Banerjee and others (2016) on the National Rural Employment Guarantee Act in the Indian state of Bihar. While overt corruption, like skimming off the payroll before it is handed out, may be reduced by various forms of e-governance, there is nothing to stop the skimming from happening outside the gaze of the electronic eye. It is encouraging that Banerjee and others (2016) find that "local program officials' self-reported median personal assets fell." But the general point remains, that digitalization can only do so much to address deep-seated norms and practices that reflect longstanding power relations in society.

CONCLUSION

Sounding a note of caution, this chapter has examined whether the digital revolution can help mitigate the significant trade-offs in aiming for fine targeting of anti-poverty transfers to the poor and only to the poor. Many studies have identified the trade-offs and ground-level experience in the implementation of several programs, as well as conventional empirical evidence, confirm and highlights them.

Clearly, new information technology can help mitigate some of the information-al and administrative costs of targeting—one of three trade-offs scrutinized here—for example by facilitating the maintenance and updating of local databases on individual characteristics on which targeting relies. But the system is only as good as the information put into it. Income information is problematic in countries with a significant informal sector, and the issues of ground-level assessment and valida-tion of the proxies used in proxy means tests are not overcome by new technology, which can only record and process the information once it has been generated.

To the extent that digitalization can allow better use of observable and unal-terable individual characteristics to segment the population into groups, across which there is a variation of transfer but within each of which there is the univer-salism of an identical transfer, this can help to mitigate the tension between fine targeting and high implicit marginal tax rates, the second of the chap-ter's main issues.

The political economy of targeting, meanwhile, relates to the relationship between the nature of the targeting (fine or not) and the resources that the political system will generate for poverty reduction. It is not clear that new technology will affect this trade-off greatly. However, proxy means targeting and group-based targeting can create new tensions on the ground and new forms of political economy based on the groups used for targeting. These unintended consequences will have to be taken on board in any assessment of the consequences of easier group-based targeting because of the digital revolution.

Thus, the hype around the digital revolution needs to be duly mitigated by the lessons that the conventional literature presents on targeting anti-poverty transfers.

REFERENCES

Adato, Michelle. 2011. "Combining Quantitative and Qualitative Methods for Program Monitoring and Evaluation: Why Are Mixed-Method Designs Best?" World Bank Other Operational Studies 11063, World Bank, Washington, DC.

Anand, Sudhir, and Ravi Kanbur. 1991. "Public Policy and Basic Needs Provision in Sri Lanka." In *The Political Economy of Hunger, Volume III: Endemic Hunger*, edited by J. Dreze and A. Sen. Oxford: Clarendon Press.

Banerjee, Abhijit, Esther Duflo, Clement Imbert, Santhosh Mathew, and Rohini Pande. 2016. "E-Governance, Accountability, and Leakage in Public Programs: Experimental Evidence from a Financial Management Reform in India." NBER Working Paper 22803, National Bureau of Economic Research, Cambridge, MA.

Banerjee, Abhijit, Rema Hanna, Gabriel Kreindler, and Benjamin A. Olken. 2015. "Debunking the Stereotype of the Lazy Welfare Recipient: Evidence from Cash Transfer Programs." MIT Working Paper, Massachusetts Institute of Technology, Cambridge, MA.

Besley, Timothy, and Ravi Kanbur. 1988. "Food Subsidies and Poverty Alleviation." *Economic Journal* 98 (392): 701–19.

———. 1993. "The Principles of Targeting." In *Including the Poor*, edited by M. Lipton and J. Van der Gaag. Washington, DC: World Bank.

Bourguignon, Francois, and Gary Fields. 1990. "Poverty Measures and Anti-Poverty Policy." *Recherches Economique de Louvain* 56 (3/4): 409–27.

Chao, Kalvin, and Martin Ravallion. 1989. "Targeted Policies for Poverty Alleviation under Imperfect Information: Algorithms and Applications." *Journal of Policy Modeling* 11: 213–24.

Coady, David, Margaret Grosh, and John Hoddinott. 2004. *Targeting of Transfers in Developing Countries: Review of Lessons and Experience*. Washington, DC: World Bank and International Food Policy Research Institute.

Daley, Suzanne. 2015. "Speeding in Finland Can Cost a Fortune, If You Already Have One." *New York Times*, April 25.

Dasgupta, Indraneel, and Ravi Kanbur. 2005. "Community and Anti-Poverty Targeting." *Journal of Economic Inequality* 3 (3): 281–302.

Fiszbein, Ariel, Norbert Schady, Francisco H. G. Ferreira, Margaret Grosh, Niall Keleher, Pedro Olinto, and Emmanuel Skoufias. 2009. "Conditional Cash Transfers: Reducing Present and Future Poverty." World Bank Policy Research Report, World Bank, Washington, DC.

Fiszbein, Ariel, Ravi Kanbur, and Ruslan Yemtsov. 2014. "Social Protection, Poverty and the Post-2015 Agenda." *World Development* 61: 167–77.

Foster, James, Joel Greer, and Erik Thorbecke. 1984. "A Class of Decomposable Poverty Measures." *Econometrica* 3 (52): 761–66.

Gelb, Alan, and Anna Diofasi. 2015. "Preliminary Discussion Paper on the Future of Identification and Development." Discussion Paper, Center for Global Development, Washington, DC.

Gelbach, Jonah, and Lant Pritchett. 2002. "Is More for the Poor Less for the Poor? The Politics of Means-Tested Targeting." *The B.E. Journal of Economic Analysis & Policy* 2 (1): 1–28.

Government of India. 2017. *Economic Survey 2016–17.* New Delhi: Ministry of Finance, Department of Economic Affairs.

Grosh, Margaret, C. Del Ninno, E. Tesliuc, and A. Ouerghi. 2008. *For Protection and Promotion: The Design and Implementation of Effective Safety Nets.* Washington, DC: World Bank.

Immonen, Ritva, Ravi Kanbur, Michael Keen, and Matti Tuomala. 1998. "Tagging and Taxing: The Optimal Use of Categorical and Income Information in Designing Tax/Transfer Schemes." *Economica* 65 (258): 179–92.

Kanbur, Ravi. 1987. "Measurement and Alleviation of Poverty: With an Application to the Impact of Macroeconomic Adjustment." IMF Staff Papers, International Monetary Fund, Washington, DC.

———. 2010. "Macro Crises and Targeting Transfers to the Poor." In *Globalization and Growth: Implications for a Post-Crisis World,* edited by Michael Spence and Danny Leipziger. Washington, DC: World Bank.

———. 2015. "Informality: Causes, Consequences and Policy Responses." CEPR Discussion Paper 10509, Centre for Economic Policy Research, London.

Kanbur, Ravi, and Michael Keen. 1989. "Poverty, Incentives and Linear Income Taxation." In *The Economics of Social Security Reform,* edited by A. Dilnot and I. Walker. Oxford: Oxford University Press.

Kanbur, Ravi, Michael Keen, and Matti Tuomala. 1994. "Labor Supply and Targeting in Poverty Alleviation Programs." *World Bank Economic Review* 8 (2): 191–211.

Kanbur, Ravi, Michael Keen, and Matti Tuomala. 2016. "Groupings and the Gains from Targeting." *Research in Economics* 70: 53–63.

Nazara, Suahasil, and Sri Kusumastuti Rahayu. 2013. "Program Keluarga Harapan (PKH): Indonesian Conditional Cash Transfer Programme." Policy Research Brief 42, International Policy Centre for Inclusive Growth, Brasilia.

Radcliff, Dan. 2016. "Digital Payments as a Platform for Improving State Capacity." Background Paper, Center for Global Development, Washington, DC.

Ravallion, Martin. 1989. "Land-Contingent Policies for Rural Poverty Alleviation." *World Development* 17 (August): 1223–33.

———. 1991. "Reaching the Rural Poor through Public Employment: Arguments, Evidence, and Lessons from South Asia." *World Bank Research Observer* 6 (2): 153–76.

Reality Check Approach + Project Team. 2015. *People's Views and Experience of the National Social Assistance Programmes.* Jakarta: Effective Development Group.

Rodriguez-Castelan, Carlos. 2017. "Conditionality as Targeting? Participation and Distributional Effects of Conditional Cash Transfers." World Bank Policy Research Paper 7940, World Bank, Washington, DC.

PART IV

Country Case Studies

CHAPTER 10

Digitalization in Kenya

Revolutionizing Tax Design and Revenue Administration

NJUGUNA NDUNG'U

INTRODUCTION

The digital revolution has paved the way for profound changes in tax policy design and revenue administration. In several developing countries, digital technologies have transformed how payments are made, enabling financial inclusion through easy virtual access to bank accounts.

Kenya has been among the success stories, leading the way with a mobile-phone-based financial services platform, set in motion by the inception of the M-Pesa, a money-transfer system that gradually advanced into real-time retail payments and further into a virtual savings and credit supply platform. These innovations have led to a broad retail payment platform, which has made payments more efficient, transparent, and safe, facilitating financial inclusion regardless of income level. The broader platform has been useful for functions including e-commerce, tax payments, and revenue administration. Digitalization has also begun to change the way fiscal policy works, with the March 2017 launch of M-Akiba for micro-investment in government securities using the mobile-phone platform.[1]

This chapter explores developments in Kenya—from M-Pesa to national retail payments, to the positive impact of digitalization on financial inclusion and the

---

The author acknowledges the excellent research assistance of Alex Oguso, Ph.D. student at the University of Nairobi.

[1]M-Akiba is a government-issued retail bond that investors can purchase using their mobile phones. It is aimed at small investors to build financial inclusion for economic development. The money raised from issuance will go toward infrastructural development projects. Traditionally, of course, investing and trading in government securities has been a major business for banks and brokerage firms. The idea that small savers could invest their savings in government securities with good returns underscores the success of digitalization in the country.

rollout of a range of products made possible by the M-Pesa payments platform. The chapter further shows that M-Pesa and pressure for institutional reform were the catalysts for innovation that revolutionized tax designs and revenue adminis- tration. The acceleration of digitalization after the introduction of M-Pesa has pushed reforms in different directions, but the data are too limited to disentangle the effects of institutional reforms in the KRA (Kenya Revenue Authority) from the nationwide success in digitalization.

The next section discusses the preconditions for the reform of tax design and revenue administration in Kenya, how digitalization has progressed, the role of government, and reforms of the KRA. The chapter then reviews the impact of the reforms and the iTax system, the KRA M-Service, and the outcomes of digitali- zation at the KRA.

The chapter posits that tax design and revenue administration cannot work efficiently without an effective payments system. In some years in Kenya, the national payments system was thought to be adequate, but mobile-phone-based retail payments have provided important lessons and pointed the way forward. In countries like Kenya, the starting point for financial inclusion is the existence of a financial transactions platform that, in addition to payments, improves and broadens the availability of savings and investment. This is the innovation that M-Pesa has provided.

PRECONDITIONS FOR TAX DESIGN AND REVENUE ADMINISTRATION REFORMS

Technological advances and innovations have vast potential to transform fiscal formulation and implementation, but several preconditions exist before reforms to tax design and revenue administration can take place.

How Digitalization Progressed in Kenya

The year 2017 marks a decade of rapid development in Kenya's financial sec- tor, driven by the desire for financial inclusion and, as noted, spearheaded by M-Pesa (from the words for "mobile money").

M-Pesa was launched in March 2007 as a bank product in partnership with Safaricom, a telecommunication company, and the Commercial Bank of Africa, a commercial bank in Kenya. M-Pesa enabled users to store value on their mobile phone or mobile account as electronic currency for multiple uses, including trans- fers to other users, payments for goods and services, and conversion to and from cash.

The structure of M-Pesa was based on a person-to-person money transfer system by Safaricom that enabled millions of Kenyans to use the M-Pesa platform to make payments and send remittances. Safaricom supervised and regulated its network of agents, who formed the point-of-service countrywide, and another class of agents, the aggregators, who ensured efficient, effective, and transparent liquidity distribution across the country.

Box 10.1. M-Pesa and the Digital Financial System

M-Pesa developed in four stages, shaping financial market developments in Kenya and what is now referred to as the Digital Financial System:

- **First stage:** using the M-Pesa technological platform for transfers, payments, and settlement. This led to an expansion of the platform for more person-to-person transfers, payments, and settlements, as well as participants in the transaction platform.
- **Second stage:** introduction of virtual savings accounts using the M-Pesa platform, complemented by virtual banking services. That is, the phone could be used to deposit or withdraw from personal savings accounts. Subsequently, virtual banking services enabled costless transfer of money from M-Pesa to a savings account. A technological platform to manage micro-savings accounts was therefore now in place and developing for small savers with low and irregular income who were previously excluded.
- **Third stage:** a natural progression of supply and disbursement of short-term credit through the M-Pesa technological platform. Banks and telecommunication companies invested in a more versatile platform that used the transactions and savings data to generate credit scores to evaluate savers and to price short-term credit at an individual level, changing the costly collateral technology that had inhibited development of the credit market in most African economies. As of June 2016, this platform had 15.2 million accounts and Kenyans ages 18–34 were the main drivers.
- **Fourth stage:** expansion of the technological platform to enable cross-border and international remittances. The immediate impact of this development has been the transformation of the informal *Hawala* money transfer system into a network of formal money remittances companies as well as standalone payments units.

Funds were held in a trust account with the Commercial Bank of Africa that formed the transaction platform. Safaricom issued electronic money in exchange for cash at par value, and this was stored in the SIM card for the customer and simultaneously loaded into the trust account at the Commercial Bank of Africa. The trust account was under the custody of trustees, its funds separated from Safaricom business account funds, meaning that Safaricom could not access them.

Trust accounts became the payments system platform in commercial banks, separating regulatory issues for banks from those of telecommunication companies. This gave the market confidence that cash and transactions were secure.

The M-Pesa platform quickly developed into a platform for payments of goods and services and subsequently to mobile-banking functions. Box 10.1 explains the evolution and its support for financial inclusion and retail payments.

Commercial and microfinance banks in Kenya have leveraged the Digital Financial System platform to manage micro-accounts, build up deposits, and extend financial services to the previously unbanked and underserved. The innovative financial products and services they have provided have broadened financial inclusion (Figure 10.1).

As the figure shows, the adult population served by formal financial service providers increased to 75.3 percent in 2016 from 66.9 percent in 2013,

Figure 10.1. Kenya's Financial Inclusion Profile: 2000–16

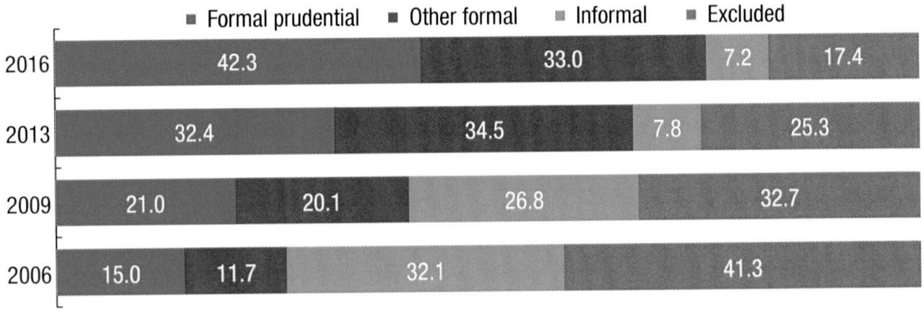

■ Formal prudential   ■ Other formal   ■ Informal   ■ Excluded

Year	Formal prudential	Other formal	Informal	Excluded
2016	42.3	33.0	7.2	17.4
2013	32.4	34.5	7.8	25.3
2009	21.0	20.1	26.8	32.7
2006	15.0	11.7	32.1	41.3

Source: Various FinAccess surveys.

30.5 percent in 2009, and 27.4 percent in 2006. Informal financial channels were serving only 7.2 percent of the adult population in 2016, from 35.2 percent in 2006. And the financially excluded population, though still high, declined to 17.4 percent of the adult population in 2016, from 41.3 percent in 2006.

Moreover, information and data from the Central Bank of Kenya show that commercial banks' branch outlets increased from 534 in 2005 to 1,443 in 2015; deposit accounts increased from 2.55 million in 2005 to nearly 34 million in 2016, with more than 90 percent of them micro-accounts. Since 2009, when Safaricom launched its pay-bill service on the M-Pesa platform, Safaricom has partnered with 25 banks and more than 700 businesses to facilitate fund deposits, bank transfers, and the regular payment of utility bills, insurance premiums, and loan installments.

Financial access touch points in Kenya have also continued to expand, with more bank branches, ATMs, telecommunication agents, and an agency network for banks. According to FSD (2013), about 76.7 percent of Kenyans are within five kilometers of financial access points, compared with 35.1 percent of Tanzanians, 42.7 percent of Ugandans, and 47.3 percent of Nigerians.

THE ROLE OF GOVERNMENT

The digital economy requires a strong analog foundation consisting of regulations that create a vibrant environment for economic agents to leverage digital technologies (World Bank 2016). The rapid digital revolution in Kenya's financial sector was supported by the "test-and-learn" approach adopted by the Central Bank of Kenya and the Communications Authority of Kenya, the telecommunications regulator. The approach combined a supportive policy environment with a sound regulatory and supervisory framework that allowed innovators and entrepreneurs to introduce financial innovations and to

> ### Box 10.2. Role of Government
>
> - The Central Bank of Kenya and the Communications Authority of Kenya worked together. This collaboration was necessary because the Digital Financial System involved commercial banks as a transactions platform and telecommunications companies as transmitters of transactions to this platform.
> - This system required a national payments and settlement legal framework and guidelines for the market. But parliament had not passed such legislation. To overcome the legal vacuum, the Central Bank of Kenya invoked the Trust Law that required development of the payment platform as a trust account owned by trustees and provided guidelines on how it would be operated.
> - The Central Bank of Kenya ensured that regulations were in place so that the M-Pesa platform remained a low-risk money transfer system, and hence improved the regime for anti–money laundering and countering the financing of terrorism. The data trails from M-Pesa transactions make it easier to detect fraud. These trails also help tax authorities to ensure tax compliance.
> - The Central Bank of Kenya maintained a ceiling on transactions and on how much money could be stored on the SIM card and provided guidelines on a tiered, know-your-customer framework for account holders, for both M-Pesa and savings products. These thresholds included limiting the size (value) of mobile transactions, set at 35,000 Kenyan shillings (KSh) (then about $500) per transaction at any one time and maximum limit of KSh 50,000 that a SIM card could hold (about $700) at any one time. These thresholds were later revised to KSh 70,000 per transaction and a maximum of KSh 14,000 transactions per day and can hold a maximum of KSh 100,000 on the SIM card.

diversify products (Ndung'u 2017). Box 10.2 summarizes the government's role during the digital revolution.

KRA Revenue Administration Reforms

To improve domestic resource mobilization, the KRA has implemented initiatives and reforms to modernize Kenya's tax system. Before 2003, the KRA achieved little in digitalizing tax administration, lacking as it did the appropriate developments in the national payments system. After 2003, the KRA laid the groundwork for the current momentum of digitalization and reforms in tax design and revenue administration launched under the Revenue Administration Reforms and Modernization Program.

The reform strategy was based on six components: customs reform and modernization, domestic taxes reform and modernization, road transport reform and modernization, business automation, human resources revitalization, and infrastructure development (KRA 2010). Box 10.3 describes the main digitalization initiatives that preceded the iTax system and KRA M-Service.

The reforms described in this section, made possible by the technological revolution, were the prerequisites for development and adoption of the iTax system and the KRA M-Service. The financial sector has become more inclusive,

Box 10.3. Pre-iTax KRA Reform Agenda

- The Kenya Revenue Authority (KRA) implemented the Withholding VAT Agency System in October 2003. It was introduced in order to capture credit, zero credit, and non-filers and reduce uncollected debts. In July 2005, the Electronic Tax Register system was introduced to enforce record keeping for business transactions.
- The Simba system (System of Information Management and Banking) was introduced in 2005, enabling automation of about 90 percent of the customs operations by introducing online lodging of manifests and entries, electronic processing, automated reports and reconciliations, electronic presentation of customs entries, automated calculation of duties and taxes, and internal accounting (KRA 2010).
- The Simba system also enabled an interface with the Vehicle Management System, which allowed the seamless flow of motor vehicle details into the system to facilitate clearance, registration, and duty payments.
- The KRA introduced electronic banking to expedite payment of duties and taxes through a secure electronic process. The authority developed the Common Cash Receipting System for direct revenue collection through commercial banks, which was interfaced with relevant KRA business systems (Simba, Integrated Tax Management System, and Vehicle Management System). The Common Cash Receipting System allowed a single view of the taxpayer, reduced human intervention in the payments process, improved reconciliations, matched payment and bank reports online, and enabled real-time monitoring of revenue collection (KRA 2010).
- In September 2007, the authority began implementation of the Integrated Tax Management System, rolled out in December 2008. Through it, registration and issuance of personal tax identification numbers was automated. Additionally, the system allowed taxpayers to electronically file their tax returns for value-added tax and PAYE (Pay As You Earn), which was later upgraded to cover electronic filing of corporate tax, stamp duty, and turnover tax, which became mandatory in October 2015.
- The KRA improved the Integrated Tax Management System in 2010 through development and implementation of an additional 11 modules, which form the current iTax system.

banks have integrated the Digital Financial System as an efficient platform to manage micro-savings accounts, and a retail payments system has emerged that does not require a bank account.

A retail payment system has emerged that has allowed formal transactions, and Kenyans have opened virtual savings accounts in banks, raising the national financial inclusion profile. Moving to a digital payments system (away from cash and check payments) is a major boost to financial inclusion, and effective, efficient, transparent, and safe payments and settlements set the stage for other innovations, including improvement in fiscal policy, tax design, and revenue administration. These developments have given market participants and government agencies leeway to develop products and payment lines such as targeted social protection for the aged and the physically challenged, tax payment, and payment of government licenses and fees.

DIGITALIZING TAX ADMINISTRATION

The iTax System

The technological revolution taking place across the world has changed how tax authorities and taxpayers relate. It has allowed authorities to obtain and cross-reference critical taxpayer information in real time or near real time. Prior to 2013, the KRA mainly relied on the Integrated Tax Management System for domestic tax administration. But with further developments in that system and the launch of iTax, the profile of taxation and tax payments has changed. This section describes the iTax system and KRA M-Service and how they have revolutionized tax design and payment, and revenue administration in Kenya through digitalization.

The iTax is a user-friendly, web-enabled, secure application that provides fully integrated and automated administration of all domestic taxes. It allows the taxpayer to register, file, pay, and inquire about status online with real-time monitoring of accounts. The system confirms successful registration, electronic filing, and actual tax payment. It also enables online back-office processing of all Domestic Tax Department transactions. Access is restricted based on the different tax categories. Figure 10.2 outlines the 18 modules of the system.

The iTax system registers taxpayers based on a unique personal identification number (PIN) acquired through the system. Once registered, a taxpayer account is created that forms the core of the iTax system through its comprehensive information about all taxpayer activities. The commercial banks have integrated with iTax (the KRA Payment Gateway), allowing taxpayers to make payments conveniently through online banking, cash, check, or real-time gross settlement. The system allows real-time access and update of ledgers upon payment registration and submission by partner banks.

Currently, tax payments to all government agencies, ministries, and county governments are made through the central bank's "G-Pay" platform. Integration of iTax with the Central Bank of Kenya and Integrated Financial Management Information System is in the process of ensuring that the system captures tax payments to all levels of government. The Integrated Financial Management Information System is already integrated with the central bank's G-Pay system, which remits the money directly from the respective ministries, state agencies, and county government accounts.

The iTax system has also enabled several online services through the portal,[2] and provides tools for processing tax returns and tax amendments for all domestic taxes. It also generates estimated assessments, which applies for several taxes.

---

[2] These include PIN application and checker, withholding tax certificate checker, tax compliance certificate application, tax compliance certificate checker, generation of e-slip, electronic filing and amending returns, viewing of tax returns filed, viewing of taxpayer account/ledger, e-query, application for refund, transfer of tax credits, application for payment plan, application for waivers and write-offs, and tax agents verification/services.

Figure 10.2. iTax System Modules

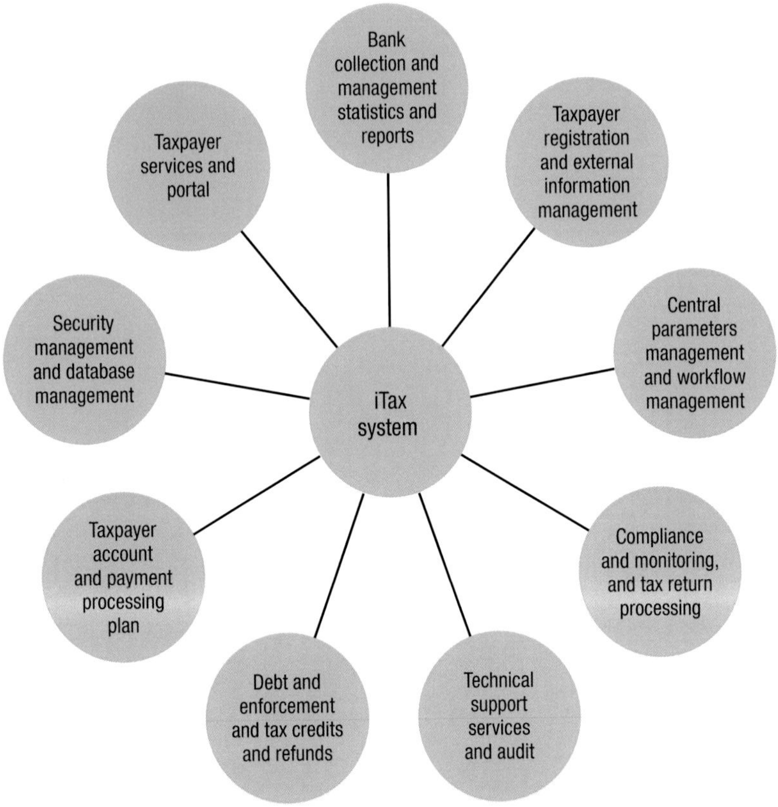

Source: Author's presentation of the iTax modules.

The system has enabled the KRA to easily generate weekly, monthly, quarterly, or yearly revenue and audit reports. The system prepares notices to taxpayers and records the time needed for the audit, as well as the audit results. This system has also enabled authorities to easily reconcile payments with assessment debits, identify defaulters, issue reminder letters and demand notices, compute fines and interest for late and nonpayment, and propose additional enforcement.

iTax restricts accessibility of certain modules only to specific users who have permission to view or edit different data to system security and the confidentiality of taxpayers' information. Additionally, its central management module enables incorporation of legal tax changes and amendments into the system without having to change the program code. The iTax system is secure and can be customized to cover all taxes and fees for national and local governments.

Seelmann and others (2010) show that iTax has enabled various tax authorities to move from the traditional tax administration systems based on a specific type of tax—which led to many different systems for different taxes, resulting in data duplication and inconsistency—to an integrated, "future-proof" system in which new technological developments can easily be incorporated to offer new functionalities and to integrate new tax categories.

KRA M-Service Platform

In October 2014, the KRA launched the KRA M-Service platform, a mobile phone application that facilitates tax payment and taxpayers' access to tax information.

It has two service components: informational services, and mobile payment of all taxes and e-slip generation for traffic revenue fees. The informational service enables taxpayers to access specific information from the KRA by text message. The mobile payment of all taxes and e-slip generation component conveniently allows taxpayers to make quick, simple payments of up to 140,000 Kenyan shillings (KSh) (currently about $1,373) per day through their mobile phones. The service is available on Safaricom M-Pesa and Airtel Money platforms. The payments made are cleared, processed, and credited to the KRA account in real time, and the taxpayer retains the payment confirmation SMS from the mobile financial services provider as proof of payment to the KRA. At the individual level, once a tax assessment or fees are determined, it becomes easier to move back to the M-Pesa platform to effect payments and receive responses from the iTax system.

The M-Service platform has encouraged institutional reforms at the KRA that go hand in hand with the institutional capacity.

THE IMPACT OF DIGITALIZATION AND THE KRA REFORMS

The chapter has already shown that digitalization has supported tax design and revenue collection. In assessing the impact, the chapter relies on trend analysis of various tax revenue streams as well as total tax effort over time.

The results realized so far seem to suggest huge potential in digitalization for tax payments and revenue administration. Figure 10.3 shows the trend in volume of transactions and the proportion of total tax payments made through the KRA M-Service platform between launch on 2014 and 2016.

The first two quarters in the figure were basically the test period. The information available shows that when the system was launched in October 2014, only 1,411 tax payment transactions were made through the mobile phone financial services in a month with a value of KSh 5.23 million (about $51,274.50). Transactions since increased to over 40,000 by October 2016, with a value of KSh 71.4 million (about $700,000.00). The figure also shows that the proportion of tax revenue remitted through the KRA M-Service platform has increased since the

Figure 10.3. Tax Remittance through KRA M-Service

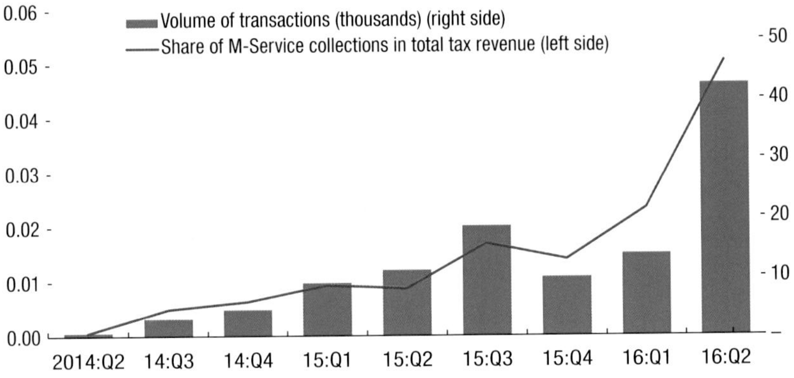

Source: Author's analysis of Kenya Revenue Authority (KRA) data.

second quarter of 2015, reflecting taxpayers' growing confidence in using the platform for tax payments.

Impact on Tax Design

The digital platform has affected the design of new taxes and improved overall tax collection, but it would be difficult to disentangle other positive factors. Evidently, the tax base for the KRA has expanded, as confirmed by the introduction of new tax categories, such as excise tax on money transfers. This tax was introduced in the third quarter of 2013 and has more than tripled in the three years since its introduction, moving from KSh 896 million ($8.78 million) in the third quarter of 2013 to KSh 3,187 million ($31.25 million) in the second quarter of 2016. This steady revenue growth has not been witnessed in other new tax categories introduced at the same time, except withholding value-added tax (VAT). Figure 10.4 shows the quarterly trend in contribution of the new tax categories to total tax revenue.

Put together, the performance trend of the new tax categories (Figure 10.5)—turnover tax from fiscal year (FY) 2007/08, excise tax on money transfers from FY2013/14, withholding VAT from FY2014/15, capital gains tax from FY2014/15, and rental income from FY2015/16—show that the aggregate tax effort (tax-revenue-to-GDP ratio) has increased since FY2012/13. The increase in the tax effort and the percentage share in total tax revenue for the new tax categories from FY2012/13 seems to have been in part because of the introduction of the iTax system in 2013.

Figure 10.4. Contribution of New Tax Categories to Total Tax Revenue

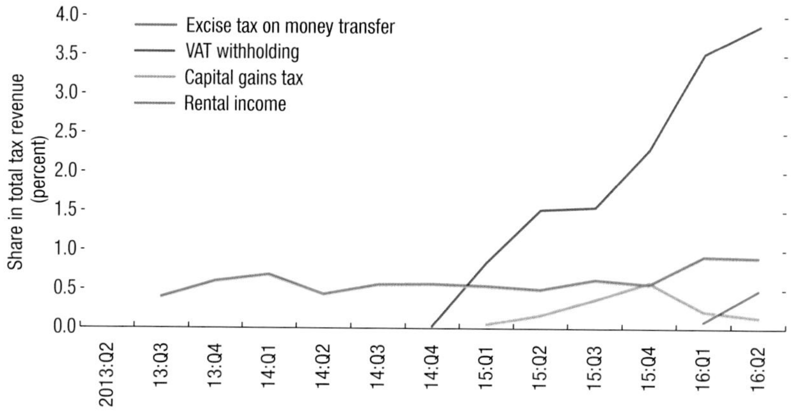

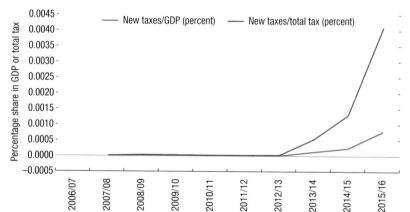

Source: Author's analysis of KRA data.

Figure 10.5. Annual Performance of New Tax Categories

Source: Author's analysis of KRA data.

Impact on the informal sector

Like any other developing country, the informal sector plays a major role in the Kenyan economy. The sector consists of small-scale traders generally operating at subsistence with few employees (World Bank 2006). Their myriad activities include selling or hawking food and clothes, running food stalls and small kiosks, and selling home supplies and fuels. They engage in small manufacturing, production, construction, or repair of goods (World Bank 2006).

The informal sector also has high revenue-generation potential. But informality remains a challenge to domestic resource mobilization in Kenya given the large number of unregistered taxpayers and unreported transactions and incomes associated with it. The Kenya National Bureau of Statistics estimated in 1993 that 910,000 small and medium enterprises (SMEs) operated, employing up to 2 million people, according to a baseline survey in that year. This had expanded dramatically by 2015, with the *Economic Survey 2016* showing that the informal economy employed an estimated 12.5 million people in the year, or 82.8 percent of the workforce (KNBS 2016a).

The statistics bureau's 2016 Micro, Small and Medium Enterprises (MSME) Survey showed that the sector in Kenya had evolved into a highly vibrant and dynamic one. The survey revealed that about 1.56 million licensed MSMEs and 5.85 million unlicensed businesses employed about 14.9 million people. Monthly expenditure on salaries and wages for licensed businesses was reported at KSh 64.1 billion (about $628.40 million), and unlicensed MSMEs spent KSh 9.0 billion ($88.24 million) (KNBS 2016b), a significant portion of untapped income tax revenue.

Part of the solution to the challenges in taxing informal businesses lies in ensuring that businesses formalize and grow from micro to small, and small to macro, enterprises. But such progression has not evidently occurred. However, even though this progression is deterred by structural as well as institutional constraints, digitalization allows such businesses to participate in formal financial transactions and to pay their requisite taxes electronically—with time, these formal transactions will translate to formalization of the businesses themselves.

Indeed, it can be shown that, over time, the number of taxpayers has increased, but to assess the impact of M-Pesa on informality would require survey data. Nonetheless, the available literature shows that the banking industry, through the Digital Financial System, is playing an important role in helping SMEs to formalize and grow.

The Digital Financial System platform has made it easier and more convenient for small taxpayers, mainly in the informal sector, to meet their tax obligations. Small taxpayers with no platform of payment had to physically visit KRA offices to make small transactions, a costly bureaucratic process that took time away from business. Booming digital financial services (particularly online and mobile banking), however, allow informal sector business owners to conveniently make small transactions at their marketplaces. GrowthCap and FSD Kenya (2016) show that, on top of the financial services mainly offered through the Digital Financial System, most banks also offer relationship management and business advice (face-to-face and online) to SME clients to help them to formalize and grow their businesses.

Formal and informal businesses have embraced mobile-phone-based solutions in their operations, influencing the design of taxes at the KRA. The businesses use phones to contact customers and suppliers, make money transfers, apply for microcredit, access micro-savings, and make tax payments. They also pay levies and charges to the various county governments, some of which have embraced

Figure 10.6. Kenya's Tax Effort, Tax to GDP
(Percent)

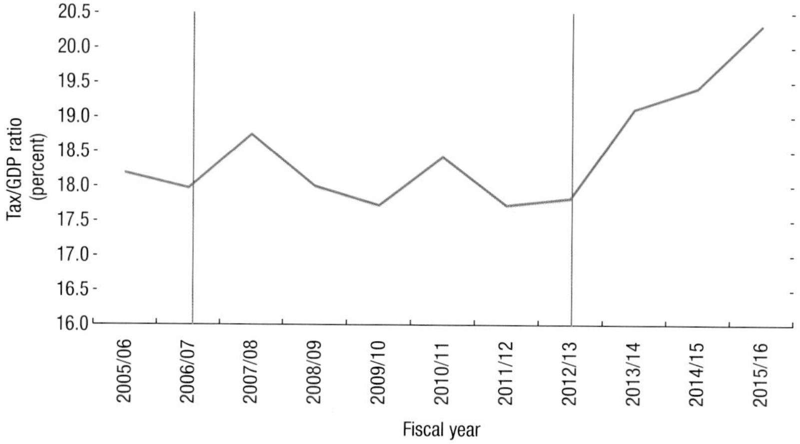

Source: Author's analysis of KRA data.

receipt of such payments through the Digital Financial System. These mobile phone transactions leave data trails, opening a window onto a large segment of the informal economy.

Impact on tax administration

Figure 10.6 shows tax trends. The line at FY2006/07 demarcates when M-Pesa was introduced, setting the pace for digitalization and financial inclusion. It is the same period as when the KRA started to implement the Integrated Tax Management System for domestic tax administration. The second line at FY2012/13 shows when the KRA rolled out the iTax system. The figure shows that Kenya's tax-to-GDP ratio had averaged 18.1 percent from the FY2005/06 to FY2012/13 before the iTax introduction in September 2013. Over the same period, GDP growth (at constant prices) averaged 5.13 percent.

The expanded tax base, institutional reforms, and the ease of tax payment supported by the digital platform enabled the KRA to boost tax collection from KSh 695.9 billion (about $6.82 billion) in FY2011/12 to KSh 911.8 billion (about $8.94 billion) in 2013/14. In FY2014/15, it passed the trillion mark for the first time, hitting KSh 1.02 trillion (about $10 billion).

Tax-to-GDP improved from 19.1 percent in FY2013/14 to about 20.3 percent in FY2015/16, and GDP growth (at constant prices) averaged 5.66 percent. It may also be that this trend is consistent with economic growth, but we show that there is no significant shift in GDP growth in the demarcated periods during 2007–13, with GDP growth averaging 5.02 percent a year and 5.66 percent in 2014–16.

Figure 10.7. Cost of Revenue Collection Including Capital Expenditure
(Percent)

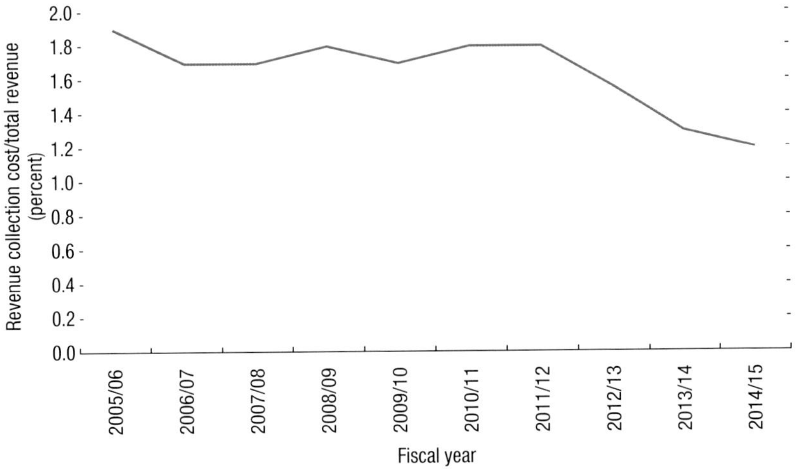

Source: Author's analysis of KRA data.

By 2018, the KRA aims to reduce its cost of revenue collection to less than 1 percent of total revenue collected, a target it intends to achieve by automating all its processes and taking advantage of the Digital Financial System to reduce operational and compliance costs for taxpayers.

The trend in Figure 10.7 shows that the cost of revenue collection has been declining since 2011. The reduction may reflect improved efficiency in the tax system through KRA digitalization reforms, which have aided simplification of tax processes, making it easier for taxpayers to comply and reducing opportunities for fraud and tax evasions. This has also improved accuracy of taxpayer accounting data, reduced the time taken by taxpayers when dealing with the KRA, and enhanced speed and accuracy of the KRA to extract data and information on revenue. This has improved the confidentiality of taxpayer information and enhanced taxpayer acceptance.

Specifically, the iTax system is cost-effective because it can handle many taxpayers and has enabled the KRA to reduce workload and operational costs such as for processing, storing, and handling tax returns. The system has helped speed up tax assessment and service delivery and made tax administration more efficient. Currently, taxpayers with internet access can easily file returns anywhere and anytime.

Moreover, the digitalization of tax design and tax collection has reduced taxpayer–tax officer interactions, minimizing opportunities for tax fraud (collusion and tax evasion). Before digitalization, the KRA relied heavily on tax agents. With digitalization, rogue agents who were previously defrauding taxpayers and the KRA have been eliminated, and it is now easier to certify

Figure 10.8. Perceived Corruption of Tax Officials
(Percent)

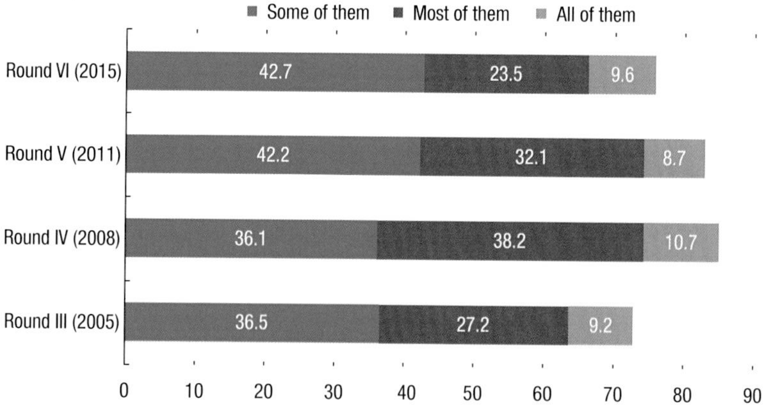

Source: Author's analysis of Kenya's Afrobarometer survey data.

online that a tax agent is registered by the KRA. Taxpayers who have internet are now able to monitor their accounts in real time and remotely.

The digital platform and implementation of the KRA integrity program have enabled the KRA to increase transparency in its operations and reduce opportunities for corruption within the tax system. Figure 10.8 shows the past four rounds of survey results on public perception of corruption, from Afrobarometer. The research network has surveyed 37 countries in Africa on various aspects of democracy and governance.

Each of the surveys covers a sample size of about 2,400 respondents. The results look at how many tax officials (KRA officials or local government tax collectors) Kenyan citizens perceive to be corrupt. Interesting to note is that, since 2008, the number perceived as such has generally gone down. The Afrobarometer survey results show that respondents who feel that at least some tax officials are corrupt has declined from 85 percent in 2008 to 75.8 percent in 2015.

More specifically, those who felt that most tax officials were corrupt declined from 38.2 percent in 2008 to 23.5 percent in 2015, and those who felt that all tax officials were corrupt declined from 10.7 percent to 9.6 percent. Although these responses capture only the *perceived* number of corrupt KRA officials and local government tax collectors, they clearly indicate that the digitalization of KRA processes and the use of available payments systems for tax revenue collection have significantly reduced opportunities for personal interaction with tax officials and hence incidences of fraud and evasion.

LESSONS FROM THE KENYAN CASE

This chapter has made clear that digitalization has supported the design of potentially more efficient and effective tax categories and revenue administration. The iTax system and the KRA M-Service have enabled a single view of the taxpayer's records, improved reconciliations, matched payment and bank reports online, allowed real-time monitoring of revenue collection, introduced system checks and audit trails, and minimized interaction between taxpayers and tax officers, reducing breaches in integrity in the organization.

Digitalization has given the KRA an opportunity to strengthen and revamp its tax enforcement mechanisms through third-party sharing of information. Currently, the iTax system is already integrated with the Integrated Financial Management Information System and Central Bank of Kenya and plans are under way to integrate with other systems such as the National Social Security Fund, National Health Insurance Fund, and the eCitizen digital platform. This integration will facilitate identification of potential tax defaulters, unregistered businesses, and individuals, and increase active taxpayers and tax compliance.

The Digital Financial System as a nationwide transactions platform has made it easier and convenient for taxpayers to meet their tax obligations wherever they are, improving tax receipts. Taxpayers do not have to visit KRA offices to pay taxes or visit their banks to effect payments. The Digital Financial System also presents a platform the tax authority can use to pay tax refunds promptly and directly into taxpayers' bank accounts or through their mobile phones. This module is yet to be implemented in iTax. This is an opportunity for using the Digital Financial System to shorten the time for refunds to reduce complaints and dissatisfaction with handling of tax refund claims and the reduction in tax revenue distortions associated with tax refunds.

Most developing countries have narrow tax bases owing to many factors, but one clear reason is their large informal markets. In this area, the Digital Financial System is expected to play a major role in helping to formalize informal enterprises and to expand countries' tax bases. Formalization here does not automatically mean that these informal businesses will be registered. But bringing transactions onto the formal platform will allow the government to design incentives to formalize all aspects of such informal businesses. As banks bring SMEs and MSMEs on board through the Digital Financial System platform, most of them are expected to formalize and grow into stable formal enterprises that will grow and become potential taxpayers.

Institutional reforms at the KRA have strengthened its capacity to mobilize domestic resources in the country. Also, corruption, an institutional failure, has been checked through the digitalization of KRA processes, reducing taxpayer–tax official contacts, which many viewed as opportunities for fraud. The decline in perceived corruption by Kenyan tax officials since 2008 confirms this. In addition, revenue administration through the Integrated Financial Management Information System, supported by Central Banks' G-Pay system, has enabled efficient revenue administration in central and county governments and efficient payments to suppliers and the tendering process.

However, as recognized in the 2016/17 Budget Policy Statement, the Digital Financial System also poses a fiscal risk to the country. The risk is linked to the volume of transactions and the number of taxpayers employed in the system, the thousands of businesses supported by the system, and the tax revenue that consequently accrues to the government. This implies that it is an important source of tax revenue and so the risk of failure will have a significant effect on overall fiscal revenue or the fiscal position of the country.

Generally, the Digital Financial System has changed the game through the opportunities it has generated for greater savings and investment for the previously unbanked, through settlement of payments, including tax payments, and government payments through targeted social protection. Studies so far (Suri and Jack 2016) show that the Digital Financial System driven by M-Pesa has lifted 2 percent of the population out of poverty. The government has slowly moved from cash payments to embrace digitalization, which has made a great difference in revenue administration in Kenya. Moreover, there remains great potential for Kenya to fully automate tax administration and allow integration with other third-party systems.

REFERENCES

GrowthCap, and FSD Kenya. 2016. *SME Banking in Kenya.*

Financial Sector Deepening (FSD) Kenya. 2013. *Kenya Financial Diaries 2012–2013: Socio-Economic and Demographic Datasets.* Nairobi.

Kenyan Bureau of Statistics (KNBS). 2016a. *Economic Survey 2016.* Nairobi.

———. 2016b. *Micro, Small and Medium Establishment (MSME) Survey.* Nairobi.

Kenyan Revenue Authority (KRA). 2010. *Revenue Administration Reforms in Kenya: Experience and Lessons.* Nairobi.

———. 2015. "Sixth Corporate Plan 2015/16–2017/18, Trust through Facilitation." Nairobi.

Ndung'u, Njuguna. 2017. "Boosting Transformational Technology: Creating Supportive Environment for Game-Changing Innovations." In *Foresight Africa: Top Priorities for the Continent in 2017*, edited by Amadou Sy and Christina Golubski. Washington, DC: Brookings Institute.

Njoroge, Kiarie. 2016. "Treasury Report Reveals Fears over M-Pesa's Critical Role in Economy." *Business Daily.* November 30.

Seelmann, Jürgen, Dietrich Lerche, Anja Kiefer, and Pierre Lucante. 2010. *Benefits of a Computerized Integrated System for Taxation: iTax Case Study.* Bonn: Federal Ministry for Economic Cooperation and Development.

Suri, Tavneet, and William Jack. 2016. "The Long-Run Poverty and Gender Impacts of Mobile Money." *Science* 354 (6317): 1288–92.

World Bank. 2006. "Kenya Inside Informality: Poverty, Jobs, Housing and Services in Nairobi's Slums." Water and Urban Unit 1, Africa Region, Report 36347. Washington, DC.

———. 2016. *World Development Report 2016: Digital Dividends.* Washington, DC: World Bank.

CHAPTER 11

Fiscal Policy Consequences of Digitalization and Demonetization in India

Rathin Roy and Suyash Rai

DIGITALIZATION IN INDIA

In recent years, initiatives and trends have been enabling large-scale digitalization of the Indian economy. The country leapfrogged to widespread use of mobile phones in the past decade or so, given a lift as liberalization of the telecommunications sector occurred alongside booming mobile technology and amid relatively low penetration of fixed-line technology.

By February 2017, more than 1.16 billion Indians had subscribed to mobile services, for a "mobile teledensity" of 85.9 (Telecom Regulatory Authority of India 2017).[1] Teledensity has risen as much as tenfold in slightly more than a decade and prices of mobile services have fallen sharply. By February, 261 million people had become broadband subscribers, up from 1.4 million in March 2006.

Several government projects are catalyzing this digitalization. Among them, a national biometric identity program (*Aadhaar*) has reached about 1.15 billion residents,[2] and enables identification and authentication of residents. In banking, two programs are helping bring the "unbanked" into the economy. And under the *Pradhan Mantri Jan Dhan Yojana* of August 2014, more than 280 million bank accounts had been opened by March 2017, while another 243 million accounts were opened under a government financial inclusion plan before this. Many of these accounts are held by people who never had bank accounts before,[3] while

---

The authors thank Meghna Paul of the National Institute for Public Finance and Policy for research assistance.

[1] The number of subscribers for every 100 residents.

[2] Data from Unique Identification Authority of India.

[3] According to Sharma, Giri, and Chadha (2016), 67 percent of account holders surveyed said that the Jan Dhan account was their first bank account.

about 60 percent of the *Pradhan Mantri Jan Dhan Yojana* accounts were opened in rural areas.

Banking and payments are also undergoing considerable change. In 2006, new rules allowed banks to appoint agents (called business correspondents and business facilitators),[4] enabling innovations that have brought down the cost of banking and payment services to low-income households and enterprises. Authorities have also recently allowed licensing of payment banks and various types of prepaid instruments.

Following the demonetization of its 500 and 1,000 rupee (Rs) notes in November 2016, the government announced several measures to increase the pace of digitalization of storage of value and payments. It has reduced the maximum value of cash transactions, lowered permissible cash donations to political parties, and announced various incentives for making electronic payments, such as a service tax waiver for certain values of digital payments. In addition, it waived transaction charges for digital payments made to government agencies and offered discounts and rewards for making digital payments. The Reserve Bank of India also relaxed customer charges for various modes of digital payment.

STATUS OF DIGITALIZATION

Yet despite a widespread perception of India as a leader in digitalization, the economy remains relatively less digitized. On the World Economic Forum's Networked Readiness Index, India ranked 91st among 139 countries in 2016 on "how well (it) is using information and communications technologies to boost competitiveness and well-being." China ranked 59th, Brazil 72nd, and South Africa 65th. India ranked well on affordability of digital services (8th), but mediocre or poor on all other parameters (Table 11.1).

India has a long way to go for digitalization of payments. The penetration of point-of-sales machines is among the lowest in the world and much lower than countries such as Brazil and China (BIS 2016). Surveys have reported that most people in India have never used digital transaction methods.

The process of digitalization in India raises concerns. India lacks a comprehensive legal framework to protect the privacy of users of digital services (Bhandari and Sane 2016), leaving their information vulnerable to misuse. This is a significant concern given the poor skills of users. For example, with literacy at relatively low levels—slightly more than 74 percent in 2011—users may be unable to protect their privacy. And because of weaknesses in redress, enforcement, and adjudication systems, users may be unable to get compensation for abuse or fraud.

The legal framework also enables state surveillance, with little recourse (Bhandari and Sane 2016). And although recent trends suggest India is set for

---

[4]Business correspondents are agents who conduct transactions on behalf of banks. These transactions typically include accepting deposits, redeeming deposits, and facilitating payments. Business facilitators do only sourcing of business and are not allowed to conduct transactions.

Table 11.1. India's Ranking on Networked Readiness Index

Parameter	India's Ranking
Affordability of digital services	8
Business and innovation environment	110
Infrastructure	114
Skills	101
Individual usage	120
Business usage	75
Government usage	59
Economic impact	80
Social impact	69

Source: World Economic Forum, Networked Readiness Index.
Note: The index measures performance on drivers of digital technologies under three subindices: overall environment, readiness (infrastructure, affordability, skills), and usage (individuals, business, government). The drivers considered for the environment subindex are political and regulatory environment, and business and innovation environment; under the readiness subindex are infrastructure and digital content, affordability, and skills; under the usage subindex are individual, business, and government usage.

rapid digitalization, it seems likely that this will be marked by a "digital divide." It is estimated that about 9.3 percent of villages do not have mobile network coverage (Parliament of India 2017). Several states have much lower teledensity than the national average—Assam, Bihar, Madhya Pradesh, and Uttar Pradesh have teledensity of 70—while states with teledensity of more than 100 drive up the national average, such as Tamil Nadu and Punjab.

POTENTIAL BENEFITS OF DIGITALIZATION FOR FISCAL POLICY

Digitalization could benefit fiscal policy in many ways, including under the six following categories:

1. **Government payments to individuals:** The government can improve the efficiency of financial payments made to citizens and residents under various schemes and may improve the effectiveness of these schemes by better identification of beneficiaries. Reports have suggested significant leakage from government schemes, which could reduce use of digital authentication methods. For example, a government study estimated that 58 percent of subsidized food grains issued under the Public Distribution System do not reach the targeted beneficiaries (Government of India 2005). Use of digital databases to identify beneficiaries of schemes could help improve the effectiveness of some.

2. **Public procurement:** The government can improve the efficiency and integrity of public procurements by relying on electronic systems that improve transparency and competition.

3. **Nontax revenues:** The government can improve the efficiency of collection of nontax receipts (such as user charges) with digital payment. These methods may reduce the costs associated with handling cash and human resources for collecting these revenues.

4. **Tax collection:** The government can improve efficiency of tax collection with digital methods. For example, electronic filing of taxes may reduce the costs of collection and the resources that it requires.

5. **Tax intelligence and enforcement:** Access to real-time or near real-time information on financial transactions could help improve tax enforcement by the government. As individuals and businesses integrate with the digital economy and accept and make digital payments, it should become easier to create transaction trails that can reveal avoidance or evasion of taxes.

6. **E-governance:** The government could use digitalization to improve efficiency of governance. This may include digitalization of procedures and better information access for citizens and residents. For example, digitalization of land records can help better govern land resources by making such information available to residents online, and possibly by improving procedures for land-record mutations and land transactions.

The next section describes government efforts to realize these benefits of digitalization.

GOVERNMENT RESPONSE TO DIGITALIZATION

As noted, digitalization has created opportunities for greater government efficiency and effectiveness. The central government has launched major and minor programs to integrate use of information technology into its systems and processes, and in 2015 brought all such initiatives under the common "Digital India" program, which now includes 115 major and minor initiatives of the government.[5]

Government Payments to Individuals

The Direct Benefit Transfer program, which commenced in 2013, aims to make government payments directly to beneficiary accounts. It strives to reform the government delivery system by re-engineering the existing process in welfare schemes to simplify and speed up the flow of information and funds. It also aims to ensure accurate targeting of beneficiaries, remove duplication, and reduce fraud.

By March 16, 2017, 99 schemes from 20 ministries had been integrated with the Direct Benefit Transfer system.[6] Eventually, the system is expected to cover all schemes involving cash transfers to individuals, which will mean integrating 536 schemes across 65 ministries and departments out of 1,182 schemes administered by 75 ministries and departments of the central government.

From January 2013 to December 2016, government payments worth about 1.1 percent of GDP had been transferred through the Direct Benefit Transfer system (Centre for Policy Research 2017). About half of this amount was

---

[5]The complete list is available at the Ministry of Electronics and Information Technology at http://www.digitalindia.gov.in/di-initiatives.

[6]The list is available at https://dbtbharat.gov.in/scheme/schemelist.

transferred under the national rural employment guarantee scheme. Other major schemes involving direct benefit transfers include cooking gas subsidies and the National Social Assistance Programme, which provides financial assistance to the elderly, widows, and people with disabilities, and provides scholarships.

The government has also established various portals for end-to-end processing under various schemes. For example, it launched the National Scholarship Portal for scholarship processing, which includes submission of student applications, verification, sanction, and disbursal to the end beneficiary for the government scholarship. Similarly, Jeevan Pramaan, an Aadhar-based biometric-enabled digital service for government pensioners is designed to improve the issuing of life certificates for pensioners.

In addition, the government has started linking different databases for policy decisions about beneficiaries, using the tax database to deny cooking gas subsidies to higher-income households, for example. Such initiatives may help better target subsidies.

The government has also made gradual yet considerable progress in making payments electronically. About 98 percent of all government payments made so far in fiscal year (FY) 2016/17 were electronic, according to the Controller General of Accounts on March 1, 2017 (BGR 2017).

Public Procurement

The government launched the online Central Public Procurement Portal in October 2012, mandating ministries to channel all procurements with an estimated value of Rs 1 million ($58,000 in purchasing power parity terms) or more through the portal or through other e-procurement solutions they may be using. The threshold was reduced to Rs 0.5 million ($29,000) in April 2015 and Rs 0.2 million ($11,600) in April 2016, both in purchasing power parity terms. The government also mandated public sector undertakings and autonomous and statutory bodies under the administrative control of ministries to use e-procurement.

In 2016, the central government launched the Government e-Marketplace for single-window online procurement of commonly used, small-value goods and services. The Central Public Procurement Portal facilitates e-procurement for larger-value items (Rs 0.2 million or higher). The government e-Marketplace enables direct purchase, e-bidding, and reverse e-auctions to help achieve best value. The portal offers online registration facilities for government users, product sellers, and service providers. It is expected to help overcome information asymmetry across vendors by making information about procurements by various departments and agencies available to those purchasing similar goods and services.

Nontax Revenues

The government has also launched the national payment service platform, PayGov India, a transactional facility that allows customers to access various services through the internet. Government departments and agencies can use the platform to offer services through their portals, with a facility to make online payment.

Nonetheless, many user charges levied by government agencies are presently not collected electronically. Some departments have implemented electronic payments with greater success than others. For example, more than 50 percent of passenger ticketing and more than 95 percent of freight ticketing in railways is now online. But most museums and archaeological sites managed by Archaeological Survey of India do not accept electronic payments. Reports by the Comptroller and Auditor General (Audit Report No. 18 of 2013 and Report No. 17 of 2014) have pointed out instances and risks of misappropriation of cash in the Archaeological Survey of India and Department of Posts.

Tax Collection

Most taxes the central government collects are deposited and returns filed electronically. Indeed, the government has mandated electronic filing for certain categories of taxpayers, and most organizations and individuals are now required to file electronically, with conditions based on which electronic filing is mandated. For example, any individual with an income of more than Rs 0.5 million ($29,000), about five times per capita income, is required to file electronically.

A major reform launched in FY 2017/18 is the introduction of a goods and services tax (GST). This entails a considerable effort to migrate taxpayers from the present system of indirect taxes to the GST system. The government has created the Goods and Services Tax Network, a nonprofit organization that maintains a single portal for all GST stakeholders, including the government and taxpayers. The portal is accessible to the central government to track down every transaction, while taxpayers file their taxes. The system is completely online and is designed to, among other things, provide invoice matching to enable matching of taxable supplies shipped out against all the taxable supplies received. This should help reduce tax evasion.

Tax Intelligence and Enforcement

In 2004, India established a Financial Intelligence Unit under the Financial Action Task Force. It gathers and analyzes information about transactions suspected of involving money laundering. The unit gets data from various financial firms and produces intelligence reports that feed into revenue investigation and enforcement processes.

E-governance

The government has launched several schemes to use digital technologies to improve governance.

For example, it has substantially automated the management of public finances through the Public Financial Management System. It has begun a program to digitize land records across the country and launched a platform (Digilocker) for digital issuance and verification of documents and certificates.

In addition, the government started the National Digital Literacy Mission Scheme to impart information technology training to 5.25 million people working at the front end of government service delivery, including childcare workers, health workers, and others. The e-District Mission Mode Project has been launched to strengthen district administrations through centralized software applications for citizen services and training for staff in departments. And community service centers in village local governments (*Panchayat)* will strengthen a network of 250,000 centers to deliver services. The government has also launched e-Panchayat to provide software for automation of local rural functions.

Challenges of a Digital Economy

Digitalization may also pose certain fiscal challenges. The main, widely acknowledged challenge is in the difficulty of taxation that a digital economy creates. Digitalization provides opportunities for profit-shifting to low-tax locations where a company may in fact be doing no significant business.

In 2016, a committee constituted by the Central Board of Direct Taxes submitted its recommendations on taxation of business models for e-commerce. The committee recommended an equalization levy on payments to nonresidents for certain specified services. From June 1, 2016, the government introduced an equalization levy of 6 percent on specified cross-border, business-to-business transactions exceeding Rs 100,000. By December 31, 2016, Rs 1.46 billion had been collected.

FISCAL CONSEQUENCES OF GOVERNMENT INITIATIVES

Evidence of the impact of digitalization for government fiscal policy is sparse, with little research done. This is partly because most initiatives are new. But the potential is great for research studies of the initiatives described above. These could range from descriptive case studies of design and implementation to rigorous impact studies.

Muralidharan, Niehaus, and Sukhtankar (2016), evaluating biometrically authenticated payments infrastructure for employment and pension programs in Andhra Pradesh, reveal positive fiscal consequences. The new system delivered faster, more predictable, and less corrupt payments without hurting access. The study also found that the investment was cost-effective, as time savings to beneficiaries alone were equal to the cost of the intervention, and leakage of funds between the government and beneficiaries was reduced significantly, indeed, by 12.7 percent in the employment program.

The government says the Direct Benefit Transfer program led to cumulative savings of Rs 0.5 trillion from 2014–15 and 2016–17,[7] about 1 percent of total government expenditure. However, the quality of these estimates cannot be verified as detailed workings have not been released. In 2016, the government estimated cumulative savings of Rs 0.21 trillion during 2014–15 and 2015–16, arising out of the direct transfer of the cooking gas subsidy,[8] about 0.4 percent of total expenditure.

THE DEMONETIZATION DECISION

Indian Finance Minister Arun Jaitley explained the reasons for demonetization in his budget speech in February 2017 (Box 11.1). The proximate objective was fiscal, to expand the tax base. "Tax evasion for many years has become a way of life. This compromises the larger public interest and creates unjust enrichment in favor of the tax evader, to the detriment of the poor and deprived. This has bred a parallel economy which is unacceptable for an inclusive society. Demonetization seeks to create a new 'normal' wherein the GDP would be bigger, cleaner and real." He concluded: "We are largely a tax noncompliant society. The predominance of cash in the economy makes it possible for the people to evade their taxes. When too many people evade taxes, the burden of their share falls on those who are honest and compliant" (Jaitley 2017).

The government had for some time been concerned about the size of the unaccounted, and therefore non-tax-paying, income base. The National Institute for Public Finance and Policy's (2013) report for the Ministry of Finance, while still confidential (and therefore not cited in detail), showed that unaccounted wealth and income inside the country was large. Yet, the World Bank found that in terms of the size of its shadow economy, India compares favorably with most other developing countries (Schneider, Buehn, and Montenegro 2010). India ranked 15th among 98 developing countries,[9] and the study found that between 1999 and 2007, the shadow economy shrank from 23.2 percent of GDP to 20.7 percent.

In addition, the National Institute for Public Finance and Policy, using an analytical model commissioned by the government for widening the tax base, indicated that scope existed to do so. But given the large informal sector, such widening could only be of a limited nature if the instruments currently available were deployed. The Finance Ministry considered new forms of instrumentation, even shock therapy such as demonetization.

---

[7]See the statement published at http://pib.nic.in/ndagov/Comprehensive-Materials/compr20.pdf.

[8]See the press release at http://pib.nic.in/newsite/PrintRelease.aspx?relid=147384.

[9]Rank 1 means the smallest shadow economy as a percentage of GDP.

Box 11.1. Demonetization of High-Denomination Currency Notes

On November 8, 2016, the Government of India invoked the 1934 Reserve Bank of India Act to withdraw the legal tender status of Rs 500 and Rs 1,000 denomination notes. All those holding these notes were expected to deposit them in their bank accounts or with the central bank, and the amount was credited to their bank accounts.

These high-denomination notes comprised about 87 percent of currency in circulation and amounted to about $235 billion (nominal conversion), or 10 percent of GDP. The government also introduced Rs 2,000 notes and circulation of a new series of Rs 500 notes. The remonetization of the economy, which is ongoing at the time of writing, is primarily happening through these notes.

On December 28, 2016, the government issued the Specified Bank Notes (Cessation of Liabilities) Ordinance, 2016 to cease the liability of the government for the currency notes whose legal tender status had already been canceled. The ordinance also imposed fines on people transacting with or holding such notes. This ordinance was later confirmed by the parliament as The Specified Bank Notes Cessation of Liabilities Act, 2017.

Sources: Prime Minister's speech delivered on November 8, 2016, to announce the decision to demonetize, and the Specified Bank Notes Cessation of Liabilities Act, 2017.

Even if there is unaccounted wealth in India, it may not be easy to extract a considerably larger amount of tax from the economy. As the government's Economic Survey 2015–16 pointed out, income tax collection is significantly better than expected for the country's level of economic development (Government of India 2017).

To account for the theory that democracies tend to tax and spend more, the survey controlled for democracy as a variable. The finding on personal income tax still holds, albeit the overall tax-to-GDP ratio is lower than it should be. While the percentage of individuals paying taxes is much smaller than expected, the amount of personal income tax collected is actually better than one would expect at this per capita income. This mismatch between satisfactory income tax collection and low number of income tax payers may be because income is concentrated in a smaller number of individuals and because agriculture, which employs a lot of people, is not taxed at all, as taxes are not levied on income from agriculture.

After demonetization, the Department of Revenue issued notices to all who had deposited amounts above Rs 250,000, asking them to show how they had acquired these resources. The government also put in place two amnesties, albeit with heavy penalties as discussed below.

Demonetization was a bold decision and was expected to have considerable short- and long-term consequences. The expected consequences and what the data available to date say about them is discussed in the next section.

Impact on Tax Collection

The impact of demonetization on tax collection and the tax base can be considered in the short term (2016–17) or the medium to long term (2017–18 and beyond). It was expected to hurt growth by reducing demand because of a lack of cash to make payments. It was also expected to reduce production because of cash-flow problems, especially in labor-intensive sectors such as construction or textiles, since casual workers in the informal sector are paid in cash. The government argued, however, that the move would improve tax compliance and help expand the tax base in the long term.

Short-term impact on tax collection

Table 11.2 presents a snapshot of estimates of the negative impact on GDP growth of demonetization in 2016–17. Most organizations expected a big impact, with recovery in 2017–18.

Table 11.2. GDP Growth Estimates by Various Agencies
(Percent, year-over-year growth)

Agency	2016–17		2017–18	
	Pre-demonetization	Post-demonetization	Pre-demonetization	Post-demonetization
IMF	7.6	6.6	7.6	7.2
World Bank	7.6	7.0	7.7	7.6
Asian Development Bank	7.4	7.0	7.8	7.8
Economic Survey, India	7.0–7.75	6.5–6.75		6.75–7.5
Morgan Stanley	7.7	7.3	7.8	7.7
HSBC	7.4	6.3	7.2	7.1
Nomura	7.8	7.1	7.6	7.1
Goldman Sachs	7.6	6.3	...	...
ICRA	7.9	6.8	...	...
CARE Ratings	7.8	6.8	...	...
CRISIL	...	6.9	...	...
FITCH	7.4	6.9	8.0	7.7
BofA-ML	7.4	6.9	7.6	7.2
Ambit Capital	6.8	3.5	7.3	5.8
RBI	7.7	...	7.6	7.1
Central Statistical Office	...	...	7.6	7.1

Source: Reddy (2017).
Note: ... = not available; BofA-ML = Bank of America-Merrill Lynch; CARE = CARE Ratings; ICRA = India Credit Rating Agency; RBI = Reserve Bank of India.

Table 11.3 shows the latest estimates of growth in GDP growth. As can be seen, growth in GDP and GVA began decelerating after the fourth quarter of 2015–16. However, the pace of deceleration seems to have accentuated in the fourth quarter of 2016–17, the quarter in which the full impact of demonetization was expected. Provisional estimates show that in the first quarter of 2012–18, GDP and GVA growth further decelerated to 5.7 and 5.6 percent, respectively. Although it is difficult to say how much of this deceleration results from demonetization, other indicators suggest that economic activity did decline after the

Figure 11.1. Industrial Production
(Percent, year-over-year growth)

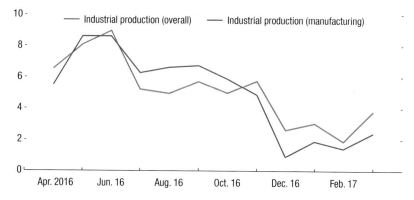

Source: Centre for Monitoring of Indian Economy.

decision. Figure 11.1 shows considerable deceleration in growth of industrial production following demonetization.

Table 11.3. GDP and Gross Value-Added Growth Estimates
(Percent, year-over-year growth)

	GDP Growth		Gross Value-Added Growth	
	2015–16	2016–17	2015–16	2016–17
Full year	8.01	7.11	7.94	6.62
First half	7.79	7.73	7.89	7.17
Second half	8.21	6.53	7.98	6.10
First quarter	7.58	7.92	7.59	7.56
Second quarter	8.01	7.53	8.20	6.77
Third quarter	7.25	6.97	7.29	6.65
Fourth quarter	9.13	6.12	8.65	5.57

Source: Central Statistics Office, Government of India.

Despite this deceleration, growth in tax collection was good in 2016–17 (see Figure 11.2), and almost the same as in the previous year. Indeed, growth in income tax collection was higher than it had been in recent years. This may have been because of the government's additional revenue mobilization measures: tax rates applicable on petroleum products in the second half of 2016–17 were higher than those for the same period in 2015–16, for example, which may explain higher collections of excise duties. In addition, collections under a tax amnesty scheme that closed in September 2016 raised income tax collections. And enhanced revenue enforcement efforts following demonetization may also have boosted collections. Each of these may have blunted the impact of economic deceleration on tax collections in 2016–17.

Figure 11.2. Tax Collection Growth
(Percent, year-over-year)

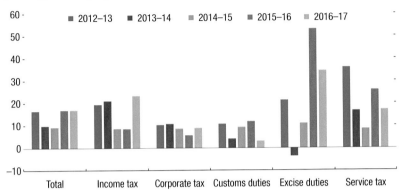

Source: Economic Outlook Database (maintained by the Centre for Monitoring of Indian Economy).

Long-term impact on tax base

Yet, even though tax collection appears not to have been affected, demonetization may have affected the tax base, as indicated by the GDP and GVA data.

It is worth noting that the national accounts statistics shown in Table 11.3 do not account for the impact of demonetization on the informal sector, which is where its impact was expected to be significant. The commonly held view in policy circles was that the informal sector largely operated using high-denomination cash. Demonetization was therefore expected to undermine output and, thereby, factor payments, as well as the income and consumption tax base. This is because the quarterly numbers published by the Central Statistics Office estimate growth by extrapolating from events in the formal sector. Thus, the Economic Survey for fiscal year 2017–18 noted: "The national income accounts estimate informal sector activity on the basis of formal sector indicators, which have not suffered to the same extent. But the costs have nonetheless been real and significant." However, since the first-order contribution of the informal sector to direct and indirect tax revenue is much lower than the formal sector, any slowdown in informal sector activity that is not replaced by the migration of that activity to the formal sector will, at best, have a small impact on revenue. Equally, the impact on revenue will be positive to the extent that such migration happens.

In addition to the formalization of the economy, the government also expects greater tax compliance and is expecting to use data from bank deposits made after the demonetization to generate intelligence for tax enforcement. The government has a record of 1.8 million people whose cash transactions do not appear in line with their profiles (Department of Revenue 2017). Assessing the responses received from depositors is ongoing. In addition, the government has augmented departmental capability to analyze large volumes of cash deposit data, tracking the compliance status of taxpayers and reporting entities.

Such efforts might yield better tax compliance in the medium to long term. The 2017–18 budget detailed the government's expectations for the positive long-term impact of demonetization on tax revenues. While the tax-to-GDP ratio in 2017–18 was projected to rise by just 0.06 percent of GDP, the numbers flagged an important structural change in GDP.[10] Taxes on personal income have been projected to rise by 0.28 percent of GDP, while all other taxes would either fall or stay constant. The share of personal income taxes is projected to be 16 percent of total revenue receipts in 2017–18, up from 14 percent in 2016–17, while the share of service and indirect taxes was projected to fall. We therefore infer that this is what the government sees as the main fiscal gain from demonetization. If successful, this would be in keeping with the stated aim of the finance minister, which was to ensure that increases in the tax-to-GDP ratio happened through increases in the share of taxes on income, secured by widening the tax base.

Impact on Bank Credit

Figure 11.3 shows that while bank deposits, especially demand deposits, grew sharply after demonetization, credit growth slumped. The credit-to-deposit ratio dropped from 74.35 percent in October 2016 to 69.26 percent in November 2016. By July 2017, the credit-to-deposit ratio had risen to 72.23 percent. A large part of the incremental amount collected as deposits was deployed in liquid assets. It is difficult to say if the banks view the increase in deposits as temporary or if this reflects continued weak demand for credit arising from such sources as weak private investment demand and balance sheet difficulties faced by banks, restricting their risk appetite. In this context, notably, between October 2016 and April 2017 the one-year median, marginal cost of funds based lending rate declined by 78 basis points. But this decline did not raise demand for credit, such that, while borrowing has become cheaper, credit growth has decelerated significantly.

Impact on Unaccounted Income

The Economic Survey of 2016–17 argues that demonetization can be viewed as a tax on unaccounted income. This is because the government required depositors of cash above a minimum threshold to account for the source of these deposits. Thus, holders of unaccounted income or wealth could:

- Declare their unaccounted wealth and pay taxes at a penalty rate;

---

[10]FY2016–17 revised estimates projected the tax-to-GDP ratio to be 11.3 percent of GDP, up from 10.8 percent in the budget estimates. This rise was due entirely to higher-than-expected collections of indirect taxes on goods and services. Therefore, in the budget estimates of FY2017–18, the government has perhaps been cautious in projecting further increases in indirect tax revenues, also mindful of the uncertainty associated with the introduction of the new goods and services tax in FY2017–18.

Figure 11.3. Bank Credit and Deposit Growth
(Percent, year-over-year growth)

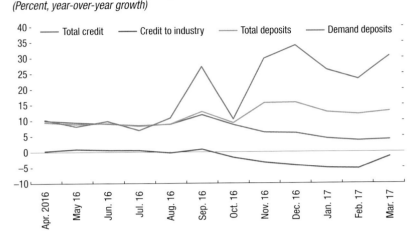

Source: Database on Indian Economy, Reserve Bank of India.

- Continue to hide it, not converting their old notes and thereby suffering a tax rate of 100 percent;
- Launder their black money, paying a cost to do so

The government has been optimistic about getting holders of unaccounted wealth to "come clean." The Prime Minister's Welfare of the Poor scheme allowed people to declare cash deposits, of which 50 percent would immediately be taken by the government and the government would withhold a further 25 percent in noninterest-bearing deposits for four years.

Newspaper reports suggested that the government was optimistic that this scheme would net Rs 500 billion to Rs 1,000 billion (15–30 percent of total income tax collection in 2016–17).[11] Indeed, according to the government, the scheme has collected only Rs 23 billion (about 0.67 percent of total income tax collection in 2016–17) in additional taxes and surcharges. This suggests that the government's efforts to encourage people to admit their unaccounted wealth have not generated a good response. Further, the government has announced that it has detected Rs 164 billion in wealth suspected of being unaccounted. Only after investigation and the judicial process will it become clear how much of this is really unaccounted wealth. However, even if this amounts to just about 1.1 percent of the total value of demonetized notes, it raises questions about the efficacy of this method for solving the problem of unaccounted wealth.

---

[11]For example, see Moneycontrol: http://www.moneycontrol.com/news/business/economy/pmgky -flop-why-black-money-holders-dont-mind-taking-on-the-i-t-department-2249931.html.

Figure 11.4. Electronic Payments, November–March
(Percent, year-over-year)

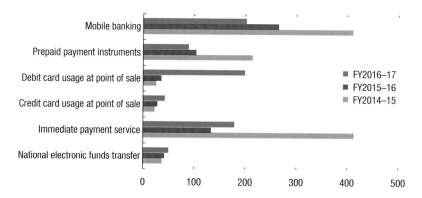

Source: Reserve Bank of India.
Note: FY = fiscal year.

The Reserve Bank of India's FY2016/17 annual report notes that about 99 percent of the demonetized currency notes have been deposited in the banking system. Thus, it would appear that most holders of unaccounted wealth have been able to find ways to show their unaccounted wealth as legitimate wealth, or perhaps there was not much unaccounted wealth in cash form to begin with. It is possible that the government may be able to take enforcement actions against those who deposited unaccounted cash. However, since tax evaders would have taken the necessary precautions to protect themselves, it would not be easy to generate substantial additional revenue from this source. At this stage, it appears that the demonetization scheme did not make much headway in reducing unaccounted wealth.

Impact on Digitalization

In the wake of demonetization, and the measures to encourage the digital store of value and digital payments that followed, a permanent shift to digital payments would be possible. Government leaders expressed this several times, including in the Economic Survey of February 2017. It is too early to say whether these expectations will be realized in the long term, but trends so far are mixed.

Since the impact was expected after demonetization, we have plotted growth in the November–March period over the corresponding period of the previous year for the past three years. Only for card payments does improvement seem to be significant, for November 2016 to March 2017, compared to corresponding periods in previous years (Figure 11.4). For most of the instruments, the growth rate has been less than what it was in previous years. So, while the steady-state impact of demonetization on digitalization remains to be seen, the information available to date suggests that the signs are not encouraging.

CONSEQUENCES OF BETTING TOO MUCH TOO SOON

As discussed previously, although the government and private sector have taken initiatives to expedite digitalization of the economy, India lags comparable countries on many important parameters. Further, the expected push to digitalization because of demonetization cannot be taken for granted. Even though there may be an improvement in the steady state, it may not turn out to be as large as expected. Still, the central government has launched various initiatives to benefit from digitalization, and it is rapidly launching schemes to integrate digital methods of collecting and transacting information.

India's digitalization initiatives may be categorized into two sets: those that involve direct interaction with citizens, residents, and private organizations, and those that are meant only to improve the government's own internal processes (Table 11.4). Initiatives such as establishment of the National Digital Literacy Mission Scheme fall in the latter set, while the remaining are in the former. The schemes in the former set can be further categorized into those that lead to a mandate for citizens and residents, and those that create a digital option while leaving the nondigital option available.

Table 11.4. Classification of Government Schemes on Digitalization

Who Does the Scheme Deal With?	Is the Digital Method Mandated?	Mandate on Whom?	Examples
Government to person/enterprise	Mandated	Low-income individuals Higher-income individuals and enterprises	Direct benefit transfer E-procurement, submission of information to Financial Intelligence Unit, electronic tax payment, e-filing of taxes, and so on
	Optional	Not applicable	Land record digitalization, community service centers
Government to government	Not applicable	Not applicable	National Digital Literacy Mission

Source: Authors' analysis using information available on initiatives under Digital India.

Most of the e-governance initiatives and digitalization of systems for collecting nontax revenues fall into the category of optional use of digital methods. In the mandated set, there is a case for distinguishing between those that impose the mandate on ordinary citizens and residents and those that impose it on businesses and better-off citizens and residents. In the former set, the biggest initiative is the Direct Benefit Transfer program, which is rapidly integrating government schemes where payments are made to citizens. Mandatory e-procurement, mandatory submission of information to the Financial Intelligence Unit, and electronic payment and filing of taxes are in the latter set.

As long as they are well-implemented, it is hard to argue against technology-based initiatives that improve internal government processes. However, for schemes that concern citizens, residents, and private organizations, close scrutiny is required. Particularly for schemes where ordinary citizens are being mandated to go digital, there is a need to study the unintended consequences and see what can be done to ensure sound implementation. Some of the potential unintended consequences may include false exclusion of recipients because of infrastructure constraints, compromise of systems because of data integrity and security problems, and mistakes by beneficiaries because of low awareness. The demonetization decision and its consequences also show many unintended consequences of trying to push an ambitious solution quickly through a complex system.

CONCLUSION

India's intensive digitalization seeks to leverage the remarkable increase in access to mobile services of recent years. While digital services are affordable, the country still has a long way to go to achieving universal access, owing to inadequate infrastructure and less-than-universal coverage. With the introduction of Aadhaar, the government has sought to improve the effectiveness of public expenditure, especially transfers. It has also sought to use digitalization to improve tax collection and enforcement. The fiscal policy consequences of these government initiatives are yet to be measured, although the limited research available shows that there have been cost savings in direct benefit transfers.

In 2016, the Government of India made the decision to withdraw the Rs 500 and Rs 1,000 notes in circulation. This event had a momentous impact on both fiscal policy and digitalization. In the short term, the move was expected to have a negative impact on the tax base, principally because demonetization was temporarily expected by nearly all forecasting agencies to reduce economic growth. Although the national accounts statistics show significant deceleration in growth of output, growth in tax collections has not decelerated. This may be because of additional revenue mobilization measures and enhanced enforcement efforts during the year. So, even though growth in tax collection may have remained stable, the underlying economic activity has decelerated.

The impact of demonetization was expected to be significant on the informal sector, but this would, at best, have had a small impact on revenue. The informal sector does not contribute much to corporate taxes, and the impact would therefore be on consumption taxes, due to a loss of output and, therefore, lower disposable income among those employed in this sector. Since the demonetization, growth in bank credit has significantly decelerated. The impact on unaccounted income also appears to be small.

Although demonetization was expected to result in a permanent shift to digital payments, it is too early to say whether this has been realized, as the data show considerable volatility. It is becoming increasingly clear that for most payment instruments, demonetization did not have a positive impact.

Mandating use of digital methods has many benefits, but the pace at which these initiatives are being implemented poses risks. For example, given the digital divide in India, it is possible that there may be exclusion errors in the new system, especially when money is being transferred to a citizen or resident. Several anecdotal media reports note how expeditious implementation of the Direct Benefit

Transfer program has led to exclusions.[12] Further, because protections against privacy breaches are weak in India, forcing so many citizens and residents to digitize their personal information and finances may have unintended negative consequences. Similarly, if there is fraud or other crimes, the weaknesses of redress and adjudication systems may lead to denial of relief for citizens and residents.

Given that India still has a long way to go before achieving a satisfactory level of digitalization of its economy, and the weaknesses in its implementation of digitalization measures, a different and more gradual approach may be better. If the government indeed wants to make use of digitalization for salutary fiscal consequences while avoiding the risks of false exclusions and other inequitable consequences, it should make or encourage investments in better infrastructure so that the digital divide can be minimized. Further, it should put in place a comprehensive consumer protection framework, including privacy protections, and develop systems of redress, enforcement, and adjudication that make the digital experience of users more secure.

REFERENCES

Bank for International Settlements (BIS). 2016. *Statistics on Payment, Clearing and Settlement Systems in the CPMI Countries*. Basel.

BGR. 2017. "98% of Government Payments Made Digitally in 2016–17: CGA." June 22.

Bhandari, Vrinda, and Renuka Sane. 2016. "Towards a Privacy Framework for India in the Age of the Internet." Working Paper 179, National Institute for Public Finance and Policy, New Delhi.

Centre for Policy Research. 2017. "Direct Benefit Transfer (DBT), Jan Dhan, Aadhaar and Mobile (JAM) GOI, 2017–18." *Budget Briefs* 9 (6).

Department of Revenue. 2017. "Income Tax Department (ITD) Launches Operation Clean Money." Press Release, Ministry of Finance, Government of India, January 31.

Government of India. 2017. "Economic Survey 2016–17." Ministry of Finance, Department of Economic Affairs Economic Division. New Delhi.

———. 2016. "Economic Survey 2015–16." Ministry of Finance, Department of Economic Affairs Economic Division. New Delhi.

———. 2005. "Performance Evaluation of Targeted Public Distribution System." Planning Commission, New Delhi.

HBX. 2016. "Rajastnan Presses on with Aadhaar after Fingerprint Readers Fail: We'll Buy Iris Scanners." April 10.

Jaitley, Arun. 2017. *Union Budget Speech*. Speech of the Minister of Finance, Government of India.

Muralidharan, Karthik, Paul Niehaus, and Sandip Sukhtankar. 2016. "Building State Capacity: Evidence from Biometric Smartcards in India." *The American Economic Review* 106 (10): 2895–929.

National Institute for Public Finance and Policy. 2013. "A Study on Unaccounted Incomes in India." New Delhi.

Parliament of India. 2017. "Statement by the Minister of State for Communications in Response to a Question in the Parliament." New Delhi.

Reddy, C. Rammanohar. 2017. *Demonetisation and Black Money*. Mumbai: Orient Blackswan Private Limited.

---

[12]See, for example, HBX (2016).

Reserve Bank of India. 2017. "Macroeconomic Impact of Demonetisation: A Preliminary Assessment." New Delhi.

Schneider, F., A. Buehn, and C.E. Montenegro. 2010. "Shadow Economies All over the World: New Estimates for 162 Countries from 1999 to 2007." Policy Research Working Paper 5356, World Bank, Washington, DC.

Sharma, Manoj, Anurodh Giri, Sakshi Chadha. 2016. "Pradhan Mantri Jan Dhan Yojana (PMJDY) Wave III Assessment." MicroSave.

Telecom Regulatory Authority of India. 2017. "Highlights of Telecom Subscription Data as on 30th November, 2016." Press Release 09/2017, February 1.

CHAPTER 12

Integration of Government Digitalization and Public Financial Management—Initial Evidence

Marco Cangiano, Alan Gelb, and Ruth Goodwin-Groen

Payments are central to how governments transfer financial resources for various programs. The ways such payments are conducted have largely been peripheral to developments in modern public financial management (PFM) systems. Nonetheless, some governments are striving to digitize payments as part of financial inclusion or efficiency agendas, as digitalization is understood to contribute indirectly to growth and poverty reduction.

This chapter argues that it is time to mainstream digitalization of payments as part of functional PFM to improve those systems and broaden reform goals.

Every year governments, the private sector, and development organizations make billions of dollars in cash payments to people in low-income and emerging market economies. It is estimated that in 2014 over a billion people were receiving government transfers and other payments and that the average developing country operated some 20 social safety net programs at an annual cost of 1.6 percent of GDP (World Bank 2015). Considering transfers, subsidies, payroll, and pension payments together, public payments to individuals typically represent 12 percent of GDP in developing countries and often far more.

Experience indicates that shifting from cash to electronic payments is generally safer, especially for women, and more efficient in reaching the financially excluded. The shift can provide a pathway to a broader range of financial services, and electronic payments can reduce costs and increase transparency for governments, development organizations, and corporations. What is more, this shift, and maximizing the benefits, can be done more quickly if the effort is part of a broader management of public resources aimed at meeting government goals and objectives.

Despite rapid progress in the technology for digitalizing payments and leadership by governments such as China and Mexico, results in other emerging economies have been mixed pr governments have been slow in adopting digitalization. This is in part because governments and companies have lacked a coherent and tailored framework showing them how to realize these gains, as the Better Than Cash Alliance noted in a recent report reviewing the experience of digitalization in 25 countries (Janis and Shah

2016).[1] Without a broad and cohesive analytical framework, governments and companies have been unable to leverage the experiences of other markets and players to implement digital payments effectively. The report identifies 10 steps, or "accelerators," to implement digital payments effectively across an economy.[2] Of relevance for this chapter is the digitalization of government payments and receipts.[3]

Leaders committed to digitalization and inclusion at the Group of Twenty (G20) 2016 Hangzhou Summit and endorsed eight High Level Principles for Digital Financial Inclusion. These included the recommendation to provide incentives to digitize all payments to and from governments (where feasible) (GPFI 2016b).[4] So far, however, digitalization has been pursued and largely implemented outside the complex network of systems and processes that constitute the emerging architecture of PFM (Cangiano and others 2013).

This chapter argues that digitalization of payments should become an integral component of a modern PFM system by presenting four case studies.

The chapter first defines digitalizing payments and its main objectives, then shows that digitalization and PFM are two sides of the same coin. It provides a cautionary tale from the challenges of developing and implementing large financial management information systems and presents case studies for Estonia, Ghana, India, and Mexico.[5] These studies show that successful joint implementation of digitalization of payments and PFM holds significant benefits. The chapter concludes with a look at the important lessons from the case studies and challenges and directions for future research.

WHAT DOES DIGITALIZATION OF PAYMENTS MEAN?

Governments, businesses, and international organizations distribute and receive billions in cash payments worldwide in payrolls, benefits, pensions, social programs, humanitarian aid, fines, taxes, and much more. With the speed of mobile phone distribution and usage, and the rapid expansion of innovative

---

[1] The Better Than Cash Alliance was launched in 2012 in response to public and private sector demand for more strategic advocacy, research, and guidance on digitalizing cash payments to accelerate the shift from cash to electronic payments. It is funded by the Bill & Melinda Gates Foundation, Citi, MasterCard, Omidyar Network, United States Agency for International Development, and Visa. The UN Capital Development Fund is the secretariat.

[2] Transaction volumes in the 25 countries grew an average of 32 percent annually over the past decade.

[3] The literature classifies these financial flows as government to person (G2P), government to business (G2B), and vice versa (P2G and B2G).

[4] The Better Than Cash Alliance is an Implementing Partner of the G20 Global Partnership for Financial Inclusion, working closely with the Markets and Payments Systems Subgroup.

[5] Ghana, India, and Mexico are members of the Better than Cash Alliance.

> **Box 12.1. Electronic Payment Instruments: Definition and Classification**
>
> The Bank for International Settlements' Committee on Payments and Market Infrastructures (CPMI) promotes the safety and efficiency of payment, clearing, settlement, and related arrangements for financial stability and the wider economy. CPMI (2015, 12) recognizes that "payment services providers include banks and other deposit-taking institutions, as well as specialized entities such as money transfer operators and e-money issuers." It classifies electronic payment instruments in three broad categories:
> - **Electronic funds transfer–based instruments:** These are direct (that is, account-to-account) credit transfers and direct debit transfers. As account-to-account payments, these instruments can be processed fully electronically.
> - **Payment card–based instruments:** These include credit, charge, and debit card payments, and typically still involve a plastic card. With few exceptions, payments with cards are initiated, authorized, authenticated, cleared, and settled fully electronically.
> - **Electronic money (e-money)–based instruments:** In general terms, these instruments involve the payer maintaining a prefunded transaction account with a payment service provider (PSP), often a nonbank. Specific products include online money when the payment instruction is initiated by internet, mobile money when by mobile phone, and prepaid cards.
>
> Source: CPMI 2015, page 13.

payment options with internet access, the possibility of digitalizing each of these is expanding rapidly.[6]

This chapter sees digitalization of payments as the shifting of cash payments to some form of electronic or digital payment (BTCA 2012). Box 12.1 presents the definition and classification of electronic or digital payments of the Committee on Payments and Markets Infrastructures.

Table 12.1 provides a framework for understanding the multiple types of payers and payees. It includes payments from governments to businesses and individuals as well as between government agencies and from businesses and individuals to governments.

---

[6]In the first quarter of 2000, there were 467 million unique mobile phone subscribers (7.7 percent of the population). By the same quarter of 2017, there were 4.97 billion unique subscribers (66.3 percent), for 15 percent annualized growth (GSMA 2017). In 1995, 1.6 mobile subscriptions existed for every 100 people in the world. By 2015, that number had reached 98.3 (23 percent annual growth), and today there are more mobile subscriptions than there are people in the world (International Telecommunication Union through World Bank, World Development Indicators). Compared to growth in ownership of mobile phones, the International Telecommunication Union estimates the number of internet users per 100 people increased from 0.8 in 1995 to 43.8 in 2015.

Table 12.1. Payment Grid: Types of Payments by Payer and Payee

		Payee		
		Government	Business	Person (individual)
Payer	Government	G2G Budgetary allocations, funding	G2B Grants, payments for goods and services	G2P Welfare programs, salaries, pensions
	Business	B2G Taxes, fees for licenses	B2B Payments for goods and services	B2P Salaries and benefits
	Person (individual)	P2G Taxes, utilities	P2B Purchases	P2P Remittances, gifts
	Development community	D2G Taxes	D2B Payments for goods and services	D2P Cash transfers

Source: Better Than Cash Alliance (2012).
Note: B = business (nonfinancial private sector); D = development community partner; G = government; P = person. For further explanation of the payment grid, see Better Than Cash Alliance (2012).

By digitalizing payments, a government aims mainly to foster a modern and inclusive economy.[7] The benefits of digitalizing payments for governments—enhanced transparency and accountability[8] and cost savings—have been well identified by the G20 (Klapper 2014). It is also clear that the transparency of payments under digitalization enhances accountability between governments and citizens, more clearly linking the services governments provide and taxes levied (Pillai 2016). In addition, the opportunity for driving financial inclusion through digitalization of payments, such as in Kenya,[9] benefits households (Suri and Jack 2017) and entire economies.[10]

DIGITALIZATION OF PAYMENTS AND PUBLIC FINANCIAL MANAGEMENT: COMPLEMENTARITY AND CAUTION

Complementarity—Two Sides of the Same Coin

Digitalization of payments should be integrated into complex government PFM systems to leverage the full potential gain in effectiveness and functionality

---

[7]Digitalization of payments may be a key element of a government's digital economy initiatives. Open data portals, which provide open access to government data online (of which Mexico is a good example, OECD 2016), are another digital government initiative. Importantly, while neither initiative is synonymous with a digital economy, they are both helping build a digital economy.

[8]On transparency, Rogoff (2016) is an outspoken advocate for digitalization to overcome shadow economies worth billions of dollars.

[9]Johnson (2016) provides valuable ethnographic insights into Kenyans' use of mobile money.

[10]According to IMF Managing Director Christine Lagarde: "greater financial inclusion has tangible economic benefits, such as higher GDP growth and lower income inequality. By providing access to accounts, credit, infrastructure, women and low-income users, financial inclusion helps make growth more inclusive" (Opening Remarks—IMF CGD event, "Financial Inclusion: Macroeconomic and Regulatory Challenges." April 11, 2016).

these systems offer.[11,12] When integrated with PFM, digitalization of payments can benefit governments both directly and indirectly. Directly, effective digitalization expedites basic PFM functions—payroll management, reaching correct beneficiaries, accounting and reporting through faster reconciliation with government bank accounts—and strengthens accountability by providing a more reliable audit trail.

Digitalization can also be important in enhancing the quality of information from fiscal events.[13] Indirect benefits include accelerating the production of in-year budget execution reports, providing more timely information on the government's cash position (enhancing cash management functions), and greatly facilitating the reconciliation of above-the-line information for a bank's transactions (see Chapter 6 for further discussion of these issues).

By drastically reducing the use of cash, digitalization can also help shrink the size of shadow economies and, hence, opportunities for tax evasion (Rogoff 2016). Similarly, it can help shift remittances away from informal mechanisms and money transfer operators, closing a notorious leak in balance of payment transactions—another avenue for tax evasion. P2P digital remittances between identified participants could also strengthen compliance with the recommendations of the Financial Action Task Force and reduce the likelihood of "de-risking" by correspondent banks.[14]

Although digitalization initiatives can emerge within government or the private sector, it is only the combination and coordination between the two spheres that maximizes benefits within and across countries. This allows governments to not only recognize that digitalization of payments fully

---

[11]In essence, PFM "relates to the way governments manage public resources (both revenue and expenditure) and the immediate and medium- to-long-term impact of such resources on the economy or society. As such, PFM has to do with both process (how governments manage) and results (short, medium, and long-term implications of financial flows)" (Andrews and others 2014, 1). The modalities by which payments and transfers are carried out are often overlooked. It is not by chance that in the wave of PFM books and publications (such as Allen, Hemming, and Potter 2014; Cangiano, Curristine, and Lazare 2013) of the past five years the very word "digitalization" is hardly found.

[12]This definition raises the question, what makes a PFM system effective in pursuing its objectives? Andrews and others (2014, 6) clarify that a " . . . PFM system needs to record and distribute (financial resources) to the right places in a reliable and timely manner so that they can be audited (to ensure that) money is being used properly." In the same paper, Andrews and associates characterize a functional PFM system as one that promotes (1) prudent fiscal decisions, (2) credible budgets, (3) reliable and efficient resource flows and transactions, and (4) institutionalized accountability. Digitalization of payments falls squarely under the last two factors since it helps ensure that payments and transfers are processed efficiently and effectively.

[13]Quality of fiscal information is at the core of fiscal transparency. In reformulating its 2014 Fiscal Transparency Code, the IMF defined it as the comprehensiveness, clarity, reliability, timeliness, and relevance of public reporting on the past, present, and future state of public finances.

[14]De-risking is the withdrawal of correspondent banking relationships in response to perceived risks of sanctions for violating anti–money laundering and combating the financing of terrorism regulations (Center for Global Development 2015).

supports PFM and is indeed the other side of the same coin, but to take leadership in integrating digitalization agendas to better serve government goals.

Cautions—Learning from FMIS Implementation

A government's Financial Management Information System (FMIS) tracks financial events and summarizes financial information (Diamond and Khemani 2015).[15] Core FMIS may or may not contain the payment/transfer functions, including tax collection, that are relevant for a functional PFM system.[16] The World Bank, IMF, and Inter-American Development Bank have produced several studies assessing the relative strengths and weaknesses of integrated FMIS introduction across many countries.[17]

The World Bank Independent Evaluation Group's evaluation (IEG 2016) and Hashim and Piatti (2016) identified the following prerequisites for successful FMIS project implementation:

- improved budget classification
- a unified chart of accounts integrated with budget classification
- better treasury single-account operations
- commitment control and monitoring mechanisms
- establishment of cash management functions

Another crucial prerequisite for successful FMIS implementation, directly applicable to digitalization, is a unitary vision of government objectives within public financial management architecture. If that is not in place, governments risk confusing ends with means, processes with objectives, and procedures with

---

[15]Diamond and Khemani (2015) define an FMIS as the "computerization of public expenditure management processes including budget formulation, budget execution, and accounting with the help of a fully integrated system for financial management of the line ministries and other spending agencies. The full system should also secure integration and communication with other relevant information systems." They also clarify that "because of the integration requirement, the FMIS is commonly characterized as an integrated financial management information system. Unfortunately, using the term 'integrated financial management information system' can sometimes be erroneously interpreted as describing a system that can capture all the functional processes, and the relevant financial flows, within public expenditure management."

[16]According to Khan and Pessoa (2010); Diamond and Khemani (2015); Dener, Watkins, and Dorotinsky (2011); and Una and Pimenta (2016), "core" modules typically include general ledger, budgetary accounting, and accounts payable and receivable. "Noncore" modules include areas such as payroll, procurement, project ledger, and asset registry.

[17]During 1984–2010, the World Bank financed 87 integrated FMIS projects in 51 countries with an average cost of $25 million (Dener, Watkins, and Dorotinsky 2011; Dorotinsky and Watkins 2013). In Latin America, the Inter-American Development Bank has funded 47 PFM reform projects envisaging the adoption of an integrated FMIS at an average cost of $26 million (Una and Pimenta 2016). Both studies put the average length of such projects at six to seven years, thus often crossing more than one political cycle.

Box 12.2. Malawi FMIS Project

Malwai set up and rolled out a Financial Management Information System (FMIS) starting in 2010, covering most of the budget and the key core modules, including a commitment control system. A recent review of this World Bank–funded FMIS project shows how even a well-managed FMIS project may not by itself be conducive to a well-functioning public financial managament (PFM) system (IEG 2016).

The review found that while the FMIS was under development, the complementary PFM environment, although satisfactory on paper, did not change behaviors. For instance, even though controls were in place, commitments continued to be processed outside the system; spending units were reported to maintain an off-FMIS registry and upload funding limits on an as-needed basis; and evidence suggests that spending units generated local purchase orders and payment vouchers simultaneously, using pro-forma invoices despite directives to the contrary. Over time, large payment arrears accumulated, to an estimated 9.2 percent of GDP in 2014, and $32 million was embezzled in the so-called cashgate scandal.

Weaknesses in PFM systems, processes, and controls around the FMIS environment caused these outcomes. IEG 2016 notes that a few technical factors were at play that were more directly associated with the FMIS, such as weak system access controls, inadequate data capture, poor system performance due to erratic power supply, inadequate server capacity, and unreliable connectivity. But these were not crucial in explaining the outcomes. It was a more diffuse disregard of the regulatory framework and a breakdown of internal controls that were at the root of the problems. These in turn reflected a general lack of understanding of the overall PFM architecture and the interrelationship among its many components that failed to focus on basic control procedures, such as bank reconciliation.

The independent review of Malawi's FMIS project provides two main lessons:

- Information technology solutions cannot be pursued without addressing fundamental PFM problems in parallel. In Malawi, as elsewhere, unrealistic expectations that the FMIS would solve all the issues created a tendency to blame FMIS when problems occurred.
- Even a well-designed and functioning FMIS is not sufficient to support good public financial management. The breakdown of the accountability chain that led to a major corruption episode in Malawi was chiefly because of a disregard of processes rather than a technical failure of the FMIS.

functions. Unless mindful, a digitalization agenda can also fall into this trap. The Malawi story in Box 12.2 illustrates the point.

As noted above, digitalizing payments and transfers should acknowledge the lessons of FMIS implementation. Diamond and Khemani (2015) have found that computerization promotes two kinds of reform: efficiency reforms that accelerate the operation of existing procedures, and effectiveness reforms that change existing procedures. Information technology (IT) truly pays off when it makes organizations more effective, not simply more efficient.

Digitalization cannot be IT-driven or donor-driven. Rather, to realize its potential for boosting effectiveness, it needs to be driven by the functionalities that can address problems while keeping in mind the medium- to long-term objectives. Those using digitalization should accept a certain degree of endogeneity and learning by doing, in which capacities and capabilities have to be developed in parallel with the proposed solutions, as argued by Andrews (2013). It should also accept that the need for some cash transfers will persist in the face of challenging contextual factors (ODI 2016; Sturge 2017).

Since the core function of government digitalization is processing payments and collecting revenues, the risks of developing "silos"—in which different systems and IT infrastructure become an impediment to reconciling the *whole* relationship between the government and the citizen—should be avoided.

Finally, very little work has been done on the cost benefit of introducing large computerization systems, meaning that the importance of building in the assessment of the efficiency and effectiveness at the beginning of digitalization efforts is another valuable lesson.[18]

SELECTED COUNTRY CASES

The four country case studies described in this section illustrate how PFM and digitalization of government payments are indeed two sides of the same coin, and point to the factors that have helped determine their success.

Table 12.2 summarizes the country cases. Although each case is different, they point to very similar factors that the previous section identified as desirable to any computerization project: identifying problems and needs, developing customized solutions, and strengthening institutional capacity. Perhaps most importantly, the cases also point to the way problems beyond the specific ambit of the existing PFM systems were addressed and how digitalization contributed to a unitary vision of government priorities and objectives.

India's fast-track digitalization approach combining the unique identity, Aadhaar, and financial inclusion to drive both efficiency and effectiveness in

---

[18]The IEG (forthcoming) review of reforming FMIS concludes that "researching available options and carefully weighing benefits against risks and costs is crucial for selecting an appropriate country specific strategy for application software development (off the shelf versus developing an application in house" and that "the attribution to improved PFM outcomes can be facilitated through good monitoring and evaluation frameworks."

government benefits has generated noteworthy gains by reducing the number of illegitimate beneficiaries under social welfare programs (see Chapter 11).[19,20]

Mexico's long-term development of its single treasury account and the digitalization of payments—developed at first in parallel before becoming aligned—significantly improved efficiency and effectiveness and both are now contributing to inclusion goals. Estonia's infrastructural digitalization has significantly benefited the government's effectiveness. And Ghana's efforts to standardize digital identification and shift away from a cash-based economy are still facing challenges, but ghost workers from public payrolls have largely been eliminated where the approach has been applied.

Together, these cases (representing four continents) illustrate the many common challenges in aligning PFM and digitalization. While substantial, the estimated savings from the initiatives set out in Table 12.2 are nonetheless indicative, as they are not always grounded in rigorous analysis and are not comparable. Far more rigorous, comparable research is needed to reveal the economic impact of digitalization, including in developing economies.

India

In 2009, India created the Unique Identification Authority of India with the mandate to issue a unique identifying number, the Aadhaar, to every resident. *Aadhaar* was introduced, together with digital payments, as part of an ambitious project to shift the country toward an inclusive digital economy, with a strong initial focus on reforming and rationalizing a massive array of subsidy and payments schemes. Together these accounted for some $60 billion in annual public expenditures, with studies suggesting huge leakage and diversion in many programs. The strategy was to link subsidies and benefits to identified individuals and to pay all benefits and transfers through financial accounts, and then to provide additional financial services such as savings and insurance so those accounts could be used.

By early 2017, the number of people enrolled had topped 1.1 billion, largely achieving the objectives. The program now includes almost all adults and is being extended to children. Aadhaar relies on digital technology and biometrics to uniquely identify people and to enable them to authenticate themselves for transactions. It is the largest identity management program in the world.

---

[19]Many countries tried increasingly to consolidate their safety-net programs, or at least to rationalize them by moving toward an integrated register of beneficiaries. This requires consistent and unique identification of beneficiaries while integrating payment mechanisms to reap economies of scale and prevent overlap and duplication. However, non-government organizations focused on privacy have questioned the desirability of a common identification system, often a national ID or similar nationwide system, because it represents coercive enrollment, since the poor beneficiaries have little option, in practice, but to sign up.

[20]Many other countries, including Pakistan and South Africa, have moved toward digital identification and payments to deliver social grants more effectively. For more on such cases see Gelb and Decker (2012) and Gelb and Diofasi (forthcoming).

Table 12.2. Summary of Country Cases

Country	Years	Main Objectives	Main Reforms	Indications of Effect	Estimated Savings
India	2009– ongoing	Financial inclusion, reducing leakage and corruption, rationalizing subsidy programs, improving tax collection	Unique digital identification, financial inclusion, reforming subsidies and transfers, enhancing payments and interoperability	More than 1.1 billion enrolled, 280 million accounts by March 2017, comprehensive reform of liquefied petroleum gas subsidies including elimination of duplicates, rollout of subsidy and payment reforms across states	$7 Billion over 2.5 years
Mexico	2007–13 and ongoing	Modern public financial management transparency, cost savings, financial inclusion	Single treasury account, digital payments, measures to enable financial inclusion	Payments now through single treasury account and digital at federal level	$1.27 billion per year
Estonia	2001– ongoing	Efficient government, inclusion in economy, digital platform for private economy	Unique universal identification, X-road: a digital data framework and regulatory regime	Unique virtual identity for all, X-Road connects 170 public sector databases for 1,571 public and private services, 98% digital tax filing	820 years' working time, 2% of GDP from electronic signatures
Ghana	2008– ongoing	Financial inclusion, eliminating ghost workers, improving tax collection	e-Zwich smart-card system, de-duplication of identities, public wage payments through e-Zwich	Increasing use of e-Zwich to deliver payments, elimination of 40% of public payroll where applied	$35 million per year from one application

Source: Authors' compilations.

To enable this, the JAM strategy links (1) financial accounts under the Pradhan Mantri Jan Dhan Yojana program[21] (hence the J from Jan), (2) Aadhaar (hence the A), and (3) a mobile number (the M). Digital identity and payments come together in several ways. First, digital know-your-customer procedures have drastically reduced the cost of gaining new bank customers and enabled the opening of some 280 million Jan Dhan accounts by March 2017, used to receive digital transfers. Electronic know-your-customer has also helped expand mobile banking and create new payment banks, an essential step to increase the density of the payments infrastructure.

Second, with Aadhaar Payments Bridge G2P, payments are easily made to any identified individual without having to key in the details of his or her account.

---

[21]See the Pradhan Mantri Jan Dhan Yojana website for more information: https://pmjdy.gov.in/.

Third, extending this further, the Aadhaar-Enabled Payments Service enables seamless P2P digital payments between any two accounts linked to Aadhaar numbers or the associated mobile numbers, even if they are with different banks.

Partly because of the way in which Aadhaar was introduced—as a voluntary credential or authentication service—debate is ongoing about the appropriate scope of this digital system, and it faces several challenges in the Supreme Court. But its use is being expanded to other areas relevant for PFM, most recently to strengthen tax administration. For instance, in April 2017 it became compulsory for all tax filings to be accompanied by an Aadhaar number (if the person had no Aadhaar number it was not compulsory to obtain one) and further measures are under way to integrate Aadhaar into asset registration. This will make it possible to build a full economic profile of an individual, helping to identify potential taxpayers who have chosen not to file.

A particularly interesting feature of the digitalization program is how it has been rolled out. While the Aadhaar itself, its associated Aadhaar Payments Bridge, and Aadhaar-Enabled Payments Service are integrated technology projects, individual states and even some districts have been free to adopt it in their own way, applying the technology toward problems and priorities they have identified. Reforms are moving forward rapidly in some areas but more slowly in others, and may involve a good deal of experimentation and innovation in implementation. In the most advanced states, reforms have been ongoing for five years or more; in the least advanced, they have barely gotten off the ground. Incentives also exist to move forward at the state level, where discretionary spending power is increasing as more tax revenue is devolved to states thanks to awards by the Fourteenth Finance Commission.[22]

States that save money by strengthening the administration of their social programs will have resources available for other purposes. Krishna District, Andhra Pradesh, offers perhaps the most advanced example of these reforms. The subsidy, benefit, and pension system has been digitized, as has the supply chain for subsidized commodities provided through an extensive system of Fair Price Shops. This enables real-time monitoring of payments and subsidies effected through the system.

The disbursement of payments and subsidized rations can be monitored in the aggregate, by town, by individual bank, or by "Fair Price Shop"—and, drilling down, even by individual beneficiary—creating a complete audit trail for each transaction. No longer can shopkeepers divert unclaimed products for private gain; the system reconciles stocks and flows to ensure that they are held over for the subsequent month's distribution.

Krishna District also offers examples of adaption and innovation, for example, to improve connectivity of mobile point-of-service devices (sometimes referred to as mobile ATMs, although they are capable of multiple functions) with portable aerials and dual subscriber identity modules (typically known as SIMs).

---

[22]For more information, see http://indiabudget.nic.in/es2014-15/echapvol1-10.pdf.

Krishna and other regions also offer lessons for how to address opposition to reforms from vested interests that have benefited from the previous system. These may include entities on the front line of delivering payments, subsidies, and services that are no longer able to divert public spending for their own advantage. In some cases, they can be bought off with increases in service margins—if these are not set at reasonable levels there will be no incentive to implement the transfers. In other cases, they can be bypassed by concluding new contracts with competitors enthusiastic about providing services under the new systems.

As with FMIS, implementation involves far more than technology. It requires vision, clear objectives, and sustained commitment.

Another example of the application of these systems in India is the area of fuel subsidies. For reasons of equity, and to cushion households against volatile prices and reduce deforestation, the country has long provided subsidized fuel to households. Liquefied petroleum gas (LPG) is a favored clean fuel, relative to kerosene. In the first stage of reform, the Pratyaksh Hanstantrit Labh scheme changed the form of subsidy on LPG cooking gas cylinders, transferring this directly into the financial accounts of beneficiary households for up to 12 cylinders per year. This allowed market forces to set pricing of the cylinders rather than reflecting the subsidized price. The reform is known to have weeded out a considerable number of duplicate and fake connections and to have reduced diversion to unsubsidized commercial users. The second stage involves a massive rollout of the LPG program (the Pradhan Mantri Ujjwala Yojana *Ujjwala* scheme) to more households.[23]

Among various estimates of the fiscal savings of these digital systems, the Ministry of Communications and Information Technology in March 2017 put savings at Rs 49,000 *crore*, (about $7 billion) over the previous two and a half years. The detailed basis for this estimate has not been made available and it is probably optimistic, but even a modest fraction of such savings would represent an enormous return on the investments made in digital technology.[24]

Several factors complicate estimates of savings, however, including difficulty specifying the counterfactual and whether savings are to be considered *ex ante* or *ex post*. Savings from the LPG reforms, for example, depend highly on the per-cylinder subsidy, which fell sharply with a sharp decline in world energy prices as the reform moved forward. Energy markets are unpredictable, nonetheless, and the reform has put in place a system that will better enable the government to respond to future price shocks.

Another complication is that the objective of that reform was not simply to cut subsidies—it was to strengthen the administration of the program so that it could be rolled out more widely across India. As the scheme is rolled out, subsidies increase proportionately, but more slowly than they would have done

---

[23]The Ujjwala program is a scheme rolled out under Prime Minister Narendra Modi in 2016 to expand access to LPG—a clean cooking fuel—by poorer and rural households.

[24]The costs of the Aadhaar system through its first billion-plus registrations were about $1.16 per head. The overall costs have been projected at about $2 billion. For more discussion of costs and benefits, see Gelb and Diofasi (forthcoming 2017).

without the elimination of spurious connections. The use of the common identifier also enables households that had previously received kerosene subsidies to be struck off the list as they are provided with LPG connections. This generates further savings relative to the counterfactual of providing subsidies through controlled prices rather than direct transfers into identified financial accounts.

Public savings are, of course, not the only relevant measure of successful digitalization. Equally important is whether the reforms have improved service delivery. This is still an open question for many programs. Especially at the start, some beneficiaries are likely to experience inconvenience as the new systems settle down. But there is little doubt of the potential gains.

One rigorous study evaluates the impact of the adopted biometrically authenticated payments infrastructure (known as Smartcards) on beneficiaries of employment (the National Rural Employment Guarantee Scheme or NREGS) and Social Security Pension (SSP) schemes. A large-scale randomized control trial was carried out for the rollout of Smartcards over 158 subdistricts and 19 million people. The new system delivered a faster, more predictable, and less corrupt NREGS payments process without undermining program access. For each of these outcomes, treatment group distributions first-order stochastically dominated those of the control group. The investment was cost-effective, as time savings to NREGS beneficiaries alone were equal to the cost of the intervention. Leakage of funds between the government and beneficiaries in both NREGS and SSP programs was also significantly reduced. Beneficiaries overwhelmingly preferred the new system for both programs (Muralidharan, Niehaus, and Sukhtankar 2014).

Mexico

Mexico clearly illustrates the benefits of combining PFM modernization with the digitalization of government payments to drive efficiency and financial inclusion.[25] The Mexican government's 2013 National Digital Strategy, known as Digital Mexico, was championed by the president as part of the 2013–18 National Development Plan. It included a commitment to "encourage the innovation of digital services through the democratization of public spending" and to financial inclusion. This 2013 strategy reflected over 15 years of successive presidents' commitments to centralization through a single treasury account, the digitalization of government revenues and expenses as part of building a modern PFM system, and a more recent government focus on financial inclusion.[26]

---

[25]This section draws from Babatz (2013).

[26]In 1997, President Ernesto Zedillo had mandated all *Dependencias* of the federal government to collaborate with the Ministry of Finance to implement the Sistema Integral de Administración Financiera Federal. This was the start of the process to develop both the IT infrastructure and the business process re-engineering for an efficient Single Treasury Account. In 2007, President Felipe Calderon and the head of the Treasury, Gina Casar, with the support of the Central Bank Governor Agustín Carstens, enshrined the Single Treasury Account into law. In 2010, a presidential budget decree mandated all government departments to shift to centralized electronic payments. This was the first time the "promotion of the use of electronic payments and the *bankarization*

Prior to the 2013 Strategy, Mexico's commitment to financial inclusion had been on a parallel track. The 2007–12 National Development Plan specifically cites the long-term objectives of increasing the number of people and enterprises with access to financial services and protecting such newcomers. In 2007, the Mexican Congress issued the new Transparency of Financial Services Law, which established more precise transparency standards for the fees charged by financial institutions, disclosure statements principles, and the obligation for banks to offer basic savings products. In 2008, the Mexican Congress approved reform of the Banking Law to enable the use of nonfinancial entities as banking agents (Goodwin-Groen 2010). A presidential decree in September 2011 created the National Council for Financial Inclusion. Then, as president of the G20 in 2011, Mexico led the Maya Declaration on financial inclusion. This all contributed to the launch of the president's National Financial Inclusion Policy in 2016, which clearly committed to merging both agendas by promoting the use of electronic payments for greater efficiency.

Mexico's experience clearly pointed to the synergies between digitalization and PFM when the two came together after 2013. It also indicated the role of consistent senior-level sponsorship and support and the need to coordinate across agencies. At a technical level, the shift was designed and supported by a core group of skilled senior civil servants within Tesorería de la Federación (the Mexican Federal Treasury), in cooperation with other key agencies such as the central bank. Without this technical competence, the complexity of the process may well have caused it to stall.[27] Overall, it has been estimated that the Mexican government is saving at least $1.27 billion a year, or 3.3 percent of its combined spending on wages, pensions, and social transfers. The methodology and assumptions behind these estimates are carefully described in Babatz (2013),[28] but they are still estimates and as such should be understood as indicative, not definitive. Nonetheless, this order of magnitude of savings is hard to ignore.

Estonia

Estonia has prioritized digitalization across the whole government for almost 20 years. As Lindpere (2017) notes, the objective was to bring all citizens into the national digital economy to get the full cost-effectiveness benefit for the economy. Unlike many other countries with extensive legacy systems, as a newly

---

of beneficiaries," that is, financial inclusion, is mentioned as one of the objectives of developing a modern PFM system.

[27]For instance, the 2011 presidential decree could not have forced the shift overnight. But it was a decisive moment, alongside sustained pressure by senior champions.

[28]Cost savings estimates in Babatz (2013) were calculated for salaries, pensions, and transfer programs using data and assumptions on three line items: (1) the interest earned by not having to deposit funds in advance of payments (the cost of the float), (2) the savings through not having to pay fees to banks for effecting transfers, and (3) the estimated savings from reduction in losses due to unauthorized or incorrect payments.

independent country, Estonia was able to initiate its transition to a digital economy in a remarkably comprehensive way.

One essential step was the creation of the X-Road in 2001, a data exchange layer that enables secure internet-based data exchange between information systems. Public and private sector enterprises and institutions can all connect their information systems with the X-Road without a fee. This is shared infrastructure hosted by the government, making it easier for public and private institutions to innovate together, as they can leverage the existing infrastructure for data exchange, saving resources (Janis and Shah 2016).[29] Another essential step was the creation of an advanced digital identity system so that citizens could authenticate themselves for digital transactions. Estonia's system is the most highly developed in the world, allowing not only authentication, but also signing documents digitally and remotely. Currently, 1.1 million of 1.3 million citizens have an electronic ID or digital identity (Margetts and Naumann 2017).

Data on the cost-effectiveness of this initiative, which has been run as Estonia modernized its entire PFM system,[30] are compelling, even if not all estimates are the result of rigorous analysis against a fully specified counterfactual. By eliminating the need for in-person interactions, X-Road estimates it saved the equivalent of 820 years of working time in 2016 (Government of Estonia 2017).[31]

The digital tax return statistic also sets Estonia apart. In 2016, over 98 percent of returns came in through the e-Tax, the electronic tax filing system set up by the Estonian Tax and Customs Board, through X-Road (Margetts and Naumann 2017). X-Road has enabled a digitized income-tax declaration system by linking employment tax records to each citizen's tax records.

Ghana

Ghana offers an example of the use of digital payments to eliminate ghost workers. Despite many years of effort to implement public sector reforms, the country has long struggled to contain recurrent spending, which is high relative to GDP compared with countries at a comparable income level. Overstaffing is chronic and the public sector wage and benefits bill has been a particular

---

[29]As of May 2017, X-Road had connected 170 public sector databases and provided 1,571 public and private services, all based on one standard, obligatory digital identity for each citizen. X-Road receives more than 1 million requests per day and processed more than 500 million transactions in 2016 (Government of Estonia 2017).

[30]Estonia has been and remains a frontrunner in reforming its PFM systems since the 1991 restoration of independence. From an early adoption of results-oriented budgeting to accrual accounting and, more recently, accrual budgeting, reforms have been supported by an effective treasury and budget execution system and a remarkable degree of transparency and accountability.

[31]The 820 years number assumes that every request to the X-Road saves 15 minutes of an officials' time and 5 percent of requests submitted through the X-Road involve communication between people. Using e-services then helped save 7,182,262 working hours in the previous year (Government of Estonia 2017). These are obviously simplistic assumptions, but they usefully indicate the magnitude of savings.

challenge, absorbing over 9 percent of GDP. Another PFM challenge for Ghana has been the prevalence of cash-based payments across the economy, weakening tax administration and thus reducing tax collection.

As Breckenridge (2010) explains, Ghana's e-Zwich payment system, "the world's first biometric money," drew on a technology developed in South Africa to transition toward digital payments even without full or reliable connectivity. It also aimed to extend financial inclusion to people who were not literate and less able to cope with personal identification numbers (PINs) for managing their transactions.

The e-Zwich system captures clients' fingerprints during enrollment, de-duplicates them, and stores the template on a smartcard. For each withdrawal from an ATM equipped with a biometric reader, for example, cardholders' fingerprints are checked against the template stored on their card. The system can work offline, reconciling the card balance with that of the underlying account when connectivity is available. To ensure an auditable trail, the ATM records the last 10 transactions on the card and the card records the last 10 transactions on the ATM.

The e-Zwich system was anticipated to serve two key PFM objectives. First, it would clean up government payrolls by consolidating all salary payments into a single, de-duplicated,[32] digital system. This would immediately flag multiple payments, since the different accounts belonging to a single individual would all be mapped to the same identity. Second, as it was rolled out across the economy, initially to large employers, it was anticipated that it would strengthen tax administration by ensuring that a greater number of employees saw their wages and salaries being paid into digital accounts.

e-Zwich has been a mixed success. Its take-up has grown more slowly than anticipated, although growth has been higher in recent years. Transactions went up from 2.2 million in 2014 to 5.3 million in 2016 as its usage increased to pay beneficiaries of public programs (Citifmonline 2017). But as IMF (2016) notes, plans to use e-Zwich to pay all public salaries have encountered opposition, particularly from Ghana's public sector unions. They argue that the system imposes additional costs and inconveniences payees, in that it does not yet have a sufficiently dense network of service points.

In retrospect, it would have been better to have separated out the unique identification system from a particular financial technology, the approach taken by India. Nevertheless, it is reported that one single application, to Ghana's scandal-plagued National Service System, uncovered 35,000 fictitious employees—almost half the initial payroll of 75,000—potentially saving the Ghanaian government $35 million a year.[33] This would only be a small gain rel-

---

[32] A de-duplicated system is one in which identities are statistically unique, in the sense that the probability that any individual has two or more distinct identities is extremely small. De-duplication is possible even for very large populations through multimodal biometrics.

[33] *B&FT Online*. 2016. "E-Zwich Helps Flush Out 35,000 Ghost Names from Payroll ... Saves Gov't GH?146m." April 21, 2016.

ative to the $3.5 billion public sector wage bill, but it would represent a huge rate of return on the initial investment in the e-Zwich program.[34]

DIGITALIZATION CHALLENGES: WHAT CAN WE LEARN AND WHERE DO WE GO FROM HERE?

Traditional approaches to PFM have not paid detailed attention to the digitalization of payments, particularly to entities external to the government. However, as outlined in the case studies, the problems addressed using digital payments, together with (unique) identification technology, are highly relevant for the sound management of public finances. In fact, most of the questions about payments external to the government are essentially the same as for payments internal to the government and at the core of a functional PFM system (as discussed in the section What Does Digitalization of Payments Mean?):

- Are payments delivered securely, in a timely manner, and at reasonable administrative cost?
- Are there serious problems of ghost workers, leakage, or corruption?
- Can government "follow the money" in real time as resources flow through banks or other intermediaries to the ultimate recipients? Is there an auditable trail?

In addition, one needs to consider the wider role of digital payments in helping to shift away from a cash-based economy, which remains largely outside the tax net.

The four case studies—Estonia, Ghana, India, and Mexico—present a diverse range of approaches to developing a functional PFM that could meet such policy objectives.

Through consolidating payments services and going digital, Mexico aimed to rationalize payments and increase efficiency.

In Estonia, digitalization has gone far beyond payments, to encompass virtually all government functions and engagement with citizens. The aim, again, has been to govern effectively and inclusively at lower cost.

India's digital transition is driven by multiple objectives, but the first and most important has been to improve the efficiency of its vast array of subsidies, transfers, and schemes by eliminating leakage and redundancy, as well as creating auditable trails. Financial inclusion has also been a major focus. Improving tax administration through facilitating digital payments more widely is emerging as the next priority.

---

[34]Net-1, the provider of the system, was paid an upfront fee of $20 million plus $3 per card. Wide coverage, at about 7 million cards for the whole of Ghana, would involve payment of $41 million (Gelb and Clark 2013). This does not of course include all costs of instituting the system, but it is indicative.

Ghana's program, though far more limited in scope, had similar objectives, in the first instance to substitute for shortcomings in managing public payrolls through channeling payments into biometrically enabled accounts. Building on financial inclusion, the next stage intended to focus on broadening the tax net to include all formal wages and salaries.

This transition toward digital payments and the wider digital economy is happening naturally to some extent with the adoption of new technology, but often far less rapidly and comprehensively than possible, especially in the countries where the potential benefits are greatest. The transition also needs to avoid common mistakes and draw from recent reviews of efforts to introduce large computerization programs within governments, as discussed previously.

In addition, the case studies largely confirm the need for high-level leadership, an integrated and comprehensive approach to digitalization and PFM whereby the former becomes a constituent element of the latter, and an appreciation of the risks and challenges. These key success factors are briefly discussed below.

High-Level Leadership

Only senior and sustained political and technical leadership that brings together these agendas and co-opts international expert agendas to support it can produce success. As Mexico and Estonia illustrate, these reforms take time. And, as India shows, senior political and technical leadership is required to deal with the various problems that will inevitably arise. These will include the need to neutralize the opposition of those who have benefited from the previous system. Technology alone is ineffective without political will. Ghana's inability to apply its digital payments system more widely across the public sector illustrates this point.

The approach in India shows how much more there is to these reforms than simply installing a new computer system or payments infrastructure. It is more about developing a strategy to use digital payments effectively, which requires a top-down view and a broad framework of reference. Digitalization is being driven largely at the subnational level, with the added spur of greater devolution of fiscal revenues to subnational levels.

The other cases mentioned above faced different problems and priorities, but they also had specific and broader PFM objectives in mind when developing aspects of their digital strategies.

An Integrated, Comprehensive Approach

It is important to build a comprehensive digital and regulatory infrastructure that will permit an inclusive approach to PFM. Each of the examples provides compelling evidence of this—whether X-Road, E-Zwich, or the India Stack. Notably, digitalization of government payments, as in Mexico and India, is only one stage of a wider transition toward digital (noncash) payments across the economy. It is a critical stage, however, since they often build and sustain a first round of infrastructure needed for wider P2P digital payments, including POS and cash-in-cash-out facilities. Digital government payments can also increase a population's familiarity with digital systems, including through the opening of large numbers of accounts for new clients of the financial system. In the first years, many of these accounts will not be used for purposes other than receiving government payments, but this will slowly change.

Causality is not one-way, however. In turn, wider P2P digitalization complements the initial G2P stage to start to build the digital ecosystem. It reduces the need to cash out payments and transfers immediately and lowers reliance on cash-in-cash-out infrastructure. It also increases the transparency of payments and transactions across the economy to improve tax administration further down the road. If and when it is decided to actively reduce the role of cash in the economy, through eliminating large-denomination banknotes and other measures, the digital infrastructure will be ready (see Chapter 11 for a discussion of India's recent demonetization).

One regulatory priority is a telecommunications regime that encourages universal connectivity. Even with the astonishing spread of mobile devices—now almost one for every man, woman, and child on earth—some less densely populated areas of poor countries lack basic connectivity, and higher-capacity broadband internet is still costly in many countries.

A second regulatory requirement is a level playing field for financial providers, one that encourages entry and competition and facilitates the inclusion of low-income clients. For example, countries should apply a risk-based approach to know-your-customer, graduating the requirements so that small accounts that provide basic services to low-income clients face less stringent customer due diligence requirements.[35]

Interoperability should be another strong focus to enable cross-provider payments with negotiated and low-interchange fees. There are advantages and disadvantages in setting up the equivalent of a regulated public utility. One example is India's Unified Payments Interface, the payment system launched by National Payments Corporation of India and regulated by the Reserve Bank of India that facilitates the instant transfers of funds between all users of the mobile platform. Interoperability can also help ensure a sufficiently dense network of financial agents to enable convenient cash-in-cash-out transactions and other services.[36]

Based on these examples, unique identification is another prerequisite for a well-functioning digital payments system. And without a centralized database to verify identities, it is difficult to develop a strong digital payments ecosystem.

In Ghana, for example, 98 percent of people report having at least one form of ID, but market participants across the country struggle with the numerous forms of identification and identity databases. With nine separate biometric databases in use across government and public entities, it is difficult to perform efficient know-your-customer functions. To verify either the form of ID or the

---

[35]For further discussion of financial regulation to improve financial inclusion, see Center for Global Development (2016) as well as GPFI (2016b).

[36]It is logical to permit reasonable interchange fees for access to agents of another network, as this involves the provision of real (non-virtual) services.

holder of a current account, the company must be able to access the accompanying database. Yet, Ghana lacks a national, centralized identification method and database, hampering the development of its inclusive digital payments ecosystem (Janis and Shah 2016).

Indeed, such a system could benefit PFM in many other ways, and it is surprising to see governments sometimes supporting a diverse and costly range of identification systems that are not interoperable, rather than focusing attention on the core systems of civil registration and national identification.

Appreciation of the Risks

The movement toward a digitized economy also comes with risks, to both citizens and government systems. For citizens, digital transactions and interactions leave a trail—in contrast to cash, which is anonymous—potentially extending to all aspects of an individual's life. The "Responsible Digital Payment Guidelines" (2016), of the Better Than Cash Alliance, document eight good practices for digital payments that, if followed, would significantly reduce risks to citizens. Guideline 7 to protect client data, for example, should not be an issue for G2P payments, but it is a consideration for the wider payments ecosystem. Where one shops, what one buys, who one pays—all these become matters of record and translate into data of considerable commercial value.

Countries need to take steps to ensure the security and safety of these data, and to ensure that the growing digital cloud of information does not unduly compromise either the privacy of citizens or the privacy of classified government information, as both engage in the digital economy. This raises legal and regulatory issues that go far beyond the scope of this paper, but it is important to stress them since only about half of all developing countries have data privacy laws in place. The need for continuous upgrading of digital security is now a *sine qua non* for all such systems and the importance of qualified internal experts cannot be overemphasized.

Directions for Future Work

The very limitations of these cases from Estonia, Ghana, India, and Mexico serve to highlight the urgent need for more rigorous, comparable research to document, and then systematize, how governments are building inclusive digital economies in which the PFM and broader inclusion agenda work together. The speed of innovation in payments makes the importance of robust research all the more important so the learning is substantive, not superficial.

Perhaps more urgent, though, is the need for research on the counterfactual of not integrating PFM with the broader government digitalization agenda and of not digitally connecting the increasingly complex relations between government and citizens, for which PFM is the foundation. These examples also highlight the imperative for training national and international PFM experts to position a modern functional PFM at the center of the government's broader digitalization and inclusion agendas and address the evolving risks.

This is a call to action for the skills development agenda of the IMF, World Bank, United Nations, and bilateral funders active in this sector.

CONCLUSION

The train toward a digital economy has left the station and is moving rapidly. Its destination is a more inclusive society where everyone can benefit from lower costs, increased speed in processing financial transactions, and greater effectiveness in delivering government services.

That future can be reached faster if digitalization becomes a constituent element of a modern and functioning PFM and is combined with broader reform agendas such as financial and social inclusion or digital identification. When embarking on these initiatives, there is much to be learned from the record of large government computerization initiatives in managing risks and from the experience of leaders in digital services.

Digital payments are not a "silver bullet." It will take significant intellectual capital and infrastructure investment. But if the digitalization agenda runs on a parallel track to PFM, the greater risk is a missed opportunity. The cases presented in this chapter from Estonia, Ghana, India, and Mexico are concrete examples of the components of an integrated approach between digitalization and more traditional PFM objectives and the benefits of integration. The call is to mainstream digitalization of payments as part of a functional PFM system that will, in turn, facilitate achievement of PFM goals and a broader inclusion agenda.

REFERENCES

Allen, Richard, Richard Hemming, and Barry H. Potter (eds). 2014. *The International Handbook of Public Financial Management*. New York: Palgrave Macmillan.

Andrews, Matt. 2013. *The Limits of Institutional Reform in Developing Countries: Changing Rules for Realistic Solutions*. Cambridge, MA: Cambridge University Press.

Andrews, Matt, Marco Cangiano, Neil Cole, Paolo de Renzio, Philipp Krause, and Renaud Seligmann. 2014. "This Is PFM." CID Working Paper 285, Center for International Development, Harvard University, Cambridge, MA.

Babatz, Guillermo. 2013. "Sustained Effort, Saving Billions: Lessons from the Mexican Government's Shift to Electronic Payments." Better Than Cash Alliance, New York.

Better Than Cash Alliance (BTCA). 2012. "The Journey Toward 'Cash Lite': Addressing Poverty, Saving Money and Increasing Transparency by Accelerating the Shift to Electronic Payments." New York.

———. 2016. "Responsible Digital Payments Guidelines." July 20.

Breckenridge, Keith. 2010. "The World's First Biometric Money: Ghana's E-Zwich and The Contemporary Influence of South African Biometrics." *Africa* 80 (4): 642–62.

Cangiano, Marco, Teresa Curristine, and Michel Lazare. 2013. *Public Financial Management and Its Emerging Architecture*. Washington, DC: International Monetary Fund.

Center for Global Development. 2015. "Unintended Consequences of Anti–Money Laundering Policies for Poor Countries." CGD Working Group Report, Center for Global Development, Washington, DC.

———. 2016. "Financial Regulations for Improving Financial Inclusion." CGD Task Force Report, Center for Global Development, Washington, DC.

Chang, Ha-Joon. 2006. "Understanding the Relationship between Institutions and Economic Development." WIDER Discussion Paper No. 2006/05, United Nations University World Institute for Development Economics Research, Helsinki.

Chang, Ha-Joon, Antonio Andreoni, and Ming Leong Kuan. 2013. "International Industrial Policy Experiences and the Lessons for the UK." Evidence Paper for the Government Office for Science, London.

Cirasino, Massimo, Hermnat Baijal, Jose Antonio, Garcia Garcia Luna, and Rahul Kitchlu. 2012. "General Guidelines for the Development of Government Payment Programs." World Bank Working Paper 96463, World Bank, Washington, DC.

Citifmonline. 2017. "E-Zwich Patronage Grew by 140% in 2016." February 15.

Committee on Payments and Market Infrastructures (CPMI) and World Bank. 2015. "Payment Aspects of Financial Inclusion." Consultative Report, World Bank, Washington, DC.

Dener, Cem, Joanna Watkins, and William Leslie Dorotinsky. 2011. "Financial Management Information Systems: 25 Years of World Bank Experience on What Works and What Doesn't." World Bank Study, World Bank, Washington, DC.

Diamond, Jack, and Pokar Khemani. 2015. "Introducing Financial Management Information Systems in Developing Countries." IMF Working Paper 05/196, International Monetary Fund, Washington, DC.

Dorotinsky, W., and J. Watkins. 2013. "Government Financial Management Information Systems." *The International Handbook of Public Financial Management,* edited by R. Allen, R. Hemming, and B. Potter. New York: Palgrave Macmillan.

Gelb, Alan, and Julia Clark. 2013. "Identification for Development: The Biometrics Revolution." Center for Global Development Working Paper 315, Center for Global Development, Washington, DC.

Gelb, Alan, and Caroline Decker. 2012. "Cash at Your Fingertips: Biometric Technology for Transfers in Developing Countries." *Review of Policy Research* 29 (1): 91–117.

Gelb, Alan, and Anna Diofasi. Forthcoming. "Biometric Revolution: Towards Sustainable Development in the Digital Age." Center for Global Development, Washington, DC.

G20 Global Partnership for Financial Inclusion (GPFI). 2016a. *Global Standard-Setting Bodies and Financial Inclusion: The Evolving Landscape.* Washington, DC: GFPI.

———. 2016b. "G20 High-Level Principles on Digital Financial Inclusion." Washington, DC: GFPI.

Goodwin-Groen, Ruth (ed.). 2010. "Innovative Financial Inclusion: Principles and Report on Innovative Financial Inclusion from the Access through Innovation Sub-Group of the G20 Financial Inclusion Experts Group." Consultative Group to Assist the Poor, Washington, DC.

Government of Estonia. 2017. "X-Road. Republic of Estonia Information Systems Authority Facts about the X-Road."

Government of India. 2017. "Direct Benefit Transfer." Savings Report to the Prime Minister's Office. New Delhi.

GSMA. 2017. "GSMA Intelligence Data."

Hashim, Ali, and Moritz Piatti. 2016. "A Diagnostic Framework to Assess the Capacity of a Government's Financial Management Information System as a Budget Management Tool." IEG Working Paper, World Bank, Washington, DC.

Independent Evaluation Group (IEG). 2016. "Project Performance Assessment Report: Malawi." Financial Management, Transparency, and Accountability Project. World Bank, Washington, DC.

———. Forthcoming. "A Review of Lessons in Reforming Financial Management Information Systems." World Bank, Washington, DC.

International Monetary Fund (IMF). 2016. "Ghana: Third Review under the Extended Credit Facility Arrangement." Country Report 16/321, Washington, DC.

Janis, William, and Reeya Shah. 2016. "Accelerators to an Inclusive Digital Payments Ecosystem." Better Than Cash Alliance, New York.

Johnson, Susan. 2016. "Competing Visions of Financial Inclusion in Kenya: The Rift Revealed by Mobile Money Transfer." *Canadian Journal of Development Studies* 37 (1): 83–100.

Khan, Abdul, and Mario Pessoa. 2010. "Conceptual Design: A Critical Element of a Government Financial Management Information System Project." IMF Technical Notes and Manuals 10, International Monetary Fund, Washington, DC.

Klapper, Leora. 2014. *The Opportunities for Digitizing Payments: How Digitization of Payments, Transfers, and Remittances Contributes to the G20 Goals of Broad-Based Economic Growth, Financial Inclusion, and Women's Economic Empowerment.* Washington, DC: World Bank.

Lindpere, Martin. 2017. "Summary of Estonia's Digitization Revolution." Remarks at IMF 2017 Fiscal Forum: Digital Revolutions in Public Finance. April 22–23.

Malik, Tariq. 2014. "Technology in the Service of Development: The NADRA Story." Center for Global Development, Washington, DC.

Margetts, Helen, and Andre Naumann. 2017. "Government as a Platform: What Can Estonia Show the World?" Research Paper, University of Oxford, Oxford.

Muralidharan, Karthik, Paul Niehaus, and Sandip Sukhtankar. 2014. "Payments Infrastructure and the Performance of Public Programs: Evidence from Biometric Smartcards in India." NBER Working Paper, National Bureau of Economic Research, Cambridge, MA.

Organisation for Economic Co-operation and Development (OECD). 2016. *Open Government Data Review of Mexico: Data Reuse for Public Sector Impact and Innovation.* Paris: OECD Publishing.

Overseas Development Institute (ODI). 2016. "Cash Transfers: What Does the Evidence Say?" London.

Pillai, Rashmi. 2016. "Person to Government Payments: Lessons from Tanzania's Digitization Efforts." Case Study, Better Than Cash Alliance, New York.

Rogoff, Kenneth S. 2016. *The Curse of Cash.* Princeton, NJ: Princeton University Press.

Sahay, Ratna, Martin Čihák, Papa N'Diaye, Adolfo Barajas, Srobona Mitra, Annette Kyobe, Yen Nian Mooi, and Seyed Reza Yousefi. 2015. "Financial Inclusion: Can It Meet Multiple Macroeconomic Goals?" IMF Staff Discussion Note 15/17, International Monetary Fund, Washington, DC.

Sturge, Georgina. 2017. *Five Myths about Cash Transfers.* London: Overseas Development Institute.

Suri, Tavneet, and William Jack. 2017. "The Long-Run Poverty and Gender Impacts of Mobile Money." *Science* 354 (6317): 1288–92.

Una, Gerardo, and Carlos Pimenta. 2016. "Integrated Financial Management Information Systems in Latin America: Strategic Aspects and Challenges." In *Public Financial Management in Latin America,* edited by Carlos Pimenta and Mario Pessoa. Washington, DC: Inter-American Development Bank.

World Bank. 2015. *The State of Social Safety Nets.* Washington, DC.

———. 2017. *World Development Indicators.* Washington, DC.

.

PART V

How Much Is It All Worth?

CHAPTER 13

The Value of Digitalizing Government Payments in Developing Economies

SUSAN LUND, OLIVIA WHITE, AND JASON LAMB

In 2009, Afghan police officers were surprised that, when the government started delivering their salaries digitally—by mobile phone rather than in cash—the payment method was not the issue. Rather, the electronic bank account deposits were significantly larger than they had ever been. Some officers thought it was an error; others took it as an unexpected pay raise.

The real surprise: the officers were receiving their full pay—for the first time.

The new digital delivery stymied superior officers and clerks who had been routinely skimming off some of the payroll cash passing through their offices—taking up to 30 percent of some officers' earnings (USAID 2014). Government paymasters were equally surprised to discover that as much as 10 percent of the country's police force consisted of "ghost cops"—nonexistent entities created solely to let corrupt authorities collect money they did not earn (World Economic Forum 2014).

This story illustrates the potential for governments in developing countries to use digital payments to plug leaky payment systems. Money is lost on its way into government accounts as well, as tax collectors accept bribes to underreport taxes owed or skim from payments by businesses and individuals. Digital transactions complicate fraud and eliminate leakage in government expenditures and receipts.

This chapter quantifies the potential value at stake when government payment transactions shift from cash to digital. The analysis here finds that digitalizing government payments in developing countries could save roughly 0.8–1.1 percent of GDP, equivalent to $220–$320 billion annually.[1] This is equal to 1.5 percent of the value of all government payment transactions and is more than all official development aid to emerging market economies in 2015.

---

[1] The chapter builds on research found in McKinsey Global Institute (2016a). The results are larger than those in the report, as the authors used updated data from 2015 and expanded the scope of the analysis to include a reduction in fraud and savings in payments processing as well as government-to-government transactions.

Moreover, these calculations are likely to underestimate the true value at stake, as there are substantial indirect benefits that we do not attempt to measure. Of the total value, roughly 0.5 percent of GDP, about $105–$155 Billion, would accrue directly to the government and improve fiscal balances, while the remainder would benefit individuals and businesses as government spending reached its intended targets.

These figures are not meant to be a forecast, since capturing the value will depend on upfront investments and operational changes within governments. Incomplete data hamper the analysis; a range of estimates is presented of the potential value at stake. Nonetheless, the chapter provides one of the first comprehensive, cross-countries estimates of the potential benefits of digitalizing government payments, using the best available data. It is important to understand the potential magnitude of these benefits when weighing them against the cost of investments in information technology and hardware that will be required.

The chapter first looks at the extent to which government payments in developing countries are made in cash and digitally. It focuses on seven countries that span income levels and geographies: Brazil, China, India, Indonesia, Mexico, Nigeria, and South Africa. It then details the methodology for calculating the potential value from digitalizing payments to and from governments. Subsequent sections describe the data used, present the results of calculations, and discuss other potential benefits not included in the calculations. The conclusion discusses limitations to the calculations and reveals thoughts on future research.

CASH IS COMMON IN GOVERNMENT EXPENDITURES AND REVENUE IN DEVELOPING COUNTRIES

In developing countries, a large share of government payment transactions to and from individuals and businesses and between government entities are transacted in cash or by check when payments are measured by volume or by the number of transactions. Digital payments—which include automated clearing house transfers directly between financial accounts, payments made by credit and debit cards, wire transactions, mobile money transactions, and other noncash payments—are still a small share in many countries (Figure 13.1). In Nigeria and Indonesia, for example, only 20 to 25 percent of government payment expenditures and about 10 to 15 percent of tax receipts were made using digital channels in 2015.[2] In Brazil, China, and Mexico, use of digital payments in government is more advanced. In South Africa, the share of digital payments in government transactions has already reached advanced-economy levels.

---

[2]The analysis here includes all levels of government—central, state or provincial, and local—to the extent that such data are available.

Figure 13.1. Developing Economies Have a Significant Opportunity to Digitalize Government Payments
(Share of digital in government payments by number, 2015, percent[1])

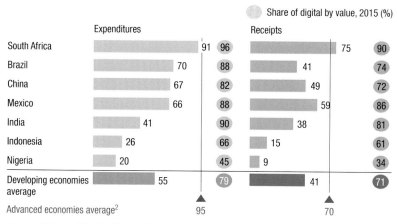

Sources: McKinsey Global Institute analysis; and McKinsey Payments Map 2015.
[1]Total excluding cash, checks, and paper-based transactions by number. Total excluding cash and checks by value. G2G transactions not included.
[2]Based on data from 20 advanced economies. Weighted average.

When we measure government payments by value rather than by volume, the share of digital transactions increases significantly. This is not surprising, as the largest payments, particularly between governments and businesses and between different branches of government, are already digital. The columns of figures in circles in Figure 13.1 show the share of payments by value that are digital today. In Nigeria, for example, roughly half of the value of government expenditure was transacted with digital payments, although only 20 percent of the volume of transactions was digital. Similarly, an estimated 34 percent of tax receipts were collected through digital payments in 2015, while only 9 percent of transactions were digital. On average, 79 percent of the value of government expenditures and 71 percent of tax receipts were digital in 2015 in the seven developing countries shown in the figure.

While governments around the world have begun shifting their payments to digital channels, scope remains for further digitalization. This is not surprising, given that many advanced economies adopted widespread use of digital payments for government transactions only in the past decade or so. In the United States, for example, the federal government completely phased out paper checks for recipients of Social Security, veterans' benefits, and other federal assistance in 2013. In Spain and Italy, 8 percent and 7 percent, respectively, of all government expenditures by value still occur in cash or by check.

METHODOLOGY FOR CALCULATING VALUE FROM DIGITALIZING GOVERNMENT PAYMENTS AND RECEIPTS

Digital payments promise to plug a variety of government expenditure and revenue "leaks." Cash payrolls, for example, only invite clerks, bosses, and others to skim off wages before employees receive them. The same is true of social security and pension benefits and payments to vendors. Revenue streams are also vulnerable to leakage: value-added tax can be collected in cash and never reported to the government. Income taxes and fees paid in cash can also be stolen before reaching the government. Beyond plugging such leaks, moving from manual cash processing of payments to digital processing can result in significant operational gains. In this analysis, we attempt to measure the full set of benefits across both government expenditures and tax receipts.

Framework for Measuring the Value

Moving from cash to digital for government payment expenditures and receipts yields three main types of benefits: reducing leakage, eliminating fraudulent payments and tax evasion, and reducing the costs of payment processing within the government. Table 13.1 describes these three sources of value in government expenditures, government receipts, and payments in different government organizations. Many studies from around the world provide estimates of the size of these effects and the value obtained by digitalizing payments. This research section describes some of this work.

Reducing leakage in government payments and tax receipts

A system that pays workers, pensioners, vendors, and household social programs in cash is vulnerable to losses through corruption. In addition to embezzlement, risks include robbery and simply misplacing currency. Electronic payment transfers greatly reduce the risk of funds being skimmed by officials or bribes paid by users. This leakage can be quite costly. Using a randomized control trial, researchers in India found that after digitalizing wage payments for workers in the National Rural Employment Guarantee Scheme, the leakage rate in Andhra Pradesh fell from 30.7 percent to 18.5 percent on average (Muralidharan, Niehaus, and Sukhtankar 2016).

In Côte d'Ivoire, after that country's 2011 civil war, school fees were paid almost exclusively in cash and were subject to high levels of bribery, theft, and other security issues, eroding the quality of the education system. Between 2011 and 2014, the Ministry of National and Technical Education began requiring that school payments be made digitally, with most parents using mobile wallets to do so. In 2014, 99 percent of secondary school students paid their fees digitally. The result was a significant reduction in lost payments, fraud, theft, and the administrative burden of managing cash (Frydrych, Scharwatt, and Vonthron 2015).

Table 13.1. The Three Main Sources of Potential Savings in Government Payment Transactions

		Potential Sources of Savings		
		Leakage	Fraud and Tax Evasion	Processing Costs
Expenditures	To public employees	• Salaries skimmed or stolen by government finance employees	• Fake or deceased employees to whom salaries are paid	
	To individuals	• Subsidies and pensions skimmed or stolen by government finance employees	• Transfers to individuals who do not qualify for the subsidy or pension	
	To businesses	• Subsidy payments or payments for procurement contracts skimmed or stolen by government finance employees	• Overbilling for goods and services • Billing for work not performed	
Receipts	From businesses	• Income tax payments skimmed or stolen by tax collectors or government finance employees	• Value-added taxes collected by business but not paid to government • Tax evasion in informal economy	• Back-office cost savings from automated payments (including FTE cost for processing and transportation, paperwork, errors, and rework)
	From individuals	• Income tax payments skimmed or stolen by tax collectors or government finance employees	• Income tax evasion by individuals	
Intragovernmental payments	Between government entities	• Public sector institutions and municipalities do not receive full transfers • Payments for public goods and services (e.g., parks, museums) not reported and transferred to budgets	• n/a	

Source: McKinsey Global Institute analysis.

The Ebola virus outbreak in 2014 exposed the weaknesses of Sierra Leone's use of cash to pay health care workers. Some emergency responders had to leave patients for days and walk many miles to collect their pay from a regional office, sometimes to discover that someone else had claimed their cash before they arrived. The country introduced e-payments through mobile wallets in December

2014, saving the government and health care workers $10.7 million over the last 13 months of the outbreak (Bangura 2016).

Relying on cash or even checks as payment for taxes and fees is often just as troublesome, as some of the revenue generated ends up in the pockets of tax officials themselves rather than in the national treasury. In Tanzania, authorities sought to stem corruption by tax collectors by printing receipt books and requiring collectors to document every payment and deliver the amount documented before they received another book. By the year's end, 30 percent of the books—and 35 percent of expected revenue—were missing (Fjeldstad and Semboja 2000). Collecting taxes through digital payments rather than cash would eliminate this leakage, boosting government revenue.

Reducing fraudulent payments and tax evasion

Fraud is a second problem in government payments. This includes paying salaries to fake or deceased employees, payment for work not performed by vendors and contractors, and other fraudulent payments. In Zimbabwe, an estimated 40 percent of the central government payroll consisted of fake employees in 2011 (BBC 2011). In Honduras, nearly one-quarter of teacher salaries go to so-called ghost workers (World Bank 2010). Sometimes the extent of the problem is not apparent until a government takes steps to eradicate it. After Botswana, South Africa, and the Indian state of Andhra Pradesh adopted biometric identification to weed out nonexistent claimants from their benefit rolls, for example, the number of beneficiaries dropped 12–25 percent (Gelb and Decker 2012). Digital payments allow government auditors to better spot fraud, since such payments create a data trail that they can analyze. The examples in Table 13.2 illustrate the extent of the problem.

Fraud also occurs in revenue collection, mainly through tax evasion. Examples include retail sales and professional service fees paid in cash that are not reported to tax authorities, businesses that fail to collect or pay value-added or sales taxes, and individuals who underreport their income. By definition, knowing the extent of tax evasion is difficult. If citizens pay with credit or debit cards, or business owners are required to record cash sales electronically, they create a digital trail that tax authorities can follow. In this analysis, we do not attempt to measure tax evasion because of a lack of data on its magnitude and because reducing it requires digitalizing payments by individuals and businesses throughout the economy.

Cost savings to government operations from digitalizing payment processing

Digital payments relieve governments of many burdens associated with cash, which in turn can create considerable savings. This includes the manual processes involved in collecting, counting, recording, and transporting cash—all of which can happen almost instantaneously and at zero marginal cost once digital payment infrastructure is in place. The US government cut the cost of issuing

Table 13.2. Leakage and Fraudulent Payments Can Reach Half of Government Transfers to a Particular Group of Individuals

	Examples
Fraudulent Payments for Ghost Workers	40% of central government payroll, Zimbabwe 23% of teachers in Honduras 19% of Nairobi city payroll, Kenya 18% of National Rural Employment Guarantee Scheme, India (ranges from 5% in Chattisgarh to almost 80% in Uttar Pradesh) 15% of teachers in Papua New Guinea 10% of police in Afghanistan 10% of civil servants in Ghana
Leakage in Government-to-Government Payments	87% of schools' nonwage spending in Uganda 76% of discretionary education spending in Zambia 73% of nonwage recurrent spending budgeted for regional health directorates in Chad 40% of Ngorongoro Conservation Area revenues, Tanzania 38% of health spending in Kenya 8% of municipal spending in Brazil
Leakage in Household Subsidies	58% of targeted Public Distribution System food subsidies, India 44% of social programs, India 31% of National Rural Employee Guarantee Scheme, Andhra Pradesh, India 25–50% in IAY (social welfare program) subsidies to build and renovate houses, India

Sources: Arze del Granado, Coady, and Gillingham 2010; Banerjee 2015; BBC 2003, 2011; Ghana Ministry of Finance 2012; Government of India 2005; McKinsey & Company 2010; PricewaterhouseCoopers 1999; Reinikka and Svensson 2004, 2006; World Bank 2004, 2010; World Economic Forum 2014.

federal benefits payments by more than 90 percent after it began requiring all recipients to receive federal benefit payments electronically in 2013 (US Treasury 2011). The Philippines saved $0.51 per transaction by digitalizing payments distributed through its 4Ps social-benefits program—electronic transaction costs $0.45, while cash costs $0.96 (Zimmerman, Bohling, and Rotman Parker (2014).[3] In Haiti, where an electronic transaction costs $0.50, the government saved $1.17 per transaction for the Ti Manman Cheri social assistance program (Zimmerman, Bohling, and Rotman Parker 2014).

Methodology for Calculating the Potential Value of Digitalizing Government Payments

The following equation calculates the potential value of moving from cash to digital payments for governments:

$$V_{i,t} = \sum_k (PV_{i,k,t} {}^* c_{i,k,t}^v {}^* \rho_k + PN_{i,t} {}^* c_{i,k,t}^n {}^* \Phi)$$

where i represents country i, t the current year, and k the type of government payment transaction.

---

[3]4Ps refers to the Filipino-language Pantawid Pamilyang Pilipino Program.

$V_{i,t}$ is the total value of savings for the government and for individuals and businesses in the economy from digitalizing government payment transactions that today are made in cash. This includes prevention of leakage and fraud as well as reducing payment processing costs.

The first component in the equation measures the potential savings from reducing leakage and fraud.

$PV_{i,k,t}$ is the value of government payment transactions of type k for country i for year t.

$c^{v}_{i,k,t}$ is the share of government payment transactions by value of type k that are made in cash or check.

ρ_{k} is the percent savings from reducing leakage and fraud for payment type k. We use a range for ρ_k based on empirical estimates found in the literature, discussed below.

The second term in the equation measures the reduction in processing costs by moving from cash to digital payments.

$PN_{i,k,t}$ is the number of government payment transactions of type k for country i for year t.

$c^{n}_{i,k,t}$ is the share of government payment transactions by number of type k that occur in cash or check (that is, non-digital).

Φ are the savings per transaction from increasing processing efficiency by moving from cash to digital. We use a range of values for Φ based on empirical estimates found in other studies, discussed below. We assume the value of Φ is the same for all payment types.

This analysis distinguishes between five types of government payments (represented by k in the equation above):

- G2C: payments from governments to consumers. This includes payments of salaries to government employees, cash subsidies to households and individuals, and other government payments to individuals.

- G2B: payments from governments to businesses. This includes government procurement costs paid to vendors, contractors, and other suppliers of goods and services to the government.

- C2G: payments from consumers to the government as income and other taxes and fees.

- B2G: payments from businesses to the government, from corporate income taxes, value-added taxes, and other fees.

- G2G: payments from one government entity to another, such as payments from a central government to state or local governments, or transfers to public educational and health care institutions.

A key variable in our analysis is ρ_{k}, which represents the magnitude of leakage and fraud in government expenditures and receipts that can be eliminated from digitalizing government payments. We reviewed the available literature for empirical estimates of the scale of leakage and fraud for different types of payments. Admittedly, only a limited number of such studies exist, and there is a wide range of reported figures for the scale of such leakage. Table 13.2 shows examples from the literature on the scale of leakage for government payments to individuals and businesses.

This analysis uses a range of values for ρ_k, reflecting the uncertainty of the true size. For government payments to consumers (mainly salaries of government employees and household subsidy payments), we assume that leakage and fraud amount to 15–25 percent of the total value of payments. For government payments to businesses (mainly for procurement of goods and services purchased by the government), we assume that the leakage rate is smaller at 5–15 percent of the value of such payments. This reflects the fact that such payments are typically larger in scale and more likely to be audited today. For payments between government entities, we similarly assume that 5–15 percent of the value of payments is lost, for similar reasons.

Finally, for payments from consumers to the government and from businesses to the government (taxes and fees collected), we assume that 5 percent of payments are skimmed by officials or lost to bribery, based on the few reports we could find. This figure may be an underestimate. Moreover, importantly, it does not include the far larger amounts of government revenue that may be lost to tax evasion—in other words, underreporting individual or business income or sales. We do not attempt to measure the value of tax evasion, because reducing such evasion requires digitalizing incomes of individuals and businesses from all sources, which is beyond the scope of the chapter. In the section below on other potential benefits not included in our analysis, we discuss how more widespread use of digital payments across an economy could reduce tax evasion.

Another key variable in our analysis is Φ, which represents the reduction in processing costs per payment transaction from moving from cash to digital payments. As discussed above, estimates of the processing cost reduction vary. Estimates from advanced economies, such as the United States and European Union, tend to show higher cost savings of $2–$3 per payment transaction, reflecting higher labor costs in those areas. In developing countries, where labor costs are lower, the cost savings are less. Based on the experience of the Philippines and Haiti, we choose a range of $0.50 to $1.20 as the cost savings per transaction.

Focus Countries and Extrapolation of Results to All Developing Countries

As noted, the analysis focuses on seven developing countries that span geographies: Brazil, China, India, Indonesia, Mexico, Nigeria, and South Africa. The choice partly reflects the quality and granularity of available data, as well as the ability to have payment experts within each country check the results. While we would have liked to include more low-income countries in the sample, incomplete data prevented that.

The seven focus countries account for 61 percent of GDP of all developing countries. To estimate the potential value for all developing countries, the analysis extrapolates the results using their share of GDP. Ideally, we would have granular data on the share of cash versus digital payments in all developing countries, which would make the extrapolation more precise. But lacking such data, we instead make the simplifying assumption of extrapolating results from the seven countries to all developing countries based on their GDP. This puts a downward bias on the results, as low-income countries are more likely to be using cash payments today and thus may derive a larger benefit from digitalizing government payments.

THE DATA

We draw data from two main sources. We obtain data on the value of different types of government expenditures and receipts in 2015 from national income accounts. We get these data from Haver Analytics, which sources the data directly from country financial statements. It covers data on all levels of government—central, state or provincial, and local. Data on government expenditures include, among others, social services, payroll, subsidies, and grants to individuals and businesses as well as public security expenses. Data on government revenue primarily include tax revenue, revenue from fiscal services, and other dividends and payments. We cross-checked and enriched these data based on the International Monetary Fund *Fiscal Monitor* and the World Development Indicators database of the World Bank.[4]

The McKinsey Global Payments Map is another key source of data. McKinsey & Company created this proprietary database to provide a granular view of the global payment business. The data are drawn from both public and private sources, with more than 200 in total. The data include, among other things, payment flows (volume and value) between individuals, businesses, and government entities; the channel for each payment flow (for example, cash, check, prepaid cards, credit cards, debit cards, automated clearing house payments [credit transfers and direct debits], wire transfers); the revenue and costs for providers generated through payment activities (various types of fees and interest income); and stocks of payment-related equipment (for example, number of credit and debit cards). The database covers 45 countries around the world. By applying consistent definitions and measurements across different geographies, the map is able to provide a globally consistent view of the payment industry. This chapter used the most recent release of the map, with data through 2015.

For the analysis, we obtain two key data series from the McKinsey Global Payments Map. First is the number of government payment transactions of different types, including payments both to and from the government. We also obtain estimates of the share of government payments that are made in cash and digitally. In the map, these shares are estimated using a variety of sources, starting

---

[4]Figures on government expenditure receipts differ from the IMF *Fiscal Monitor* for Brazil and India. For Brazil, figures are lower, as we exclude state-owned enterprises such as Petrobras. Figures differ for India because we include state government expenditures and receipts as well.

with the Bank for International Settlements *Red Book* and incorporating national data for each country drawn from industry sources.

RESULTS: THE VALUE OF DIGITALIZING GOVERNMENT PAYMENTS

Our calculations show that digitalizing government payments could create value of roughly 1 percent of GDP for most countries, equivalent to $220–$320 billion of value annually for all developing countries (Figure 13.2).[5] This includes the value of reducing leakage and fraud, and increasing efficiency of payments for governments. The range reflects different assumptions about the potential savings of each of the sources.

Nearly half of the total value—approximately 0.5 percent of GDP for most countries and $105–$155 billion across all emerging markets annually—accrues to governments, by reducing processing costs, leakage in tax receipts and government-to-government payments, and fraudulent payments (Figure 13.3). Of these sources, reducing leakage in tax receipts and reducing fraudulent payments account for roughly two-thirds of the value in most countries. This money directly boosts fiscal balances and could be used to reduce deficits, invest in infrastructure, fund social programs, and more.

The remainder of the value, or $115–$165 billion annually or roughly 0.5 percent GDP at the country level, comes from reducing leakage in payments to a wider range of actors across the economy. Individuals would derive some of the benefit, receiving their full salaries and subsidy payments. Businesses would benefit from preventing officials from skimming payments for their goods and services. Society would also benefit as more public spending reached its intended targets—for instance, roads and other infrastructure, health care, and education.

The potential value of digitalizing government payments varies by country, reflecting the value of government expenditures and receipts that are paid in cash or by check today. The value is particularly large in countries with a low share of digital payments in government transactions, such as Indonesia and Nigeria. Indonesia could gain $6–$10 billion annually, or as much as 1.1 percent of GDP. This reflects the large share of government subsidy programs and other payments and receipts still made in cash. This value is comparable to the annual value added of Indonesia's mineral-based products industry. Nigeria similarly has a high share of cash payments and receipts. Digitalizing government payments could generate $5–$9 billion in value each year for Nigeria, equivalent to 1.7 percent of GDP for the high end of that range.

---

[5]The results in the chapter are larger than those in McKinsey Global Institute (2016a), the *Digital Finance for All* report of September 2016. The chapter uses updated data and expands the analysis to include a reduction in fraud and savings in payments processing, and includes G2G transactions.

Figure 13.2. The Value of Digitalizing Government Payments in Developing Countries is $220 Billion to $320 Billion Annually
(Annual savings in government payment transactions)

■ Expenditures ■ Receipts ■ Government-to-government payments ■ Increase in processing efficiency

	Savings by source (percent)	Total savings (billions, US dollars)	Savings in government payment transactions/GDP (percent)
China	44 43 12 1	94–134	0.9–1.2
India	32 43 12 14	11–17	0.5–0.8
Brazil	65 23 10 3	10–16	0.6–0.9
Indonesia	64 24 4 8	6–10	0.7–1.1
Mexico	75 17 5 2	6–10	0.5–0.9
Nigeria	65 22 1 12	5–9	1.0–1.7
South Africa	59 33 5 3	0.8–1.2	0.2–0.4
Total sample		130–200	0.8–1.1
Total emerging economies[1]		220–320	0.8–1.1

Sources: McKinsey Global Institute analysis; and McKinsey Payments Map 2015.
Note: Numbers may not sum due to rounding.
[1]Extrapolation on potential savings based on the share of sample in total GDP.

In South Africa, the share of digital government payments is comparable to the share in advanced economies, and there is less room for further gains. Still, our analysis suggests that South Africa's government could reap up to $1.2 billion annually (0.4 percent of GDP) by digitalizing government payments that are still in cash.

OTHER POTENTIAL BENEFITS NOT INCLUDED IN THE ANALYSIS

Our estimate of the potential benefits obtained from digitalizing government payments, while large, is likely a conservative figure in that it does not attempt to quantify potentially significant second-order effects. There are three important categories: improving government service delivery, for instance by improved targeting of social subsidies and reducing absenteeism; encouraging more widespread adoption of digital finance by businesses and individuals throughout the economy; and reducing tax evasion and shifting economic activity from the informal economy to the official one.

Figure 13.3. Almost Half of Savings from Digitalizing Government Payment Transactions Accrues to Government

(Annual savings in government payment transaction in developing countries, 100% = $220 billion–$320 billion)

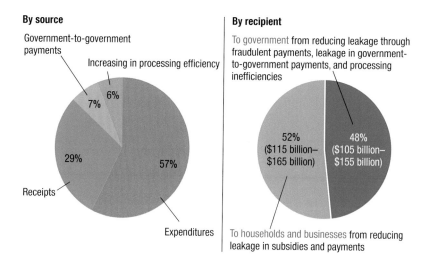

By source

Government-to-Government payments

Increasing in processing efficiency

6%

7%

29%

57%

Receipts

Expenditures

By recipient

To government from reducing leakage through fraudulent payments, leakage in government-to-government payments, and processing inefficiencies

52%
($115 billion–
$165 billion)

48%
($105 billion–
$155 billion)

To households and businesses from reducing leakage in subsidies and payments

Sources: McKinsey Global Institute analysis; and McKinsey Payments Map 2015.

Improving Government Service Delivery

Shifting to digital payments enables governments to improve delivery of services in several ways. First, digital payment of salaries for teachers, health care workers, and other government employees allows them to receive their wages regularly rather than sporadically. This simple act has been shown to reduce absenteeism of government workers. In India, for example, one study found that teachers' attendance rate is 90 percent in states with reliable digital salary payments, but only 60 to 80 percent in other states (McKinsey & Company 2010). Higher attendance by teachers improves the quality of education delivered and enables students to learn more, lifting the quality of human capital in the economy. The same effect has been observed in systems that pay health care workers digitally. Over the long term, improvements in human capital have been shown empirically to have a strongly positive effect on GDP growth.

Digital payments also enable governments to target social benefits to the poorest households. Brazil, for instance, improved the delivery of aid to its poorest citizens by switching to digital payments after consolidating four existing cash-transfer programs into one, called *Bolsa Família*, in 2003. The new system delivers 80 percent of its benefits to the poorest quartile of Brazilians, up from 64 percent under previous arrangements (Lindert and others 2010). At the same time, the administrative cost of serving Bolsa Família's 12.4 million eligible households has declined by more than three-fourths—to 2.6 percent of the benefits delivered from 14.7 percent for its predecessor agencies (Pickens, Porteous, and Rotman Parker 2009). A final benefit of digitalizing subsidy payments has been to increase financial inclusion. In 2000, about 20 percent of Brazilian adults had bank accounts (von Mettenheim and de Lima 2014). By 2014, that had risen to 68 percent for the general population—and 99 percent for adults in families served by Bolsa Família.

Throughout the developing world, it is common for governments to use price subsidies rather than delivering cash to those in need. Using digital payments to help poor households buy basic commodities avoids market distortions that can come from direct subsidization of food, fuel, and other commodities, and significantly reduces the cost of the program. IMF researchers estimate that 43 percent of the benefit of fuel subsidies around the world went to the wealthiest quintile, because of their relatively higher consumption, while only 7 percent of the benefit went to the poorest quintile (Coady and others 2015). Globally, the research finds that ending fuel subsidies could raise government revenue by $2.9 trillion while cutting global carbon dioxide emissions by 20 percent and reducing premature deaths related to air pollution by 55 percent.

Finally, digital payments to households in need can also replace subsidies that have been distributed in kind, such as programs that deliver wheat, rice, and other grains to the poor. These programs create massive logistical challenges and are subject to leakage. The government of India, for example, spends $21 billion annually on food subsidies—but 54 percent of subsidized wheat, 48 percent of subsidized sugar, and 15 percent of subsidized rice is lost as leakage before it reaches the poor (Radcliffe 2016). Providing households in poverty with digital cash transfers instead dramatically lowers these costs. A randomized control trial in four countries (Ecuador, Niger, Uganda, and Yemen) found that cash transfers via debit cards resulted in better nutritional outcomes in all countries except Niger, and resulted in savings in all four countries that ranged from $2.96 per transfer in Uganda to $8.91 per transfer in Niger (Hoddinott and others 2013).

Spurring Broader Use of Digital Payments by Individuals and Businesses

Beyond the direct value of digitalizing government payments, a potentially larger benefit is to spur development of digital payment infrastructure across the economy and prompt broader adoption among businesses and individuals. To accelerate this process, India launched the Pradhan Mantri Jan Dhan Yojana financial inclusion initiative in 2014, leading people to open more than 280 million new bank accounts to receive government subsidy payments digitally (Government of India 2017). In November 2016, India went further by removing 500 and 1,000 rupee notes from circulation. The surprise move created short-term disruptions in supply chains based predominantly on cash, but it has also prompted millions of individuals and small businesses to sign up for mobile payment programs. Paytm, a mobile wallet provider, added 50 million new subscribers in the three months after the cash ban was imposed, bringing its total user base to over 200 million by March 2017.

MGI Research has estimated that widespread adoption of digital finance by individuals, businesses, and governments could raise the aggregate GDP of emerging market economies over 10 years by $3.7 trillion, or 6 percent (McKinsey Global Institute 2016a). This is because shifting to digital finance produces enormous time and cost savings for businesses, financial institutions, and individuals as they conduct economic transactions. Nearly two-thirds of the GDP increase would come from raising the productivity of financial and nonfinancial businesses, as well as governments, because of digital payments. One-third of the impact comes from the additional investment across the economy that results from broader financial inclusion of people and micro, small, and medium-sized businesses. The small remainder would come from time savings by individuals enabling more hours of work. Given these enormous economy-wide benefits, the cost and investment needed to digitize government payments seems modest.

Digitalizing Payments Enables Better Tax Enforcement and Can Reduce the Size of the Informal Economy

The predominance of cash transactions spawns a large informal, or "shadow," economy of businesses that do not register their entities, pay taxes, or comply with product- or labor-market regulations. The World Bank estimated that the size of the informal economy in 2007 ranged from about 18 percent of GDP in advanced economies to as much as 50 percent of GDP in developing countries (Schneider, Buehn, and Montenegro 2010). The costs of such tax evasion can be quite high. India, for example, says its aggregate shortfall in tax collections was $117 billion in 2016 due to tax evasion. That is equal to about 6 percent of the country's $2 trillion GDP and is more than the total amount—$90 billion—that the government planned to borrow in the capital markets that year (Kumar 2016). In Mexico, one report estimates that reducing the informal economy by just 1 percent would represent $560 million of new tax revenue with no changes to tax rates (Mazzotta and Chakravorti 2014).

Shifting from cash to digital payments for businesses and consumers creates a digital trail for tax auditors to review. By using new analytical tools that can detect patterns in the digital data trail of taxpayers, auditors can greatly enhance their ability to detect fraud. In most countries, tax authorities audit 5 percent of returns filed each year or less, but they do not know if they are targeting the biggest tax evaders. Digital payments can help by generating more transactional data. Using these data in analytical models can improve detection of likely tax evasion, thereby increasing the average additional revenue captured per audit case. New machine learning algorithms that continually improve their performance based on past results have shown extraordinary improvements in fraud detection as compared to earlier algorithms.

Beyond increasing tax revenue, bringing informal businesses into the formal economy can boost economy-wide productivity by giving these casual businesses access to capital and enabling them to invest and grow—or to fold, opening opportunities for more efficient enterprises. Once businesses are in the formal economy, compliance with health and safety regulations also improves. Of course, governments will have to tread a fine line as they seek to expand digital payments while also reducing tax evasion: sudden step-ups in tax enforcement have been shown to have unintended consequences, including a reduction in the use of digital payments by informal firms.

CONCLUSION

Digitalizing government payments and receipts can help the public sector in emerging market economies substantially increase revenue without raising tax rates, and eliminate tens of billions of dollars in waste and fraud. In addition, digitalizing payments can help reduce corruption and bribery, enabling government spending to reach its intended target. This analysis estimates that the value for all developing countries is equivalent to around 1 percent of their GDP, or equivalent to more than all official development aid in 2015.

Our findings come with several caveats. First, while we employ the best data available, gaps exist, particularly in valuing cash payments by local and provincial governments. Second, important second-order benefits exist that we do not attempt to quantify, such as improving government service delivery, reducing tax evasion, and catalyzing broader adoption of digital finance among businesses and consumers. Calculating the value of these benefits, particularly over the long term, would increase the value of digitalizing government payments considerably. Finally, capturing the value of digitalizing payments requires more than investing in technology. While digital payments make it more difficult for officials to skim from government payments and increase the ability of governments to detect fraud, political will is required. The significant vested interests among those currently benefiting from corruption will resist change.

Digitalizing government payments is not a small task and will come with risks that need to be managed. Purchasing and implementing new accounting and payment systems is a significant undertaking in cost and time. For businesses as well as governments, the value of such systems is often derived from redesigning operational processes while implementing new systems. Risks include those associated with cybersecurity and IT robustness against crashes or even power failure. The shift toward digital payments also requires governments to establish thoughtful approaches to developing privacy laws to both protect and maintain the trust of citizens and other residents.

We recognize that this will be a major undertaking for governments, many of which already face unmet demand for public services and have large fiscal deficits. But the results of this chapter suggest that the potential value will far outweigh the costs and generate significantly positive returns for government fiscal balances and for society.

The need is considerable for further research on the impact of digitalizing government payments and the most effective ways to do so. Much of the evidence on leakage in payments for household subsidies comes from a series of studies in India since 2010. More research is needed on the impact of digitalizing government payments on reducing leakage, fraud, and program administration costs in more countries around the world. There have been at least two randomized control trials, but trials in different settings are important to see how local settings affect results. Research is also needed on the second-order benefits of digitalizing government payments, particularly in improving government service delivery, and the impact on education and health outcomes. Finally, new technologies are emerging, such as blockchains, which may open new avenues for efficiency in payments and in creating secure, transparent contracts of all kinds. Developing countries that currently lack digital payment systems may have an opportunity to leapfrog to the next generation of technologies.

Digital payments are the lifeblood of a modern economy, enabling efficient, secure transactions. Governments can improve their fiscal balances and play a positive role in catalyzing adoption of digital finance across society by adopting digital for their own payments—a win-win for all.

REFERENCES

Aker, Jenny, Rachid Boumnijel, Amanda McClelland, and Niall Tierney. 2015. "Payment Mechanisms and Anti-Poverty Programs: Evidence from a Mobile Money Cash Transfer Experiment in Niger." Working Paper, Center for Global Development, Washington, DC.

Arze del Granado, Javier, David Coady, and Robert Gillingham. 2010. "The Unequal Benefits of Fuel Subsidies: A Review of Evidence for Developing Countries." IMF Working Paper 10/202, International Monetary Fund, Washington, DC.

Babatz, Guillermo. 2013. "Sustained Effort, Saving Billions: Lessons from the Mexican Government's Shift to Electronic Payments." Better Than Cash Alliance, New York.

Banerjee, Abhijit, Esther Duflo, Nathanael Goldberg, Dean Karlan, Robert Osei, William Parienté, Jeremy Shapiro, Bram Thuysbaert, and Christopher Udry. 2015. "A Multifaceted Program Causes Lasting Progress for the Very Poor: Evidence from Six Countries." *Science* 348 (6236).

Banerjee, Shweta S. 2015. "From Cash to Digital Transfers in India: The Story So Far." CGAP Brief, Consultative Group to Assist the Poor, Washington, DC.

Bangura, Joe Abass. 2016. "Saving Money, Saving Lives: A Case Study on the Benefits of Digitizing Payments to Ebola Response Workers in Sierra Leone." Better Than Cash Alliance, New York.

BBC. 2003. "Headcount Reveals Nairobi Scam." March 11.

———. 2011. "World Bank Report Exposes Zimbabwe Ghost Workers." May 13.

British Broadcasting Corporation (BBC). 2011. "Zimbabwe Civil Servants Exposed by World Bank Report." May 13.

Coady, David, Ian Parry, Louis Sears, and Baoping Shang. 2015. "How Large Are Global Energy Subsidies?" IMF Working Paper 15/105, International Monetary Fund, Washington, DC.

Demirgüç-Kunt, Asli, Leora Klapper, Dorothe Singer, and Peter Van Oudheusden. 2015. "The Global Findex Database 2014: Measuring Financial Inclusion around the World." World Bank Policy Research Working Paper 7255, World Bank, Washington, DC.

Fjeldstad, Odd-Helge, and Joseph Semboja. 2000. "Dilemmas of Fiscal Decentralisation: A Study of Local Government Taxation in Tanzania." *Forum for Development Studies* 27 (1): 7–41.

Frydrych, Jennifer, Claire Scharwatt, and Nicolas Vonthron. 2015. "Paying School Fees with Mobile Money in Côte d'Ivoire: A Public-Private Partnership to Achieve Greater Efficiency." GSMA, London.

Gauthier, Bernard, and Ritva Reinikka. 2007. "Methodological Approaches to the Study of Institutions and Service Delivery: A Review of PETS, QSDS and CRCS." AER Working Paper, African Economic Research Consortium, Nairobi.

Gauthier, Bernard, and Waly Wane. 2007. "Leakage of Public Resources in the Health Sector: An Empirical Investigation of Chad." World Bank Policy Research Working Paper 4351, World Bank, Washington, DC.

Gelb, Alan, and Caroline Decker. 2012. "Cash at Your Fingertips: Biometric Technology for Transfers in Developing Countries." *Review of Policy Research* 29 (1): 91–117.

Ghana Ministry of Finance. 2012. *Budget Statement and Economic Policy of the Government of Ghana for the 2002 Financial Year.* Accra, Ghana.

Government of India. 2017. *Pradhan Mantri Jan Dhan Yojana—Progress Report.* Ministry of Finance, New Delhi.

———. 2005. "Performance Evaluation of Targeted Public Distribution System." Programme Evaluation Organisation, New Delhi.

Hoddinott, John, Daniel Gilligan, Melissa Hidrobo, Amy Margolies, Shalini Roy, Susanna Sandström, Benjamin Schwab, and Joanna Upton. 2013. "Enhancing WFP's Capacity and Experience to Design, Implement, Monitor and Evaluate Vouchers and Cash Transfer Programmes: Study Summary." International Food Policy Research Institute, Washington, DC.

Kireyev, Alexei. 2017. "The Macroeconomics of De-Cashing." IMF Working Paper 17/71, International Monetary Fund, Washington, DC.

Kumar, M. 2016. "In Need of Cash, India Chases $117 Billion in Elusive Back Taxes." Reuters, April 17.

Lindert, Kathy, Anja Linder, Jason Hobbs, and Bénédicte de la Brière. 2007. "The Nuts and Bolts of Brazil's Bolsa Família Program: Implementing Conditional Cash Transfers in a Decentralized Context." SP Discussion Paper 0709, World Bank, Washington, DC.

Mazzotta, Benjamin D., and Bhaskar Chakravorti. 2014. *The Cost of Cash in Mexico, The Institute for Business in the Global Context.* Medford, MA: Fletcher School of Law and Diplomacy, Tufts University.

McKinsey & Company. 2016. *Global Payments Map.* Washington, DC.

———. 2010. "Inclusive Growth and Financial Security: The Benefits of E-Payments to Indian Society." McKinsey & Company, Washington, DC.

McKinsey Global Institute. 2016a. "Digital Finance for All: Powering Inclusive Growth in Emerging Economies." Washington, DC.

———. 2016b. "The Age of Analytics: Competing in a Data-Driven World." Washington, DC.

Muchichwa, Nyasha. 2016. *Working without Pay: Wage Theft in Zimbabwe.* Washington, DC: Solidarity Center.

Muralidharan, Karthik, Paul Niehaus, and Sandip Sukhtankar. 2016. "Building State Capacity: Evidence from Biometric Smartcards in India." *American Economic Review* 106 (10): 2895–929.

National Institute of Public Finance and Policy (NIPFP). 2012. "A Cost-Benefit Analysis of Aadhaar." New Delhi.

Pickens, Mark, David Porteous, and Sarah Rotman. 2009. "Banking the Poor Via G2P Payments." CGAP Focus Note 58. Consultative Group to Assist the Poor, Washington, DC.

PricewaterhouseCoopers. 1999. *Tanzania Public Expenditure Review: Health and Education Financial Tracking Study.* Dar es Salaam.

Radcliffe, Dan. 2016. "Digital Payments as a Platform for Improving State Capacity." Center for Global Development, Washington, DC.

Reinikka, Ritva, and Jakob Svensson. 2004. "Local Capture: Evidence from a Central Government Transfer Program in Uganda." *The Quarterly Journal of Economics* 119 (2): 679–705.

———. 2006. "Using Micro-Surveys to Measure and Explain Corruption." *World Development* 34 (2): 357–70.

Schneider, Friedrich, Andreas Buehn, and Claudio E. Montenegro. 2010. "Shadow Economies All Over the World: New Estimates for 162 Countries from 1999 to 2007." World Bank Policy Research Working Paper 356, World Bank, Washington, DC.

US Agency for International Development (USAID). 2014. *Digital Finance for Development: A Handbook for USAID Staff.* Washington, DC.

US Department of Treasury. 2011. Press Release, April 26.

von Mettenheim, Kurt Eberhart, and Maria Fernanda Freire de Lima. 2014. "Monetary Channels of Social Inclusion: A Case Study of Basic Income and The Caixa Econômica Federal in Brazil." *Revista de Administração Pública* 48 (6): 1451–74.

World Bank. 2004. *Papua New Guinea: Public Expenditure and Service Delivery.* Washington, DC.

———. 2010. *Public Expenditure Tracking and Service Delivery Survey: Education and Health in Honduras–Main Report.* Washington, DC: World Bank.

World Economic Forum. 2014. *Future of Government Smart Toolbox.* Geneva.

Zimmerman, Jamie M., Kristy Bohling, and Sarah Rotman Parker. 2014. "Electronic G2P Payments: Evidence from Four Lower-Income Countries." Consultative Group to Assist the Poor, Washington, DC.

Index

market failures relating to,
202, 205–6, 206*n*9
with social protection
programs, 204–5, 204*n*7
studies about, 203
with transportation, 203
Economic experiments, 117*b*
Economic impact, of P2P activities, 72
Economics
outcomes of, 25–26, 28
welfare, 33
Economic Survey, of 2016–17, 271–72
Economic Survey 2016, 252
Economies, 188, 188*n*8
developing, 83*b*, 305–7, 305*n*1
government stabilization of, 1
in Kenya, 191–93
in Nigeria, 190–93
P2P activities and development of, 83*b*
in South Africa, 190–93
ECUs. *See* Experimental currency rates
e-District Mission Mode Project, 265
Education, 214
with digital public service
provision, 210–12, 211*f*
digital technologies for, 202,
212, 212*nn*17–18
with economic development, 204
e-governance, 262, 264–65, 274
Electronic digitalization,
payments with, 281*b*
Electronic filing, 3
Electronic know-your-customer
procedures, 288
Electronic payments
cash to, 279, 306–7
information about, 32
Electronic tracking, tax
administration for, 3–4
Electronic transaction systems, 34
Empirical results, of P2P economy,
65–67, 65*n*10, 67*n*11
Employees, P2P activities of,
67–69, 68*f*, 69*n*13
Employment, with economic
development, 205, 205*n*8
Employment guarantee schemes, 228
Enforcement. *See* Tax enforcement
e-Panchayat, 265

Equalization levy, 92
Equity-efficiency trade-off, 32, 35, 36
alleviation of, 26–27, 26*n*1, 34, 34*n*9
improvement of, 51
e-Residence, 180
Error reduction, with policy
innovation, 134
Estonia
blockchain in, 179–80
case study on, 280, 287, 292–93,
293*nn*29–31, 295
European Commission Expert Group on
Taxation of the Digital Economy, 91
Everledger, 180
Expenditure savings, 309*t*
Experimental currency
rates (ECUs), 126
Experiments
with digital tax administration, 113*n*1,
113*n*4, 115–24, 115*n*8
economic, 117*b*
natural, 119
See also Pre-population experiments;
Taxpayer guidance experiments
Externalities, correcting for,
70–71, 71*n*16, 83*b*
e-Zwich payment system, in Ghana,
294–95, 295*n*34, 296

F
Facebook, 108
Fair Price Shop, 289
Finance. *See* Public finance, reshaping of
Financial Action Task Force, 283
Financial inclusion, 318
Financial institutions, as third-party
reporters, 31–32, 51
Financial Intelligence Unit, 264
Financial Management Information
Systems (FMIS), 165
general ledger with, 151
government coverage
with, 151–52, 152*n*3
investment level with, 151, 151*n*2
public accounting systems
with, 152, 152*n*4
reporting with, 152, 152*nn*5–6
World Bank relating to, 151
Financial services, 210, 211*f*